THE GRANDEUR THAT WAS ROME:

SECOND FLORILEGIUM

THE GRANDEUR THAT WAS ROME:

SECOND FLORILEGIUM

EDITED BY

JEFFREY C. KALB, JR.

HONORS HISTORY SERIES, VOLUME 6

ISBN: 9781074420833

TABLE OF CONTENTS

TABLE OF CONTENTS
(CONTINUED)

TABLE OF CONTENTS
(CONTINUED)

INTRODUCTION TO THE *HONORS HISTORY SERIES*

To the Parent, Teacher, and Student:

The value of historical instruction is threefold: First, it allows the student to locate himself within the broader story of humanity. Second, it instructs him through concrete examples of virtue and vice, wisdom and foolishness. Third, it transmits to the student whatever elements of previous cultures are worthy of adoption or imitation.

The *Honors History Series* is a projected five-course study in which the flowers of the historical record are examined for their cultural value and moral lessons. In the first course, students are immersed in the aesthetic and investigative spirit of the ancient Greeks. In the second, they observe the Roman political, military, and legal genius. In the third course, they study the rise and flourishing of Christendom. In the fourth, students follow the political, intellectual, and cultural development of Europe from the Age of Exploration to modern times. Finally, they explore the distinctive history, character, and government of their own American nation. In discovering their ancient and modern origins, students arrive at deeper self-knowledge and a better appreciation of their cultural patrimony. What is here called the Florilegium approach to history is no educational novelty, but rather the methodical application and intensification of what many excellent instructors have always practiced. It is best understood by contrasting it to the "textbook" and "great book" methods. These are the extremes of secondary education to which the Florilegium method is a mean. Consider first the strengths and weakness of these other two methods.

The "textbook" (or "lecture") method conveys the primary facts of history, as best as these have been ascertained, together with a coherent and temporally progressive interpretation of the whole subject. This method has the virtue of simplifying and clearly organizing the material for consumption by students. If done well, it can provide a framework for the student to meaningfully locate himself, the current culture, and his nation within the larger course of human events. The deficiencies of this system are also manifest to anyone who has examined a contemporary history textbook. Textbook authors naturally project into the past our present attitudes and biases, thereby unconsciously making ourselves the term, purpose, and meaning of all history. The consequent familiarity bores the student and vitiates genuine learning. Only a single perspective is presented, and quite often not the traditional one. In the worst case, the textbook becomes a mere platform for the authors to preach their own idiosyncratic values. By no means are these texts able carry the student beyond the horizon of our debased modern culture.

In response not only to the inherent weakness of such a method, but also its present abuse, the "great book" (or "tutorial") method is favored by many who attach signal importance to literary excellence and active rational inquiry. Great teachers of the past, it is said, have left behind for us profound works that even today inform and educate. Our education should therefore consist principally in reading and studying these texts. With rhetorical flourish, the image is presented of Thucydides and Plutarch, Livy and Tacitus, Hamilton and De Tocqueville, eagerly attending to the devouring intellects of our students. The real teachers, it is said, and with some truth, are these great minds. Practice, however, is unequal to the theory. Students are left without a common framework or timeline to unify these histories. Visual aids are discounted, making imaginative synthesis all the more difficult. Art and architecture are generally passed over in silence. Moreover, excepting perhaps one in a thousand, the minds of adolescents are unprepared to absorb lofty genius unaided. Common sense tells us that too little learning takes place, and experience confirms it. Ideas and aphorisms, poorly comprehended, are merely parroted. Minds obtain a veneer of learning which, when scratched, discloses a lack of depth, integration, and coordination. Indeed, early exposure to "great books" without adequate guidance can produce an allergy to all such reading or, worse yet, the presumption of having mastered what is still above one's understanding.

The excellence of the writing notwithstanding, much that is compassed by these authors is irrelevant to the student and tedious in its detail. Let it be granted than an author is insightful and elegant; nevertheless, his intent in writing will not likely conform to our intentions in educating. Much of the narration may have served well the original audience but has little value today to anyone but the professional historian. The funeral oration of Pericles, the death of Cæsar, the battle of Agincourt, and Edmund Burke's observations on the character of the American colonies can make indelible marks upon young minds. But endless parades of Athenian military skirmishes, Roman consuls, French dynastic squabbles, or New Deal legislation produce no improvement in the student. He would be wholly justified in asking, "Why am I studying this?" Finally, the moral standards of many significant authors depart radically from those we would impart to our students. We cannot surrender children to perverse and dangerous authors simply because the latter have been inscribed into a canon of *historically* important writers.

An effective answer to these difficulties is the Florilegium method. The ideal remains to read the best that has been written: the most significant, the most beautiful, the most edifying. Yet even the greatest of authors cannot maintain himself perpetually on that high plane of wisdom; for lesser authors, brilliance is the exception rather than the rule. Given the limited time of the student and the mountain of cultural material available to the instructor, a selection process is inevitable. To demand that historical records be read in their entirety is to guarantee that much of serious value is kept entirely out of view. The *Florilegium* excerpts and collates what is worthy of the student's time, thereby increasing his cultural exposure. With proper help and encouragement as an adolescent, he will acquire a taste for such reading, in which case he may, as an adult already proficient in the necessary intellectual tools, read these same works in their entirety.

To address the remaining weaknesses of the "great book" method, the readings are indexed to concise *Outlines*, thereby supplying a framework in which they may hang together coherently. The *Outlines* also supply the visual helps that are necessary to better appreciate the history of a bygone era or the culture of a foreign people. A pronunciation guide is appended as an aid to mastery. The student will typically read each chapter of the *Outlines*, mastering names, dates, and facts to be tested by the instructor. He will then read the corresponding passages of the *Florilegium* to perfect and deepen his understanding. The *Florilegium* serves as a starting point for discussion and written essays. It is not intended to convey easily tested historical fact of the sort presented in the *Outlines*, but rather the historical, cultural, and simply human perspective that students should obtain before becoming adults. All the while, students are steeped in fine English. For the student preparing for higher learning and an intellectually engaged life, this is a method of study more fruitful than either the "textbook" or "great book" method.

Beatae Mariae Semper Virgini
Mediatrici, Coredemptrici, et Advocatae

Jeffrey C. Kalb, Jr.
Honors History Series Editor

CHAPTER XVIII

ROME AS A WORLD POWER

The Róman Government, I.—Rome and the Provinces, II.—The New Civilization, III.

The Character of Cáto the Cénsor

Cáto grew more and more powerful by his eloquence, so that he was commonly called the Róman Demósthenes but his manner of life was yet more famous and talked of. For oratorical skill was, as an accomplishment, commonly studied and sought after by all young men; but he was very rare who would cultivate the old habits of bodily labor, or prefer a light supper, and a breakfast which never saw the fire; or be in love with poor clothes and a homely lodging, or could set his ambition rather on doing without luxuries than on possessing them. For now the state, unable to keep its purity by reason of its greatness, and having so many affairs, and people from all parts under its government, was fain to admit many mixed customs, and new examples of living.

With reason, therefore, everybody admired Cáto, when they saw others sink under labors, and grow effeminate by pleasures; and yet beheld him unconquered by either, and that not only when he was young and desirous of honor, but also when old and grey headed, after a cónsulship and triumph; like some famous victor in the games, persevering in his exercise and maintaining his character to the very last. He himself says, that he never wore a suit of clothes which cost more than a hundred dráchmas; and that, when he was general and cónsul, he drank the same wine which his workmen did; and that the meat or fish which was bought in the market for his dinner, did not cost above thirty *áses*. All which was for the sake of the commonwealth, that so his body might be the hardier for the war. Having a piece of embroidered Babylónian tapestry left him, he sold it; because none of his farmhouses were so much as plastered. Nor did he ever buy a slave for above fifteen hundred dráchmas; as he did not seek for effeminate and handsome ones, but able, sturdy workmen, horse keepers and cow-herds: and these he thought ought to be sold again, when they grew old, and no useless servants fed in a house.

In short, he reckoned nothing a good bargain, which was superfluous; but whatever it was, though sold for a farthing, he would think it a great price, if you had no need of it; and was for the purchase of lands for sowing and feeding, rather than grounds for sweeping and watering. Some imputed these things to petty avarice, but others approved of him, as if he had only the more strictly denied himself for the rectifying and amending of others. Yet certainly, in my judgment, it marks an over-rigid temper, for a man to take the work out of his servants as out of brute beasts, turning them off and selling them in their old age, and thinking there ought to be no further commerce between man and man, than whilst there arises some profit by it. We see that kindness or humanity has a larger field than bare justice to exercise itself in; law and justice we cannot, in the nature of things, employ on others than men; but we may extend our goodness and charity even to irrational creatures; and such acts flow from a gentle nature, as water from an abundant spring. It is doubtless the part of a kind-natured man to keep even worn-out horses and dogs, and not only take care of them when they are foals and whelps, but also when they are grown old....

For his general temperance, however, and self-control, he really deserves the highest admiration. For when he commanded the army, he never took for himself, and those that belonged to him, above three bushels of wheat for a month, and somewhat less than a bushel and a half a day of barley for his baggage-cattle. And when he entered upon the government of Sardínia, where his predecessors had been used to require tents, bedding, and clothes upon the public account, and to charge the state heavily with the cost of provisions and entertainments for a great train of servants and friends, the difference he showed in his economy was something incredible. There was nothing of any sort for which he put the public to expense; he would walk without a carriage to visit the cities, with one only of the common town officers, who carried his dress, and a cup to offer libation with.

Yet, though he seemed thus easy and sparing to all who were under his power, he, on the other hand, showed most inflexible severity and strictness, in what related to public justice, and was rigorous, and precise in what concerned the ordinances of the commonwealth; so that the Róman government, never seemed more terrible, nor yet more mild, than under his administration. His very manner of speaking seemed to have such a kind of idea with it; for it was courteous, and yet forcible; pleasant, yet overwhelming; facetious, yet austere; sententious, and yet vehement: like Sócrates, in the description of Pláto, who seemed outwardly to those about him to be but a simple, talkative, blunt fellow; whilst at the bottom he was full of such gravity and matter, as would even move tears, and touch the very hearts of his auditors...

He was also a good father, an excellent husband to his wife, and an extraordinary economist; and as he did not manage his affairs of this kind carelessly, and as things of little moment, I think I ought to record a little further whatever was commendable in him in these points. He married a wife more noble than rich; being of opinion, that the rich and the high-born are equally haughty and proud; but that those of noble blood, would be more ashamed of base things, and consequently more obedient to their husbands in all that was fit and right. A man who beat his wife or child, laid violent hands, he said, on what was most sacred; and a good husband he reckoned worthy of more praise than a great senator; and he admired the ancient Sócrates for nothing so much, as for having lived a temperate and contented life with a wife who was a scold, and children who were half-witted. As soon as he had a son born, though he had never such urgent business upon his hands, unless it were some public matter, he would be by when his wife washed it, and dressed it in its swaddling clothes. For she herself suckled it, nay, she often too gave her breast to her servants' children, to produce, by sucking the same milk, a kind of natural love in them to her son.

When he began to come to years of discretion, Cáto himself would teach him to read, although he had a servant, a very good grammarian, called Chílo, who taught many others; but he thought not fit, as he himself said, to have his son reprimanded by a slave, or pulled, it may be, by the ears when found tardy in his lesson: nor would he have him owe to a servant the obligation of so great a thing as his learning; he himself, therefore, (as we were saying,) taught him his grammar, law, and his gymnastic exercises. Nor did he only show him, too, how to throw a dart, to fight in armor, and to ride, but to box also and to endure both heat and cold, and to swim over the most rapid and rough rivers. He says, likewise, that he wrote histories, in large characters, with his own hand, that so his son, without stirring out of the house, might learn to know about his countrymen and forefathers: nor did he less abstain from speaking any thing obscene before his son, than if it had been in the presence of the sacred virgins, called véstals.

He was now grown old, when Carnéades the Académic, and Diógenes the Stóic, came as deputies from Áthens to Rome, praying for release from a penalty of five hundred talents laid on the Athénians, in a suit, to which they did not appear, in which the Orópians were plaintiffs, and Sicyónians judges. All the most studious youth immediately waited on these philosophers, and frequently, with admiration, heard them speak. But the gracefulness of Carnéades's oratory, whose ability was really greatest, and his reputation equal to it, gathered large and favorable audiences, and erelong filled, like a wind, all the city with the sound of it. So that it soon began to be told, that a Greek, famous even to admiration, winning and carrying all before him, had impressed so strange a love upon the young men, that quitting all their pleasures and pastimes, they ran mad, as it were, after philosophy; which indeed much pleased the Rómans in general; nor could they but with much pleasure see the youth receive so welcomely the Greek literature, and frequent the company of learned men.

But Cáto, on the other side, seeing this passion for words flowing into the city, from the beginning, took it ill, fearing lest the youth should be diverted that way, and so should prefer the glory of speaking well before that of arms, and doing well. And when the fame of the philosophers increased in the city, and Gáius Acílius, a person of distinction, at his own request, became their interpreter to the senate at their first audience, Cáto resolved, under some specious pretense, to have all philosophers cleared out of the city; and, coming into the senate, blamed the magistrates for letting these deputies stay so long a time without being dispatched, though they were persons that could easily persuade the people to what they pleased; that therefore in all haste something should be determined about their petition, that so they might go home again to their own schools, and declaim to the Greek children, and leave the Róman youth, to be obedient, as hitherto, to their own laws and governors.

Yet he did this not out of any anger, as some think, to Carnéades; but because he wholly despised philosophy, and out of a kind of pride, scoffed at the Greek studies and literature; as, for example, he would say, that Sócrates was a prating seditious fellow, who did his best to tyrannize over his country, to undermine the ancient customs, and to entice and withdraw the citizens to opinions contrary to the laws. Ridiculing the school of Isócrates, he would add, that his scholars grew old men before they had done learning with him, as if they were to use their art and plead causes in the court of Mínos in the next world. And to frighten his son from any thing that was Greek, in a more vehement tone than became one of his age, he pronounced, as it were, with the voice of an oracle, that the Rómans would certainly be destroyed when they began once to be infected with Greek literature; though time indeed has shown the vanity of this his prophecy; as, in truth, the city of Rome has risen to its highest fortune, while entertaining Grécian learning.

Plútarch, *Life of Cáto* (translated by John Dryden)

Cáto Defends the Óppian Law

34.1 While the State was preoccupied by serious wars, some hardly yet over and others threatening, an incident occurred which though unimportant in itself resulted in a violent party conflict. Two of the tríbunes of the plebs, M. Fundánius and L. Valérius, had brought in a proposal to repeal the Óppian Law. This law had been made on the motion of M. Óppius, a tríbune of the plebs, during the cónsulship of Q. Fábius and Tibérius Semprónius, when the strain of the Púnic War was most severely felt. It forbade any woman to have in her possession more than half an ounce of gold, to wear a dress of various colors or to ride in a two-horsed vehicle within a mile of the City or of any Róman town unless she was going to take part in some religious function.

The two Brútuses—M. Június and T. Június—both tríbunes of the plebs, defended the law and declared that they would not allow it to be repealed; many of the nobility came forward to speak in favor of the repeal or against it; the Cápitol was crowded with supporters and opponents of the proposal; the matrons could not be kept indoors either by the authority of the magistrates or the orders of their husbands or their own sense of propriety. They filled all the streets and blocked the approaches to the Fórum; they implored the men who were on their way thither to allow the women to resume their former adornments now that the commonwealth was flourishing and private fortunes increasing every day. Their numbers were daily augmented by those who came up from the country towns. At last they ventured to approach the cónsuls and prætors and other magistrates with their demands. One of the cónsuls at all events was inexorably opposed to their request—M. Pórcius Cáto. He spoke as follows in defense of the law:

34.2 "If we had, each one of us, made it a rule to uphold the rights and authority of the husband in our own households we should not now have this trouble with the whole body of our women. As things are now our liberty of action, which has been checked and rendered powerless by female despotism at home, is actually crushed and trampled on here in the Fórum, and because we were unable to withstand them individually we have now to dread their united strength. I used to think that it was a fabulous story which tells us that in a certain island the whole of the male sex was extirpated by a conspiracy amongst the women; there is no class of women from whom the gravest dangers may not arise, if once you allow intrigues, plots, secret cabals to go on. I can hardly make up my mind which is worse, the affair itself or the disastrous precedent set up. The latter concerns us as cónsuls and magistrates; the former has to do more with you, Quirítes.

Whether the measure before you is for the good of the commonwealth or not is for you to determine by your votes; this tumult amongst the women, whether a spontaneous movement or due to your instigation, M. Fundánius and L. Valérius, certainly points to failure on the part of the magistrates, but whether it reflects more on you tríbunes or on the cónsuls I do not know. It brings the greater discredit on you if you have carried your tribunícian agitation so far as to create unrest among the women, but more disgrace upon us if we have to submit to laws being imposed upon us through fear of a secession on their part, as we had to do formerly on occasions of the secession of the plebs. It was not without a feeling of shame that I made my way into the Fórum through a regular army of women.

Had not my respect for the dignity and modesty of some amongst them, more than any consideration for them as a whole, restrained me from letting them be publicly rebuked by a cónsul, I should have said, 'What is this habit you have formed of running abroad and blocking the streets and accosting men who are strangers to you? Could you not each of you put the very same question to your husbands at home? Surely you do not make yourselves more attractive in public than in private, to other women's husbands more than to your own? If matrons were kept by their natural modesty within the limits of their rights, it would be most unbecoming for you to trouble yourselves even at home about the laws which may be passed or repealed here.' Our ancestors would have no woman transact even private business except through her guardian, they placed them under the tutelage of parents or brothers or husbands.

We suffer them now to dabble in politics and mix themselves up with the business of the Fórum and public debates and election contests. What are they doing now in the public roads and at the street corners but recommending to the plebs the proposal of their tríbunes and voting for the repeal of the law. Give the reins to a headstrong nature, to a creature that has not been tamed, and then hope that they will themselves set bounds to their license if you do not do it yourselves. This is the smallest of those restrictions which have been imposed upon women by ancestral custom or by laws, and which they submit to with such impatience. What they really want is unrestricted freedom, or to speak the truth, license, and if they win on this occasion what is there that they will not attempt?

34.3 "Call to mind all the regulations respecting women by which our ancestors curbed their license and made them obedient to their husbands, and yet in spite of all those restrictions you can scarcely hold them in. If you allow them to pull away these restraints and wrench them out one after another, and finally put themselves on an equality with their husbands, do you imagine that you will be able to tolerate them? From the moment that they become your fellows they will become your masters. But surely, you say, what they object to is having a new restriction imposed upon them, they are not deprecating the assertion of a right but the infliction of a wrong. No, they are demanding the abrogation of a law which you enacted by your suffrages and which the practical experience of all these years has approved and justified. This they would have you repeal; that means that by rescinding this they would have you weaken all. No law is equally agreeable to everybody, the only question is whether it is beneficial on the whole and good for the majority.

If everyone who feels himself personally aggrieved by a law is to destroy it and get rid of it, what is gained by the whole body of citizens making laws which those against whom they are enacted can in a short time repeal? I want, however, to learn the reason why these excited matrons have run out into the streets and scarcely keep away from the Fórum and the Assembly. Is it that those taken prisoners by Hánnibal—their fathers and husbands and children and brothers—may be ransomed? The republic is a long way from this misfortune, and may it ever remain so! Still, when this did happen, you refused to do so in spite of their dutiful entreaties. But, you may say, it is not dutiful affection and solicitude for those they love that has brought them together; they are going to welcome Máter Idǽa on her way from Phrýgian Pessínus. What pretext in the least degree respectable is put forward for this female insurrection? 'That we may shine,' they say, 'in gold and purple, that we may ride in carriages on festal and ordinary days alike, as though in triumph for having defeated and repealed a law after capturing and forcing from you your votes.'

34.4 "You have often heard me complain of the expensive habits of women and often, too, of those of men, not only private citizens but even magistrates, and I have often said that the community suffers from two opposite vices—avarice and luxury—pestilential diseases which have proved the ruin of all great empires. The brighter and better the fortunes of the republic become day by day, and the greater the growth of its dominion—and now we are penetrating into Greece and Ásia, regions filled with everything that can tempt appetite or excite desire, and are even laying hands on the treasures of kings—so much the more do I dread the prospect of these things taking us captive rather than we them. It was a bad day for this City, believe me, when the statues were brought from Sýracuse. I hear far too many people praising and admiring those which adorn Áthens and Córinth and laughing at the clay images of our gods standing in front of their temples. I for my part prefer these gods who are propitious to us, and I trust that they will continue to be so as long as we allow them to remain in their present abodes.

In the days of our forefathers Pýrrhus attempted, through his ambassador Cíneas, to tamper with the loyalty of women as well as men by means of bribes. The Law of Óppius in restraint of female extravagance had not then been passed, still not a single woman accepted a bribe. What do you think was the reason? The same reason which our forefathers had for not making any law on the subject; there was no extravagance to be restrained. Diseases must be recognized before remedies are applied, and so the passion for self-indulgence must be in existence before the laws which are to curb it. What called out the Licínian Law which restricted estates to 500 iúgera except the keen desire of adding field to field? What led to the passing of the Cíncian Law concerning presents and fees except the condition of the plebéians who had become tributaries and taxpayers to the senate? It is not therefore in the least surprising that neither the Óppian nor any other law was in those days required to set limits to the expensive habits of women when they refused to accept the gold and purple that was freely offered to them. If Cíneas were to go in these days about the City with his gifts, he would find women standing in the streets quite ready to accept them.

There are some desires of which I cannot penetrate either the motive or the reason. That what is permitted to another should be forbidden to you may naturally create a feeling of shame or indignation, but when all are upon the same level as far as dress is concerned why should any one of you fear that you will not attract notice? The very last things to be ashamed of are thriftiness and poverty, but this law relieves you of both since you do not possess what it forbids you to possess. The wealthy woman says, 'This levelling down is just what I do not tolerate. Why am I not to be admired and looked at for my gold and purple? Why is the poverty of others disguised under this appearance of law so that they may be thought to have possessed, had the law allowed it, what it was quite out of their power to possess?'

Do you want, Quirítes, to plunge your wives into a rivalry of this nature, where the rich desire to have what no one else can afford, and the poor, that they may not be despised for their poverty, stretch their expenses beyond their means? Depend upon it, as soon as a woman begins to be ashamed of what she ought not to be ashamed of she will cease to feel shame at what she ought to be ashamed of. She who is in a position to do so will get what she wants with her own money, she who cannot do this will ask her husband. The husband is in a pitiable plight whether he yields or refuses; in the latter case he will see another giving what he refused to give.

Now they are soliciting other women's husbands, and what is worse they are soliciting votes for the repeal of a law, and are getting them from some, against the interest of you and your property and your children. When once the law has ceased to fix a limit to your wife's expenses, you will never fix one. Do not imagine that things will be the same as they were before the law was made. It is safer for an evil-doer not to be prosecuted than for him to be tried and then acquitted, and luxury and extravagance would have been more tolerable had they never been interfered with than they will be now, just like wild beasts which have been irritated by their chains and then released. I give my vote against every attempt to repeal the law, and pray that all the gods may give your action a fortunate result."

Lívy, *The History of Rome*, 34.1-34.4 (translated by Rev. Canon Roberts)

Corínthian Brass

The other kinds [of copper] are made artificially, all of which will be described in the appropriate places, the more celebrated kinds first coming under our notice. Formerly a mixture was made of copper fused with gold and silver, and the workmanship in this metal was considered even more valuable than the material itself; but, at the present day, it is difficult to say whether the workmanship in it, or the material, is the worst. Indeed, it is wonderful, that while the value of these works has so infinitely increased, the reputation of the art itself is nearly extinct. But it would appear, that in this, as in everything else, what was formerly done for the sake of reputation, is now undertaken for the mere purpose of gain. For whereas this art was ascribed to the gods themselves, and men of rank in all countries endeavored to acquire fame by the practice of it, we have now so entirely lost the method of making this valuable compound by fusion, that, for this long time past, not even chance itself has assumed, in this department, the privilege which formerly belonged to art.

Next after the above compound, so celebrated in antiquity, the Corínthian metal has been the most highly esteemed. This was a compound produced by accident, when Córinth was burnt at the time of its capture. There has been a wonderful mania with many for gaining possession of this metal. It is even said, that Vérres, whom M. Cícero caused to be condemned, was proscribed by Antónius, along with Cícero, for no other reason than his refusal to give up some specimens of Corínthian metal, which were in his possession. But most of these people seem to me to make a pretense of their discernment in reference to this metal, rather for the purpose of distinguishing themselves from the multitude, than from any real knowledge which they possess...

Plíny the Elder, *Natural History*, 34.3 (translated by John Bostock and H. T. Riley)

CHAPTER XIX

THE TIMES OF THE GRÁCCHI

The Causes of Civil Strife, I.—The Reforms of Tibérius Grácchus, II.—The Reforms of Gáius Grácchus, III.

Cornélia, Mother of the Grácchi

Having completed the first two narratives, we now may proceed to take a view of misfortunes, not less remarkable, in the Róman couple, and with the lives of Ágis and Cleómenes, compare these of Tibérius and Gáius. They were the sons of Tibérius Grácchus, who though he had been once cénsor, twice cónsul, and twice had triumphed, yet was more renowned and esteemed for his virtue than his honors. Upon this account, after the death of Scípio who overthrew Hánnibal, he was thought worthy to match with his daughter Cornélia, though there had been no friendship or familiarity between Scípio and him, but rather the contrary. There is a story told that he once found in his bed-chamber a couple of snakes, and that the soothsayers, being consulted concerning the prodigy, advised that he should neither kill them both nor let them both escape; adding, that if the male serpent was killed, Tibérius should die, and if the female, Cornélia. And that therefore Tibérius, who extremely loved his wife, and thought, besides, that it was much more his part, who was an old man, to die, than it was hers, who as yet was but a young woman, killed the male serpent, and let the female escape; and soon after himself died, leaving behind him twelve children borne to him by Cornélia.

Cornélia, taking upon herself all the care of the household and the education of her children, proved herself so discreet a matron, so affectionate a mother, and so constant and noble-spirited a widow, that Tibérius seemed to all men to have done nothing unreasonable in choosing to die for such a woman; who, when King Ptólemy himself proffered her his crown, and would have married her, refused it, and chose rather to live a widow. In this state she continued, and lost all her children, except one daughter, who was married to Scípio the younger, and two sons, Tibérius and Gáius, whose lives we are now writing. These she brought up with such care, that though they were without dispute in natural endowments and dispositions the first among the Rómans of their time, yet they seemed to owe their virtues even more to their education than to their birth. And as, in the statues and pictures made of Cástor and Póllux, though the brothers resemble one another, yet there is a difference to be perceived in their countenances, between the one, who delighted in the céstus, and the other, that was famous in the course, so between these two noble youths, though there was a strong general likeness in their common love of fortitude and temperance, in their liberality, their eloquence, and their greatness of mind, yet in their actions and administrations of public affairs, a considerable variation showed itself. It will not be amiss before we proceed to mark the difference between them.

Plútarch, *Life of Tibérius Grácchus* (translated by John Dryden)

A Comparison of Tibérius and Gáius Grácchus

Tibérius, in the form and expression of his countenance, and in his gesture and motion, was gentle and composed; but Gáius, earnest and vehement. And so in their public speeches to the people, the one spoke in a quiet, orderly manner, standing throughout on the same spot; the other would walk about on the hustings, and in the heat of his orations pull his gown off his shoulders, and was the first of all the Rómans that used such gestures; as Cléon is said to have been the first orator among the Athénians that pulled off his cloak and smote his thigh, when addressing the people. Gáius's oratory was impetuous and passionate, making everything tell to the utmost, whereas Tibérius was gentle and persuasive, awakening emotions of pity. His diction was pure and carefully correct, while that of Gáius was vehement and rich. So likewise in their way of living and at their tables, Tibérius was frugal and plain, Gáius, compared with other men, temperate and even austere, but contrasting with his brother in a fondness for new fashions and rarities, as appears in Drúsus's charge against him, that he had bought some silver dolphins, to the value of twelve hundred and fifty dráchmas for every pound weight.

The same difference that appeared in their diction was observable also in their tempers. The one was mild and reasonable, the other rough and passionate, and to that degree, that often, in the midst of speaking, he was so hurried away by his passion against his judgment, that his voice lost its tone, and he began to pass into mere abusive talking, spoiling his whole speech. As a remedy to this excess, he made use of an ingenious servant of his, one Licínius, who stood constantly behind him with a sort of pitch-pipe, or instrument to regulate the voice by, and whenever he perceived his master's tone alter and break with anger, he struck a soft note with his pipe, on hearing which Gáius immediately checked the vehemence of his passion, and his voice, grew quieter, and allowed himself to be recalled to temper. Such are the differences between the two brothers; but their valor in war against their country's enemies, their justice in the government of its subjects, their care and industry in office, and their self-command in all that regarded their pleasures, were equally remarkable in both.

Tibérius was the elder by nine years; owing to which their actions as public men were divided by the difference of the times in which those of the one and those of the other were performed. And one of the principal causes of the failure of their enterprises was this interval between their careers, and the want of combination of their efforts. The power they would have exercised, had they flourished both together, could scarcely have failed to overcome all resistance. We must therefore give an account of each of them singly, and first of the eldest.

Plútarch, *Life of Tibérius Grácchus* (translated by John Dryden)

The Young Tibérius Grácchus

Tibérius, immediately on his attaining manhood, had such a reputation that he was admitted into the college of the áugurs, and that in consideration more of his early virtue than of his noble birth. This appeared by what Áppius Cláudius did, who, though he had been cónsul and cénsor, and was now the head of the Róman senate, and had the highest sense of his own place and merit, at a public feast of the áugurs, addressed himself openly to Tibérius, and with great expressions of kindness, offered him his daughter in marriage. And when Tibérius gladly accepted, and the agreement had thus been completed, Áppius returning home, no sooner had reached his door, but he called to his wife and cried out in a loud voice, "O Antístia, I have contracted our daughter Cláudia to a husband." She, being amazed, answered, "But why so suddenly, or what means this haste? Unless you have provided Tibérius Grácchus for her husband." I am not ignorant that some apply this story to Tibérius, the father of the Grácchi, and Scípio Africánus; but most relate it as we have done. And Polýbius writes, that after the death of Scípio Africánus, the nearest relations of Cornélia, preferring Tibérius to all other competitors, gave her to him in marriage, not having been engaged or promised to any one by her father.

This young Tibérius, accordingly, serving in África under the younger Scípio, who had married his sister, and living there under the same tent with him, soon learned to estimate the noble spirit of his commander, which was so fit to inspire strong feelings of emulation in virtue and desire to prove merit in action, and in a short time he excelled all the young men of the army in obedience and courage; and he was the first that mounted the enemy's wall, as Fánnius says, who writes that he himself climbed up with him, and was partaker in the achievement. He was regarded, while he continued with the army, with great affection; and left behind him on his departure a strong desire for his return.

After that expedition, being chosen paymaster, it was his fortune to serve in the war against the Númantines, under the command of Gáius Mancínus, the cónsul, a person of no bad character, but the most unfortunate of all the Róman generals. Notwithstanding, amidst the greatest misfortunes, and in the most unsuccessful enterprises, not only the discretion and valor of Tibérius, but also, which was still more to be admired, the great respect and honor which he showed for his general, were most eminently remarkable; though the general himself, when reduced in straits, forgot his own dignity and office. For being beaten in various great battles, he endeavored to dislodge by night and leave his camp; which the Númantines perceiving, immediately possessed themselves of his camp, and pursuing that part of the forces which was in flight, slew those that were in the rear, hedged the whole army in on every side, and forced them into difficult ground, whence there could be no possibility of an escape. Mancínus, despairing to make his way through by force, sent a messenger to desire a truce and conditions of peace. But they refused to give their confidence to anyone except Tibérius and required that he should be sent to treat with them. This was not only in regard to the young man's own character, for he had a great reputation amongst the soldiers, but also in remembrance of his father Tibérius, who, in his command against the Spániards, had reduced great numbers of them to subjection, but granted a peace to the Númantines, and prevailed upon the Rómans to keep it punctually and inviolably.

Tibérius was accordingly dispatched to the enemy, whom he persuaded to accept of several conditions, and he himself complied with others; and by this means, it is beyond a question, that he saved twenty thousand of the Róman citizens, besides attendants and camp followers. However, the Númantines retained possession of all the property they had found and plundered in the encampment; and amongst other things were Tibérius's books of accounts, containing the whole transactions of his quæstorship, which he was extremely anxious to recover. And therefore, when the army were already upon their march, he returned to Numántia, accompanied with only three or four of his friends; and making his application to the officers of the Númantines, he entreated that they would return him his books, lest his enemies should have it in their power to reproach him with not being able to give an account of the moneys entrusted to him.

The Númantines joyfully embraced this opportunity of obliging him, and invited him into the city; as he stood hesitating, they came up and took him by the hands, and begged that he would no longer look upon them as enemies, but believe them to be his friends, and treat them as such. Tibérius thought it well to consent, desirous as he was to have his books returned, and was afraid lest he should disoblige them by showing any distrust. As soon as he entered into the city, they first offered him food, and made every kind of entreaty that he would sit down and eat something in their company. Afterwards they returned his books and gave him the liberty to take whatever he wished for in the remaining spoils. He, on the other hand, would accept of nothing but some frankincense, which he used in his public sacrifices, and bidding them farewell with every expression of kindness, departed.

When he returned to Rome, he found the whole transaction censured and reproached, as a proceeding that was base and scandalous to the Rómans. But the relations and friends of the soldiers, forming a large body among the people, came flocking to Tibérius, whom they acknowledged as the preserver of so many citizens, imputing to the general all the miscarriages which had happened. Those who cried out against what had been done, urged for imitation the example of their ancestors, who stripped and handed over to the Sámnites not only the generals who had consented to the terms of release, but also all the quæstors, for example, and tríbunes, who had in any way implicated themselves in the agreement, laying the guilt of perjury and breach of conditions on their heads. But, in this all the populace, showing an extraordinary kindness and affection for Tibérius, indeed voted that the cónsul should be stripped and put in irons, and so delivered to the Númantines; but, for the sake of Tibérius, spared all the other officers.

It may be probable, also, that Scípio, who at that time was the greatest and most powerful man among the Rómans, contributed to save him, though indeed he was also censured for not protecting Mancínus too, and that he did not exert himself to maintain the observance of the articles of peace which had been agreed upon by his kinsman and friend Tibérius. But it may be presumed that the difference between them was for the most part due to ambitious feelings, and to the friends and reasoners who urged on Tibérius, and, as it was, it never amounted to anything that might not have been remedied, or that was really bad. Nor can I think that Tibérius would ever have met with his misfortunes, if Scípio had been concerned in dealing with his measures; but he was away fighting at Numántia when Tibérius, upon the following occasion, first came forward as a legislator.

Plútarch, *Life of Tibérius Grácchus* (translated by John Dryden)

The Land Reform of Tibérius Grácchus

Of the land which the Rómans gained by conquest from their neighbors, part they sold publicly, and turned the remainder into common; this common land they assigned to such of the citizens as were poor and indigent, for which they were to pay only a small acknowledgment into the public treasury. But when the wealthy men began to offer larger rents, and drive the poorer people out, it was enacted by law that no person whatever should enjoy more than five hundred acres of ground. This act for some time checked the avarice of the richer, and was of great assistance to the poorer people, who retained under it their respective proportions of ground, as they had been formerly rented by them.

Afterwards the rich men of the neighborhood contrived to get these lands again into their possession, under other people's names, and at last would not stick to claim most of them publicly in their own. The poor, who were thus deprived of their farms, were no longer either ready, as they had formerly been, to serve in war or careful in the education of their children; insomuch that in a short time there were comparatively few freemen remaining in all Ítaly, which swarmed with workhouses full of foreign-born slaves. These the rich men employed in cultivating their ground of which they dispossessed the citizens. Gáius Lælius, the intimate friend of Scípio, undertook to reform this abuse; but meeting with opposition from men of authority, and fearing a disturbance, he soon desisted, and received the name of the Wise or the Prudent, both which meanings belong to the Látin word Sápiens.

But Tibérius, being elected tríbune of the people, entered upon that design without delay, at the instigation, as is most commonly stated, of Dióphanes, the rhetorician, and Blóssius, the philosopher. Dióphanes was a refugee from Mityléne, the other was an Itálian, of the city of Cúma, and was educated there under Antípater of Társus, who afterwards did him the honor to dedicate some of his philosophical lectures to him.

Some have also charged Cornélia, the mother of Tibérius, with contributing towards it, because she frequently upbraided her sons, that the Rómans as yet rather called her the daughter of Scípio, than the mother of the Grácchi. Others again say that Spúrius Postúmius was the chief occasion. He was a man of the same age with Tibérius, and his rival for reputation as a public speaker; and when Tibérius, at his return from the campaign, found him to have got far beyond him in fame and influence, and to be much looked up to, he thought to outdo him, by attempting a popular enterprise of this difficulty and of such great consequence. But his brother Gáius has left it us in writing, that when Tibérius went through Túscany to Numántia, and found the country almost depopulated, there being hardly any free husbandmen or shepherds, but for the most part only barbarian, imported slaves, he then first conceived the course of policy which in the sequel proved so fatal to his family. Though it is also most certain that the people themselves chiefly excited his zeal and determination in the prosecution of it, by setting up writings upon the porches, walls, and monuments, calling upon him to reinstate the poor citizens in their former possessions.

However, he did not draw up his law without the advice and assistance of those citizens that were then most eminent for their virtue and authority; amongst whom were Crássus, the high-priest, Múcius Scævola, the lawyer, who at that time was cónsul, and Cláudius Áppius, his father-in-law. Never did any law appear more moderate and gentle, especially being enacted against such great oppression and avarice. For they who ought to have been severely punished for transgressing the former laws, and should at least have lost all their titles to such lands which they had unjustly usurped, were notwithstanding to receive a price for quitting their unlawful claims, and giving up their lands to those fit owners who stood in need of help. But though this reformation was managed with so much tenderness that, all the former transactions being passed over, the people were only thankful to prevent abuses of the like nature for the future, yet, on the other hand, the moneyed men, and those of great estates, were exasperated, through their covetous feelings against the law itself, and against the lawgiver, through anger and party-spirit. They therefore endeavored to seduce the people, declaring that Tibérius was designing a general redivision of lands, to overthrow the government, and cut all things into confusion.

But they had no success. For Tibérius, maintaining an honorable and just cause, and possessed of eloquence sufficient to have made a less creditable action appear plausible, was no safe or easy antagonist, when, with the people crowding around the hustings, he took his place, and spoke in behalf of the poor. "The savage beasts," said he, "in Ítaly, have their particular dens, they have their places of repose and refuge; but the men who bear arms, and expose their lives for the safety of their country, enjoy in the meantime nothing more in it but the air and light and, having no houses or settlements of their own, are constrained to wander from place to place with their wives and children." He told them that the commanders were guilty of a ridiculous error, when, at the head of their armies, they exhorted the common soldiers to fight for their sepulchers and altars; when not any amongst so many Rómans is possessed of either altar or monument, neither have they any houses of their own, or hearths of their ancestors to defend. They fought indeed and were slain, but it was to maintain the luxury and the wealth of other men. They were styled the masters of the world, but in the meantime had not one foot of ground which they could call their own.

A harangue of this nature, spoken to an enthusiastic and sympathizing audience, by a person of commanding spirit and genuine feelings, no adversaries at that time were competent to oppose. Forbearing, therefore, all discussion and debate, they addressed themselves to Márcus Octávius, his fellow-tríbune, who being a young man of a steady, orderly character, and an intimate friend of Tibérius, upon this account declined at first the task of opposing him; but at length, over-persuaded with the repeated importunities of numerous considerable persons, he was prevailed upon to do so, and hindered the passing of the law; it being the rule that any tríbune has a power to hinder an act, and that all the rest can effect nothing, if only one of them dissents. Tibérius, irritated at these proceedings, presently laid aside this milder bill, but at the same time preferred another; which, as it was more grateful to the common people, so it was much more severe against the wrongdoers, commanding them to make an immediate surrender of all lands which, contrary to former laws, had come into their possession. Hence there arose daily contentions between him and Octávius in their orations. However, though they expressed themselves with the utmost heat and determination, they yet were never known to descend to any personal reproaches, or in their passion to let slip any indecent expressions, so as to derogate from one another.

For not alone, "in revelings and Bácchic play," but also in contentions and political animosities, a noble nature and a temperate education stay and compose the mind. Observing that Octávius himself was an offender against this law, and detained a great quantity of ground from the commonalty, Tibérius desired him to forbear opposing him any further, and proffered, for the public good, though he himself had but an indifferent estate, to pay a price for Octávius's share at his own cost and charges. But upon the refusal of this proffer by Octávius, he then interposed an edict, prohibiting all magistrates to exercise their respective functions, till such time as the law was either ratified or rejected by public votes. He further sealed up the gates of Sáturn's temple, so that the treasurers could neither take any money out from thence, nor put any in. He threatened to impose a severe fine upon those of the prǽtors who presumed to disobey his commands, insomuch that all the officers, for fear of this penalty, intermitted the exercise of their several jurisdictions. Upon this the rich proprietors put themselves into mourning, and went up and down melancholy and dejected; they entered also into a conspiracy against Tibérius, and procured men to murder him; so that he also, with all men's knowledge, whenever he went abroad, took with him a sword-staff, such as robbers use, called in Látin a "dólo."

Plútarch, Life of Tibérius Grácchus (translated by John Dryden)

Tibérius Deposes the Tríbune Octávius

When the day appointed was come, and the people summoned to give their votes, the rich men seized upon the voting urns and carried them away by force; thus all things were in confusion. But when Tibérius's party appeared strong enough to oppose the contrary faction, and drew together in a body, with the resolution to do so, Mánlius and Fúlvius, two of the cónsular quality, threw themselves before Tibérius, took him by the hand, and, with tears in their eyes, begged of him to desist. Tibérius, considering the mischiefs that were all but now occurring, and having a great respect for two such eminent persons, demanded of them what they would advise him to do. They acknowledged themselves unfit to advise in a matter of so great importance, but earnestly entreated him to leave it to the determination of the senate. But when the senate assembled, and could not bring the business to any result, through the prevalence of the rich faction, he then was driven to a course neither legal nor fair, and proposed to deprive Octávius of his tríbuneship, it being impossible for him in any other way to get the law brought to the vote.

At first he addressed him publicly, with entreaties couched in the kindest terms, and taking him by his hands, besought him, that now, in the presence of all the people, he would take this opportunity to oblige them, in granting only that request which was in itself so just and reasonable, being but a small recompense in regard of those many dangers and hardships which they had undergone for the public safety. Octávius, however, would by no means be persuaded to compliance; upon which Tibérius declared openly, that, seeing they two were united in the same office, and of equal authority, it would be a difficult matter to compose their difference on so weighty a matter without a civil war; and that the only remedy which he knew must be the deposing one of them from their office. He desired, therefore, that Octávius would summon the people to pass their verdict upon him first, averring that he would willingly relinquish his authority if the citizens desired it. Octávius refused; and Tibérius then said he would himself put to the people the question of Octávius's deposition, if upon mature deliberation he did not alter his mind and after this declaration he adjourned the assembly till the next day.

When the people were met together again, Tibérius placed himself in the róstra, and endeavored a second time to persuade Octávius. But all being to no purpose, he referred the whole matter to the people, calling on them to vote at once, whether Octávius should be deposed or not; and when seventeen of the thirty-five tribes had already voted against him, and there wanted only the votes of one tribe more for his final deprivation, Tibérius put a short stop to the proceedings, and once more renewed his importunities; he embraced and kissed him before all the assembly, begging with all the earnestness imaginable, that he would neither suffer himself to incur the dishonor, nor him to be reputed the author and promoter of so odious a measure. Octávius, we are told, did seem a little softened and moved with these entreaties; his eyes filled with tears, and he continued silent for a considerable time. But presently looking towards the rich men and proprietors of estates, who stood gathered in a body together, partly for shame, and partly for fear of disgracing himself with them, he boldly bade Tibérius use any severity he pleased. The law for his deprivation being thus voted, Tibérius ordered one of his servants, whom he had made a freeman, to remove Octávius from the róstra, employing his own domestic freed servants in the stead of the public officers. And it made the action seem all the sadder, that Octávius was dragged out in such an ignominious manner. The people immediately assaulted him, whilst the rich men ran in to his assistance. Octávius, with some difficulty, was snatched away and safely conveyed out of the crowd; though a trusty servant of his, who had placed himself in front of his master that he might assist his escape, in keeping off the multitude, had his eyes struck out, much to the displeasure of Tibérius, who ran with all haste, when he perceived the disturbance, to appease the rioters.

This being done, the law concerning the lands was ratified and confirmed, and three commissioners were appointed, to make a survey of the grounds, and see the same equally divided. These were Tibérius himself, Cláudius Áppius, his father-in-law and his brother, Gáius Grácchus, who at this time was not at Rome, but in the army under the command of Scípio Africánus before Numántia. These things were transacted by Tibérius without any disturbance, none daring to offer any resistance to him; besides which, he gave the appointment as tríbune in Octávius's place, not to any person of distinction, but to a certain Múcius, one of his own clients. The great men of the city were therefore utterly offended, and, fearing lest he grew yet more popular, they took all opportunities of affronting him publicly in the senate-house. For when he requested, as was usual, to have a tent provided at the public charge for his use, while dividing the lands, though it was a favor commonly granted to persons employed in business of much less importance, it was peremptorily refused to him; and the allowance made him for his daily expenses was fixed to nine obols only.

The chief promoter of these affronts was Públius Nasíca, who openly abandoned himself to his feelings of hatred against Tibérius, being a large holder of the public lands, and not a little resenting now to be turned out of them by force. The people, on the other hand, were still more and more excited, insomuch that a little after this, it happening that one of Tibérius's friends died suddenly, and his body being marked with malignant-looking spots, they ran, in a tumultuous manner, to his funeral, crying aloud that the man was poisoned. They took the bier upon their shoulders, and stood over it, while it was placed on the pile, and really seemed to have fair grounds for their suspicion of foul play. For the body burst open, and such a quantity of corrupt humors issued out, that the funeral fire was extinguished, and when it was again kindled, the wood still would not burn; insomuch that they were constrained to carry the corpse to another place, where with much difficulty it took fire. Besides this, Tibérius, that he might incense the people yet more, put himself into mourning, brought his children amongst the crowd, and entreated the people to provide for them and their mother, as if he now despaired of his own security.

Plútarch, Life of Tibérius Grácchus (translated by John Dryden)

The Death of Tibérius Grácchus

About this time king Áttalus, surnamed Philómetor, died, and Éudemus, a Pergaménian, brought his last will to Rome, by which he had made the Róman people his heirs. Tibérius, to please the people, immediately proposed making a law, that all the money which Áttalus left should be distributed amongst such poor citizens as were to be sharers of the public lands, for the better enabling them to proceed in stocking and cultivating their ground; and as for the cities that were in the territories of Áttalus, he declared that the disposal of them did not at all belong to the senate, but to the people, and that he himself would ask their pleasure herein. By this he offended the senate more than ever he had done before, and Pompéius stood up and acquainted them that he was the next neighbor to Tibérius, and so had the opportunity of knowing that Éudemus, the Pergaménian, had presented Tibérius with a royal diadem and a purple robe, as before long he was to be king of Rome.

Quíntus Metéllus also upbraided him, saying, that when his father was cénsor, the Rómans, whenever he happened to be going home from a supper, used to put out all their lights, lest they should be seen to have indulged themselves in feasting and drinking at unseasonable hours, whereas now the most indigent and audacious of the people were found with their torches at night, following Tibérius home. Títus Ánnius, a man of no great repute for either justice or temperance, but famous for his skill in putting and answering questions, challenged Tibérius to the proof by wager, declaring him to have deposed a magistrate who by law was sacred and inviolable. Loud clamor ensued, and Tibérius, quitting the senate hastily, called together the people, and summoning Ánnius to appear, was proceeding to accuse him. But Ánnius, being no great speaker, nor of any repute compared to him, sheltered himself in his own particular art, and desired that he might propose one or two questions to Tibérius before he entered upon the chief argument. This liberty being granted, and silence proclaimed, Ánnius proposed his question. "If you," said he, "had a design to disgrace and defame me, and I should apply myself to one of your colleagues for redress, and he should come forward to my assistance, would you for that reason fall into a passion, and depose him?" Tibérius, they say, was so much disconcerted at this question, that, though at other times his assurance as his readiness of speech was always remarkable, yet now he was silent and made no reply.

For the present he dismissed the assembly. But beginning to understand that the course he had taken with Octávius had created offence even among the populace as well as the nobility, because the dignity of the tríbunes seemed to be violated, which had always continued till that day sacred and honorable, he made a speech to the people in justification of himself; out of which it may not be improper to collect some particulars, to give an impression of his force and persuasiveness in speaking. "A tríbune," he said, "of the people, is sacred indeed, and ought to be inviolable, because in a manner consecrated to be the guardian and protector of them; but if he degenerate so far as to oppress the people, abridge their powers, and take away their liberty of voting, he stands deprived by his own act of honors and immunities, by the neglect of the duty for which the honor was bestowed upon him. Otherwise we should be under the obligation to let a tríbune do this pleasure, though he should proceed to destroy the Cápitol or set fire to the arsenal. He who should make these attempts would be a bad tríbune. He who assails the power of the people is no longer a tríbune at all. Is it not inconceivable that a tríbune should have power to imprison a cónsul, and the people have no authority to degrade him when he uses that honor which he received from them, to their detriment? For the tríbunes, as well as the cónsuls, hold office by the people's votes.

The kingly government, which comprehends all sorts of authority in itself alone, is moreover elevated by the greatest and most religious solemnity imaginable into a condition of sanctity. But the citizens, notwithstanding this, deposed Tárquin, when he acted wrongfully; and for the crime of one single man, the ancient government under which Rome was built was abolished for ever. What is there in all Rome so sacred and venerable as the véstal virgins, to whose care alone the preservation of the eternal fire is committed? yet if one of these transgress she is buried alive; the sanctity which for the gods' sakes is allowed them, is forfeited when they offend against the gods. So likewise a tríbune retains not his inviolability, which for the people's sake was accorded to him, when he offends against the people, and attacks the foundations of that authority from whence he derived his own. We esteem him to be legally chosen tríbune who is elected only by the majority of votes; and is not therefore the same person much more lawfully degraded when, by a general consent of them all, they agreed to depose him? Nothing is so sacred as religious offerings; yet the people were never prohibited to make use of them, but suffered to remove and carry them wherever they pleased; so likewise, as it were some sacred present, they have lawful power to transfer the tríbuneship from one man's hands to another's. Nor can that authority be thought inviolable and irremovable which many of those who have held it, have of their own act surrendered and desired to be discharged from."

These were the principal heads of Tibérius's apology. But his friends, apprehending the dangers which seemed to threaten him, and the conspiracy that was gathering head against him, were of opinion that the safest way would be for him to petition that he might be continued tríbune for the year ensuing. Upon this consideration he again endeavored to secure the people's good-will with fresh laws, making the years of serving in the war fewer than formerly, granting liberty of appeal from the judges to the people, and joining to the senators, who were judges at that time, an equal number of citizens of the horsemen's degree, endeavoring as much as in him lay to lessen the power of the senate, rather from passion and partisanship than from any rational regard to equity and the public good. And when it came to the question whether these laws should be passed, and they perceived that the opposite party were strongest, the people as yet being not got together in a full body, they began first of all to gain time by speeches in accusation of some of their fellow-magistrates and at length adjourned the assembly till the day following.

Tibérius then went down into the market-place amongst the people, and made his addresses to them humbly and with tears in his eyes; and told them he had just reason to suspect that his adversaries would attempt in the night-time to break open his house and murder him. This worked so strongly with the multitude, that several of them pitched tents round about his house, and kept guard all night for the security of his person. By break of day came one of the soothsayers, who prognosticate good or bad success by the pecking of fowls, and threw them something to eat. The soothsayer used his utmost endeavors to fright the fowls out of their coop; but none of them except one would venture out, which fluttered with his left wing, and stretched out its leg, and ran back again into the coop, without eating anything. This put Tibérius in mind of another ill-omen which had formerly happened to him.

He had a very costly headpiece, which he made use of when he engaged in any battle, and into this piece of armor two serpents crawled, laid eggs, and brought forth young ones. The remembrance of which made Tibérius more concerned now than otherwise he would have been. However, he went towards the Cápitol as soon as he understood that the people were assembled there; but before he got out of the house he stumbled upon the threshold with such violence, that he broke the nail of his great toe, insomuch that blood gushed out of his shoes. He was not gone very far before he saw two ravens fighting on the top of a house which stood on his left hand as he passed along; and though he was surrounded with a number of people, a stone struck from its place by one of the ravens, fell just at his foot. This even the boldest men about him felt as a check. But Blóssius of Cúma, who was present, told him that it would be a shame and an ignominious thing for Tibérius, who was a son of Grácchus, the grandson of Scípio Africánus, and the protector of the Róman people to refuse, for fear of a silly bird, to answer when his countrymen called to him; and that his adversaries would represent it not as a mere matter for their ridicule, but would declaim about it to the people as the mark of a tyrannical temper, which felt a pride in taking liberties with the people. At the same time several messengers came also from his friends, to desire his presence at the Cápitol, saying that all things went there according to expectation.

And indeed Tibérius's first entrance there was in every way successful; as soon as ever he appeared, the people welcomed him with loud acclamations, and as he went up to his place, they repeated their expressions of joy, and gathered in a body around him, so that no one who was not well known to be his friend might approach. Múcius then began to put the business again to the vote; but nothing could be performed in the usual course and order, because of the disturbance caused by those who were on the outside of the crowd, where there was a struggle going on with those of the opposite party, who were pushing on and trying to force their way in and establish themselves among them.

Whilst things were in this confusion, Flávius Fláccus, a senator, standing in a place where he could be seen, but at such a distance from Tibérius that he could not make him hear, signified to him by motions of his hand, that he wished to impart something of consequence to him in private. Tibérius ordered the multitude to make way for him, by which means, though not without some difficulty, Flávius got to him, and informed him that the rich men, in a sitting of the senate, seeing they could not prevail upon the cónsul to espouse their quarrel, had come to a final determination amongst themselves that he should be assassinated, and to that purpose had a great number of their friends and servants ready armed to accomplish it. Tibérius no sooner communicated this confederacy to those about him, but they immediately tucked up their gowns, broke the halberds which the officers used to keep the crowd off into pieces, and distributed them among themselves, resolving to resist the attack with these. Those who stood at a distance wondered, and asked what was the occasion; Tibérius, knowing that they could not hear him at that distance, lifted his hand to his head wishing to intimate the great danger which he apprehended himself to be in.

His adversaries, taking notice of that action, ran off at once to the senate-house, and declared that Tibérius desired the people to bestow a crown upon him, as if this were the meaning of his touching his head. This news created general confusion in the senators, and Nasíca at once called upon the cónsul to punish this tyrant and defend the government. The cónsul mildly replied, that he would not be the first to do any violence; and as he would not suffer any freeman to be put to death, before sentence had lawfully passed upon him, so neither would he allow any measure to be carried into effect, if by persuasion or compulsion on the part of Tibérius the people had been induced to pass an unlawful vote. But Nasíca, rising from his seat, "Since the cónsul," said he, "regards not the safety of the commonwealth, let everyone who will defend the laws, follow me." He then, casting the skirt of his gown over his head, hastened to the Cápitol; those who bore him company, wrapped their gowns also about their arms, and forced their way after him.

And as they were persons of the greatest authority in the city, the common people did not venture to obstruct their passing but were rather so eager to clear the way for them, that they tumbled over one another in haste. The attendants they brought with them had furnished themselves with clubs and staves from their houses, and they themselves picked up the feet and other fragments of stools and chairs, which were broken by the hasty flight of the common people. Thus armed, they made towards Tibérius, knocking down those whom they found in front of him, and those were soon wholly dispersed and many of them slain. Tibérius tried to save himself by flight. As he was running, he was stopped by one who caught hold of him by the gown; but he threw it off and fled in his under-garment only. And stumbling over those who before had been knocked down, as he was endeavoring to get up again, Públius Saturéius, a tríbune, one of his colleagues, was observed to give him the first fatal stroke, by hitting him upon the head with the foot of a stool. The second blow was claimed, as though it had been a deed to be proud of, by Lúcius Rúfus. And of the rest there fell above three hundred killed by clubs and staves only, none by an iron weapon.

This, we are told, was the first sedition amongst the Rómans, since the abrogation of kingly government, that ended in the effusion of blood. All former quarrels which were neither small nor about trivial matters, were always amicably composed, by mutual concessions on either side, the senate yielding for fear of the commons, and the commons out of respect to the senate. And it is probable indeed that Tibérius himself might then have been easily induced, by mere persuasion, to give way, and certainly, if attacked at all, must have yielded without any recourse to violence and bloodshed, as he had not at that time above three thousand men to support him. But it is evident, that this conspiracy was fomented against him, more out of the hatred and malice which the rich men had to his person, than for the reasons which they commonly pretended against him. In testimony of which we may adduce the cruelty and unnatural insults which they used to his dead body. For they would not suffer his own brother, though he earnestly begged the favor, to bury him in the night, but threw him, together with the other corpses, into the river.

Neither did their animosity stop here; for they banished some of his friends without legal process, and slew as many of the others as they could lay their hands on; amongst whom Dióphanes, the orator, was slain, and one Gáius Víllius cruelly murdered by being shut up in a large tun with vipers and serpents. Blóssius of Cúma, indeed, was carried before the cónsuls, and examined touching what had happened, and freely confessed that he had done, without scruple, whatever Tibérius bade him. "What," cried Nasíca, "then if Tibérius had bidden you burn the Cápitol, would you have burnt it?" His first answer was, that Tibérius never would have ordered any such thing; but being pressed with the same question by several, he declared, "If Tibérius had commanded it, it would have been right for me to do it; for he never would have commanded it, if it had not been for the people's good." Blóssius at this time was pardoned, and afterwards went away to Aristónicus in Ásia, and when Aristónicus was overthrown and ruined, killed himself.

The senate, to soothe the people after these transactions, did not oppose the division of the public lands, and permitted them to choose another commissioner in the room of Tibérius. So they elected Públius Crássus, who was Grácchus's near connection, as his daughter Licínia was married to Gáius Grácchus; although Cornélius Népos says, that it was not Crássus's daughter whom Gáius married, but Brútus's, who triumphed for his victories over the Lusitánians: but most writers state it as we have done. The people, however, showed evident marks of their anger at Tibérius's death; and were clearly waiting only for the opportunity to be revenged, and Nasíca was already threatened with an impeachment. The senate, therefore, fearing lest some mischief should befall him, sent him ambassador into Ásia, though there was no occasion for his going thither. For the people did not conceal their indignation even in the open streets, but railed at him, whenever they met him abroad calling him a murderer and a tyrant, one who had polluted the most holy and religious spot in Rome with the blood of a sacred and inviolable magistrate.

And so Nasíca left Ítaly, although he was bound, being the chief priest, to officiate in all principal sacrifices. Thus wandering wretchedly and ignominiously from one place to another, he died in a short time after, not far from Pérgamus. It is no wonder that the people had such an aversion to Nasíca, when even Scípio Africánus, though so much and so deservedly beloved by the Rómans, was in danger of quite losing the good opinion which the people had of him, only for repeating, when the news of Tibérius's death was first brought to Numántia, the verse out of Hómer—"Even so perish all who do the same." And afterwards, being asked by Gáius and Fúlvius, in a great assembly, what he thought of Tibérius's death, he gave an answer adverse to Tibérius's public actions. Upon which account, the people thenceforth used to interrupt him when he spoke, which, until that time, they had never done, and he, on the other hand, was induced to speak ill of the people.

Plútarch, *Life of Tibérius Grácchus* (translated by John Dryden)

The Young Gáius Grácchus

Gáius Grácchus at first, either for fear of his brother's enemies, or designing to render them more odious to the people, absented himself from the public assemblies, and lived quietly in his own house, as if he were not only reduced for the present to live unambitiously, but was disposed in general to pass his life in inaction. And some indeed, went so far as to say that he disliked his brother's measures, and had wholly abandoned the defense of them. However, he was not but very young, being not so old as Tibérius by nine years; and he was not yet thirty when he was slain.

In some little time, however, he quietly let his temper appear, which was one of an utter antipathy to a lazy retirement and effeminacy, and not the least likely to be contented with a life of eating, drinking, and money-getting. He gave great pains to the study of eloquence, as wings upon which he might aspire to public business; and it was very apparent that he did not intend to pass his days in obscurity. When Véttius, a friend of his, was on his trial, he defended his cause, and the people were in an ecstasy, and transported with joy, finding him master of such eloquence that the other orators seemed like children in comparison, and jealousies and fears on the other hand began to be felt by the powerful citizens; and it was generally spoken of amongst them that they must hinder Gáius from being made tríbune.

But soon after, it happened that he was elected quæstor, and obliged to attend Oréstes, the cónsul, into Sardínia. This, as it pleased his enemies, so it was not ungrateful to him, being naturally of a warlike character, and as well trained in the art of war as in that of pleading. And, besides, as yet he very much dreaded meddling with state affairs, and appearing publicly in the róstra, which, because of the importunity of the people and his friends, he could not otherwise avoid than by taking this journey. He was therefore most thankful for the opportunity of absenting himself. Notwithstanding which, it is the prevailing opinion that Gáius was a far more thorough demagogue, and more ambitious than ever Tibérius had been, of popular applause; yet it is certain that he was borne rather by a sort of necessity than by any purpose of his own into public business. And Cícero, the orator, relates, that when he declined all such concerns, and would have lived privately, his brother appeared to him in a dream, and calling him by his name, said, "Why do you tarry, Gáius? There is no escape; one life and one death is appointed for us both, to spend the one and to meet the other in the service of the people."

Gáius was no sooner arrived in Sardínia, but he gave exemplary proofs of his high merit; he not only excelled all the young men of his age in his actions against his enemies, in doing justice to his inferiors, and in showing all obedience and respect to his superior officer; but likewise in temperance, frugality, and industry, he surpassed even those who were much older than himself. It happened to be a sharp and sickly winter in Sardínia, insomuch that the general was forced to lay an imposition upon several towns to supply the soldiers with necessary clothes. The cities sent to Rome, petitioning to be excused from that burden; the senate found their request reasonable, and ordered the general to find some other way of clothing the army. While he was at a loss what course to take in this affair, the soldiers were reduced to great distress; but Gáius went from one city to another, and by his mere representations he prevailed with them, that of their own accord they clothed the Róman army.

This again being reported to Rome, and seeming to be only an intimation of what was to be expected of him as a popular leader hereafter, raised new jealousies amongst the senators. And, besides, there came ambassadors out of África from King Micípsa to acquaint the senate that their master, out of respect to Gáius Grácchus, had sent a considerable quantity of corn to the general in Sardínia; at which the senators were so much offended that they turned the ambassadors out of the senate-house and made an order that the soldiers should be relieved by sending others in their room; but that Oréstes should continue at his post, with whom Gáius, also, as they presumed, being his quæstor, would remain. But he, finding how things were carried, immediately in anger took ship for Rome, where his unexpected appearance obtained him the censure not only of his enemies, but also of the people; who thought it strange that a quæstor should leave before his commander. Nevertheless, when some accusation upon this ground was made against him to the cénsors, he desired leave to defend himself, and did it so effectually, that, when he ended, he was regarded as one who had been very much injured. He made it then appear that he had served twelve years in the army whereas others are obliged to serve only ten; that he had continued quæstor to the general three years, whereas he might by law have returned at the end of one year; and alone of all who went on the expedition, he had carried out a full and had brought home an empty purse, while others, after drinking up the wine they had carried out with them, brought back the wine-jars filled again with gold and silver from the war.

Plútarch, Life of Gáius Grácchus (translated by John Dryden)

Gáius Grácchus, the Tríbune

After this they brought other accusations and writs against him, for exciting insurrection amongst the allies, and being engaged in the conspiracy that was discovered about Fregéllæ. But having cleared himself of every suspicion, and proved his entire innocence, he now at once came forward to ask for the tríbuneship; in which, though he was universally opposed by all persons of distinction, yet there came such infinite numbers of people from all parts of Ítaly to vote for Gáius, that lodgings for them could not be supplied in the city; and the Cámpus being not large enough to contain the assembly, there were numbers who climbed upon the roofs and the tilings of the houses to use their voices in his favor. However, the nobility so far forced the people to their pleasure and disappointed Gáius's hope, that he was not returned the first, as was expected, but the fourth tríbune.

But when he came to the execution of his office, it was seen presently who was really first tríbune, as he was a better orator than any of his contemporaries, and the passion with which he still lamented his brother's death made him the bolder in speaking. He used on all occasions to remind the people of what had happened in that tumult, and laid before them the examples of their ancestors, how they declared war against the Falíscans, only for giving scurrilous language to one Genúcius, a tríbune of the people; and sentenced Gáius Vetúrius to death, for refusing to give way in the fórum to a tríbune; "Whereas," said he, "these men did, in the presence of you all, murder Tibérius with clubs, and dragged the slaughtered body through the middle of the city, to be cast into the river. Even his friends, as many as could be taken, were put to death immediately, without any trial, notwithstanding that just and ancient custom, which has always been observed in our city, that whenever any one is accused of a capital crime, and does not make his personal appearance in court, a trumpeter is sent in the morning to his lodging, to summon him by sound of trumpet to appear; and before this ceremony is performed, the judges do not proceed to the vote; so cautious and reserved were our ancestors about business of life and death."

Having moved the people's passion with such addresses (and his voice was of the loudest and strongest), he proposed two laws. The first was, that whoever was turned out of any public office by the people, should be thereby rendered incapable of bearing any office afterwards; the second, that if any magistrate condemn a Róman to be banished without a legal trial, the people be authorized to take cognizance thereof.

One of these laws was manifestly level at Márcus Octávius, who, at the instigation of Tibérius, had been deprived of his tríbuneship. The other touched Popílius, who, in his prætorship, had banished all Tibérius's friends; whereupon Popílius, being unwilling to stand the hazard of a trial, fled out of Ítaly. As for the former law, it was withdrawn by Gáius himself, who said he yielded in the case of Octávius, at the request of his mother Cornélia. This was very acceptable and pleasing to the people, who had a great veneration for Cornélia, not more for the sake of her father than for that of her children; and they afterwards erected a statue of brass in honor of her, with this inscription, Cornélia, the mother of the Grácchi. There are several expressions recorded, in which he used her name perhaps with too much rhetoric, and too little self-respect, in his attacks upon his adversaries. "How," said he, "dare you presume to reflect upon Cornélia, the mother of Tibérius?" And because the person who made the reflections had been suspected of effeminate courses, "With what face," said he, "can you compare Cornélia with yourself? Have you brought forth children as she has done? And yet all Rome knows that she has refrained from the conversation of men longer than you yourself have done." Such was the bitterness he used in his language; and numerous similar expressions might be adduced from his written remains.

Of the laws which he now proposed, with the object of gratifying the people and abridging the power of the senate, the first was concerning the public lands, which were to be divided amongst the poor citizens; another was concerning the common soldiers, that they should be clothed at the public charge, without any diminution of their pay, and that none should be obliged to serve in the army who was not full seventeen years old; another gave the same right to all the Itálians in general, of voting at elections, as was enjoyed by the citizens of Rome; a fourth related to the price of corn, which was to be sold at a lower rate than formerly to the poor; and a fifth regulated the courts of justice, greatly reducing the power of the senators. For hitherto, in all causes, senators only sat as judges, and were therefore much dreaded by the Róman knights and the people.

But Gáius joined three hundred ordinary citizens of equestrian rank with the senators, who were three hundred likewise in number, and ordained that the judicial authority should be equally invested in the six hundred. While he was arguing for the ratification of this law, his behavior was observed to show in many respects unusual earnestness, and whereas other popular leaders had always hitherto, when speaking, turned their faces towards the senate-house, and the place called the comítium, he, on the contrary, was the first man that in his harangue to the people turned himself the other way, towards them, and continued after that time to do so. An insignificant movement and change of posture, yet it marked no small revolution in state affairs, the conversion, in a manner, of the whole government from an aristocracy to a democracy, his action intimating that public speakers should address themselves to the people, not the senate.

When the commonalty ratified this law, and gave him power to select those of the knights whom he approved of, to be judges, he was invested with a sort of a kingly power, and the senate itself submitted to receive his advice in matters of difficulty; nor did he advise anything that might derogate from the honor of that body. As, for example, his resolution about the corn which Fábius the proprætor sent from Spain, was very just and honorable; for he persuaded the senate to sell the corn, and return the money to the same provinces which had furnished them with it; and also that Fábius should be censured for rendering the Róman government odious and insupportable. This got him extraordinary respect and favor among the provinces. Besides all this, he proposed measures for the colonization of several cities, for making roads, and for building public granaries; of all which works he himself undertook the management and superintendence, and was never wanting to give necessary orders for the dispatch of all these different and great undertakings; and that with such wonderful expedition and diligence, as if he had been but engaged upon one of them; insomuch that all persons, even those who hated or feared him, stood amazed to see what a capacity he had for effecting and completing all he undertook. As for the people themselves, they were transported at the very sight, when they saw him surrounded with a crowd of contractors, artificers, public deputies, military officers, soldiers, and scholars. All these he treated with an easy familiarity, yet without abandoning his dignity in his gentleness; and so accommodated his nature to the wants and occasions of every one who addressed him, that those were looked upon as no better than envious detractors, who had represented him as a terrible, assuming, and violent character. He was even a greater master of the popular leader's art in his common talk and his actions, than he was in his public addresses.

His most especial exertions were given to constructing the roads, which he was careful to make beautiful and pleasant, as well as convenient. They were drawn by his directions through the fields, exactly in a straight line, partly paved with hewn stone, and partly laid with solid masses of gravel. When he met with any valleys or deep watercourses crossing the line, he either caused them to be filled up with rubbish, or bridges to be built over them, so well level, that all being of an equal height on both sides, the work presented one uniform and beautiful prospect. Besides this, he caused the roads to be all divided into miles (each mile containing little less than eight furlongs), and erected pillars of stone to signify the distance from one place to another. He likewise placed other stones at small distances from one another, on both sides of the way, by the help of which travelers might get easily on horseback without wanting a groom.

Plútarch, *Life of Gáius Grácchus* (translated by John Dryden)

The Confederacy Against Gáius

For these reasons, the people highly extolled him, and were ready upon all occasions to express their affection towards him. One day, in an oration to them, he declared that he had only one favor to request, which if they granted, he should think the greatest obligation in the world; yet if it were denied, he would never blame them for the refusal. This expression made the world believe that his ambition was to be cónsul; and it was generally expected that he wished to be both cónsul and tríbune at the same time. When the day for election of cónsuls was at hand, and all in great expectation, he appeared in the Cámpus with Gáius Fánnius, canvassing together with his friends for his election. This was of great effect in Fánnius's favor. He was chosen cónsul, and Gáius elected tríbune the second time, without his own seeking or petitioning for it, but at the voluntary motion of the people.

But when he understood that the senators were his declared enemies, and that Fánnius himself was none of the most zealous of friends, he began again to rouse the people with other new laws. He proposed that a colony of Róman citizens might be sent to re-people Taréntum and Cápua, and that the Látins should enjoy the same privileges with the citizens of Rome. But the senate, apprehending that he would at last grow too powerful and dangerous, took a new and unusual course to alienate the people's affections from him, by playing the demagogue in opposition to him, and offering favors contrary to all good policy. Lívius Drúsus was fellow-tríbune with Gáius, a person of as good a family and as well educated as any amongst the Rómans, and noways inferior to those who for their eloquence and riches were the most honored and most powerful men of that time. To him, therefore, the chief senators made their application, exhorting him to attack Gáius, and join in their confederacy against him; which they designed to carry on, not by using any force, or opposing the common people, but by gratifying and obliging them with such unreasonable things as otherwise they would have felt it honorable for them to incur the greatest unpopularity in resisting.

Lívius offered to serve the senate with his authority in this business; and proceeded accordingly to bring forward such laws as were in reality neither honorable nor advantageous for the public; his whole design being to outdo Gáius in pleasing and cajoling the populace (as if it had been in some comedy), with obsequious flattery and every kind of gratifications; the senate thus letting it be seen plainly that they were not angry with Gáius's public measures, but only desirous to ruin him utterly, or at least to lessen his reputation. For when Gáius proposed the settlement of only two colonies, and mentioned the better class of citizens for that purpose, they accused him of abusing the people; and yet, on the contrary, were pleased with Drúsus, when he proposed the sending out of twelve colonies, each to consist of three thousand persons, and those, too, the most needy that he could find. When Gáius divided the public land amongst the poor citizens, and charged them with a small rent, annually to be paid into the exchequer, they were angry at him, as one who sought to gratify the people only for his own interest; yet afterwards they commended Lívius, though he exempted them from paying even that little acknowledgment. They were displeased with Gáius for offering the Látins an equal right with the Rómans of voting at the election of magistrates; but when Lívius proposed that it might not be lawful for a Róman captain to scourge a Látin soldier, they promoted the passing of that law. And Lívius, in all his speeches to the people, always told them that he proposed no laws but such as were agreeable to the senate, who had a particular regard to the people's advantage. And this truly was the only point in all his proceedings which was of any real service, as it created more kindly feelings towards the senate in the people; and whereas they formerly suspected and hated the principal senators, Lívius appeased and mitigated this perverseness and animosity, by his profession that he had done nothing in favor and for the benefit of the commons without their advice and approbation.

But the greatest credit which Drúsus got for kindness and justice towards the people was, that he never seemed to propose any law for his own sake, or his own advantage; he committed the charge of seeing the colonies rightly settled to other commissioners; neither did he ever concern himself with the distribution of the moneys; whereas Gáius always took the principal part in any important transactions of this kind. Rúbrius, another tríbune of the people, had proposed to have Cárthage again inhabited, which had been demolished by Scípio, and it fell to Gáius's lot to see this performed, and for that purpose he sailed to África. Drúsus took this opportunity of his absence to insinuate himself still more into the people's affections, which he did chiefly by accusing Fúlvius, who was a particular friend to Gáius, and was appointed a commissioner with him for the division of the lands. Fúlvius was a man of a turbulent spirit; and notoriously hated by the senate; and besides, he was suspected by others to have fomented the difference between the citizens and their confederates, and underhand to be inciting the Itálians to rebel; though there was little other evidence of the truth of these accusations than his being an unsettled character and of a well-known seditious temper.

This was one principal cause of Gáius's ruin; for part of the envy which fell upon Fúlvius was extended to him. And when Scípio Africánus died suddenly, and no cause of such an unexpected death could be assigned, only some marks of blows upon his body seemed to intimate that he had suffered violence, as is related in the history of his life, the greatest part of the odium attached to Fúlvius, because he was his enemy, and that very day had reflected upon Scípio in a public address to the people. Nor was Gáius himself clear from suspicion. However, this great outrage, committed too upon the person of the greatest and most considerable man in Rome, was never either punished or inquired into thoroughly, for the populace opposed and hindered any judicial investigation, for fear that Gáius should be implicated in the charge if proceedings were carried on. This, however, had happened some time before.

But in África, where at present Gáius was engaged in the re-peopling of Cárthage, which he named Junónia, many ominous appearances, which presaged mischief, are reported to have been sent from the gods. For a sudden gust of wind falling upon the first standard, and the standard-bearer holding it fast, the staff broke; another sudden storm blew away the sacrifices, which were laid upon the altars, and carried them beyond the bounds laid out for the city, and the wolves came and carried away the very marks that were set up to show the boundary. Gáius, notwithstanding all this, ordered and dispatched the whole business in the space of seventy days, and then returned to Rome, understanding how Fúlvius was prosecuted by Drúsus, and that the present juncture of affairs would not suffer him to be absent. For Lúcius Opímius, one who sided with the nobility, and was of no small authority in the senate, who had formerly sued to be cónsul, but was repulsed by Gáius's interest, at the time when Fánnius was elected, was in a fair way now of being chosen cónsul, having a numerous company of supporters. And it was generally believed, if he did obtain it, that he would wholly ruin Gáius, whose power was already in a declining condition; and the people were not so apt to admire his actions as formerly, because there were so many others who every day contrived new ways to please them, with which the senate readily complied.

After his return to Rome, he quitted his house on the Pálatine Mount, and went to live near the marketplace, endeavoring to make himself more popular in those parts, where most of the humble and poorer citizens lived. He then brought forward the remainder of his proposed laws, as intending to have them ratified by the popular vote; to support which a vast number of people collected from all quarters. But the senate persuaded Fánnius, the cónsul, to command all persons who were not born Rómans to depart the city. A new and unusual proclamation was thereupon made, prohibiting any of the allies or Confederates to appear at Rome during that time. Gáius, on the contrary, published an edict, accusing the cónsul for what he had done, and setting forth to the Confederates, that if they would continue upon the place, they might be assured of his assistance and protection. However, he was not so good as his word; for though he saw one of his own familiar friends and companions dragged to prison by Fánnius's officers, he, notwithstanding, passed by without assisting him; either because he was afraid to stand the test of his power, which was already decreased, or because, as he himself reported, he was unwilling to give his enemies an opportunity, which they very much desired, of coming to actual violence and fighting.

About that time there happened likewise a difference between him and his fellow-officers upon this occasion. A show of gladiators was to be exhibited before the people in the market-place, and most of the magistrates erected scaffolds round about, with an intention of letting them for advantage. Gáius commanded them to take down their scaffolds, that the poor people might see the sport without paying anything. But nobody obeying these orders of his, he gathered together a body of laborers, who worked for him, and overthrew all the scaffolds the very night before the contest was to take place. So that by the next morning the market-place was cleared, and the common people had an opportunity of seeing the pastime. In this, the populace thought he had acted the part of a man; but he much disobliged the tríbunes his colleagues, who regarded it as a piece of violent and presumptuous interference.

This was thought to be the chief reason that he failed of being the third time elected tríbune; not but that he had the most votes, but because his colleagues out of revenge caused false returns to be made. But as to this matter there was a controversy. Certain it is, he very much resented this repulse, and behaved with unusual arrogance towards some of his adversaries who were joyful at his defeat, telling them that all this was but a false sardonic mirth, as they little knew how much his actions threw them into obscurity.

Plútarch, Life of Gáius Grácchus (translated by John Dryden)

The Death of Gáius Grácchus

As soon as Opímius also was chosen cónsul, they presently cancelled several of Gáius's laws, and especially called in question his proceedings at Cárthage, omitting nothing that was likely to irritate him, that from some effect of his passion they might find out a tolerable pretense to put him to death. Gáius at first bore these things very patiently; but afterwards, at the instigation of his friends, especially Fúlvius, he resolved to put himself at the head of a body of supporters, to oppose the cónsul by force. They say also that on this occasion his mother, Cornélia, joined in the sedition, and assisted him by sending privately several strangers into Rome, under pretense as if they came to be hired there for harvest-men; for that intimations of this are given in her letters to him. However, it is confidently affirmed by others that Cornélia did not in the least approve of these actions.

When the day came in which Opímius designed to abrogate the laws of Gáius, both parties met very early at the Cápitol; and the cónsul having performed all the rites usual in their sacrifices, one Quíntus Antýllius, an attendant on the cónsul, carrying out the entrails of the victim, spoke to Fúlvius, and his friends who stood about him, "Ye factious citizens, make way for honest men." Some report that, besides this provoking language, he extended his naked arm towards them, as a piece of scorn and contempt. Upon this he was presently killed with the strong stiles which are commonly used in writing, though some say that on this occasion they had been manufactured for this purpose only. This murder caused a sudden consternation in the whole assembly, and the heads of each faction had their different sentiments about it. As for Gáius, he was much grieved, and severely reprimanded his own party, because they had given their adversaries a reasonable pretense to proceed against them, which they had so long hoped for. Opímius, immediately seizing the occasion thus offered, was in great delight, and urged the people to revenge; but there happening a great shower of rain on a sudden, it put an end to the business of that day.

Early the next morning, the cónsul summoned the senate, and whilst he advised with the senators in the senate-house, the corpse of Antýllius was laid upon a bier, and brought through the market-place there exposed to open view, just before the senate-house, with a great deal of crying and lamentation. Opímius was not at all ignorant that this was designed to be done; however, he seemed to be surprised, and wondered what the meaning of it should be; the senators, therefore, presently went out to know the occasion of it, and, standing about the corpse, uttered exclamations against the inhuman and barbarous act. The people, meantime, could not but feel resentment and hatred for the senators, remembering how they themselves had not only assassinated Tibérius Grácchus, as he was executing his office in the very Cápitol, but had also thrown his mangled body into the river; yet now they could honor with their presence and their public lamentations in the fórum the corpse of an ordinary hired attendant (who, though he might perhaps die wrongfully, was, however, in a great measure the occasion of it himself), by these means hoping to undermine him who was the only remaining defender and safeguard of the people.

The senators, after some time, withdrew, and presently ordered that Opímius, the cónsul, should be invested with extraordinary power to protect the commonwealth and suppress all tyrants. This being decreed, he presently commanded the senators to arm themselves, and the Róman knights to be in readiness very early the next morning, and every one of them to be attended with two servants well armed. Fúlvius, on the other side, made his preparations and collected the populace. Gáius at that time returning from the market-place, made a stop just before his father's statue, and fixing his eyes for some time upon it, remained in a deep contemplation; at length he sighed, shed tears, and departed. This made no small impression upon those who saw it, and they began to upbraid themselves that they should desert and betray so worthy a man as Gáius.

They therefore went directly to his house, remaining there as a guard about it all night, though in a different manner from those who were a guard to Fúlvius; for they passed away the night with shouting and drinking, and Fúlvius himself, being the first to get drunk, spoke and acted many things very unbecoming a man of his age and character. On the other side, the party which guarded Gáius, were quiet and diligent, relieving one another by turns, and forecasting, as in a public what the issue of things might be. As soon as daylight appeared, they took Fúlvius, who had not yet slept off the effects of his drinking; and armed themselves with the weapons hung up in his house, that were formerly taken from the Gauls, whom he conquered in the time of his cónsulship, they presently, with threats and loud acclamations, made their way towards the Áventine Mount.

Gáius could not be persuaded to arm himself, but put on his gown, as if he had been going to the assembly of the people, only with this difference, that under it he had then a short dagger by his side. As he was going out, his wife came running to him at the gate, holding him with one hand, and with the other a young child of his. She bespoke him: "Alas, Gáius, I do not now part with you to let you address the people either as a tríbune or a lawgiver, nor as if you were going to some honorable war, when, though you might perhaps have encountered that fate which all must some time or other submit to, yet you had left me this mitigation of my sorrow, that my mourning was respected and honored. You go now to expose your person to the murderers of Tibérius, unarmed indeed, and rightly so, choosing rather to suffer the worst of injuries than do the least yourself. But even your very death at this time will not be serviceable to the public good. Faction prevails; power and arms are now the only measures of justice. Had your brother fallen before Numántia, the enemy would have given back what then had remained of Tibérius; but such is my hard fate, that I probably must be an humble suppliant to the floods or the waves, that they would somewhere restore to me your relics; for since Tibérius was not spared, what trust can we place either on the laws, or in the Gods?" Licínia, thus bewailing, Gáius, by degrees getting loose from her embraces, silently withdrew himself, being accompanied by his friends; she, endeavoring to catch him by the gown, fell prostrate upon the earth, lying there for some time speechless. Her servants took her up for dead, and conveyed her to her brother Crássus.

Fúlvius, when the people were gathered together in a full body, by the advice of Gáius sent his youngest son into the market-place, with a herald's rod in his hand. He, being a very handsome youth, and modestly addressing himself, with tears in his eyes and a becoming bashfulness, offered proposals of agreement to the cónsul and the whole senate. The greatest part of the assembly were inclinable to accept of the proposals; but Opímius said, that it did not become them to send messengers and capitulate with the senate, but to surrender at discretion to the laws, like loyal citizens, and endeavor to merit their pardon by submission. He commanded the youth not to return, unless they would comply with these conditions. Gáius, as it is reported, was very forward to go and clear himself before the senate; but none of his friends consenting to it, Fúlvius sent his son a second time to intercede for them, as before.

But Opímius, who was resolved that a battle should ensue, caused the youth to be apprehended and committed into custody; and then with a company of his foot-soldiers and some Crétan archers set upon the party under Fúlvius. These archers did such execution, and inflicted so many wounds, that a rout and flight quickly ensued. Fúlvius fled into an obscure bathing-house; but shortly after being discovered, he and his eldest son were slain together. Gáius was not observed to use any violence against anyone; but extremely disliking all these outrages, retired to Diána's temple. There he attempted to kill himself, but was hindered by his faithful friends, Pompónius and Licínius; they took his sword away from him and were very urgent that he would endeavor to make his escape. It is reported that, falling upon his knee and lifting up his hands, he prayed the goddess that the Róman people, as a punishment for their ingratitude and treachery, might always remain in slavery. For as soon as a proclamation was made of a pardon, the greater part openly deserted him.

Gáius, therefore, endeavored now to make his escape, but was pursued so close by his enemies, as far as the wooden bridge, that from thence he narrowly escaped. There his two trusty friends begged of him to preserve his own person by flight, whilst they in the meantime would keep their post, and maintain the passage; neither could their enemies, until they were both slain, pass the bridge. Gáius had no other companion in his flight but one Philócrates, a servant of his. As he ran along, everybody encouraged him, and wished him success, as standers-by may do to those who are engaged in a race, but nobody either lent him any assistance, or would furnish him with a horse, though he asked for one; for his enemies had gained ground, and got very near him. However, he had still time enough to hide himself in a little grove, consecrated to the Fúries. In that place, his servant Philócrates having first slain him, presently afterwards killed himself also, and fell dead upon his master. Though some affirm it for a truth, that they were both taken alive by their enemies, and that Philócrates embraced his master so close, that they could not wound Gáius until his servant was slain.

They say that when Gáius's head was cut off, and carried away by one of his murderers, Septimuléius, Opímius's friend, met him, and forced it from him; because, before the battle began, they had made proclamation, that whoever should bring the head either of Gáius or Fúlvius, should, as a reward, receive its weight in gold. Septimuléius, therefore, having fixed Gáius's head upon the top of his spear, came and presented it to Opímius. They presently brought the scales, and it was found to weigh above seventeen pounds. But in this affair, Septimuléius gave as great signs of his knavery as he had done before of his cruelty; for having taken out the brains, he had filled the skull with lead. There were others who brought the head of Fúlvius, too, but, being mean, inconsiderable persons, were turned away without the promised reward. The bodies of these two persons, as well as of the rest who were slain, to the number of three thousand men, were all thrown into the river; their goods were confiscated, and their widows forbidden to put themselves into mourning. They dealt even more severely with Licínia, Gáius's wife, and deprived her even of her jointure; and as in addition still to all their inhumanity, they barbarously murdered Fúlvius's youngest son; his only crime being, not that he took up arms against them, or that he was present in the battle, but merely that he had come with articles of agreement; for this he was first imprisoned, then slain.

But that which angered the common people most was, that at this time, in memory of his success, Opímius built the Temple of Concord, as if he gloried and triumphed in the slaughter of so many citizens. Somebody in the night time, under the inscription of the temple added this verse: "Folly and Discord Concord's temple built." Yet this Opímius, the first who, being cónsul, presumed to usurp the power of a dictator, condemning, without any trial, with three thousand other citizens, Gáius Grácchus and Fúlvius Fláccus, one of whom had triumphed and been cónsul, the other far excelled all his contemporaries in virtue and honor, afterwards was found incapable of keeping his hands from thieving: and when he was sent ambassador to Jugúrtha, King of Numídia, he was there corrupted by presents, and at his return, being shamefully convicted of it, lost all his honors, and grew old amidst the hatred and the insults of the people; who, though humble, and affrighted at the time, did not fail before long to let everybody see what respect and veneration they had for the memory of the Grácchi. They ordered their statues to be made and set up in public view; they consecrated the places where they were slain, and thither brought the first fruits of everything, according to the season of the year, to make their offerings. Many came likewise thither to their devotions, and daily worshipped there, as at the temple of the gods.

It is reported that as Cornélia, their mother, bore the loss of her two sons with a noble and undaunted spirit, so, in reference to the holy places in which they were slain, she said, their dead bodies were well worthy of such sepulchers. She removed afterwards, and dwelt near the place called Misénum, not at all altering her former way of living. She had many friends, and hospitably received many strangers at her house; many Greeks and learned men were continually about her; nor was there any foreign prince but received gifts from her and presented her again. Those who were conversant with her, were much interested, when she pleased to entertain them with her recollections of her father Scípio Africánus, and of his habits and way of living. But it was most admirable to hear her make mention of her sons, without any tears or sign of grief, and give the full account of all their deeds and misfortunes, as if she had been relating the history of some ancient heroes. This made some imagine, that age, or the greatness of her afflictions, had made her senseless and devoid of natural feelings. But they who so thought were themselves more truly insensible not to see how much a noble nature and education avail to conquer any affliction; and though fortune may often be more successful, and may defeat the efforts of virtue to avert misfortunes, it cannot, when we incur them, prevent our hearing them reasonably.

Plútarch, Life of Gáius Grácchus (translated by John Dryden)

CHAPTER XX

THE TIMES OF MÁRIUS AND SÚLLA

The Rise of Márius, I.—The Social War and the Rise of Súlla, II.—The Civil War between Márius and Súlla, III.
The Dictatorship of Súlla (82-79 B.C.), IV.

The Military Virtues of Márius

... The cónsul Cæcílius Metéllus, being declared general in the war against Jugúrtha in África, took with him Márius for lieutenant; where, eager himself to do great deeds and services that would get him distinction, he did not, like others, consult Metéllus's glory and the serving his interest, and attributing his honor of lieutenancy not to Metéllus, but to fortune, which had presented him with a proper opportunity and theatre of great actions, he exerted his utmost courage. That war, too, affording several difficulties, he neither declined the greatest, nor disdained undertaking the least of them; but surpassing his equals in counsel and conduct, and matching the very common soldiers in labor and abstemiousness, he gained great popularity with them; as indeed any voluntary partaking with people in their labor is felt as an easing of that labor, as it seems to take away the constraint and necessity of it. It is the most obliging sight in the world to the Róman soldier to see a commander eat the same bread as himself, or lie upon an ordinary bed, or assist the work in the drawing a trench and raising a bulwark. For they do not so much admire those that confer honors and riches upon them, as those that partake of the same labor and danger with themselves; but love them better that will vouchsafe to join in their work, than those that encourage their idleness...

Plútarch, *Life of Márius* (translated by John Dryden)

Márius Enrolls the Common People

84 Now Márius, as we have already said, was chosen cónsul with the ardent support of the commons. While even before his election he had been hostile to the nobles, as soon as the people voted him the province of Numídia he attacked the aristocracy persistently and boldly, assailing now individuals and now the entire city. He boasted that he had wrested the cónsulship from them as the spoils of victory, and made other remarks calculated to glorify himself and exasperate them. All the while he gave his first attention to preparation for the war. He asked that the légions should be reinforced, summoned auxiliaries from foreign nations and kings, besides calling out the bravest men from Látium and from our allies, the greater number of whom he knew from actual service but a few only by reputation. By special inducements, too, he persuaded veterans who had served their time to join his expedition.

The senate, although it was hostile to him, did not venture to oppose any of his measures; the addition to the légions it was particularly glad to vote, because it was thought that the commons were disinclined to military service and that Márius would thus lose either resources for the war or the devotion of the people. But such a desire of following Márius had seized almost everyone, that the hopes of the senate were disappointed. Each man imagined himself enriched by booty or returning home a victor, along with other visions of the same kind. Márius too had aroused them in no slight degree by a speech of his; for when all the decrees for which he had asked had been passed and he wished to enroll soldiers, in order to encourage men to enlist and at the same time, according to his custom, to bait the nobles, he called an assembly of the people. Then he spoke in the following manner:

85 "I know, fellow citizens, that it is by very different methods that most men ask for power at your hands and exercise it after it has been secured; that at first they are industrious, humble and modest, but afterwards they lead lives of indolence and arrogance. But the right course, in my opinion, is just the opposite; for by as much as the whole commonwealth is of more value than a cónsulate or a prǽtorship, so much greater ought to be the care with which it is governed than that which is shown in seeking those offices. Nor am I unaware how great a task I am taking upon myself in accepting this signal favor of yours. To prepare for war and at the same time to spare the treasury; to force into military service those whom one would not wish to offend; to have a care for everything at home and abroad—to do all this amid envy, enmity and intrigue, is a ruder task, fellow citizens, than you might suppose. Furthermore, if others make mistakes, their ancient nobility, the brave deeds of their ancestors, the power of their kindred and relatives, their throng of clients, are all a very present help. My hopes are all vested in myself and must be maintained by my own worth and integrity; for all other supports are weak.

"This too I understand, fellow citizens, that the eyes of all are turned towards me, that the just and upright favor me because my services are a benefit to our country, while the nobles are looking for a chance to attack me. Wherefore I must strive the more earnestly that you may not be deceived and that they may be disappointed. From childhood to my present time of life I have so lived that I am familiar with every kind of hardship and danger. As to the efforts, fellow citizens, which before your favors were conferred upon me I made without recompense, it is not my intention to relax them now that they have brought me their reward. To make a moderate use of power is difficult for those who from interested motives have pretended to be virtuous; for me, who have spent my entire life in exemplary conduct, habit has made right living a second nature.

"You have bidden me conduct the war against Jugúrtha, a commission which has sorely vexed the nobles. I pray you, ponder well whether it would be better to change your minds and send on this or any similar errand one of that ring of nobles, a man of ancient lineage and many ancestral portraits—but no campaigns; in order, no doubt, that being wholly in ignorance of the duties of such an office, he might hurry and bustle about and select some one of the common people to act as his adviser. In fact, it very often happens that the man whom you have selected as a commander looks about for someone else to command him. I personally know of men, citizens, who after being elected cónsuls began for the first time to read the history of our forefathers and the military treatises of the Greeks, preposterous creatures! for though in order of time administration follows election, yet in actual practice it comes first.

"Compare me now, fellow citizens, a 'new man,' with those haughty nobles. What they know from hearsay and reading, I have either seen with my own eyes or done with my own hands. What they have learned from books I have learned by service in the field; Think now for yourself whether words or deeds are worth more. They scorn my humble birth, I their worthlessness; I am taunted with my lot in life, they with their infamies. For my part, I believe that all men have one and the same nature, but that the bravest is the best born; and if the fathers of Albínus and Béstia could now be asked whether they would prefer to have me or those men for their descendants, what do you suppose they would reply, if not that they desired to have the best possible children?

"But if they rightly look down on me, let them also look down on their own forefathers, whose nobility began, as did my own, in manly deeds. They begrudge me my office; then let them begrudge my toil, my honesty, even my dangers, since it was through those that I won the office. In fact, these men, spoiled by pride, live as if they scorned your honors, but seek them as if their own lives were honorable. Surely they are deceived when they look forward with equal confidence to things which are worlds apart, the joys of idleness and the rewards of merit. Even when they speak to you or address the senate, their theme is commonly a eulogy of their ancestors; by recounting the exploits of their forefathers they imagine themselves more glory. The very reverse is true. The more glorious was the life of their ancestors, the more shameful is their own baseness.

Assuredly the matter stands thus: the glory of ancestors is, as it were, a light shining upon their posterity, suffering neither their virtues nor their faults to be hidden. Of such glory I acknowledge my poverty, fellow citizens; but—and that is far more glorious—I have done deeds of which I have a right to speak. Now see how unfair those men are; what they demand for themselves because of others' merit they do not allow me as the result of my own, no doubt because I have no family portraits and because mine is a new nobility. And yet surely to be its creator is better than to have inherited and disgraced it.

"I am of course well aware that if they should deign to reply to me, their language would be abundantly eloquent and elaborate. But since after the great honor which you have done me they take every opportunity to rend us both with their invectives, I thought it best not to be silent, for fear that someone might interpret my reticence as due to a guilty conscience. In point of fact, I am confident that I can be injured by no speech; for if they tell the truth, they cannot but speak well of me, and falsehood my life and character refutes. But since it is your judgment in giving me your highest office and a most important commission which they criticize, consider again and yet again whether you ought to regret those acts. I cannot, to justify your confidence, display family portraits or the triumphs and cónsulships of my forefathers; but if occasion requires, I can show spears, a banner, trappings and other military prizes, as well as scars on my breast. These are my portraits, these my patent of nobility, not left me by inheritance as theirs were, but won by my own innumerable efforts and perils.

"My words are not well chosen; I care little for that. Merit shows well enough in itself. It is they who have need of art, to gloss over their shameful acts with specious words. Nor have I studied Grécian letters. I did not greatly care to become acquainted with them, since they had not taught their teachers virtue. But I have learned by far the most important lesson for my country's good—to strike down the foe, to keep watch and ward, to fear nothing save ill repute, to endure heat and cold alike, to sleep on the ground, to bear privation and fatigue at the same time. It is with these lessons that I shall encourage my soldiers; I shall not treat them stingily and myself lavishly, nor win my own glory at the price of their toil. Such leadership is helpful, such leadership is democratic; for to live in luxury oneself but control one's army by punishments is to be a master of slaves, not a commander. It was by conduct like this that your forefathers made themselves and their country famous; but the nobles, relying upon such ancestors though themselves of very different character, despise us who emulate the men of old, and claim from you all honors, not from desert, but as a debt.

"But those most arrogant of men are greatly in error. Their ancestors have left them all that they could—riches, portrait busts, their own illustrious memory; virtue they have not left them, nor could they have done so; that alone is neither bestowed nor received as a gift. They say that I am common and of rude manners, because I cannot give an elegant dinner and because I say no actor or cook higher wages than I do my overseer. This I gladly admit, fellow citizens; for I learned from my father and other righteous men that elegance is proper to women but toil to men, that all the virtuous ought to have more fame than riches, and that arms and not furniture confer honor.

"Well then, let them continue to do what pleases them and what they hold dear; ... let them pass their old age where they have spent their youth, in banquets, slaves to their belly and the most shameful parts of their body. Sweat, dust, and all such things let them leave to us, to whom they are sweeter than feasts. But they will not; for when those most shameless of men have disgraced themselves by their crimes, they come to rob the virtuous of their rewards. Thus, most unjustly, their luxury and sloth, the most abominable of faults, in no wise injure those who practice them, but are the ruin of their blameless country.

"Now that I have replied to them to the extent that my character—but not their crimes—demanded I shall say a few words about our country. First of all, be of good cheer as to Numídia, citizens; for you have put away everything which up to this time has protected Jugúrtha—avarice, incompetence, and arrogance. Furthermore, there is an army in África familiar with the country, but by heaven! more valiant than fortunate; for a great part of it has perished through the greed or rashness of its leaders. Therefore do you, who are of military age, join your efforts with mine and serve your country, and let no one feel fear because of disasters to others or the arrogance of generals. I, Márius, shall be with you on the march and in battle, at once your counsellor and the companion of your dangers, and I shall treat myself and you alike in all respects. And surely with the help of the gods everything is ripe for us—victory, spoils, glory; but even though these were uncertain or remote, yet all good men ought to fly to the aid of their fatherland. Truly, no one ever became immortal through cowardice, and no parent would wish for his children that they might live forever, but rather that their lives might be noble and honored. I would say more, citizens, if words could make cowards brave. For the resolute I think I have spoken abundantly."

86 After Márius had made a speech in these terms and saw that it had fired the spirit of the commons, he made haste to load his ships with provisions, money, arms, and other necessities, with which he bade his lieutenant Áulus Mánlius set sail. He himself in the meantime enrolled soldiers, not according to the classes in the manner of our forefathers, but allowing anyone to volunteer, for the most part the proletariat. Some say that he did this through lack of good men, others because of a desire to curry favor, since that class had given him honor and rank. As a matter of fact, to one who aspires to power the poorest man is the most helpful, since he has no regard for his property, having none, and considers anything honorable for which he receives pay. The result was that Márius set sail for África with a considerably greater contingent than had been authorized. A few days later he arrived at Útica, where the army was handed over to him by the second in command, Públius Rutílius. For Metéllus had avoided meeting Márius, that he might not see what he had been unable even to hear of with composure.

Sállust, War with Jugúrtha, 84-86 (translated by John C. Rolfe)

The Prophecy of Seven Cónsulships

... Finding himself in a great straight, especially because those that attended him were not able to go further, being spent with their long fasting, for the present he turned aside out of the road, and hid himself in a thick wood, where he passed the night in great wretchedness. The next day, pinched with hunger, and willing to make use of the little strength he had, before it were all exhausted, he travelled by the sea-side, encouraging his companions not to fall away from him before the fulfilment of his final hopes, for which, in reliance on some old predictions, he professed to be sustaining himself. For when he was yet but very young, and lived in the country, he caught in the skirt of his garment an eagle's nest, as it was falling, in which were seven young ones, which his parents seeing and much admiring, consulted the áugurs about it, who told them that he should become the greatest man in the world, and that the fates had decreed he should seven times be possessed of the supreme power and authority. Some are of opinion that this really happened to Márius, as we have related it; others say, that those who then and through the rest of his exile heard him tell these stories, and believed him, have merely repeated a story that is altogether fabulous; for an eagle never hatches more than two; and even Musæus was deceived, who, speaking of the eagle, says that, "She lays three eggs, hatches two, and rears one." However this be, it is certain Márius, in his exile and greatest extremities, would often say, that he should attain a seventh cónsulship...

Plútarch, Life of Márius (translated by John Dryden)

Súlla Marches Against Rome

56 Sulpícius would not wait for the end of the vacation, but ordered his faction to come to the fórum with concealed daggers and to do whatever the exigency might require, sparing not even the cónsuls if need be. When everything was in readiness he denounced the vacations as illegal and ordered the cónsuls, Cornélius Súlla and Quíntus Pompéius, to put an end to them at once, in order to proceed to the enactment of the laws. A tumult arose, and those who had been armed drew their daggers and threatened to kill the cónsuls, who refused to obey. Finally Pompéius escaped secretly and Súlla withdrew on the pretext of taking advice. In the meantime the son of Pompéius, who was the son-in-law of Súlla, and who was speaking his mind rather freely, was killed by the Sulpícians. Presently Súlla came on the scene and, having annulled the vacation, hurried away to Cápua, where his army was stationed, as if to cross over to Ásia to take command of the war against Mithridátes, for he knew nothing as yet of the designs against himself. As the vacation was annulled and Súlla had left the city, Sulpícius enacted his law, and Márius, for whose sake it was done, was forthwith chosen commander of the war against Mithridátes in place of Súlla.

57 When Súlla heard of this he resolved to decide the question by war, and called the army together to a conference. They were eager for the war against Mithridátes because it promised much plunder, and they feared that Márius would enlist other soldiers instead of themselves. Súlla spoke of the indignity put upon him by Sulpícius and Márius, and while he did not openly allude to anything else (for he did not dare as yet to mention this sort of war), he urged them to be ready to obey his orders. They understood what he meant, and as they feared lest they should miss the campaign they uttered boldly what Súlla had in mind, and told him to be of good courage, and to lead them to Rome. Súlla was overjoyed and led six légions thither forthwith; but all his superior officers, except one quæstor, left him and fled to the city, because they would not submit to the idea of leading an army against their country. Envoys met him on the road and asked him why he was marching with armed forces against his country. "To deliver her from tyrants," he replied. He gave the same answer to a second and third embassy that came to him, one after another, but he announced to them finally that the Senate and Márius and Sulpícius might meet him in the Cámpus Mártius if they liked, and that he would do whatever might be agreed upon after consultation. As he was approaching, his colleague, Pompéius, came to meet and congratulate him, and to offer his whole-hearted hope, for he was delighted with the steps he was taking. As Márius and Sulpícius needed some short interval for preparation, they sent other messengers, also in the guise of envoys from the Senate, directing him not to move his camp nearer than forty stades from the city until they could review the state of affairs. Súlla and Pompéius understood their motive perfectly and promised to comply, but as soon as the envoys withdrew they followed them.

58 Súlla took possession of the Ésquiline gate and of the adjoining wall with one légion of soldiers, and Pompéius occupied the Cólline gate with another. A third advanced to the Wooden bridge, and a fourth remained on guard in front of the walls. With the remainder Súlla entered the city, in appearance and in fact an enemy. Those in the neighboring houses tried to keep him off by hurling missiles from the roofs until he threatened to burn the houses; then they desisted. Márius and Sulpícius went, with some forces they had hastily armed, to meet the invaders near the Ésquiline fórum, and here a battle took place between the contending parties, the first regularly fought in Rome with bugle and standards in full military fashion, no longer like a mere faction fight. To such extremity of evil had the recklessness of party strife progressed among them.

Súlla's forces were beginning to waver when Súlla seized a standard and exposed himself to danger in the foremost ranks, so that from regard for their general and fear of ignominy, should they abandon their standard, they might rally at once. Then he ordered up the fresh troops from his camp and sent others around by the Subúrran road to take the enemy in the rear. The Márians fought feebly against these new-comers, and as they feared lest they should be surrounded they called to their aid the other citizens who were still fighting from the houses, and proclaimed freedom to slaves who would share their dangers. As nobody came forward they fell into utter despair and fled at once out of the city, together with those of the nobility who had cooperated.

59 Súlla advanced to the Vía Sácra, and there, in sight of everybody, punished at once certain soldiers for looting things they had come across. He stationed guards at intervals throughout the city, he and Pompéius keeping watch by night. Each kept moving about his own command to see that no calamity was brought about either by the frightened people or by the victorious troops. At daybreak they summoned the people to an assembly and lamented the condition of the republic, which had been so long given over to demagogues, and said that they had done what they had done as a matter of necessity. They proposed that no question should ever again be brought before the people which had not been previously considered by the Senate, an ancient practice which had been abandoned long ago; also that the voting should not be by tribes, but by centuries, as King Sérvius Túllius had ordained. They thought that by these two measures—namely, that no law should be brought before the people unless it had been previously before the Senate, and that the voting should be controlled by the well-to-do and sober-minded rather than by the pauper and reckless classes—there would no longer be left any starting-point for civil discord. They proposed many other measures for curtailing the power of the tríbunes, which had become extremely tyrannical, and enrolled 300 of the best citizens at once in the list of the senators, who had been reduced at that time to a very small number and had fallen into contempt for that reason. They also annulled all the acts performed by Sulpícius after the vacation had been proclaimed by the cónsuls, as being illegal.

60 Thus the seditions proceeded from strife and contention to murder, and from murder to open war, and now the first army of her own citizens had invaded Rome as a hostile country. From this time the seditions were decided only by the arbitrament of arms. There were frequent attacks upon the city and battles before the walls and other calamities incident to war. Henceforth there was no restraint upon violence either from the sense of shame, or regard for law, institutions, or country. This time Sulpícius, who still held the office of tríbune, together with Márius, who had been cónsul six times, and his son Márius, also Públius Cethégus, Június Brútus, Gnǽus and Quíntus Gránius, Públius Albinovánus, Márcus Lætórius, and others with them, about twelve in number, had been exiled from Rome, because they had stirred up the sedition, had borne arms against the cónsuls, had incited slaves to insurrection, and had been voted enemies of the Róman people; and anybody meeting them had been authorized to kill them with impunity or to drag them before the cónsuls, while their goods had been confiscated. Detectives, too, were hard on their tracks, who caught Sulpícius and killed him.

61 But Márius escaped them and fled to Mintúrnæ without companion or servant. While he was resting in a darkened house the magistrates of the city, whose fears were excited by the proclamation of the Róman people, but who hesitated to be the murderers of a man who had been six times cónsul and had performed so many brilliant exploits, sent a Gaul who was living there to kill him with a sword. The Gaul, it is said, was approaching the pallet of Márius in the dusk when he thought he saw the gleam and flash of fire darting from his eyes, and Márius rose from his bed and shouted to him in a thundering voice, "Do you dare to kill Gáius Márius?" He turned and fled out of doors like a madman, exclaiming, "I cannot kill Gáius Márius." The magistrates had come to their private decision with reluctance, and now a kind of religious awe came over them as they remembered the prophecy uttered while he was a boy, that he should be cónsul seven times. For it was said that while he was a boy seven eaglets alighted on his breast, and that the soothsayers predicted that he would attain the highest office seven times."

Áppian, *Civil Wars*, 1.56-1.61 (translated by Horace White)

Márius Amidst the Ruins of Cárthage

... With this news, being somewhat comforted, he ventured to pass from that isle towards Cárthage. Sextílius, a Róman, was then governor in África; one that had never received either any injury or any kindness from Márius; but who from compassion, it was hoped, might lend him some help. But he was scarce got ashore with a small retinue, when an officer met him, and said, "Sextílius, the governor, forbids you, Márius, to set foot in África; if you do, he says, he will put the decree of the senate in execution, and treat you as an enemy to the Rómans." When Márius heard this, he wanted words to express his grief and resentment, and for a good while held his peace, looking sternly upon the messenger, who asked him what he should say, or what answer he should return to the governor? Márius answered him with a deep sigh: "Go tell him that you have seen Gáius Márius sitting in exile among the ruins of Cárthage;" appositely applying the example of the fortune of that city to the change of his own condition...

Plútarch, Life of Márius (translated by John Dryden)

Súlla's Proscriptions

Súlla being thus wholly bent upon slaughter, and filling the city with executions without number or limit, many wholly uninterested persons falling a sacrifice to private enmity, through his permission and indulgence to his friends, Gáius Metéllus, one of the younger men, made bold in the senate to ask him what end there was of these evils, and at what point he might be expected to stop? "We do not ask you," said he, "to pardon any whom you have resolved to destroy, but to free from doubt those whom you are pleased to save." Súlla answering, that he knew not as yet whom to spare. "Why then," said he, "tell us whom you will punish." This Súlla said he would do. These last words, some authors say, were spoken not by Metéllus, but by Afídius, one of Súlla's fawning companions. Immediately upon this, without communicating with any of the magistrates, Súlla proscribed eighty persons, and notwithstanding the general indignation, after one day's respite, he posted two hundred and twenty more, and on the third again, as many.

In an address to the people on this occasion, he told them he had put up as many names as he could think of; those which had escaped his memory, he would publish at a future time. He issued an edict likewise, making death the punishment of humanity, proscribing any who should dare to receive and cherish a proscribed person, without exception to brother, son, or parents. And to him who should slay any one proscribed person, he ordained two talents reward, even were it a slave who had killed his master, or a son his father. And what was thought most unjust of all, he caused the attainder to pass upon their sons, and son's sons, and made open sale of all their property. Nor did the proscription prevail only at Rome, but throughout all the cities of Ítaly the effusion of blood was such, that neither sanctuary of the gods, nor hearth of hospitality, nor ancestral home escaped. Men were butchered in the embraces of their wives, children in the arms of their mothers. Those who perished through public animosity, or private enmity, were nothing in comparison of the numbers of those who suffered for their riches. Even the murderers began to say, that "his fine house killed this man, a garden that, a third, his hot baths." Quíntus Aurélius, a quiet, peaceable man, and one who thought all his part in the common calamity consisted in condoling with the misfortunes of others, coming into the fórum to read the list, and finding himself among the proscribed, cried out, "Woe is me, my Álban farm has informed against me." He had not gone far, before he was dispatched by a ruffian, sent on that errand.

In the meantime, Márius, on the point of being taken, killed himself; and Súlla, coming to Præneste, at first proceeded judicially against each particular person, till at last, finding it a work of too much time, he cooped them up together in one place, to the number of twelve thousand men, and gave order for the execution of them all, his own host alone excepted. But he, brave man, telling him he could not accept the obligation of life from the hands of one who had been the ruin of his country, went in among the rest, and submitted willingly to the stroke. What Lúcius Catilína did was thought to exceed all other acts. For having, before matters came to an issue, made away with his brother, he besought Súlla to place him in the list of proscription, as though he had been alive, which was done; and Cátiline, to return the kind office, assassinated a certain Márcus Márius, one of the adverse party, and brought the head to Súlla, as he was sitting in the fórum, and then going to the holy water of Apóllo, which was nigh, washed his hands.

There were other things, besides this bloodshed, which gave offense. For Súlla had declared himself dictator, an office which had then been laid aside for the space of one hundred and twenty years. There was, likewise, an act of grace passed on his behalf, granting indemnity for what was passed, and for the future entrusting him with the power of life and death, confiscation, division of lands, erecting and demolishing of cities, taking away of kingdoms, and bestowing them at pleasure. He conducted the sale of confiscated property after such an arbitrary, imperious way, from the tribunal, that his gifts excited greater odium even than his usurpations; women, mimes, and musicians, and the lowest of the freed slaves had presents made them of the territories of nations, and the revenues of cities; and women of rank were married against their will to some of them. Wishing to insure the fidelity of Pómpey the Great, by a nearer tie of blood, he bade him divorce his present wife, and forcing Æmília, the daughter of Scáurus and Metélla, his own wife, to leave her husband, Mánius Glábrio, he bestowed her, though then with child, on Pómpey, and she died in childbirth at his house.

Plútarch, Life of Súlla (translated by John Dryden)

CHAPTER XXI

THE TIMES OF PÓMPEY AND CÆSAR

The Rise of Pómpey, I.—The Growing Influence of Cæsar, II.—Civil War between Pómpey and Cæsar, III.
The Rule of Július Cæsar, IV.

Sertórius Defeats Pómpey

So long as he had to do with Metéllus, he was thought to owe his successes to his opponent's age and slow temper, which were ill-suited for coping with the daring and activity of one who commanded a light army more like a band of robbers than regular soldiers. But when Pómpey also passed over the Pýrenees, and Sertórius pitched his camp near him, and offered and himself accepted every occasion by which military skill could be put to the proof, and in this contest of dexterity was found to have the better, both in baffling his enemy's designs and in counter-scheming himself, the fame of him now spread even to Rome itself, as the most expert commander of his time. For the renown of Pómpey was not small, who had already won much honor by his achievements in the wars of Súlla, from whom he received the title of Mágnus, and was called Pómpey the Great; and who had risen to the honor of a triumph before the beard had grown on his face. And many cities which were under Sertórius were on the very eve of revolting and going over to Pómpey, when they were deterred from it by that great action, amongst others, which he performed near the city of Láuron, contrary to the expectation of all.

For Sertórius had laid siege to Láuron, and Pómpey came with his whole army to relieve it; and there being a hill near this city very advantageously situated, they both made haste to take it. Sertórius was beforehand, and took possession of it first, and Pómpey, having drawn down his forces, was not sorry that it had thus happened, imagining that he had hereby enclosed his enemy between his own army and the city, and sent in a messenger to the citizens of Láuron, to bid them be of good courage, and to come upon their walls, where they might see their besieger besieged. Sertórius, perceiving their intentions, smiled, and said, he would now teach Súlla's scholar, for so he called Pómpey in derision, that it was the part of a general to look as well behind him as before him, and at the same time showed them six thousand soldiers, whom he had left in his former camp, from whence he marched out to take the hill, where if Pómpey should assault him, they might fall upon his rear.

Pómpey discovered this too late, and not daring to give battle, for fear of being encompassed, and yet being ashamed to desert his friends and confederates in their extreme danger, was thus forced to sit still, and see them ruined before his face. For the besieged despaired of relief, and delivered up themselves to Sertórius, who spared their lives and granted them their liberty, but burnt their city, not out of anger or cruelty, for of all commanders that ever were, Sertórius seems least of all to have indulged these passions, but only for the greater shame and confusion of the admirers of Pómpey, and that it might be reported amongst the Spániards, that though he had been so close to the fire which burnt down the city of his confederates as actually to feel the heat of it, he still had not dared to make any opposition. Sertórius, however, sustained many losses; but he always maintained himself and those immediately with him undefeated, and it was by other commanders under him that he suffered; and he was more admired for being able to repair his losses, and for recovering the victory, than the Róman generals against him for gaining these advantages; as at the battle of the Súcro against Pómpey, and at the battle near Túttia, against him and Metéllus together. The battle near the Súcro was fought, it is said, through the impatience of Pómpey, lest Metéllus should share with him in the victory, Sertórius being also willing to engage Pómpey before the arrival of Metéllus. Sertórius delayed the time till the evening, considering that

35

the darkness of the night would be a disadvantage to his enemies, whether flying or pursuing, being strangers, and having no knowledge of the country.

When the fight began, it happened that Sertórius was not placed directly against Pómpey, but against Afránius, who had command of the left wing of the Róman army, as he commanded the right wing of his own; but when he understood that his left wing began to give way, and yield to the assault of Pómpey, he committed the care of his right wing to other commanders, and made haste to relieve those in distress; and rallying some that were flying, and encouraging others that still kept their ranks, he renewed the fight, and attacked the enemy in their pursuit so effectively as to cause a considerable rout, and brought Pómpey into great danger of his life. For after being wounded and losing his horse, he escaped unexpectedly. For the Áfricans with Sertórius, who took Pómpey's horse, set out with gold, and covered with rich trappings, fell out with one another; and upon the dividing of the spoil, gave over the pursuit. Afránius, in the mean time, as soon as Sertórius had left his right wing, to assist the other part of his army, overthrew all that opposed him; and pursuing them to their camp, fell in together with them, and plundered them till it was dark night; knowing nothing of Pómpey's overthrow, nor being able to restrain his soldiers from pillaging; when Sertórius, returning with victory, fell upon him and upon his men, who were all in disorder, and slew many of them. And the next morning he came into the field again, well armed, and offered battle, but perceiving that Metéllus was near, he drew off, and returned to his camp, saying, "If this old woman had not come up, I would have whipped that boy soundly and sent him to Rome."

Plútarch, Life of Sertórius (translated by John Dryden)

The Love of Sertórius for Rome

Sertórius, meantime, showed the loftiness of his temper in calling together all the Róman senators who had fled from Rome, and had come and resided with him, and giving them the name of a senate; and out of these he chose prætors and quæstors, and adorned his government with all the Róman laws and institutions. And though he made use of the arms, riches, and cities of the Spániards, yet he would never, even in word, remit to them the imperial authority, but set Róman officers and commanders over them, intimating his purpose to restore liberty to the Rómans, not to raise up the Spániard's power against them. For he was a sincere lover of his country, and had a great desire to return home; but in his adverse fortune he showed undaunted courage, and behaved himself towards his enemies in a manner free from all dejection and mean-spiritedness; and when he was in his prosperity, and in the height of his victories, he sent word to Metéllus and Pómpey, that he was ready to lay down his arms, and live a private life, if he were allowed to return home, declaring that he had rather live as the meanest citizen in Rome, than, exiled from it, be supreme commander of all other cities together.

And it is thought that his great desire for his country was in no small measure promoted by the tenderness he had for his mother, under whom he was brought up after the death of his father, and upon whom he had placed his entire affection. And after that his friends had sent for him into Spain to be their general, as soon as he heard of his mother's death, he had almost cast away himself and died for grief; for he lay seven days together continually in his tent, without giving the word, or being seen by the nearest of his friends; and when the chief commanders of the army, and persons of the greatest note came about his tent, with great difficulty they prevailed with him at last to come abroad, and speak to his soldiers, and to take upon him the management of affairs, which were in a prosperous condition. And thus, to many men's judgment, he seemed to have been in himself of a mild and compassionate temper, and naturally given to ease and quietness, and to have accepted of the command of military forces contrary to his own inclination, and not being able to live in safety otherwise, to have been driven by his enemies to have recourse to arms, and to espouse the wars as a necessary guard for the defense of his person.

His negotiations with king Mithridátes further argue the greatness of his mind. For when Mithridátes, recovering himself from his overthrow by Súlla, like a strong wrestler that gets up to try another fall, was again endeavoring to reestablish his power in Ásia, at this time the great fame of Sertórius was celebrated in all places; and when the merchants who came out of the western parts of Europe, bringing these, as it were, among their other foreign wares, had filled the kingdom of Póntus with their stories of his exploits in war, Mithridátes was extremely desirous to send an embassy to him, being also highly encouraged to it by the boastings of his flattering courtiers, who, comparing Mithridátes to Pýrrhus, and Sertórius to Hánnibal, professed that the Rómans would never be able to make any considerable resistance against such great forces, and such admirable commanders, when they should be set upon on both sides at once, on one by the most warlike general, and on the other by the most powerful prince in existence.

Accordingly, Mithridátes sends ambassadors into Spain to Sertórius with letters and instructions, and commission to promise ships and money towards the charge of the war, if Sertórius would confirm his pretensions upon Ásia, and authorize him to possess all that he had surrendered to the Rómans in his treaty with Súlla. Sertórius summoned a full council which he called a senate, where, when others joyfully approved of the conditions, and were desirous immediately to accept of his offer, seeing that he desired nothing of them but a name, and an empty title to places not in their power to dispose of, in recompense of which they should be supplied with what they then stood most in need of, Sertórius would by no means agree to it; declaring that he was willing that king Mithridátes should exercise all royal power and authority over Bithýnia and Cappadócia, countries accustomed to a monarchical government, and not belonging to Rome, but he could never consent that he should seize or detain a province, which, by the justest right and title, was possessed by the Rómans, which Mithridátes had formerly taken away from them, and had afterwards lost in open war to Fímbria, and quitted upon a treaty of peace with Súlla. For he looked upon it as his duty to enlarge the Róman possessions by his conquering arms, and not to increase his own power by the diminution of the Róman territories. Since a noble-minded man, though he willingly accepts of victory when it comes with honor, will never so much as endeavor to save his own life upon any dishonorable terms. When this was related to Mithridátes, he was struck with amazement, and said to his intimate friends, "What will Sertórius enjoin us to do when he comes to be seated in the Palátium in Rome, who at present, when he is driven out to the borders of the Atlántic sea, sets bounds to our kingdoms in the east, and threatens us with war, if we attempt the recovery of Ásia?"

Plútarch, *Life of Sertórius* (translated by John Dryden)

Spártacus and the Third Slave War

At the same time Spártacus, a Thrácian by birth, who had once served as a soldier with the Rómans, but had since been a prisoner and sold for a gladiator, and was in the gladiatorial training-school at Cápua, persuaded about seventy of his comrades to strike for their own freedom rather than for the amusement of spectators. They overcame the guards and ran away, arming themselves with clubs and daggers that they took from people on the roads, and took refuge on Mount Vesúvius. There many fugitive slaves and even some freemen from the fields joined Spártacus, and he plundered the neighboring country, having for subordinate officers two gladiators named Œnomáus and Críxus. As he divided the plunder impartially he soon had plenty of men. Varínius Gláber was first sent against him and afterwards Públius Valérius, not with regular armies, but with forces picked up in haste and at random, for the Rómans did not consider this a war yet, but a raid, something like an attack of robbery. They attacked Spártacus and were beaten. Spártacus even captured the horse of Varínius; so narrowly did the very general of the Rómans escape being captured by a gladiator.

After this still greater numbers flocked to Spártacus till his army numbered 70,000. For these he manufactured weapons and collected equipment, whereas Rome now sent out the cónsuls with two légions. One of them overcame Críxus with 30,000 men near Mount Gargánus, two-thirds of whom perished together with himself. Spártacus endeavored to make his way through the Ápennines to the Alps and the Gállic country, but one of the cónsuls anticipated him and hindered his flight while the other hung upon his rear. He turned upon them one after the other and beat them in detail. They retreated in confusion in different directions. Spártacus sacrificed 300 Róman prisoners to the shade of Críxus, and marched on Rome with 120,000 foot, having burned all his useless material, killed all his prisoners, and butchered his pack-animals in order to expedite his movement. Many deserters offered themselves to him, but he would not accept them. The cónsuls again met him in the country of Picénum. Here there was fought another great battle and there was, too, another great defeat for the Rómans.

Spártacus changed his intention of marching on Rome. He did not consider himself ready as yet for that kind of a fight, as his whole force was not suitably armed, for no city had joined him, but only slaves, deserters, and riff-raff. However, he occupied the mountains around Thúrii and took the city itself. He prohibited the bringing in of gold or silver by merchants, and would not allow his own men to acquire any, but he bought largely of iron and brass and did not interfere with those who dealt in these articles. Supplied with abundant material from this source his men provided themselves with plenty of arms and made frequent forays for the time being. When they next came to an engagement with the Rómans they were again victorious, and returned laden with spoils.

This war, so formidable to the Rómans (although ridiculed and despised in the beginning, as being merely the work of gladiators), had now lasted three years. When the election of new prætors came on, fear fell upon all, and nobody offered himself as a candidate until Licínius Crássus, a man distinguished among the Rómans for birth and wealth, assumed the prætorship and marched against Spártacus with six new légions. When he arrived at his destination he received also the two légions of the cónsuls, whom he decimated by lot for their bad conduct in several battles. Some say that Crássus, too, having engaged in battle with his whole army, and having been defeated, decimated the whole army and was not deterred by their numbers, but destroyed about 4000 of them. Whichever way it was, when he had once demonstrated to them that he was more dangerous to them than the enemy, he overcame immediately 10,000 of the Spártacans, who were encamped somewhere in a detached position, and killed two-thirds of them. He then marched boldly against Spártacus himself, vanquished him in a brilliant engagement, and pursued his fleeing forces to the sea, where they tried to pass over to Sícily. He overtook them and enclosed them with a line of circumvallation consisting of ditch, wall, and paling.

Spártacus tried to break through and make an incursion into the Sámnite country, but Crássus slew about 6000 of his men in the morning and as many more towards evening. Only three of the Róman army were killed and seven wounded, so great was the improvement in their morale inspired by the recent punishment. Spártacus, who was expecting a reinforcement of horse from somewhere, no longer went into battle with his whole army, but harassed the besiegers by frequent sallies here and there. He fell upon them unexpectedly and continually, threw bundles of sticks into the ditch and set them on fire and made their labor difficult. He also crucified a Róman prisoner in the space between the two armies to show his own men what fate awaited them if they did not conquer. But when the Rómans in the city heard of the siege they thought it would be disgraceful if this war against gladiators should be prolonged. Believing also that the work still to be done against Spártacus was great and severe they ordered up the army of Pómpey, which had just arrived from Spain, as a reinforcement.

On account of this vote Crássus tried in every way to come to an engagement with Spártacus so that Pómpey might not reap the glory of the war. Spártacus himself, thinking to anticipate

Pómpey, invited Crássus to come to terms with him. When his proposals were rejected with scorn he resolved to risk a battle, and as his cavalry had arrived he made a dash with his whole army through the lines of the besieging force and pushed on to Brundísium with Crássus in pursuit. When Spártacus learned that Lucúllus had just arrived in Brundísium from his victory over Mithridátes he despaired of everything and brought his forces, which were even then very numerous, to close quarters with Crássus. The battle was long and bloody, as might have been expected with so many thousands of desperate men. Spártacus was wounded in the thigh with a spear and sank upon his knee, holding his shield in front of him and contending in this way against his assailants until he and the great mass of those with him were surrounded and slain. The Róman loss was about 1000. The body of Spártacus was not found. A large number of his men fled from the battlefield to the mountains and Crássus followed them thither. They divided themselves in four parts and continued to fight until they all perished except 6000, who were captured and crucified along the whole road from Cápua to Rome.

Crássus accomplished his task within six months, whence arose a contention for honors between himself and Pómpey. Crássus did not dismiss his army, for Pómpey did not dismiss his. Both were candidates for the cónsulship. Crássus had been prætor as the law of Súlla required. Pómpey had been neither prætor nor quæstor, and was only thirty-four years old, but he had promised the tríbunes of the people that much of their former power should be restored. When they were chosen cónsuls they did not even then dismiss their armies, which were stationed near the city. Each one offered an excuse. Pómpey said that he was waiting the return of Metéllus for his Spánish triumph; Crássus said that Pómpey ought to dismiss his army first.

The people, seeing fresh seditions brewing and fearing two armies encamped round about, besought the cónsuls, while they were occupying the cúrule chairs in the fórum, to be reconciled to each other; but at first both of them repelled these solicitations. When, however, certain persons, who seemed prophetically inspired, predicted many direful consequences if the cónsuls did not come to an agreement, the people again implored them with lamentations and the greatest dejection, reminding them of the evils produced by the contentions of Márius and Súlla. Crássus yielded first. He came down from his chair, advanced to Pómpey, and offered him his hand in the way of reconciliation. Pómpey rose and hastened to meet him. They shook hands amid general acclamations and the people did not leave the assembly until the cónsuls had given orders in writing to disband their armies. Thus was the well-grounded fear of another great dissension happily dispelled. This was about the sixtieth year in the course of the civil convulsions, reckoning from the death of Tibérius Grácchus.

Áppian, *Civil Wars*, 1.116-1.121 (translated by Horace White)

The Luxury of Lucúllus

And, indeed, Lucúllus's life, like the Old Comedy, presents us at the commencement with acts of policy and of war, at the end offering nothing but good eating and drinking, feastings and revellings, and mere play. For I give no higher name to his sumptuous buildings, porticos and baths, still less to his paintings and sculptures, and all his industry about these curiosities, which he collected with vast expense, lavishly bestowing all the wealth and treasure which he got in the war upon them, insomuch that even now, with all the advance of luxury, the Lucúllian gardens are counted the noblest the emperor has. Túbero the Stóic, when he saw his buildings at Náples, where he suspended the hills upon vast tunnels, brought in the sea for moats and fishponds round his house, and built pleasure-houses in the waters, called him Xérxes in a gown. He had also fine seats in Túsculum, belvederes, and large open balconies for men's apartments, and porticos to walk in, where Pómpey coming to see him, blamed him for making a house which would be pleasant in summer, but uninhabitable in winter; whom he answered with a smile, "You think me, then, less provident than cranes and storks, not to change my home with the season." When a prætor, with great expense and pains, was preparing a spectacle for the people, and asked him to lend him some purple robes for the performers in a chorus, he told him he would go home and see, and if he had got any, would let him have them; and the next day asking how many he wanted, and being told that a hundred would suffice, bade him to take twice as many: on which the poet Hórace observes, that a house is but a poor one, where the valuables unseen and unthought of do not exceed all those that meet the eye.

Lucúllus's daily entertainments were ostentatiously extravagant, not only with purple coverlets, and plate adorned with precious stones, and dancings, and interludes, but with the greatest diversity of dishes and the most elaborate cookery, for the vulgar to admire and envy. It was a happy thought of Pómpey in his sickness, when his physician prescribed a thrush for his dinner, and his servants told him that in summer time thrushes were not to be found anywhere but in Lucúllus's fattening coops, that he would not suffer them to fetch one thence, but observing to his physician, "So if Lucúllus had not been an épicure, Pómpey had not lived," ordered something else that could easily be got to be prepared for him. Cáto was his friend and connection, but, nevertheless, so hated his life and habits, that when a young man in the senate made a long and tedious speech in praise of frugality and temperance, Cáto got up and said, "How long do you mean to go on making money like Crássus, living like Lucúllus, and talking like Cáto?" There are some, however, who say the words were said, but not by Cáto. It is plain from the anecdotes on record of him, that Lucúllus was not only pleased with, but even gloried in his way of living. For he is said to have feasted several Greeks upon their coming to Rome day after day, who, out of a true Grécian principle, being ashamed, and declining the invitation, where so great an expense was every day incurred for them, he with a smile told them, "Some of this, indeed, my Grécian friends, is for your sakes, but more for that of Lucúllus."

Once when he supped alone, there being only one course, and that but moderately furnished, he called his steward and reproved him, who, professing to have supposed that there would be no need of any great entertainment, when nobody was invited, was answered, "What, did not you know, then, that today Lucúllus dines with Lucúllus?" Which being much spoken of about the city, Cícero and Pómpey one day met him loitering in the fórum, the former his intimate friend and familiar, and, though there had been some ill-will between Pómpey and him about the command in the war, still they used to see each other and converse on easy terms together. Cícero accordingly saluted him, and asked him whether today were a good time for asking a favor of him, and on his answering, "Very much so," and begging to hear what it was, "Then," said Cícero, "we should like to dine with you today, just on the dinner that is prepared for yourself." Lucúllus being surprised, and requesting a day's time, they refused to grant it, neither suffered him to talk with his servants, for fear he should give order for more than was appointed before. But thus much they consented to, that before their faces he might tell his servant, that today he would sup in the Apóllo, (for so one of his best dining rooms was called,) and by this evasion he outwitted his guests. For every room, as it seems, had its own assessment of expenditure, dinner at such a price, and all else in accordance; so that the servants, on knowing where he would dine, knew also how much was to be expended, and in what style and form dinner was to be served. The expense for the Apóllo was fifty thousand dráchmas, and thus much being that day laid out, the greatness of the cost did not so much amaze Pómpey and Cícero, as the rapidity of the outlay. One might believe Lucúllus thought his money really captive and barbarian, so wantonly and contumeliously did he treat it.

Plútarch, *Life of Lucúllus* (translated by John Dryden)

The Conspiracy of Cátiline

1 It becomes all men, who desire to excel other animals, to strive, to the utmost of their power, not to pass through life in obscurity, like the beasts of the field, which nature has formed groveling and subservient to appetite. All our power is situated in the mind and in the body. Of the mind we rather employ the government; of the body, the service. The one is common to us with the gods; the other with the brutes. It appears to me, therefore, more reasonable to pursue glory by means of the intellect than of bodily strength, and, since the life which we enjoy is short, to make the remembrance of us as lasting as possible. For the glory of wealth and beauty is fleeting and perishable; that of intellectual power is illustrious and immortal.

Yet it was long a subject of dispute among mankind, whether military efforts were more advanced by strength of body, or by force of intellect. For, in affairs of war, it is necessary to plan before beginning to act, and, after planning, to act with promptitude and vigor. Thus, each being insufficient of itself, the one requires the assistance of the other.

2 In early times, accordingly, kings (for that was the first title of sovereignty in the world) applied themselves in different ways; some exercised the mind, others the body. At that period, however, the life of man was passed without covetousness; everyone was satisfied with his own. But after Cýrus in Ásia, and the Lacedæmónians and Athénians in Greece, began to subjugate cities and nations, to deem the lust of dominion a reason for war, and to imagine the greatest glory to be in the most extensive empire, it was then at length discovered, by proof and experience, that mental power has the greatest effect in military operations. And, indeed, if the intellectual ability of kings and magistrates were exerted to the same degree in peace as in war, human affairs would be more orderly and settled, and you would not see governments shifted from hand to hand, and things universally changed and confused. For dominion is easily secured by those qualities by which it was at first obtained. But when sloth has introduced itself in the place of industry, and covetousness and pride in that of moderation and equity, the fortune of a state is altered together with its morals; and thus authority is always transferred from the less to the more deserving.

Even in agriculture, in navigation, and in architecture, whatever man performs owns the dominion of intellect. Yet many human beings, resigned to sensuality and indolence, uninstructed and unimproved, have passed through life like travelers in a strange country; to whom, certainly, contrary to the intention of nature, the body was a gratification, and the mind a burden. Of these I hold the life and death in equal estimations, for silence is maintained concerning both. But he only, indeed, seems to me to live, and to enjoy life, who, intent upon some employment, seeks reputation from some ennobling enterprise, or honorable pursuit. But in the great abundance of occupations, nature points out different paths to different individuals.

3 To act well for the Commonwealth is noble, and even to speak well for it is not without merits. Both in peace and in war it is possible to obtain celebrity; many who have acted, and many who have recorded the actions of others, receive their tribute of praise. And to me, assuredly, though by no means equal glory attends the narrator and the performer of illustrious deeds, it yet seems in the highest degree difficult to write the history of great transactions; first, because deeds must be adequately represented by words; and next, because most readers consider that whatever errors you mention with censure, are mentioned through malevolence and envy; while, when you speak of the great virtue and glory of eminent men, every one hears with acquiescence only that which he himself thinks easy to be performed; all beyond his own conception he regards as fictitious and incredible.

I myself, however, when a young man, was at first led by inclination, like most others, to engage in political affairs; but in that pursuit many circumstances were unfavorable to me; for, instead of modesty, temperance, and integrity, there prevailed shamelessness, corruption, and rapacity. And although my mind, inexperienced in dishonest practice, detested these vices, yet, in the midst of so great corruption, my tender age was ensnared and infected by ambition; and though I shrunk from the vicious principles of those around me, yet the same eagerness for honors, the same obloquy and jealousy, which disquieted others, disquieted myself.

4 When, therefore, my mind had rest from its numerous troubles and trials, and I had determined to pass the remainder of my days unconnected with public life, it was not my intention to waste my valuable leisure in indolence and inactivity, or, engaging in servile occupations, to spend my time in agriculture or hunting; but, returning to those studies from which, at their commencement, a corrupt ambition had allured me, I determined to write, in detached portions, the transactions of the Róman people, as any occurrence should seem worthy of mention; an undertaking to which I was the rather inclined, as my mind was uninfluenced by hope, fear, or political partisanship. I shall accordingly give a brief account with as much truth as I can, of the Conspiracy of Cátiline; for I think it an enterprise eminently deserving of record, from the unusual nature both of its guilt and of its perils. But before I enter upon my narrative, I must give a short description of the character of the man.

5 Lúcius Cátiline was a man of noble birth, and of eminent mental and personal endowments, but of a vicious and depraved disposition. His delight, from his youth, had been in civil commotions, bloodshed, robbery, and sedition; and in such scenes he had spent his early years. His constitution could endure hunger, want of sleep, and cold, to a degree surpassing belief. His mind was daring, subtle, and versatile, capable of pretending or dissembling whatever he wished. He was covetous of other men's property, and prodigal of his own. He had abundance of eloquence, though but little wisdom. His insatiable ambition was always pursuing objects extravagant, romantic, and unattainable.

Since the time of Súlla's dictatorship, a strong desire of seizing the government possessed him, nor did he at all care, provided that he secured power for himself, by what means he might arrive at it. His violent spirit was daily more and more hurried on by the diminution of his patrimony, and by his consciousness of guilt; both which evils he had increased by those practices which I have mentioned above. The corrupt morals of the state, too, which extravagance and selfishness, pernicious and contending vices, rendered thoroughly depraved, furnished him with additional incentives to action.

Since the occasion has thus brought public morals under my notice, the subject itself seems to call upon me to look back, and briefly to describe the conduct of our ancestors in peace and war; how they managed the state, and how powerful they left it; and how, by gradual alteration, it became, from being the most virtuous, the most vicious and depraved.

6 Of the city of Rome, as I understand, the founders and earliest inhabitants were the Trójans, who, under the conduct of Ænéas, were wandering about as exiles from their country, without any settled abode; and with these were joined the Aborígines, a savage race of men, without laws or government, free and owning no control. How easily these two tribes, though of different origin, dissimilar language, and opposite habits of life, formed a union when they met within the same walls, is almost incredible. But when their state, from an accession of population and territory, and an improved condition of morals, showed itself tolerably flourishing and powerful, envy, as is generally the case in human affairs, was the consequence of its prosperity. The neighboring kings and people, accordingly, began to assail them in war, while a few only of their friends came to their support; for the rest, struck with alarm, shrunk from sharing their dangers. But the Rómans, active at home and in the field, prepared with alacrity for their defense. They encouraged one another, and hurried to meet the enemy. They protected with their arms, their liberty, their country, and their homes. And when they had at length repelled danger by valor, they lent assistance to their allies and supporters, and procured friendships rather by bestowing favors than by receiving them.

They had a government regulated by laws. The denomination of their government was monarchy. Chosen men, whose bodies might be enfeebled by years, but whose minds were vigorous in understanding, formed the council of the state; and these, whether from their age, or from the similarity of their duty, were called fathers. But afterwards, when the monarchical power, which had been originally established for the protection of liberty, and for the promotion of the public interest, had degenerated into tyranny and oppression, they changed their plan, and appointed two magistrates, with power only annual; for they conceived that, by this method, the human mind would be least likely to grow overbearing through want of control.

7 At this period every citizen began to seek distinction, and to display his talents with greater freedom; for, with princes, the meritorious are greater objects of suspicion than the undeserving, and to them the worth of others is a source of alarm. But when liberty was secured, it is almost incredible how much the state strengthened itself in a short space of time, so strong a passion for distinction had pervaded it. Now, for the first time, the youth, as soon as they were able to bear the toils of war, acquired military skill by actual service in the camp, and took pleasure rather in splendid arms and military steeds than in the society of mistresses and convivial indulgence. To such men no toil was unusual, no place was difficult or inaccessible, no armed enemy was formidable; their valor had overcome everything. But among themselves the grand rivalry was for glory; each sought to be first to wound an enemy, to scale a wall, and to be noticed while performing such an exploit. Distinction such as this they regarded as wealth, honor, and true nobility. They were covetous of praise, but liberal of money; they desired competent riches, but boundless glory. I could mention, but that the account would draw me too far from my subject, places in which the Róman people, with a small body of men, routed vast armies of the enemy; and cities which, though fortified by nature, they carried by assault.

8 But, assuredly, Fortune rules in all things. She makes everything famous or obscure rather from caprice than in conformity with truth. The exploits of the Athénians, as far as I can judge, were very great and glorious, yet something inferior to what fame has represented them. But because writers of great talent flourished there, the actions of the Athénians are celebrated over the world as the most splendid of achievements. Thus, the merit of those who have acted is estimated at the highest point to which illustrious intellects could exalt it in their writings.

But among the Rómans there was never any such abundance of writers; for, with them, the most able men were the most actively employed. No one exercised the mind independently of the body; every man of ability chose to act rather than narrate, and was more desirous that his own merits should be celebrated by others, than that he himself should record theirs.

9 Good morals, accordingly, were cultivated in the city and in the camp. There was the greatest possible concord, and the least possible avarice. Justice and probity prevailed among the citizens, not more from the influence of the laws than from natural inclination. They displayed animosity, enmity, and resentment only against the enemy. Citizens contended with citizens in nothing but honor. They were magnificent in their religious services, frugal in their families, and steady in their friendships.

By these two virtues, intrepidity in war, and equity in peace, they maintained themselves and their state. Of their exercise of which virtues, I consider these as the greatest proofs; that, in war, punishment was oftener inflicted on those who attacked an enemy contrary to orders, and who, when commanded to retreat, retired too slowly from the contest, than on those who had dared to desert their standards or, when pressed by the enemy, to abandon their posts; and that, in peace, they governed more by conferring benefits than by exciting terror, and, when they received an injury, chose rather to pardon than to revenge it.

10 But when, by perseverance and integrity, the republic had increased its power; when mighty princes had been vanquished in war; when barbarous tribes and populous states had been reduced to subjection; when Cárthage, the rival of Rome's dominion, had been utterly destroyed, and sea and land lay everywhere open to her sway, Fortune then began to exercise her tyranny, and to introduce universal innovation. To those who had easily endured toils, dangers, and doubtful and difficult circumstances, ease and wealth, the objects of desire to others, became a burden and a trouble. At first the love of money, and then that of power, began to prevail, and these became, as it were, the sources of every evil. For avarice subverted honesty, integrity, and other honorable principles, and, in their stead, inculcated pride, inhumanity, contempt of religion, and general venality. Ambition prompted many to become deceitful; to keep one thing concealed in the breast, and another ready on the tongue; to estimate friendships and enmities, not by their worth, but according to interest; and to carry rather a specious countenance than an honest heart. These vices at first advanced but slowly, and were sometimes restrained by correction; but afterwards, when their infection had spread like a pestilence, the state was entirely changed, and the government, from being the most equitable and praiseworthy, became rapacious and insupportable.

11 At first, however, it was ambition, rather than avarice, that influenced the minds of men; a vice which approaches nearer to virtue than the other. For of glory, honor, and power, the worthy is as desirous as the worthless; but the one pursues them by just methods; the other, being destitute of honorable qualities, works with fraud and deceit. But avarice has merely money for its object, which no wise man has ever immoderately desired. It is a vice which, as if imbued with deadly poison, enervates whatever is manly in body or mind. It is always unbounded and insatiable and is abated neither by abundance nor by want.

But after Lúcius Súlla, having recovered the government by force of arms, proceeded, after a fair commencement, to a pernicious termination, all became robbers and plunderers; some set their affections on houses, others on lands; his victorious troops knew neither restraint nor moderation, but inflicted on the citizens disgraceful and inhuman outrages. Their rapacity was increased by the circumstance that Súlla, in order to secure the attachment of the forces which he had commanded in Ásia, had treated them, contrary to the practice of our ancestors, with extraordinary indulgence, and exemption from discipline; and pleasant and luxurious quarters had easily, during seasons of idleness, enervated the minds of the soldiery. Then the armies of the Róman people first became habituated to licentiousness and intemperance, and began to admire statues, pictures, and sculptured vases; to seize such objects alike in public edifices and private dwellings; to spoil temples; and to cast off respect for everything, sacred and profane. Such troops, accordingly, when once they obtained the mastery, left nothing to the vanquished. Success unsettles the principles even of the wise, and scarcely would those of debauched habits use victory with moderation.

12 When wealth was once considered an honor, and glory, authority, and power attended on it, virtue lost her influence, poverty was thought a disgrace, and a life of innocence was regarded as a life of ill-nature. From the influence of riches, accordingly, luxury, avarice, and pride prevailed among the youth; they grew at once rapacious and prodigal; they undervalued what was their own, and coveted what was another's; they set at naught modesty and continence; they lost all distinction between sacred and profane, and threw off all consideration and self-restraint.

It furnishes much matter for reflection, after viewing our modern mansions and villas extended to the size of cities, to contemplate the temples which our ancestors, a most devout race of men, erected to the Gods. But our forefathers adorned the fanes of the deities with devotion, and their homes with their own glory, and took nothing from those whom they conquered but the power of doing harm; their descendants, on the contrary, the basest of mankind have even wrested from their allies, with the most flagrant injustice, whatever their brave and victorious ancestors had left to their vanquished enemies; as if the only use of power were to inflict injury.

13 For why should I mention those displays of extravagance, which can be believed by none but those who have seen them; as that mountains have been leveled, and seas covered with edifices, by many private citizens; men whom I consider to have made a sport of their wealth, since they were impatient to squander disreputably what they might have enjoyed with honor.

But the love of irregular gratification, open debauchery, and all kinds of luxury, had spread abroad with no less force. Men forgot their sex; women threw off all the restraints of modesty. To gratify appetite, they sought for every kind of production by land and by sea; they slept before there was any inclination for sleep; they no longer waited to feel hunger, thirst, cold, or fatigue, but anticipated them all by luxurious indulgence. Such propensities drove the youth, when their patrimonies were exhausted, to criminal practices; for their minds, impregnated with evil habits, could not easily abstain from gratifying their passions, and were thus the more inordinately devoted in every way to rapacity and extravagance.

14 In so populous and so corrupt a city, Cátiline, as it was very easy to do, kept about him, like a body-guard, crowds of the unprincipled and desperate. For all those shameless, libertine, and profligate characters, who had dissipated their patrimonies by gaming, luxury, and sensuality; all who had contracted heavy debts, to purchase immunity for their crimes or offences; all assassins or sacrilegious persons from every quarter, convicted or dreading conviction for their evil deeds; all, besides, whom their tongue or their hand maintained by perjury or civil bloodshed; all, in fine, whom wickedness, poverty, or a guilty conscience disquieted, were the associates and intimate friends of Cátiline. And if anyone, as yet of unblemished character, fell into his society, he was presently rendered, by daily intercourse and temptation, similar and equal to the rest. But it was the young whose acquaintance he chiefly courted; as their minds, ductile and unsettled from their age, were easily ensnared by his stratagems. For as the passions of each, according to his years, appeared excited, he furnished mistresses to some, bought horses and dogs for others, and spared, in a word, neither his purse nor his character, if he could but make them his devoted and trustworthy supporters. There were some, I know, who thought that the youth, who frequented the house of Cátiline, were guilty of crimes against nature; but this report arose rather from other causes than from any evidence of the fact.

15 Cátiline, in his youth, had been guilty of many criminal connections, with a virgin of noble birth, with a priestess of Vésta, and of many other offences of this nature in defiance alike of law and religion. At last, when he was smitten with a passion for Aurélia Orestílla, in whom no good man, at any time of her life, commended anything but her beauty, it is confidently believed that because she hesitated to marry him, from the dread of having a grown-up step-son, he cleared the house for their nuptials by putting his son to death. And this crime appears to me to have been the chief cause of hurrying forward the conspiracy. For his guilty mind, at peace with neither gods nor men, found no comfort either waking or sleeping; so effectually did conscience desolate his tortured spirit. His complexion, in consequence, was pale, his eyes haggard, his walk sometimes quick and sometimes slow, and distraction was plainly apparent in every feature and look.

16 The young men, whom, as I said before, he had enticed to join him, he initiated, by various methods, in evil practices. From among them he furnished false witnesses, and forgers of signatures; and he taught them all to regard, with equal unconcern, honor, property, and danger. At length, when he had stripped them of all character and shame, he led them to other and greater enormities. If a motive for crime did not readily occur, he invited them, nevertheless, to circumvent and murder inoffensive persons, just as if they had injured him; for, lest their hand or heart should grow torpid for want of employment, he chose to be gratuitously wicked and cruel.

Depending on such accomplices and adherents, and knowing that the load of debt was everywhere great, and that the veterans of Súlla, having spent their money too liberally, and remembering their spoils and former victory, were longing for a civil war, Cátiline formed the design of overthrowing the government. There was no army in Ítaly; Pómpey was fighting in a distant part of the world; he himself had great hopes of obtaining the cónsulship; the senate was wholly off its guard; everything was quiet and tranquil, and all these circumstances were exceedingly favorable for Cátiline.

17 Accordingly, about the beginning of June, in the cónsulship of Lúcius Cǽsar and Gáius Fígulus, he at first addressed each of his accomplices separately, encouraged some, and sounded others, and informed them of his own resources, of the unprepared condition of the state, and of the great prizes to be expected from the conspiracy. When he had ascertained, to his satisfaction, all that he required, he summoned all whose necessities were the most urgent, and whose spirits were the most daring, to a general conference. At that meeting there were present, of senatorial rank: Públius Léntulus Súra, Públius Autrónius, Lúcius Cássius Longínus, Gáius Cethégus, Públius and Sérvius Súlla, the sons of Sérvius Súlla, Lúcius Varguntéius, Quíntus Ánnius, Márcus Pórcius Læca, Lúcius Béstia, Quíntus Cúrius; and of the equestrian order, Márcus Fúlvius Nobílior, Lúcius Statílius, Públius Gabínius Cápito, Gáius Cornélius; with many from the colonies and municipal towns, persons of consequence in their own localities. There were many others, too, among the nobility, concerned in the plot, but less openly; men whom the hope of power, rather than poverty or any other exigence, prompted to join in the affair. But most of the young men, and especially the sons of the nobility, favored the schemes of Cátiline; they who had abundant means of living at ease, either splendidly or voluptuously, preferred uncertainties to certainties, war to peace. There were some, also, at that time, who believed that Márcus Licínius Crássus was not unacquainted with the conspiracy; because Gnæus Pómpey, whom he hated, was at the head of a large army, and he was willing that the power of anyone whomsoever should raise itself against Pómpey's influence; trusting, at the same time, that if the plot should succeed, he would easily place himself at the head of the conspirators.

18 But previously to this period, a small number of persons, among whom was Cátiline, had formed a design against the state; of which affair I shall here give as accurate an account as I am able.

Under the cónsulship of Lúcius Túllus and Márcus Lépidus, Públius Autrónius and Públius Súlla, having been tried for bribery under the laws against it, had paid the penalty of the offence. Shortly after Cátiline, being brought to trial for extortion, had been prevented from standing for the cónsulship, because he had been unable to declare himself a candidate within the legitimate number of days. There was at that time, too, a young nobleman of the most daring spirit, needy and discontented, named Gnæus Píso, whom poverty and vicious principles instigated to disturb the government. Cátiline and Autrónius, having concerted measures with this Píso, prepared to assassinate the cónsuls, Lúcius Cótta and Lúcius Torquátus, in the Cápitol, on the first of February, when they, having seized on the fasces, were to send Píso with an army to take possession of the two Spains. But their design being discovered, they postponed the assassination to the fifth of February; when they meditated the destruction, not of the cónsuls only, but of most of the senate. And had not Cátiline, who was in front of the senate-house, been too hasty to give the signal to his associates, there would that day have been perpetrated the most atrocious outrage since the city of Rome was founded. But as the armed conspirators had not yet assembled in sufficient numbers, the want of force frustrated the design.

19 Some time afterwards, Píso was sent as quæstor, with Prætórian authority, into Hither Spain; Crássus promoting the appointment, because he knew him to be a bitter enemy to Gnæus Pómpey. Nor were the senate, indeed, unwilling to grant him the province; for they wished so infamous a character to be removed from the seat of government; and many worthy men, at the same time, thought that there was some security in him against the power of Pómpey, which was then becoming formidable. But this Píso, on his march towards his province, was murdered by some Spánish cavalry whom he had in his army. These barbarians, as some say, had been unable to endure his unjust, haughty, and cruel orders; but others assert that this body of cavalry, being old and trusty adherents of Pómpey, attacked Píso at his instigation, since the Spániards, they observe, had never before committed such an outrage, but had patiently submitted to many severe commands. This question we shall leave undecided. Of the first conspiracy enough has been said.

20 When Cátiline saw those, whom I have just above mentioned, assembled, though he had often discussed many points with them singly, yet thinking it would be to his purpose to address and exhort them in a body, retired with them into a private apartment of his house, where, when all witnesses were withdrawn, he harangued them to the following effect:

"If your courage and fidelity had not been sufficiently proved by me, this favorable opportunity would have occurred to no purpose; mighty hopes, absolute power, would in vain be within our grasp; nor should I, depending on irresolution or fickle mindedness, pursue contingencies instead of certainties. But as I have, on many remarkable occasions, experienced your bravery and attachment to me, I have ventured to engage in a most important and glorious enterprise. I am aware, too, that whatever advantages or evils affect you, the same affect me, and to have the same desires and the same aversions, is assuredly a firm bond of friendship.

"What I have been meditating you have already heard separately. But my ardor for action is daily more and more excited when I consider what our future condition of life must be, unless we ourselves assert our claims to liberty. For since the government has fallen under the power and jurisdiction of a few, kings and princes have constantly been their tributaries; nations and states have paid them taxes; but all the rest of us, however brave and worthy, whether noble or plebéian, have been regarded as a mere mob, without interest or authority, and subject to those, to whom, if the state were in a sound condition, we should be a terror. Hence, all influence, power, honor, and wealth, are in their hands, or where they dispose of them; to us they have left only insults, dangers, prosecutions, and poverty. To such indignities, bravest of men, how long will you submit? Is it not better to die in a glorious attempt, than, after having been the sport of other men's insolence, to resign a wretched and degraded existence with ignominy?

"But success (I call gods and men to witness!) is in our own hands. Our years are fresh, our spirit is unbroken; among our oppressors, on the contrary, through age and wealth, a general debility has been produced. We have therefore only to make a beginning; the course of events will accomplish the rest.

"Who in the world, indeed, that has the feelings of a man, can endure that they should have a superfluity of riches, to squander in building over seas and leveling mountains, and that means should be wanting to us even for the necessaries of life, that they should join together two houses or more, and that we should not have a hearth to call our own? They, though they purchase pictures, statues, and embossed plate; though they pull down new buildings and erect others, and lavish and abase their wealth in every possible method, yet cannot, with the utmost efforts of caprice, exhaust it. But for us there is poverty at home, debts abroad; our present circumstances are bad, our prospects much worse; and what, in a word, have we left, but a miserable existence?

"Will you not, then awake to action? Behold that liberty, that liberty for which you have so often wished, with wealth, honor, and glory, are set before your eves. All these prizes fortune offers to the victorious. Let the enterprise itself, then, let the opportunity, let your poverty, your dangers, and the glorious spoils of war, animate you far more than my words. Use me either as your leader or your fellow-soldier; neither my heart nor my hand shall be wanting to you. These objects I hope to effect, in concert with you, in the character of cónsul; unless, indeed, my expectation deceives me, and you prefer to be slaves rather than masters."

21 When these men, surrounded with numberless evils but without any resources or hopes of good, had heard this address, though they thought it much for their advantage to disturb the public tranquility, yet most of them called on Cátiline to state on what terms they were to engage in the contest; what benefits they were to expect from taking up arms; and what support or encouragement they had, and in what quarters. Cátiline then promised them the abolition of their debts; a proscription of the wealthy citizens; offices, sacerdotal duties, plunder, and all other gratifications which war, and the license of conquerors, can afford. He added that Píso was in Hither Spain, and Públius Síttius Nucerínus with an army in Mauritánia, both of whom were privy to his plans; that Gáius Antónius, whom he hoped to have for a colleague, was canvassing for the cónsulship, a man with whom he was intimate, and who was involved in all manner of embarrassments; and that, in conjunction with him, he himself, when cónsul, would commence operations. He, moreover, assailed all the respectable citizens with reproaches, commended each of his associates by name, reminded one of his poverty, another of his ruling passion, several others of their danger or disgrace, and many of the spoils which they had obtained by the victory of Súlla. When he saw their spirits sufficiently elevated, he charged them to attend to his interest at the election of cónsuls and dismissed the assembly.

22 There were some, at that time, who said that Cátiline, having ended his speech, and wishing to bind his accomplices in guilt by an oath, handed round among them in goblets, the blood of a human body mixed with wine; and that when all, after an imprecation, had tasted of it, as is usual in sacred rites, he disclosed his design; and they asserted that he did this, in order that they might be the more closely attached to one another, by being mutually conscious of such an atrocity. But some thought that this report, and many others, were invented by persons who supposed that the odium against Cícero, which afterwards arose, might be lessened by imputing an enormity of guilt to the conspirators who had suffered death. The evidence which I have obtained, in support of this charge, is not at all in proportion to its magnitude.

23 Among those present at this meeting was Quíntus Cúrius, a man of no mean family, but immersed in vices and crimes, and whom the cénsors had ignominiously expelled from the senate. In this person there was not less levity than impudence; he could neither keep secret what he heard, nor conceal his own crimes; he was altogether heedless what he said or what he did. He had long had a criminal intercourse with Fúlvia, a woman of high birth, but growing less acceptable to her, because in his reduced circumstances he had less means of being liberal, he began, on a sudden, to boast, and to promise her seas and mountains; threatening her, at times, with the sword, if she were not submissive to his will; and acting, in his general conduct, with greater arrogance than ever. Fúlvia, having learned the cause of his extravagant behavior, did not keep such danger to the state a secret; but, without naming her informant, communicated to several persons what she had heard, and under what circumstances, concerning Cátiline's conspiracy. This intelligence it was that incited the feelings of the citizens to give the cónsulship to Márcus Túllius Cícero. For before this period, most of the nobility were moved with jealousy, and thought the cónsulship in some degree sullied, if a man of no family, however meritorious, obtained it. But when danger showed itself, envy and pride were laid aside.

24 Accordingly, when the comítia were held, Márcus Túllius and Gáius Antónius were declared cónsuls; an event which gave the first shock to the conspirators. The ardor of Cátiline, however, was not at all diminished; he formed every day new schemes; he deposited arms, in convenient places, throughout Ítaly; he sent sums of money, borrowed on his own credit, or that of his friends, to a certain Mánlius, at Brútti, who was subsequently the first to engage in hostilities. At this period, too, he is said to have attached to his cause great numbers of men of all classes, and some women, who had, in their earlier days, supported an expensive life by the price of their beauty, but who, when age had lessened their gains but not their extravagance, had contracted heavy debts. By the influence of these females, Cátiline hoped to gain over the slaves in Rome, to get the city set on fire, and either to secure the support of their husbands or take away their lives.

25 In the number of these ladies was Semprónia, a woman who had committed many crimes with the spirit of a man. In birth and beauty, in her husband and her children, she was extremely fortunate; she was skilled in Greek and Róman literature; she could sing, play, and dance, with greater elegance than became a woman of virtue, and possessed many other accomplishments that tend to excite the passions. But nothing was ever less valued by her than honor or chastity. Whether she was more prodigal of her money or her reputation, it would have been difficult to decide ... She had frequently, before this period, forfeited her word, forsworn debts, been privy to murder, and hurried into the utmost excesses by her extravagance and poverty. But her abilities were by no means despicable; she could compose verses, jest, and join in conversation either modest, tender, or licentious. In a word, she was distinguished by much refinement of wit, and much grace of expression.

26 Cátiline, having made these arrangements, still canvassed for the cónsulship for the following year; hoping that, if he should be elected, he would easily manage Antónius according to his pleasure. Nor did he, in the mean time, remain inactive, but devised schemes, in every possible way, against Cícero, who, however, did not want skill or policy to guard against them. For, at the very beginning of his cónsulship, he had, by making many promises through Fúlvia, prevailed on Quíntus Cúrius, whom I have already mentioned, to give him secret information of Cátiline's proceedings. He had also persuaded his colleague, Antónius, by an arrangement respecting their provinces, to entertain no sentiments of disaffection towards the state; and he kept around him, though without ostentation, a guard of his friends and dependents.

When the day of the comítia came, and neither Cátiline's efforts for the cónsulship, nor the plots which he had laid for the cónsuls in the Cámpus Mártius, were attended with success, he determined to proceed to war, and to resort to the utmost extremities, since what he had attempted secretly had ended in confusion and disgrace.

27 He accordingly dispatched Gáius Mánlius to Brútti, and the adjacent parts of Etrúria; one Septímius, of Camerínum, into the Picénian territory; Gáius Július into Apúlia; and others to various places, wherever he thought each would be most serviceable. He himself, in the mean time, was making many simultaneous efforts at Rome; he laid plots for the cónsul; he arranged schemes for burning the city; he occupied suitable posts with armed men, he went constantly armed himself, and ordered his followers to do the same; he exhorted them to be always on their guard and prepared for action; he was active and vigilant by day and by night, and was exhausted neither by sleeplessness nor by toil. At last, however, when none of his numerous projects succeeded, he again, with the aid of Márcus Pórcius Læca, convoked the leaders of the conspiracy in the dead of night, when, after many complaints of their apathy, he informed them that he had sent forward Mánlius to that body of men whom he had prepared to take up arms; and others of the confederates into other eligible places, to make a commencement of hostilities; and that he himself was eager to set out to the army, if he could but first cut off Cícero, who was the chief obstruction to his measures.

28 While, therefore, the rest were in alarm and hesitation, Gáius Cornélius, a Róman knight, who offered his services, and Lúcius Varguntéius, a senator, in company with him, agreed to go with an armed force, on that very night, and with but little delay, to the house of Cícero, under pretense of paying their respects to him, and to kill him unawares, and unprepared for defense, in his own residence. But Cúrius, when he heard of the imminent danger that threatened the cónsul, immediately gave him notice, by the agency of Fúlvia, of the treachery which was contemplated. The assassins, in consequence, were refused admission, and found that they had undertaken such an attempt only to be disappointed.

In the mean time, Mánlius was in Etrúria, stirring up the populace, who, both from poverty, and from resentment for their injuries (for, under the tyranny of Súlla, they had lost their lands and other property), were eager for a revolution. He also attached to himself all sorts of marauders, who were numerous in those parts, and some of Súlla's colonists, whose dissipation and extravagance had exhausted their enormous plunder.

29 When these proceedings were reported to Cícero, he, being alarmed at the twofold danger, since he could no longer secure the city against treachery by his private efforts, nor could gain satisfactory intelligence of the magnitude or intentions of the army of Mánlius, laid the matter, which was already a subject of discussion among the people, before the senate. The senate, accordingly, as is usual in any perilous emergency, decreed that "The cónsuls should make it their care that the commonwealth should receive no injury." This is the greatest power which, according to the practice at Rome, is granted by the senate to the magistrate, and which authorizes him to raise troops; to make war; to assume unlimited control over the allies and the citizens; to take the chief command and jurisdiction at home and in the field, rights which, without an order of the people, the cónsul is not permitted to exercise.

30 A few days afterwards, Lúcius Sǽnius, a senator, read to the senate a letter, which, he said, he had received from Brútti, and in which it was stated that Gáius Mánlius, with a large force, had taken the field by the 27th of October. Others at the same time, as is not uncommon in such a crisis, spread reports of omens and prodigies; others of meetings being held, of arms being transported, and of insurrections of the slaves at Cápua and in Apúlia. In consequence of these rumors, Quíntus Március Rex was dispatched, by a decree of the senate, to Brútti, and Quíntus Metéllus Créticus into Apúlia and the parts adjacent, both which officers, with the title of commanders, were waiting near the city, having been prevented from entering in triumph, by the malice of a cabal, whose custom was to ask a price for everything, whether honorable or infamous. The prǽtors, too, Quíntus Pompéius Rúfus, and Quíntus Metéllus Céler, were sent off, the one to Cápua, the other to Picénum, and power was given them to levy a force proportioned to the exigency and the danger. The senate also decreed, that if anyone should give information of the conspiracy which had been formed against the state, his reward should be, if a slave, his freedom and a hundred sestértia, if a freeman, a complete pardon and two hundred sestértia. They further appointed that the schools of gladiators should be distributed in Cápua and other municipal towns, according to the capacity of each; and that, at Rome, watches should be posted throughout the city, of which the inferior magistrates should have the charge.

31 By such proceedings as these the citizens were struck with alarm, and the appearance of the city was changed. In place of that extreme gaiety and dissipation, to which long tranquility had given rise, a sudden gloom spread over all classes; they became anxious and agitated; they felt secure neither in any place, nor with any person; they were not at war, yet enjoyed no peace; each measured the public danger by his own fear. The women, also, to whom, from the extent of the empire, the dread of war was new, gave way to lamentation, raised supplicating hands to heaven, mourned over their infants, made constant inquiries, trembled at everything, and, forgetting their pride and their pleasures, felt nothing but alarm for themselves and their country.

Yet the unrelenting spirit of Cátiline persisted in the same purposes, notwithstanding the precautions that were adopted against him, and though he himself was accused by Lúcius Páullus under the Pláutian law. At last, with a view to dissemble, and under pretense of clearing his character, as if he had been provoked by some attack, he walked into the senate house. It was then that Márcus Túllius, the cónsul, whether alarmed at his presence, or fired with indignation against him, delivered that splendid speech, so beneficial to the republic, which he afterwards wrote and published.

When Cícero sat down, Cátiline, being prepared to pretend ignorance of the whole matter, entreated, with downcast looks and suppliant voice, that "the Conscript Fathers would not too hastily believe anything against him;" saying "that he was sprung from such a family, and had so ordered his life from his youth, as to have every happiness in prospect; and that they were not to suppose that he, a patrícian, whose services to the Róman people, as well as those of his ancestors, had been so numerous, should want to ruin the state, where Márcus Túllius, a mere adopted citizen of Rome, was eager to preserve it." When he was proceeding to add other invectives, they all raised an outcry against him, and called him an enemy and a traitor. Being thus exasperated, "Since I am encompassed by enemies," he exclaimed, "and driven to desperation, I will extinguish the flame kindled around me in a general ruin."

32 He then hurried from the senate to his own house; and then, after much reflection with himself, thinking that, as his plots against the cónsul had been unsuccessful, and as he knew the city to be secured from fire by the watch, his best course would be to augment his army, and make provision for the war before the légions could be raised, he set out in the dead of night, and with a few attendants, to the camp of Mánlius. But he left in charge Léntulus and Cethégus, and others of whose prompt determination he was assured, to strengthen the interests of their party in every possible way, to forward the plots against the cónsul, and to make arrangements for a massacre, for firing the city, and for other destructive operations of war; promising that he himself would shortly advance on the city with a large army.

During the course of these proceedings at Rome, Gáius Mánlius dispatched some of his followers as envoys to Quíntus Március Rex, with directions to address him to the following effect:

33 "We call gods and men to witness, general, that we have taken up arms neither to injure our country, nor to occasion peril to any one, but to defend our own persons from harm, who, wretched and in want, have been deprived, most of us, of our homes, and all of us of our character and property, by the oppression and cruelty of usurers; nor has any one of us been allowed, according to the usage of our ancestors, to have the benefit of the law, or, when our property was lost, to keep our persons free. Such has been the inhumanity of the usurers and of the prǽtor.

"Often have your forefathers, taking compassion on the commonalty at Rome, relieved their distress by decrees; and very lately, within our own memory, silver, by reason of the pressure of debt, and with the consent of all respectable citizens, was paid with brass.

"Often too, have the commonalty themselves, driven by desire of power, or by the arrogance of their rulers, seceded under arms from the patrícians. But at power or wealth, for the sake of which wars, and all kinds of strife, arise among mankind, we do not aim; we desire only our liberty, which no honorable man relinquishes but with life. We therefore conjure you and the senate to befriend your unhappy fellow-citizens; to restore us the protection of the law, which the injustice of the prǽtor has taken from us and not to lay on us the necessity of considering how we may perish, so best to avenge our blood."

34 To this address Quíntus Március replied, that, "if they wished to make any petition to the senate, they must lay down their arms, and proceed as suppliants to Rome;" adding, that "such had always been the kindness and humanity of the Róman senate and people, that none had ever asked help of them in vain."

Cátiline, on his march, sent letters to most men of cónsular dignity, and to all the most respectable citizens, stating, that "as he was beset by false accusations, and unable to resist the combination of his enemies, he was submitting to the will of fortune, and going into exile at Massília (Marseilles); not that he was guilty of the great wickedness laid to his charge, but that the state might be undisturbed, and that no insurrection might arise from his defense of himself."

Quíntus Cátulus, however, read in the senate a letter of a very different character, which, he said, was delivered to him in the name of Cátiline, and of which the following is a copy:

35 "Lúcius Cátiline to Quíntus Cátulus. Your eminent integrity, known to me by experience, gives a pleasing confidence, in the midst of great perils, to my present recommendation. I have determined therefore, to make no formal defense with regard to my new course of conduct; yet I was resolved, though conscious of no guilt, to offer you some explanation, which, on my word of honor, you may receive as true. Provoked by injuries and indignities, since, being robbed of the fruit of my labor and exertion, I did not obtain the post of honor due to me, I have undertaken, according to my custom, the public cause of the distressed. Not but that I could have paid, out of my own property, the debts contracted on my own security; while the generosity of Orestílla, out of her own fortune and her daughter's, would discharge those incurred on the security of others. But because I saw unworthy men ennobled with honors, and myself proscribed on groundless suspicion, I have, for this very reason, adopted a course, amply justifiable in my present circumstances, for preserving what honor is left to me. When I was proceeding to write more, intelligence was brought that violence is preparing against me. I now commend and entrust Orestílla to your protection; entreating you, by your love for your own children, to defend her from injury. Farewell."

36 Cátiline himself, having stayed a few days with Gáius Flamínius Flámma in the neighborhood of Arrétium while he was supplying the adjacent parts, already excited to insurrection, with arms, marched with the fasces, and other ensigns of authority, to join Mánlius in his camp.

When this was known at Rome, the senate declared Cátiline and Mánlius enemies to the state, and fixed a day as to the rest of their force, before which they might lay down their arms with impunity except such as had been convicted of capital offences. They also decreed that the cónsuls should hold a levy; that Antónius, with an army, should hasten in pursuit of Cátiline; and that Cícero should protect the city.

At this period the empire of Rome appears to me to have been in an extremely deplorable condition; for though every nation, from the rising to the setting of the sun, lay in subjection to her arms, and though peace and prosperity, which mankind think the greatest blessings, were hers in abundance, there yet were found, among her citizens, men who were bent, with obstinate determination, to plunge themselves and their country into ruin; for, notwithstanding the two decrees of the senate, not one individual, out of so vast a number, was induced by the offer of reward to give information of the conspiracy; nor was there a single deserter from the camp of Cátiline. So strong a spirit of disaffection had, like a pestilence, pervaded the minds of most of the citizens.

37 Nor was this disaffected spirit confined to those who were actually concerned in the conspiracy; for the whole of the common people, from a desire of change, favored the projects of Cátiline. This they seemed to do in accordance with their general character; for, in every state, they that are poor envy those of a better class, and endeavor to exalt the factious; they dislike the established condition of things, and long for something new; they are discontented with their own circumstances, and desire a general alteration; they can support themselves amidst revolt and sedition, without anxiety, since poverty does not easily suffer loss.

As for the populace of the city, they had become disaffected from various causes. In the first place, such as everywhere took the lead in crime and profligacy, with others who had squandered their fortunes in dissipation, and, in a word, all whom vice and villainy had driven from their homes, had flocked to Rome as a general receptacle of impurity. In the next place, many, who thought of the success of Súlla, when they had seen some raised from common soldiers into senators, and others so enriched as to live in regal luxury and pomp, hoped, each for himself, similar results from victory, if they should once take up arms. In addition to this, the youth, who, in the country, had earned a scanty livelihood by manual labor, tempted by public and private largesses, had preferred idleness in the city to unwelcome toil in the field. To these and all others of similar character, public disorders would furnish subsistence. It is not at all surprising, therefore, that men in distress, of dissolute principles and extravagant expectations, should have consulted the interest of the state no further than as it was subservient to their own. Besides, those whose parents, by the victory of Súlla, had been proscribed, whose property had been confiscated, and whose civil rights had been curtailed, looked forward to the event of a war with precisely the same feelings.

All those, too, who were of any party opposed to that of the senate, were desirous rather that the state should be embroiled, than that they themselves should be out of power. This was an evil, which, after many years, had returned upon the community to the extent to which it now prevailed.

38 For after the powers of the tríbunes, in the cónsulate of Gnǽus Pómpey and Márcus Crássus, had been fully restored, certain young men, of an ardent age and temper, having obtained that high office, began to stir up the populace by inveighing against the senate, and proceeded, in course of time, by means of largesses and promises, to inflame them more and more; by which methods they became popular and powerful. On the other hand, the most of the nobility opposed their proceedings to the utmost; under pretense, indeed, of supporting the senate, but in reality for their own aggrandizement. For, to state the truth in few words whatever parties, during that period, disturbed the republic under plausible pretexts, some, as if to defend the rights of the people, others, to make the authority of the senate as great as possible, all, though affecting concern for the public good, contended everyone for his own interest. In such contests there was neither moderation nor limit; each party made a merciless use of its successes.

39 After Pómpey, however, was sent to the maritime and Mithridátic wars, the power of the people was diminished and the influence of the few increased. These few kept all public offices, the administration of the provinces, and everything else, in their own hands; they themselves lived free from harm, in flourishing circumstances, and without apprehension; overawing others, at the same time, with threats of impeachment, so that, when in office, they might be less inclined to inflame the people. But as soon as a prospect of change, in this dubious state of affairs, had presented itself, the old spirit of contention awakened their passions; and had Cátiline, in his first battle, come off victorious, or left the struggle undecided, great distress and calamity must certainly have fallen upon the state, nor would those, who might at last have gained the ascendancy, have been allowed to enjoy it long, for some superior power would have wrested dominion and liberty from them when weary and exhausted.

There were some, however, unconnected with the conspiracy, who set out to join Cátiline at an early period of his proceedings. Among these was Áulus Fúlvius, the son of a senator, whom, being arrested on his journey, his father ordered to be put to death. In Rome, at the same time Léntulus, in pursuance of Cátiline's directions, was endeavoring to gain over, by his own agency or that of others, all whom he thought adapted, either by principles or circumstances, to promote an insurrection; and not citizens only but every description of men who could be of any service in war.

40 He accordingly commissioned one Públius Umbrénus to apply to certain deputies of the Allóbroges, and to lead them, if he could, to a participation in the war; supposing that as they were nationally and individually involved in debt, and as the Gauls were naturally warlike, they might easily be drawn into such an enterprise. Umbrénus, as he had traded in Gaul, was known to most of the chief men there, and personally acquainted with them; and consequently without loss of time, as soon as he noticed the envoys in the Fórum, he asked them, after making a few inquiries about the state of their country, and affecting to commiserate its fallen condition, "what termination they expected to such calamities?" When he found that they complained of the rapacity of the magistrates, inveighed against the senate for not affording them relief, and looked to death as the only remedy for their sufferings, "Yet I," said he, "if you will but act as men, will show you a method by which you may escape these pressing difficulties." When he had said this, the Allóbroges, animated with the highest hopes, besought Umbrénus to take compassion on them; saying that there was nothing so disagreeable or difficult, which they would not most gladly perform, if it would but free their country from debt. He then conducted them to the house of Décimus Brútus, which was close to the Fórum, and, on account of Semprónia, not unsuitable to his purpose, as Brútus was then absent from Rome. In order, too, to give greater weight to his representations, he sent for Gabínius, and, in his presence, explained the objects of the conspiracy, and mentioned the names of the confederates, as well as those of many other persons, of every sort, who were guiltless of it, for the purpose of inspiring the ambassadors with greater confidence. At length, when they had promised their assistance, he let them depart.

41 Yet the Allóbroges were long in suspense what course they should adopt. On the one hand, there was debt, an inclination for war, and great advantages to be expected from victory; on the other, superior resources, safe plans, and certain rewards instead of uncertain expectations. As they were balancing these considerations, the good fortune of the state at length prevailed. They accordingly disclosed the whole affair, just as they had learned it, to Quíntus Fábius Sánga, to whose patronage their state was very greatly indebted. Cícero, being apprised of the matter by Sánga, directed the deputies to pretend a strong desire for the success of the plot, to seek interviews with the rest of the conspirators, to make them fair promises, and to endeavor to lay them open to conviction as much as possible.

42 Much about the same time there were commotions in Hither and Further Gaul, in the Picénian and Brúttian territories, and in Apúlia. For those, whom Cátiline had previously sent to those parts, had begun, without consideration and seemingly with madness, to attempt everything at once, and, by nocturnal meetings, by removing armor and weapons from place to place, and by hurrying and confusing everything, had created more alarm than danger. Of these, Quíntus Metéllus Céler, the prætor, having brought several to trial, under the decree of the senate, had thrown them into prison, as had also Gáius Muræna in Further Gaul, who governed that province in quality of legate.

43 But at Rome, in the mean time, Léntulus, with the other leaders of the conspiracy, having secured what they thought a large force, had arranged, that as soon as Cátiline should reach the neighborhood of Fǽsulæ, Lúcius Béstia, a tríbune of the people, having called an assembly, should complain of the proceedings of Cícero, and lay the odium of this most oppressive war on the excellent cónsul; and that the rest of the conspirators, taking this as a signal, should, on the following night, proceed to execute their respective parts.

These parts are said to have been thus distributed. Statílius and Gabínius, with a large force, were to set on fire twelve places of the city, convenient for their purpose, at the same time; in order that, during the consequent tumult, an easier access might be obtained to the cónsul, and to the others whose destruction was intended; Cethégus was to beset the gate of Cícero, and attack him personally with violence; others were to single out other victims; while the sons of certain families, mostly of the nobility, were to kill their fathers; and, when all were in consternation at the massacre and conflagration, they were to sally forth to join Cátiline.

While they were thus forming and settling their plans, Cethégus was incessantly complaining of the want of spirit in his associates; observing, that they wasted excellent opportunities through hesitation and delay; that, in such an enterprise, there was need, not of deliberation, but of action and that he himself, if a few would support him, would storm the senate-house while the others remained inactive. Being naturally bold, sanguine, and prompt to act, he thought that success depended on rapidity of execution.

44 The Allóbroges, according to the directions of Cícero, procured interviews, by means of Gabínius, with the other conspirators; and from Léntulus, Cethégus, Statílius, and Cássius, they demanded an oath, which they might carry under seal to their countrymen, who otherwise would hardly join in so important an affair. To this the others consented without suspicion; but Cássius promised them soon to visit their country, and, indeed, left the city a little before the deputies.

In order that the Allóbroges, before they reached home, might confirm their agreement with Cátiline, by giving and receiving pledges of faith, Léntulus sent with them one Títus Voltúrcius, a native of Cróton, he himself giving Voltúrcius a letter for Cátiline, of which the following is a copy:

"Who I am, you will learn from the person whom I have sent to you. Reflect seriously in how desperate a situation you are placed and remember that you are a man. Consider what your views demand, and seek aid from all, even the lowest. In addition, he gave him this verbal message: Since he was declared an enemy by the senate, for what reason should he reject the assistance of slaves?

That, in the city, everything which he had directed was arranged and that he should not delay to make nearer approaches to it."

45 Matters having proceeded thus far, and a night being appointed for the departure of the deputies, Cícero, being by them made acquainted with everything, directed the prætors, Lúcius Valérius Fláccus, and Gáius Pomtínus, to arrest the retinue of the Allóbroges, by lying in wait for them on the Mílvian Bridge; he gave them a full explanation of the object with which they were sent, and left them to manage the rest as occasion might require. Being military men, they placed a force, as had been directed, without disturbance, and secretly invested the bridge; when the envoys, with Voltúrcius, came to the place, and a shout was raised from each side of the bridge, the Gauls, at once comprehending the matter, surrendered themselves immediately to the prætors. Voltúrcius, at first, encouraging his companions, defended himself against numbers with his sword; but afterwards, being unsupported by the Allóbroges, he began earnestly to beg Pomtínus, to whom he was known, to save his life, and at last, terrified and despairing of safety, he surrendered himself to the prætors as unconditionally as to foreign enemies.

46 The affair being thus concluded, a full account of it was immediately transmitted to the cónsul by messengers. Great anxiety, and great joy, affected him at the same moment. He rejoiced that, by the discovery of the conspiracy, the state was freed from danger; but he was doubtful how he ought to act, when citizens of such eminence were detected in treason so atrocious. He saw that their punishment would be a weight upon himself, and their escape the destruction of the Commonwealth. Having, however, formed his resolutions he ordered Léntulus, Cethégus, Statílius, Gabínius, and one Quíntus Cœpárius of Terracína, who was preparing to go to Apúlia to raise the slaves, to be summoned before him. The others came without delay; but Cœpárius, having left his house a little before, and heard of the discovery of the conspiracy, had fled from the city. The cónsul himself conducted Léntulus, as he was prætor, holding him by the hand, and ordered the others to be brought into the Temple of Concord, under a guard. Here he assembled the senate, and in a very full attendance of that body, introduced Voltúrcius with the deputies. Hither also he ordered Valérius Fláccus, the prætor, to bring the box with the letters which he had taken from the deputies.

47 Voltúrcius, being questioned concerning his journey, concerning his letter, and lastly, what object he had had in view, and from what motives he had acted, at first began to prevaricate, and to pretend ignorance of the conspiracy; but at length, when he was told to speak on the security of the public faith, he disclosed every circumstance as it had really occurred, stating that he had been admitted as an associate a few days before, by Gabínius and Cœpárius; that he knew no more than the envoys, only that he used to hear from Gabínius, that Públius Autrónius, Sérvius Súlla, Lúcius Varguntéius, and many others, were engaged in the conspiracy. The Gauls made a similar confession, and charged Léntulus, who began to affect ignorance, not only with the letter to Cátiline, but with remarks which he was in the habit of making, "that the sovereignty of Rome, by the Síbylline books, was predestined to three Cornélii, that Cínna and Súlla had ruled already; and that he himself was the third, whose fate it would be to govern the city; and that this, too, was the twentieth year since the Cápitol was burnt; a year which the áugurs, from certain omens, had often said would be stained with the blood of civil war."

The letter then being read, the senate, when all had previously acknowledged their seals, decreed that Léntulus, being deprived of his office, should, as well as the rest, be placed in private custody. Léntulus, accordingly, was given in charge to Públius Léntulus Spínther, who was then ædile; Cethégus, to Quíntus Cornifícius; Statílius, to Gáius Cæsar; Gabínius, to Márcus Crássus; and Cœpárius, who had just before been arrested in his flight, to Gnæus Teréntius, a senator.

48 The common people, meanwhile, who had at first, from a desire of change in the government, been to much inclined to war, having, on the discovery of the plot, altered their sentiments, began to execrate the projects of Cátiline, to extol Cícero to the skies; and, as if rescued from slavery, to give proofs of joy and exultation. Other effects of war they expected as a gain rather than a loss; but the burning of the city they thought inhuman, outrageous, and fatal especially to themselves, whose whole property consisted in their daily necessaries and the clothes which they wore.

On the following day, a certain Lúcius Tarquínius was brought before the senate, who was said to have been arrested as he was setting out to join Cátiline. This person, having offered to give information of the conspiracy, if the public faith were pledged to him, and being directed by the cónsul to state what he knew, gave the senate nearly the same account as Voltúrcius had given, concerning the intended conflagration, the massacre of respectable citizens, and the approach of the enemy, adding that "he was sent by Márcus Crássus to assure Cátiline that the apprehension of Léntulus, Cethégus, and others of the conspirators, ought not to alarm him, but that he should hasten, with so much the more expedition, to the city, in order to revive the courage of the rest, and to facilitate the escape of those in custody." When Tarquínius named Crássus, a man of noble birth, of very great wealth, and of vast influence, some, thinking the statement incredible, others, though they supposed it true, yet, judging that at such a crisis a man of such power was rather to be soothed than irritated (most of them, too, from personal reasons, being under obligation to Crássus), exclaimed that he was "a false witness," and demanded that the matter should be put to the vote. Cícero, accordingly, taking their opinions, a full senate decreed, "that the testimony of Tarquínius appeared false; that he himself should be kept in prison; and that no further liberty of speaking should be granted him, unless he should name the person at whose instigation he had fabricated so shameful a calumny."

There were some, at that time, who thought that this affair was contrived by Públius Autrónius, in order that the interest of Crássus, if he were accused, might, from participation in the danger, more readily screen the rest. Others said that Tarquínius was suborned by Cícero, that Crássus might not disturb the state, by taking upon him, as was his custom, the defense of the criminals. That this attack on his character was made by Cícero, I afterwards heard Crássus himself assert.

49 Yet, at the same time, neither by interest, nor by solicitation, nor by bribes, could Quíntus Cátulus, and Gáius Píso, prevail upon Cícero to have Gáius Cǽsar falsely accused, either by means of the Allóbroges, or any other evidence. Both of these men were at bitter enmity with Cǽsar; Píso, as having been attacked by him, when he was on his trial for extortion, on a charge of having illegally put to death a Transpádane Gaul; Cátulus, as having hated him ever since he stood for the pontificate, because, at an advanced age, and after filling the highest offices, he had been defeated by Cǽsar, who was then comparatively a youth. The opportunity, too, seemed favorable for such an accusation; for Cǽsar, by extraordinary generosity in private, and by magnificent exhibitions in public, had fallen greatly into debt. But when they failed to persuade the cónsul to such injustice, they themselves, by going from one person to another, and spreading fictions of their own, which they pretended to have heard from Voltúrcius or the Allóbroges, excited such violent odium against him, that certain Róman knights, who were stationed as an armed guard round the Temple of Concord, being prompted, either by the greatness of the danger, or by the impulse of a high spirit, to testify more openly their zeal for the republic, threatened Cǽsar with their swords as he went out of the senate-house.

50 While these occurrences were passing in the senate, and while rewards were being voted, on approbation of their evidence, to the Allobrógian deputies and to Títus Voltúrcius, the freedmen, and some of the other dependents of Léntulus, were urging the artisans and slaves, in various directions throughout the city, to attempt his rescue; some, too, applied to the ringleaders of the mob, who were always ready to disturb the state for pay. Cethégus, at the same time, was soliciting, through his agents, his slaves and freedmen, men trained to deeds of audacity, to collect themselves into an armed body, and force a way into his place of confinement.

The cónsul, when he heard that these things were in agitation, having distributed armed bodies of men, as the circumstances and occasion demanded, called a meeting of the senate, and desired to know "what they wished to be done concerning those who had been committed to custody." A full senate, however, had but a short time before declared them traitors to their country. On this occasion, Décimus Június Silánus, who, as cónsul elect, was first asked his opinion, moved that capital punishment should be inflicted, not only on those who were in confinement, but also on Lúcius Cássius, Públius Fúrius, Públius Umbrénus, and Quíntus Ánnius, if they should be apprehended; but afterwards, being influenced by the speech of Gáius Cæsar, he said that he would go over to the opinion of Tibérius Néro, who had proposed that the guards should be increased, and that the senate should deliberate further on the matter. Cæsar, when it came to his turn, being asked his opinion by the cónsul, spoke to the following effect:

51 "It becomes all men, Conscript Fathers, who deliberate on dubious matters, to be influenced neither by hatred, affection, anger, nor pity. The mind, when such feelings obstruct its view, cannot easily see what is right; nor has any human being consulted, at the same moment, his passions and his interest. When the mind is freely exerted, its reasoning is sound; but passion, if it gain possession of it, becomes its tyrant, and reason is powerless.

"I could easily mention, Conscript Fathers, numerous examples of kings and nations, who, swayed by resentment or compassion, have adopted injudicious courses of conduct; but I had rather speak of those instances in which our ancestors, in opposition to the impulse of passion, acted with wisdom and sound policy.

"In the Macedónian war, which we carried on against king Pérseus, the great and powerful state of Rhodes, which had risen by the aid of the Róman people, was faithless and hostile to us; yet, when the war was ended, and the conduct of the Rhódians was taken into consideration, our forefathers left them unmolested, lest any should say that war was made upon them for the sake of seizing their wealth, rather than of punishing their faithlessness. Throughout the Púnic Wars, too, though the Carthagínians, both during peace, and in suspensions of arms, were guilty of many acts of injustice, yet our ancestors never took occasion to retaliate, but considered rather what was worthy of themselves, than what might justly be inflicted on their enemies.

"Similar caution, Conscript Fathers, is to be observed by yourselves, that the guilt of Léntulus, and the other conspirators, may not have greater weight with you than your own dignity, and that you may not regard your indignation more than your character. If, indeed, a punishment adequate to their crimes be discovered, I consent to extraordinary measures; but if the enormity of their crime exceeds, whatever can be devised, I think that we should inflict only such penalties as the laws have provided.

"Most of those, who have given their opinions before me, have deplored, in studied and impressive language, the sad fate that threatens the republic; they have recounted the barbarities of war, and the afflictions that would fall on the vanquished; they have told us that maidens would be dishonored, and youths abused; that children would be torn from the embraces of their parents; that matrons would be subjected to the pleasure of the conquerors; that temples and dwelling-houses would be plundered; that massacres and fires would follow; and that every place would be filled with arms, corpses, blood, and lamentation. But to what end, in the name of the eternal gods! was such eloquence directed? Was it intended to render you indignant at the conspiracy? A speech, no doubt, will inflame him whom so frightful and monstrous a reality has not provoked! Far from it: for to no man does evil, directed against himself, appear a light matter; many, on the contrary, have felt it more seriously than was right.

"But to different persons, Conscript Fathers, different degrees of license are allowed. If those who pass a life sunk in obscurity, commit any error, through excessive anger, few become aware of it, for their fame is as limited as their fortune; but of those who live invested with extensive power, and in an exalted station, the whole world knows the proceedings. Thus in the highest position there is the least liberty of action; and it becomes us to indulge neither partiality nor aversion, but least of all animosity; for what in others is called resentment, is in the powerful termed violence and cruelty.

"I am indeed of opinion, Conscript Fathers, that the utmost degree of torture is inadequate to punish their crime; but the generality of mankind dwell on that which happens last, and, in the case of malefactors, forget their guilt, and talk only of their punishment, should that punishment have been inordinately severe. I feel assured, too, that Décimus Silánus, a man of spirit and resolution, made the suggestions which he offered, from zeal for the state, and that he had no view, in so important a matter, to favor or to enmity; such I know to be his character, and such his discretion. Yet his proposal appears to me, I will not say cruel (for what can be cruel that is directed against such characters?), but foreign to our policy. For assuredly, Silánus, either your fears, or their treason, must have induced you, a cónsul elect, to propose this new kind of punishment. Of fear it is unnecessary to speak, when, by the prompt activity of that distinguished man our cónsul, such numerous forces are under arms, and as to the punishment, we may say, what is indeed the truth, that in trouble and distress, death is a relief from suffering, and not a torment; that it puts an end to all human woes; and that, beyond it, there is no place either for sorrow or joy.

"But why, in the name of the immortal gods, did you not add to your proposal, Silánus, that, before they were put to death, they should be punished with the scourge? Was it because the Pórcian law forbids it? But other laws forbid condemned citizens to be deprived of life and allow them to go into exile. Or was it because scourging is a severer penalty than death? Yet what can be too severe, or too harsh, towards men convicted of such an offence? But if scourging be a milder punishment than death, how is it consistent to observe the law as to the smaller point, when you disregard it as to the greater?

"But who, it may be asked, will blame any severity that shall be decreed against these parricides of their country? I answer that time, the course of events, and fortune, whose caprice governs nations, may blame it. Whatever shall fall on the traitors, will fall on them justly; but it is for you, Conscript Fathers, to consider well what you resolve to inflict on others. All precedents productive of evil effects, have had their origin from what was good; but when a government passes into the hands of the ignorant or unprincipled, any new example of severity, inflicted on deserving and suitable objects, is extended to those that are improper and undeserving of it. The Lacedæmónians, when they had conquered the Athénians, appointed thirty men to govern their state. These thirty began their administration by putting to death, even without a trial, all who were notoriously wicked, or publicly detestable; acts at which the people rejoiced, and extolled their justice. But afterwards, when their lawless power gradually increased, they proceeded, at their pleasure, to kill the good and bad indiscriminately, and to strike terror into all; and thus the state, overpowered and enslaved, paid a heavy penalty for its imprudent exultation.

"Within our own memory, too, when the victorious Súlla ordered Damasíppus, and others of similar character, who had risen by distressing their country, to be put to death, who did not commend the proceeding? All exclaimed that wicked and factious men, who had troubled the state with their seditious practices, had justly forfeited their lives. Yet this proceeding was the commencement of great bloodshed. For whenever anyone coveted the mansion or villa, or even the plate or apparel of another, he exerted his influence to have him numbered among the proscribed. Thus they, to whom the death of Damasíppus had been a subject of joy, were soon after dragged to death themselves; nor was there any cessation of slaughter, until Súlla had glutted all his partisans with riches.

"Such excesses, indeed, I do not fear from Márcus Túllius, or in these times. But in a large state there arise many men of various dispositions. At some other period, and under another cónsul, who, like the present, may have an army at his command, some false accusation may be credited as true; and when, with our example for a precedent, the cónsul shall have drawn the sword on the authority of the senate, who shall stay its progress, or moderate its fury?

"Our ancestors, Conscript Fathers, were never deficient in conduct or courage; nor did pride prevent them from imitating the customs of other nations, if they appeared deserving of regard. Their armor, and weapons of war, they borrowed from the Sámnites; their ensigns of authority, for the most part, from the Etrúrians; and, in short, whatever appeared eligible to them, whether among allies or among enemies, they adopted at home with the greatest readiness, being more inclined to emulate merit than to be jealous of it. But at the same time, adopting a practice from Greece, they punished their citizens with the scourge, and inflicted capital punishment on such as were condemned. When the republic, however, became powerful, and faction grew strong from the vast number of citizens, men began to involve the innocent in condemnation, and other like abuses were practiced; and it was then that the Pórcian and other laws were provided, by which condemned citizens were allowed to go into exile. This lenity of our ancestors, Conscript Fathers, I regard as a very strong reason why we should not adopt any new measures of severity. For assuredly there was greater merit and wisdom in those, who raised so mighty an empire from humble means, than in us, who can scarcely preserve what they so honorably acquired. Am I of opinion, then, you will ask, that the conspirators should be set free, and that the army of Cátiline should thus be increased? Far from it; my recommendation is, that their property be confiscated, and that they themselves be kept in custody in such of the municipal towns as are best able to bear the expense; that no one hereafter bring their case before the senate, or speak on it to the people; and that the senate now give their opinion, that he who shall act contrary to this, will act against the republic and the general safety."

52 When Cǽsar had ended his speech, the rest briefly expressed their assent, some to one speaker, and some to another, in support of their different proposals; but Márcus Pórcius Cáto, being asked his opinion, made a speech to the following purport:

"My feelings, Conscript Fathers, are extremely different, when I contemplate our circumstances and dangers, and when I revolve in my mind the sentiments of some who have spoken before me. Those speakers, as it seems to me, have considered only how to punish the traitors who have raised war against their country, their parents, their altars, and their homes; but the state of affairs warns us rather to secure ourselves against them, than to take counsel as to what sentence we should pass upon them. Other crimes you may punish after they have been committed; but as to this, unless you prevent its commission, you will, when it has once taken effect, in vain appeal to justice. When the city is taken, no power is left to the vanquished.

"But, in the name of the immortal gods, I call upon you who have always valued your mansions and villas, your statues and pictures, at a higher price than the welfare of your country; if you wish to preserve those possessions, of whatever kind they are, to which you are attached; if you wish to secure quiet for the enjoyment of your pleasures, arouse yourselves, and act in defense of your country. We are not now debating on the revenues, or on injuries done to our allies, but our liberty and our life is at stake.

"Often, Conscript Fathers, have I spoken at great length in this assembly; often have I complained of the luxury and avarice of our citizens, and, by that very means, have incurred the displeasure of many. I, who never excused to myself, or to my own conscience, the commission of any fault, could not easily pardon the misconduct, or indulge the licentiousness, of others. But though you little regarded my remonstrances, yet the republic remained secure; its own strength was proof against your remissness. The question, however, at present under discussion, is not whether we live in a good or bad state of morals; nor how great, or how splendid, the empire of the Róman people is; but whether these things around us, of whatever value they are, are to continue our own, or to fall, with ourselves, into the hands of the enemy.

"In such a case, does any one talk to me of gentleness and compassion? For some time past, it is true, we have lost the real names of things; for to lavish the property of others is called generosity, and audacity in wickedness is called heroism; and hence the state is reduced to the brink of ruin. But let those, who thus misname things, be liberal, since such is the practice, out of the property of our allies; let them be merciful to the robbers of the treasury; but let them not lavish our blood, and, while they spare a few criminals, bring destruction on all the guiltless.

"Gáius Cæsar, a short time ago, spoke in fair and elegant language, before this assembly, on the subject of life and death; considering as false, I suppose, what is told of the dead; that the bad, going a different way from the good, inhabit places gloomy, desolate, dreary, and full of horror. He accordingly proposed 'that the property of the conspirators should be confiscated, and themselves kept in custody in the municipal towns;' fearing, it seems, that, if they remain at Rome, they may be rescued either by their accomplices in the conspiracy, or by a hired mob; as if, forsooth, the mischievous and profligate were to be found only in the city, and not through the whole of Ítaly, or as if desperate attempts would not be more likely to succeed where there is less power to resist them. His proposal therefore, if he fears any danger from them, is absurd; but if, amidst such universal terror, he alone is free from alarm, it the more concerns me to fear for you and myself.

"Be assured, then, that when you decide on the fate of Léntulus and the other prisoners, you at the same time determine that of the army of Cátiline, and of all the conspirators. The more spirit you display in your decision, the more will their confidence be diminished; but if they shall perceive you in the smallest degree irresolute, they will advance upon you with fury. Do not suppose that our ancestors, from so small a commencement, raised the republic to greatness merely by force of arms. If such had been the case, we should enjoy it in a most excellent condition; for of allies and citizens, as well as arms and horses, we have a much greater abundance than they had. But there were other things which made them great, but which among us have no existence; such as industry at home, equitable government abroad, and minds impartial in council, uninfluenced by any immoral or improper feeling. Instead of such virtues, we have luxury and avarice, public distress, and private superfluity; we extol wealth, and yield to indolence; no distinction is made between good men and bad; and ambition usurps the honors due to virtue. Nor is this wonderful; since you study each his individual interest, and since at home you are slaves to pleasure, and here to money or favor; and hence it happens that an attack is made on the defenseless state.

"But on these subjects I shall say no more. Certain citizens, of the highest rank, have conspired to ruin their country; they are engaging the Gauls, the bitterest foes of the Róman name, to join in a war against us; the leader of the enemy is ready to make a descent upon us; and do you hesitate, even in such circumstances how to treat armed incendiaries arrested within your walls? I advise you to have mercy upon them; they are young men who have been led astray by ambition; send them away, even with arms in their hands. But such mercy, and such clemency, if they turn those arms against you, will end in misery to yourselves. The case is, assuredly, dangerous, but you do not fear it; yes, you fear it greatly, but you hesitate how to act, through weakness and want of spirit, waiting one for another, and trusting to the immortal gods, who have so often preserved your country in the greatest dangers. But the protection of the gods is not obtained by vows and effeminate supplications; it is by vigilance, activity, and prudent measures, that general welfare is secured. When you are once resigned to sloth and indolence, it is in vain that you implore the gods; for they are then indignant and threaten vengeance.

In the days of our forefathers, Títus Mánlius Torquátus, during a war with the Gauls, ordered his own son to be put to death, because he had fought with an enemy contrary to orders. That noble youth suffered for excess of bravery; and do you hesitate what sentence to pass on the most inhuman of traitors? Perhaps their former life is at variance with their present crime. Spare, then, the dignity of Léntulus, if he has ever spared his own honor or character, or had any regard for gods or for men. Pardon the youth of Cethégus, unless this be the second time that he has made war upon his country. As to Gabínius, Statílius, Cœpárius, why should I make any remark upon them? Had they ever possessed the smallest share of discretion, they would never have engaged in such a plot against their country.

"In conclusion, Conscript Fathers, if there were time to amend an error, I might easily suffer you, since you disregard words, to be corrected by experience of consequences. But we are beset by dangers on all sides; Cátiline, with his army, is ready to devour us; while there are other enemies within the walls, and in the heart of the city; nor can any measures be taken, or any plans arranged, without their knowledge. The more necessary is it, therefore, to act with promptitude. What I advise, then, is this: that since the state, by a treasonable combination of abandoned citizens, has been brought into the greatest peril; and since the conspirators have been convicted on the evidence of Títus Voltúrcius, and the envoys of the Allóbroges, and on their own confession, of having concerted massacres, conflagrations, and other horrible and cruel outrages, against their fellow-citizens and their country, punishment be inflicted, according to the usage of our ancestors, on the prisoners who have confessed their guilt, as on men convicted of capital crimes."

53 When Cáto had resumed his seat, all the senators of cónsular dignity, and a great part of the rest, applauded his opinion, and extolled his firmness of mind to the skies. With mutual reproaches, they accused one another of timidity, while Cáto was regarded as the greatest and noblest of men; and a decree of the senate was made as he had advised.

After reading and hearing of the many glorious achievements which the Róman people had performed at home and in the field, by sea as well as by land, I happened to be led to consider what had been the great foundation of such illustrious deeds. I knew that the Rómans had frequently, with small bodies of men, encountered vast armies of the enemy; I was aware that they had carried on wars with limited forces against powerful sovereigns; that they had often sustained, too, the violence of adverse fortune; yet that, while the Greeks excelled them in eloquence, the Gauls surpassed them in military glory. After much reflection, I felt convinced that the eminent virtue of a few citizens had been the cause of all these successes; and hence it had happened that poverty had triumphed over riches, and a few over a multitude. And even in later time, when the state had become corrupted by luxury and indolence, the republic still supported itself, by its own strength, under the misconduct of its generals and magistrates; when, as if the parent stock were exhausted, there was certainly not produced at Rome, for many years, a single citizen of eminent ability. Within my recollection, however, there arose two men of remarkable powers, though of very different character, Márcus Cáto and Gáius Cæsar, whom, since the subject has brought them before me, it is not my intention to pass in silence, but to describe, to the best of my ability, the disposition and manners of each.

54 Their birth, age, and eloquence, were nearly on an equality; their greatness of mind similar, as was also their reputation, though attained by different means. Cæsar grew eminent by generosity and munificence; Cáto by the integrity of his life. Cæsar was esteemed for his humanity and benevolence; austereness had given dignity to Cáto. Cæsar acquired renown by giving, relieving, and pardoning; Cáto by bestowing nothing. In Cæsar, there was a refuge for the unfortunate; in Cáto, destruction for the bad. In Cæsar, his easiness of temper was admired; in Cáto, his firmness. Cæsar, in fine, had applied himself to a life of energy and activity; intent upon the interests of his friends, he was neglectful of his own; he refused nothing to others that was worthy of acceptance, while for himself he desired great power, the command of an army, and a new war in which his talents might be displayed. But Cáto's ambition was that of temperance, discretion, and, above all, of austerity; he did not contend in splendor with the rich, or in faction with the seditious, but with the brave in fortitude, with the modest in simplicity, with the temperate in abstinence, he was more desirous to be, than to appear, virtuous; and thus, the less he courted popularity, the more it pursued him.

55 When the senate, as I have stated, had gone over to the opinion of Cáto, the cónsul, thinking it best not to wait till night, which was coming on, lest any new attempts should be made during the interval, ordered the triúmvirs to make such preparations as the execution of the conspirators required. He himself, having posted the necessary guards conducted Léntulus to the prison; and the same office was performed for the rest by the prǽtors.

There is a place in the prison, which is called the Túllian dungeon, and which, after a slight ascent to the left, is sunk about twelve feet under ground. Walls secure it on every side, and over it is a vaulted roof connected with stone arches; but its appearance is disgusting and horrible, by reason of the filth, darkness, and stench. When Léntulus had been let down into this place, certain men, to whom orders had been given, strangled him with a cord. Thus this patrícian, who was of the illustrious family of the Cornélii, and who had filled the office of cónsul at Rome, met with an end suited to his character and conduct. On Cethégus, Statílius, Gabínius, and Cœpárius, punishment was inflicted in a similar manner.

56 During these proceedings at Rome, Cátiline, out of the entire force which he himself had brought with him, and that which Mánlius had previously collected, formed two légions, filling up the cohorts as far as his numbers would allow; and afterwards, as any volunteers, or recruits from his confederates, arrived in his camp, he distributed them equally throughout the cohorts, and thus filled up his légions, in a short time, with their regular number of men, though at first he had not had more than two thousand. But, of his whole army, only about a fourth part had the proper weapons of soldiers; the rest, as chance had equipped them, carried darts, spears, or sharpened stakes.

As Antónius approached with his army, Cátiline directed his march over the hills, encamping, at one time, in the direction of Rome, at another in that of Gaul. He gave the enemy no opportunity of fighting, yet hoped himself shortly to find one, if his accomplices at Rome should succeed in their objects. Slaves, meanwhile, of whom vast numbers had at first flocked to him, he continued to reject, not only as depending on the strength of the conspiracy, but as thinking impolitic to appear to share the cause of citizens with them.

57 When it was reported in his camp, however, that the conspiracy had been discovered at Rome, and that Léntulus, Cethégus, and the rest whom I have named, had been put to death, most of those whom the hope of plunder, or the love of change, had led to join in the war, fell away. The remainder Cátiline conducted, over rugged mountains, and by forced marches, into the neighborhood of Pistória, with a view to escape covertly, by crossroads, into Gaul.

But Quíntus Metéllus Céler, with a force of three légions, had, at that time, his station in Picénum, who suspected that Cátiline, from the difficulties of his position, would adopt precisely the course which we have just described. When, therefore, he had learned his route from some deserters, he immediately broke up his camp, and took his post at the very foot of the hills, at the point where Cátiline's descent would be, in his hurried march into Gaul. Nor was Antónius far distant, as he was pursuing, though with a large army, yet through plainer ground, and with fewer hindrances, the enemy in retreat.

Cátiline, when he saw that he was surrounded by mountains and by hostile forces, that his schemes in the city had been unsuccessful, and that there was no hope either of escape or of succor, thinking it best, in such circumstances, to try the fortune of a battle, resolved upon engaging, as speedily as possible, with Antónius. Having, therefore, assembled his troops, he addressed them in the following manner:

58 "I am well aware, soldiers, that words cannot inspire courage; and that a spiritless army cannot be rendered active, or a timid army valiant, by the speech of its commander. Whatever courage is in the heart of a man, whether from nature or from habit, so much will be shown by him in the field; and on him whom neither glory nor danger can move, exhortation is bestowed in vain; for the terror in his breast stops his ears.

"I have called you together, however, to give you a few instructions, and to explain to you, at the same time, my reasons for the course which I have adopted. You all know, soldiers, how severe a penalty the inactivity and cowardice of Léntulus has brought upon himself and us; and how, while waiting for reinforcements from the city, I was unable to march into Gaul. In what situation our affairs now are, you all understand as well as myself. Two armies of the enemy, one on the side of Rome, and the other on that of Gaul, oppose our progress; while the want of grain, and of other necessaries, prevents us from remaining, however strongly we may desire to remain, in our present position. Whithersoever we would go, we must open a passage with our swords. I conjure you, therefore, to maintain a brave and resolute spirit; and to remember, when you advance to battle, that on your own right hands depend riches, honor, and glory, with the enjoyment of your liberty and of your country. If we conquer, all will be safe, we shall have provisions in abundance; and the colonies and corporate towns will open their gates to us. But if we lose the victory through want of courage, those same places will turn against us; for neither place nor friend will protect him whom his arms have not protected. Besides, soldiers, the same exigency does not press upon our adversaries, as presses upon us; we fight for our country, for our liberty, for our life; they contend for what but little concerns them, the power of a small party. Attack them, therefore, with so much the greater confidence, and call to mind your achievements of old.

"We might, with the utmost ignominy, have passed the rest of our days in exile. Some of you, after losing your property, might have waited at Rome for assistance from others. But because such a life, to men of spirit, was disgusting and unendurable, you resolved upon your present course. If you wish to quit it, you must exert all your resolution for none but conquerors have exchanged war for peace. To hope for safety in flight, when you have turned away from the enemy the arms by which the body is defended, is indeed madness. In battle, those who are most afraid are always in most danger; but courage is equivalent to a rampart.

"When I contemplate you, soldiers, and when I consider your past exploits, a strong hope of victory animates me. Your spirit, your age, your valor, give me confidence; to say nothing of necessity, which makes even cowards brave. To prevent the numbers of the enemy from surrounding us, our confined situation is sufficient. But should Fortune be unjust to your valor, take care not to lose your lives unavenged; take care not to be taken and butchered like cattle, rather than, fighting like men, to leave to your enemies a bloody and mournful victory."

59 When he had thus spoken, he ordered, after a short delay, the signal for battle to be sounded, and led down his troops, in regular order, to the level ground. Having then sent away the horses of all the cavalry, in order to increase the men's courage by making their danger equal, he himself on foot, drew up his troops suitably to their numbers and the nature of the ground. As a plain stretched between the mountains on the left, with a rugged rock on the right, he placed eight cohorts in front, and stationed the rest of his force, in close order, in the rear. From among these he removed all the ablest centúrions, the veterans, and the stoutest of the common soldiers that were regularly armed, into the foremost ranks. He ordered Gáius Mánlius to take the command on the right, and a certain officer of Brútti on the left; while he himself; with his freedmen and the colonists, took his station by the eagle, which Gáius Márius was said to have had in his army in the Címbrian war.

On the other side, Gáius Antónius, who, being lame, was unable to be present in the engagement, gave the command of the army to Márcus Petréius, his lieutenant. Petréius ranged the cohorts of veterans, which he had raised to meet the present insurrection, in front, and behind them the rest of his force in lines. Then, riding round among his troops, and addressing his men by name, he encouraged them, and bade them remember that they were to fight against unarmed marauders, in defense of their country, their children, their temples, and their homes. Being a military man, and having served with great reputation, for more than thirty years, as tríbune, prefect, lieutenant, or prǽtor, he knew most of the soldiers and their honorable actions, and, by calling these to their remembrance, roused the spirits of the men.

60 When he had made a complete survey, he gave the signal with the trumpet, and ordered the cohorts to advance slowly. The army of the enemy followed his example; and when they approached so near that the action could be commenced by the light-armed troops, both sides, with a loud shout, rushed together in a furious charge. They threw aside their missiles, and fought only with their swords. The veterans, calling to mind their deeds of old, engaged fiercely in the closest combat. The enemy made an obstinate resistance; and both sides contended with the utmost fury. Cátiline, during this time, was exerting himself with his light troops in the front, sustaining such as were pressed, substituting fresh men for the wounded, attending to every exigency, charging in person, wounding many an enemy and performing at once the duties of a valiant soldier and a skillful general.

When Petréius, contrary to his expectation, found Cátiline attacking him with such impetuosity, he led his prǽtórian cohort against the center of the enemy, amongst whom, being thus thrown into confusion, and offering but partial resistance, he made great slaughter, and ordered, at the same time, an assault on both flanks. Mánlius and the Fǽsulan, sword in hand, were among the first that fell; and Cátiline, when he saw his army routed, and himself left with but few supporters, remembering his birth and former dignity, rushed into the thickest of the enemy, where he was slain, fighting to the last.

61 When the battle was over, it was plainly seen what boldness, and what energy of spirit, had prevailed throughout the army of Cátiline; for, almost everywhere, every soldier, after yielding up his breath, covered with his corpse the spot which he had occupied when alive. A few, indeed, whom the prǽtórian cohort had dispersed, had fallen somewhat differently, but all with wounds in front. Cátiline himself was found, far in advance of his men, among the dead bodies of the enemy; he was not quite breathless, and still expressed in his countenance the fierceness of spirit which he had shown during his life. Of his whole army, neither in the battle, nor in flight, was any free-born citizen made prisoner, for they had spared their own lives no more than those of the enemy. Nor did the army of the Róman people obtain a joyful or bloodless victory; for all their bravest men were either killed in the battle or left the field severely wounded. Of many who went from the camp to view the ground, or plunder the slain, some, in turning over the bodies of the enemy, discovered a friend, others an acquaintance, others a relative; some, too, recognized their enemies. Thus, gladness and sorrow, grief and joy, were variously felt throughout the whole army.

Gáius Sallústius Críspus, *Conspiracy of Cátiline* (translated by the Rev. John Selby Watson)

Cícero's First Oration Against Cátiline

1 When, O Cátiline, do you mean to cease abusing our patience? How long is that madness of yours still to mock us? When is there to be an end of that unbridled audacity of yours, swaggering about as it does now? Do not the night guards placed on the Pálatine Hill—do not the watches posted throughout the city—does not the alarm of the people, and the union of all good men— does not the precaution taken of assembling the senate in this most defensible place—do not the looks and countenances of this venerable body here present, have any effect upon you? Do you not feel that your plans are detected? Do you not see that your conspiracy is already arrested and rendered powerless by the knowledge which every one here possesses of it? What is there that you did last night, what the night before—where is it that you were—who was there that you summoned to meet you—what design was there which was adopted by you, with which you think that any one of us is unacquainted?

Shame on the age and on its principles! The senate is aware of these things; the cónsul sees them; and yet this man lives. Lives! aye, he comes even into the senate. He takes a part in the public deliberations; he is watching and marking down and checking off for slaughter every individual among us. And we, gallant men that we are, think that we are doing our duty to the republic if we keep out of the way of his frenzied attacks.

You ought, O Cátiline, long ago to have been led to execution by command of the cónsul. That destruction which you have been long plotting against us ought to have already fallen on your own head.

What? Did not that most illustrious man, Públius Scípio, the Póntifex Máximus, in his capacity of a private citizen, put to death Tibérius Grácchus, though but slightly undermining the constitution? And shall we, who are the cónsuls, tolerate Cátiline, openly desirous to destroy the whole world with fire and slaughter? For I pass over older instances, such as how Gáius Servílius Ahála with his own hand slew Spúrius Mælius when plotting a revolution in the state. There was— there was once such virtue in this republic, that brave men would repress mischievous citizens with severer chastisement than the most bitter enemy. For we have a resolution of the senate, a formidable and authoritative decree against you, O Cátiline; the wisdom of the republic is not at fault, nor the dignity of this senatorial body. We, we alone—I say it openly—we, the cónsuls, are wanting in our duty.

2 The senate once passed a decree that Lúcius Opímius, the cónsul, should take care that the republic suffered no injury. Not one night elapsed. There was put to death, on some mere suspicion of disaffection, Gáius Grácchus, a man whose family had borne the most unblemished reputation for many generations. There was slain Márcus Fúlvius, a man of cónsular rank, and all his children. By a like decree of the senate the safety of the republic was entrusted to Gáius Márius and Lúcius Valérius, the cónsuls. Did not the vengeance of the republic, did not execution overtake Lúcius Saturnínus, a tríbune of the people, and Gáius Servílius, the prǽtor, without the delay of one single day? But we, for these twenty days, have been allowing the edge of the senate's authority to grow blunt, as it were. For we are in possession of a similar decree of the senate, but we keep it locked up in its parchment—buried, I may say, in the sheath; and according to this decree you ought, O Cátiline, to be put to death this instant. You live—and you live, not to lay aside, but to persist in your audacity.

I wish, O conscript fathers, to be merciful; I wish not to appear negligent amid such danger to the state; but I do now accuse myself of remissness and culpable inactivity. A camp is pitched in Ítaly, at the entrance of Etrúria, in hostility to the republic; the number of the enemy increases every day; and yet the general of that camp, the leader of those enemies, we see within the walls— ay, and even in the senate—planning every day some internal injury to the republic. If, O Cátiline, I should now order you to be arrested, to be put to death, I should, I suppose, have to fear lest all good men should say that I had acted tardily, rather than that any one should affirm that I acted cruelly. But yet this, which ought to have been done long since, I have good reason for not doing as yet; I will put you to death, then, when there shall be not one person possible to be found so wicked, so abandoned, as like yourself, as not to allow that it has been rightly done. As long as one person exists who can dare to defend you, you shall live; but you shall live as you do now, surrounded by my many and trusty guards, so that you shall not be able to stir one finger against the republic: many eyes and ears shall still observe and watch you, as they have hitherto done, though you shall not perceive them.

3 For what is there, O Cátiline, that you can still expect, if night is not able to veil your nefarious meetings in darkness, and if private houses cannot conceal the voice of your conspiracy within their walls; if everything is seen and displayed? Change your mind: trust me: forget the slaughter and conflagration you are meditating. You are hemmed in on all sides; all your plans are clearer than the day to us; let me remind you of them. Do you recollect that on the 21st of October I said in the senate, that on a certain day, which was to be the 27th of October, C. Mánlius, the satellite and servant of your audacity, would be in arms? Was I mistaken, Cátiline, not only in so important, so atrocious, so incredible a fact, but, what is much more remarkable, in the very day? I said also in the senate that you had fixed the massacre of the nobles for the 28th of October, when many chief men of the senate had left Rome, not so much for the sake of saving themselves as of checking your designs. Can you deny that on that very day you were so hemmed in by my guards and my vigilance, that you were unable to stir one finger against the republic; when you said that you would be content with the flight of the rest, and the slaughter of us who remained? What? when you made sure that you would be able to seize Prænéste on the first of November by a nocturnal attack, did you not find that that colony was fortified by my order, by my garrison, by my watchfulness and care? You do nothing, you plan nothing, you think of nothing which I not only do not hear, but which I do not see and know every particular of.

4 Listen while I speak of the night before. You shall now see that I watch far more actively for the safety than you do for the destruction of the republic. I say that you came the night before (I will say nothing obscurely) into the Scythe-dealers' street, to the house of Márcus Lécca; that many of your accomplices in the same insanity and wickedness came there too. Do you dare to deny it? Why are you silent? I will prove it if you do deny it; for I see here in the senate some men who were there with you.

O ye immortal gods, where on earth are we? in what city are we living? what constitution is ours? There are here—here in our body, O conscript fathers, in this the most holy and dignified assembly of the whole world, men who meditate my death, and the death of all of us, and the destruction of this city, and of the whole world. I, the cónsul, see them; I ask them their opinion about the republic, and I do not yet attack, even by words, those who ought to be put to death by the sword. You were, then, O Cátiline, at Lécca's that night; you divided Ítaly into sections; you settled where every one was to go; you fixed whom you were to leave at Rome, whom you were to take with you; you portioned out the divisions of the city for conflagration; you undertook that you yourself would at once leave the city, and said that there was then only this to delay you, that I was still alive. Two Róman knights were found to deliver you from this anxiety, and to promise that very night, before daybreak, to slay me in my bed. All this I knew almost before your meeting had broken up. I strengthened and fortified my house with a stronger guard; I refused admittance, when they came, to those whom you sent in the morning to salute me, and of whom I had foretold to many eminent men that they would come to me at that time.

5 As, then, this is the case, O Cátiline, continue as you have begun. Leave the city at last: the gates are open; depart. That Mánlian camp of yours has been waiting too long for you as its general. And lead forth with you all your friends, or at least as many as you can; purge the city of your presence; you will deliver me from a great fear, when there is a wall between me and you. Among us you can dwell no longer—I will not bear it, I will not permit it, I will not tolerate it. Great thanks are due to the immortal gods, and to this very Júpiter Státor, in whose temple we are, the most ancient protector of this city, that we have already so often escaped so foul, so horrible, and so deadly an enemy to the republic. But the safety of the commonwealth must not be too often allowed to be risked on one man. As long as you, O Cátiline, plotted against me while I was the cónsul elect, I defended myself not with a public guard, but by my own private diligence. When, in the next cónsular comítia, you wished to slay me when I was actually cónsul, and your competitors also, in the Cámpus Mártius, I checked your nefarious attempt by the assistance and resources of my own friends, without exciting any disturbance publicly. In short, as often as you attacked me, I by myself opposed you, and that, too, though I saw that my ruin was connected with great disaster to the republic. But now you are openly attacking the entire republic.

You are summoning to destruction and devastation the temples of the immortal gods, the houses of the city, the lives of all the citizens; in short, all Ítaly. Wherefore, since I do not yet venture to do that which is the best thing, and which belongs to my office and to the discipline of our ancestors, I will do that which is more merciful if we regard its rigor, and more expedient for the state. For if I order you to be put to death, the rest of the conspirators will still remain in the republic; if, as I have long been exhorting you, you depart, your companions, those worthless dregs of the republic, will be drawn off from the city too. What is the matter, Cátiline? Do you hesitate to do that when I order you which you were already doing of your own accord? The cónsul orders an enemy to depart from the city. Do you ask me, Are you to go into banishment? I do not order it; but, if you consult me, I advise it.

6 For what is there, O Cátiline, that can now afford you any pleasure in this city? for there is no one in it, except that band of profligate conspirators of yours, who does not fear you, no one who does not hate you. What brand of domestic baseness is not stamped upon your life? What disgraceful circumstance is wanting to your infamy in your private affairs? From what licentiousness have your eyes, from what atrocity have your hands, from what iniquity has your whole body ever abstained? Is there one youth, when you have once entangled him in the temptations of your corruption, to whom you have not held out a sword for audacious crime, or a torch for licentious wickedness?

What? when lately by the death of your former wife you had made your house empty and ready for a new bridal, did you not even add another incredible wickedness to this wickedness? But I pass that over, and willingly allow it to be buried in silence, that so horrible a crime may not be seen to have existed in this city, and not to have been chastised. I pass over the ruin of your fortune, which you know is hanging over you against the ides of the very next month; I come to those things which relate not to the infamy of your private vices, not to your domestic difficulties and baseness, but to the welfare of the republic and to the lives and safety of us all.

Can the light of this life, O Cátiline, can the breath of this atmosphere be pleasant to you, when you know that there is not one man of those here present who is ignorant that you, on the last day of the year, when Lépidus and Túllus were cónsuls, stood in the assembly armed; that you had prepared your hand for the slaughter of the cónsuls and chief men of the state, and that no reason or fear of yours hindered your crime and madness, but the fortune of the republic? And I say no more of these things, for they are not unknown to every one. How often have you endeavored to slay me, both as cónsul elect and as actual cónsul? how many shots of yours, so aimed that they seemed impossible to be escaped, have I avoided by some slight stooping aside, and some dodging, as it were, of my body? You attempt nothing, you execute nothing, you devise nothing that can be kept hid from me at the proper time; and yet you do not cease to attempt and to contrive. How often already has that dagger of yours been wrested from your hands? how often has it slipped through them by some chance, and dropped down? and yet you cannot any longer do without it; and to what sacred mysteries it is consecrated and devoted by you I know not, that you think it necessary to plunge it in the body of the cónsul.

7 But now, what is that life of yours that you are leading? For I will speak to you not so as to seem influenced by the hatred I ought to feel, but by pity, nothing of which is due to you. You came a little while ago into the senate: in so numerous an assembly, who of so many friends and connections of yours saluted you? If this in the memory of man never happened to any one else, are you waiting for insults by word of mouth, when you are overwhelmed by the most irresistible condemnation of silence? Is it nothing that at your arrival all those seats were vacated? that all the men of cónsular rank, who had often been marked out by you for slaughter, the very moment you sat down, left that part of the benches bare and vacant? With what feelings do you think you ought to bear this? On my honor, if my slaves feared me as all your fellow-citizens fear you, I should think I must leave my house. Do not you think you should leave the city? If I saw that I was even undeservedly so suspected and hated by my fellow-citizens, I would rather flee from their sight than be gazed at by the hostile eyes of every one. And do you, who, from the consciousness of your wickedness, know that the hatred of all men is just and has been long due to you, hesitate to avoid the sight and presence of those men whose minds and senses you offend? If your parents feared and hated you, and if you could by no means pacify them, you would, I think, depart somewhere out of their sight. Now, your country, which is the common parent of all of us, hates and fears you, and has no other opinion of you, than that you are meditating parricide in her case; and will you neither feel awe of her authority, nor deference for her judgment, nor fear of her power?

And she, O Cátiline, thus pleads with you, and after a manner silently speaks to you: "There has now for many years been no crime committed but by you; no atrocity has taken place without you; you alone unpunished and unquestioned have murdered the citizens, have harassed and plundered the allies; you alone have had power not only to neglect all laws and investigations, but to overthrow and break through them. Your former actions, though they ought not to have been borne, yet I did bear as well as I could; but now that I should be wholly occupied with fear of you alone, that at every sound I should dread Cátiline, that no design should seem possible to be entertained against me which does not proceed from your wickedness, this is no longer endurable. Depart, then, and deliver me from this fear; that, if it be a just one, I may not be destroyed; if an imaginary one, that at least I may at last cease to fear."

8 If, as I have said, your country were thus to address you, ought she not to obtain her request, even if she were not able to enforce it? What shall I say of your having given yourself into custody? what of your having said, for the sake of avoiding suspicion, that you were willing to dwell in the house of Márcus Lépidus? And when you were not received by him, you dared even to come to me, and begged me to keep you in my house; and when you had received answer from me that I could not possibly be safe in the same house with you, when I considered myself in great danger as long as we were in the same city, you came to Quíntus Metéllus, the prǽtor, and being rejected by him, you passed on to your associate, that most excellent man, Márcus Marcéllus, who would be, I suppose you thought, most diligent in guarding you, most sagacious in suspecting you, and most bold in punishing you; but how far can we think that man ought to be from bonds and imprisonment who has already judged himself deserving of being given into custody?

Since, then, this is the case, do you hesitate, O Cátiline, if you cannot remain here with tranquility, to depart to some distant land, and to trust your life, saved from just and deserved punishment, to flight and solitude? Make a motion, say you, to the senate, (for that is what you demand,) and if this body votes that you ought to go into banishment, you say that you will obey. I will not make such a motion, it is contrary to my principles, and yet I will let you see what these men think of you. Be gone from the city, O Cátiline, deliver the republic from fear; depart into banishment, if that is the word you are waiting for. What now, O Cátiline? Do you not perceive, do you not see the silence of these men; they permit it, they say nothing; why wait you for the authority of their words when you see their wishes in their silence?

But had I said the same to this excellent young man, Públius Séxtius, or to that brave man, Márcus Marcéllus, before this time the senate would deservedly have laid violent hands on me, cónsul though I be, in this very temple. But as to you, Cátiline, while they are quiet they approve, while they permit me to speak they vote, while they are silent they are loud and eloquent. And not they alone, whose authority forsooth is dear to you, though their lives are unimportant, but the Róman knights too, those most honorable and excellent men, and the other virtuous citizens who are now surrounding the senate, whose numbers you could see, whose desires you could know, and whose voices you a few minutes ago could hear—ay, whose very hands and weapons I have for some time been scarcely able to keep off from you; but those, too, I will easily bring to attend you to the gates if you leave these places you have been long desiring to lay waste.

9 And yet, why am I speaking? that anything may change your purpose? that you may ever amend your life? that you may meditate flight or think of voluntary banishment? I wish the gods may give you such a mind; though I see, if alarmed at my words you bring your mind to go into banishment, what a storm of unpopularity hangs over me, if not at present, while the memory of your wickedness is fresh, at all events hereafter. But it is worth while to incur that, as long as that is but a private misfortune of my own, and is unconnected with the dangers of the republic. But we cannot expect that you should be concerned at your own vices, that you should fear the penalties of the laws, or that you should yield to the necessities of the republic, for you are not, O Cátiline, one whom either shame can recall from infamy, or fear from danger, or reason from madness.

Wherefore, as I have said before, go forth, and if you wish to make me, your enemy as you call me, unpopular, go straight into banishment. I shall scarcely be able to endure all that will be said if you do so; I shall scarcely be able to support my load of unpopularity if you do go into banishment at the command of the cónsul; but if you wish to serve my credit and reputation, go forth with your ill-omened band of profligates; betake yourself to Mánlius, rouse up the abandoned citizens, separate yourself from the good ones, wage war against your country, exult in your impious banditti, so that you may not seem to have been driven out by me and gone to strangers, but to have gone invited to your own friends.

Though why should I invite you, by whom I know men have been already sent on to wait in arms for you at the Fórum Aurélium; who I know has fixed and agreed with Mánlius upon a settled day; by whom I know that that silver eagle, which I trust will be ruinous and fatal to you and to all your friends, and to which there was set up in your house a shrine as it were of your crimes, has been already sent forward. Need I fear that you can long do without that which you used to worship when going out to murder, and from whose altars you have often transferred your impious hand to the slaughter of citizens?

10 You will go at last where your unbridled and mad desire has been long hurrying you. And this causes you no grief, but an incredible pleasure. Nature has formed you, desire has trained you, fortune has preserved you for this insanity. Not only did you never desire quiet, but you never even desired any war but a criminal one; you have collected a band of profligates and worthless men, abandoned not only by all fortune but even by hope.

Then what happiness will you enjoy! with what delight will you exult! in what pleasure will you revel! when in so numerous a body of friends, you neither hear nor see one good man. All the toils you have gone through have always pointed to this sort of life; your lying on the ground not merely to lie in wait to gratify your unclean desires, but even to accomplish crimes; your vigilance, not only when plotting against the sleep of husbands, but also against the goods of your murdered victims, have all been preparations for this. Now you have an opportunity of displaying your splendid endurance of hunger, of cold, of want of everything; by which in a short time you will find yourself worn out. All this I effected when I procured your rejection from the cónsulship, that you should be reduced to make attempts on your country as an exile, instead of being able to distress it as cónsul, and that that which had been wickedly undertaken by you should be called piracy rather than war.

11 Now that I may remove and avert, O conscript fathers, any in the least reasonable complaint from myself, listen, I beseech you, carefully to what I say, and lay it up in your inmost hearts and minds. In truth, if my country, which is far dearer to me than my life—if all Ítaly—if the whole republic were to address me, "Márcus Túllius, what are you doing? will you permit that man to depart whom you have ascertained to be an enemy? whom you see ready to become the general of the war? whom you know to be expected in the camp of the enemy as their chief, the author of all this wickedness, the head of the conspiracy, the instigator of the slaves and abandoned citizens, so that he shall seem not driven out of the city by you, but let loose by you against the city? Will you not order him to be thrown into prison, to be hurried off to execution, to be put to death with the most prompt severity? What hinders you? Is it the customs of our ancestors? But even private men have often in this republic slain mischievous citizens. Is it the laws which have been passed about the punishment of Róman citizens? But in this city those who have rebelled against the republic have never had the rights of citizens. Do you fear odium with posterity? You are showing fine gratitude to the Róman people which has raised you, a man known only by your own actions, of no ancestral renown, through all the degrees of honor at so early an age to the very highest office, if from fear of unpopularity or of any danger you neglect the safety of your fellow-citizens. But if you have a fear of unpopularity, is that arising from the imputation of vigor and boldness, or that arising from that of inactivity and indecision most to be feared? When Ítaly is laid waste by war, when cities are attacked and houses in flames, do you not think that you will be then consumed by a perfect conflagration of hatred?"

12 To this holy address of the republic, and to the feelings of those men who entertain the same opinion, I will make this short answer: If, O conscript fathers, I thought it best that Cátiline should be punished with death, I would not have given the space of one hour to this gladiator to live in. If, forsooth, those excellent men and most illustrious cities not only did not pollute themselves, but even glorified themselves by the blood of Saturnínus, and the Grácchi, and Fláccus, and many others of old time, surely I had no cause to fear lest for slaying this parricidal murderer of the citizens any unpopularity should accrue to me with posterity. And if it did threaten me to ever so great a degree, yet I have always been of the disposition to think unpopularity earned by virtue and glory, not unpopularity.

Though there are some men in this body who either do not see what threatens, or dissemble what they do see; who have fed the hope of Cátiline by mild sentiments, and have strengthened the rising conspiracy by not believing it; influenced by whose authority many, and they not wicked, but only ignorant, if I punished him would say that I had acted cruelly and tyrannically. But I know that if he arrives at the camp of Mánlius to which he is going, there will be no one so stupid as not to see that there has been a conspiracy, no one so hardened as not to confess it. But if this man alone were put to death, I know that this disease of the republic would be only checked for awhile, not eradicated for ever. But if he banishes himself, and takes with him all his friends, and collects at one point all the ruined men from every quarter, then not only will this full-grown plague of the republic be extinguished and eradicated, but also the root and seed of all future evils.

13 We have now for a long time, O conscript fathers, lived among these dangers and machinations of conspiracy; but somehow or other, the ripeness of all wickedness, and of this long-standing madness and audacity, has come to a head at the time of my cónsulship. But if this man alone is removed from this piratical crew, we may appear, perhaps, for a short time relieved from fear and anxiety, but the danger will settle down and lie hid in the veins and bowels of the republic. As it often happens that men afflicted with a severe disease, when they are tortured with heat and fever, if they drink cold water, seem at first to be relieved, but afterwards suffer more and more severely; so this disease which is in the republic, if relieved by the punishment of this man, will only get worse and worse, as the rest will be still alive.

Wherefore, O conscript fathers, let the worthless begone—let them separate themselves from the good—let them collect in one place—let them, as I have often said before, be separated from us by a wall; let them cease to plot against the cónsul in his own house—to surround the tribunal of the city prǽtor—to besiege the senate-house with swords—to prepare brands and torches to burn the city; let it, in short, be written on the brow of every citizen, what are his sentiments about the republic. I promise you this, O conscript fathers, that there shall be so much diligence in us the cónsuls, so much authority in you, so much virtue in the Róman knights, so much unanimity in all good men, that you shall see everything made plain and manifest by the departure of Cátiline— everything checked and punished.

With these omens, O Cátiline, begone to your impious and nefarious war, to the great safety of the republic, to your own misfortune and injury, and to the destruction of those who have joined themselves to you in every wickedness and atrocity. Then do you, O Júpiter, who were consecrated by Rómulus with the same auspices as this city, whom we rightly call the stay of this city and empire, repel this man and his companions from your altars and from the other temples—from the houses and walls of the city—from the lives and fortunes of all the citizens; and overwhelm all the enemies of good men, the foes of the republic, the robbers of Ítaly, men bound together by a treaty and infamous alliance of crimes, dead and alive, with eternal punishments.

Márcus Túllius Cícero, First Oration Against Cátiline (translated by Charles Duke Yonge)

The Simultaneous Appearance of Great Talents

1.16 Although this portion of my work has already, as it were, outgrown my plan, and although I am aware that in my headlong haste—which, just like a revolving wheel or a down-rushing and eddying stream, never suffers me of stop—I am almost obliged to omit matters of essential importance rather than to include unessential details, yet I cannot refrain from noting a subject which has often occupied my thoughts but has never been clearly reasoned out. For who can marvel sufficiently that the most distinguished minds in a branch of human achievement have happened to adopt the same form of effort, and to have fallen within the same narrow space of time? Just as animals of different species when shut in the same pen or other enclosure still segregate themselves from those which are not of their kind, and gather together each in its own group, so the minds that have had the capacity for distinguished achievement of each kind have set themselves apart from the rest by doing like things in the same period of time. A single epoch, and that only of a few years' duration, gave luster to tragedy through three men of divine inspiration, Æschylus, Sóphocles, and Eurípides. So, with Comedy, a single age brought to perfection that early form, the Old Comedy, through the agency of Cratínus, Aristóphanes, and Éupolis; while Menánder, and Philémon and Díphilus, his equals in age rather than in performance, within the space of a very few years invented the New Comedy and left it to defy imitation. The great philosophers, too, who received their inspiration from the lips of Sócrates—their names we gave a moment ago—how long did they flourish after the death of Pláto and of Áristotle? What distinction was there in oratory before Isócrates, or after the time of his disciples and in turn of their pupils? So crowded were they into a brief epoch that there were no two worthy of mention who could not have seen each other.

1.17 This phenomenon occurred among the Rómans as well as among the Greeks. For, unless one goes back to the rough and crude beginnings, and to men whose sole claim to praise is that they were the pioneers, Róman tragedy centers in and about Áccius; and the sweet pleasantry of Látin humor reached its zenith in practically the same range under Cæcílius, Teréntius, and Afránius. In the case of the historians also, if one adds Lívy to the period of the older writers, a single epoch, comprised within the limits of eighty years, produced them all, with the exception of Cáto and some of the old and obscure authors. Likewise the period which was productive of poets does not go back to an earlier date or continue to a later. Take oratory and the forensic art at its best, the perfected splendor of eloquence in prose, if we again except Cáto—and this I say with due respect to Públius Crássus, Scípio, Lælius, the Grácchi, Fánnius, and Sérvius Gálba— eloquence, I say, in all its branches burst into flower under Cícero, its chief exponent, so that there are few before his day whom one can read with pleasure, and none whom one can admire, except men who had either seen Cícero or had been seen by him. One will also find, if he follows up the dates closely, that the same thing holds true of the grammarians, the workers in clay, the painters, the sculptors, and that pre-eminence in each phase of art is confined within the narrowest limits of time.

Though I frequently search for the reasons why men of similar talents occur exclusively in certain epochs and not only flock to one pursuit but also attain like success, I can never find any of whose truth I am certain, though I do find some which perhaps seem likely, and particularly the following. Genius is fostered by emulation, and it is now envy, now admiration, which enkindles imitation, and, in the nature of things, that which is cultivated with the highest zeal advances to the highest perfection; but it is difficult to continue at the point of perfection, and naturally that which cannot advance must recede. And as in the beginning we are fired with the ambition to overtake those whom we regard as leaders, so when we have despaired of being able either to surpass or even to equal them, our zeal wanes with our hope; it ceases to follow what it cannot overtake, and abandoning the old field as though pre-empted, it seeks a new one. Passing over that in which we cannot be pre-eminent, we seek for some new object of our effort. It follows that the greatest obstacle in the way of perfection in any work is our fickle way of passing on at frequent intervals to something else.

Velléius Patérculus, *The Róman History*, 1.16-1.17 (translated by Frederick W. Shipley)

Július Cæsar Invades Brítain

4.20 During the short part of summer which remained, Cæsar, although in these countries, as all Gaul lies toward the north, the winters are early, nevertheless resolved to proceed into Brítain, because he discovered that in almost all the wars with the Gauls succors had been furnished to our enemy from that country; and even if the time of year should be insufficient for carrying on the war, yet he thought it would be of great service to him if he only entered the island, and saw into the character of the people, and got knowledge of their localities, harbors, and landing-places, all which were for the most part unknown to the Gauls. For neither does any one except merchants generally go thither, nor even to them was any portion of it known, except the sea-coast and those parts which are opposite to Gaul. Therefore, after having called up to him the merchants from all parts, he could learn neither what was the size of the island, nor what or how numerous were the nations which inhabited it, nor what system of war they followed, nor what customs they used, nor what harbors were convenient for a great number of large ships.

4.21 He sends before him Gáius Volusénus with a ship of war, to acquire a knowledge of these particulars before he in person should make a descent into the island, as he was convinced that this was a judicious measure. He commissioned him to thoroughly examine into all matters, and then return to him as soon as possible. He himself proceeds to the Mórini with all his forces. He orders ships from all parts of the neighboring countries, and the fleet which the preceding summer he had built for the war with the Véneti, to assemble in this place. In the mean time, his purpose having been discovered, and reported to the Brítons by merchants, ambassadors come to him from several states of the island, to promise that they will give hostages, and submit to the government of the Róman people. Having given them an audience, he after promising liberally, and exhorting them to continue in that purpose, sends them back to their own country, and [dispatches] with them Cómmius, whom, upon subduing the Atrébates, he had created king there, a man whose courage and conduct he esteemed, and who he thought would be faithful to him, and whose influence ranked highly in those countries. He orders him to visit as many states as he could, and persuade them to embrace the protection of the Róman people, and apprize them that he would shortly come thither. Volusénus, having viewed the localities as far as means could be afforded one who dared not leave his ship and trust himself to barbarians, returns to Cæsar on the fifth day, and reports what he had there observed.

4.22 While Cæsar remains in these parts for the purpose of procuring ships, ambassadors come to him from a great portion of the Mórini, to plead their excuse respecting their conduct on the late occasion; alleging that it was as men uncivilized, and as those who were unacquainted with our custom, that they had made war upon the Róman people, and promising to perform what he should command. Cæsar, thinking that this had happened fortunately enough for him, because he neither wished to leave an enemy behind him, nor had an opportunity for carrying on a war, by reason of the time of year, nor considered that employment in such trifling matters was to be preferred to his enterprise on Brítain, imposes a large number of hostages; and when these were brought, he received them to his protection. Having collected together, and provided about eighty transport ships, as many as he thought necessary for conveying over two légions, he assigned such [ships] of war as he had besides to the quæstor, his lieutenants, and officers of cavalry. There were in addition to these eighteen ships of burden which were prevented, eight miles from that place, by winds, from being able to reach the same port. These he distributed among the horse; the rest of the army, he delivered to Q. Titúrius Sabínus and L. Aurunculéius Cótta, his lieutenants, to lead into the territories of the Menápii and those cantons of the Mórini from which ambassadors had not come to him. He ordered P. Sulpícius Rúfus, his lieutenant, to hold possession of the harbor, with such a garrison as he thought sufficient.

4.23 These matters being arranged, finding the weather favorable for his voyage, he set sail about the third watch, and ordered the horse to march forward to the further port, and there embark and follow him. As this was performed rather tardily by them, he himself reached Brítain with the first squadron of ships, about the fourth hour of the day, and there saw the forces of the enemy drawn up in arms on all the hills. The nature of the place was this: the sea was confined by mountains so close to it that a dart could be thrown from their summit upon the shore. Considering this by no means a fit place for disembarking, he remained at anchor till the ninth hour, for the other ships to arrive there. Having in the mean time assembled the lieutenants and military tríbunes, he told them both what he had learned from Volusénus, and what he wished to be done; and enjoined them (as the principle of military matters, and especially as maritime affairs, which have a precipitate and uncertain action, required) that all things should be performed by them at a nod and at the instant. Having dismissed them, meeting both with wind and tide favorable at the same time, the signal being given and the anchor weighed, he advanced about seven miles from that place, and stationed his fleet over against an open and level shore.

4.24 But the barbarians, upon perceiving the design of the Rómans, sent forward their cavalry and charioteers, a class of warriors of whom it is their practice to make great use in their battles, and following with the rest of their forces, endeavored to prevent our men landing. In this was the greatest difficulty, for the following reasons, namely, because our ships, on account of their great size, could be stationed only in deep water; and our soldiers, in places unknown to them, with their hands embarrassed, oppressed with a large and heavy weight of armor, had at the same time to leap from the ships, stand amid the waves, and encounter the enemy; whereas they, either on dry ground, or advancing a little way into the water, free in all their limbs in places thoroughly known to them, could confidently throw their weapons and spur on their horses, which were accustomed to this kind of service. Dismayed by these circumstances and altogether untrained in this mode of battle, our men did not all exert the same vigor and eagerness which they had been wont to exert in engagements on dry ground.

4.25 When Cæsar observed this, he ordered the ships of war, the appearance of which was somewhat strange to the barbarians and the motion more ready for service, to be withdrawn a little from the transport vessels, and to be propelled by their oars, and be stationed toward the open flank of the enemy, and the enemy to be beaten off and driven away, with slings, arrows, and engines: which plan was of great service to our men; for the barbarians being startled by the form of our ships and the motions of our oars and the nature of our engines, which was strange to them, stopped, and shortly after retreated a little. And while our men were hesitating [whether they should advance to the shore], chiefly on account of the depth of the sea, he who carried the eagle of the tenth légion, after supplicating the gods that the matter might turn out favorably to the légion, exclaimed, "Leap, fellow soldiers, unless you wish to betray your eagle to the enemy. I, for my part, will perform my duty to the commonwealth and my general." When he had said this with a loud voice, he leaped from the ship and proceeded to bear the eagle toward the enemy. Then our men, exhorting one another that so great a disgrace should not be incurred, all leaped from the ship. When those in the nearest vessels saw them, they speedily followed and approached the enemy.

4.26 The battle was maintained vigorously on both sides. Our men, however, as they could neither keep their ranks, nor get firm footing, nor follow their standards, and as one from one ship and another from another assembled around whatever standards they met, were thrown into great confusion. But the enemy, who were acquainted with all the shallows, when from the shore they saw any coming from a ship one by one, spurred on their horses, and attacked them while embarrassed; many surrounded a few, others threw their weapons upon our collected forces on their exposed flank. When Cæsar observed this, he ordered the boats of the ships of war and the spy sloops to be filled with soldiers, and sent them up to the succor of those whom he had observed in distress. Our men, as soon as they made good their footing on dry ground, and all their comrades had joined them, made an attack upon the enemy, and put them to flight, but could not pursue them very far, because the horse had not been able to maintain their course at sea and reach the island. This alone was wanting to Cæsar's accustomed success.

4.27 The enemy being thus vanquished in battle, as soon as they recovered after their flight, instantly sent ambassadors to Cæsar to negotiate about peace. They promised to give hostages and perform what he should command. Together with these ambassadors came Cómmius the Atrebátian, who, as I have above said, had been sent by Cæsar into Brítain. Him they had seized upon when leaving his ship, although in the character of ambassador he bore the general's commission to them, and thrown into chains: then after the battle was fought, they sent him back, and in suing for peace cast the blame of that act upon the common people, and entreated that it might be pardoned on account of their indiscretion. Cæsar, complaining, that after they had sued for peace, and had voluntarily sent ambassadors into the continent for that purpose, they had made war without a reason, said that he would pardon their indiscretion, and imposed hostages, a part of whom they gave immediately; the rest they said they would give in a few days, since they were sent for from remote places. In the mean time they ordered their people to return to the country parts, and the chiefs assembled from all quarter, and proceeded to surrender themselves and their states to Cæsar.

4.28 A peace being established by these proceedings four days after we had come into Brítain, the eighteen ships, to which reference has been made above, and which conveyed the cavalry, set sail from the upper port with a gentle gale, when, however, they were approaching Brítain and were seen from the camp, so great a storm suddenly arose that none of them could maintain their course at sea; and some were taken back to the same port from which they had started; others, to their great danger, were driven to the lower part of the island, nearer to the west; which, however, after having cast anchor, as they were getting filled with water, put out to sea through necessity in a stormy night, and made for the continent.

4.29 It happened that night to be full moon, which usually occasions very high tides in that ocean; and that circumstance was unknown to our men. Thus, at the same time, the tide began to fill the ships of war which Cæsar had provided to convey over his army, and which he had drawn up on the strand; and the storm began to dash the ships of burden which were riding at anchor against each other; nor was any means afforded our men of either managing them or of rendering any service. A great many ships having been wrecked, inasmuch as the rest, having lost their cables, anchors, and other tackling, were unfit for sailing, a great confusion, as would necessarily happen, arose throughout the army; for there were no other ships in which they could be conveyed back, and all things which are of service in repairing vessels were wanting, and, corn for the winter had not been provided in those places, because it was understood by all that they would certainly winter in Gaul.

4.30 On discovering these things the chiefs of Brítain, who had come up after the battle was fought to perform those conditions which Cæsar had imposed, held a conference, when they perceived that cavalry, and ships, and corn were wanting to the Rómans, and discovered the small number of our soldiers from the small extent of the camp (which, too, was on this account more limited than ordinary, because Cæsar had conveyed over his légions without baggage), and thought that the best plan was to renew the war, and cut off our men from corn and provisions and protract the affair till winter; because they felt confident, that, if they were vanquished or cut off from a return, no one would afterward pass over into Brítain for the purpose of making war. Therefore, again entering into a conspiracy, they began to depart from the camp by degrees and secretly bring up their people from the country parts.

4.31 But Cæsar, although he had not as yet discovered their measures, yet, both from what had occurred to his ships, and from the circumstance that they had neglected to give the promised hostages, suspected that the thing would come to pass which really did happen. He therefore provided remedies against all contingencies; for he daily conveyed corn from the country parts into the camp, used the timber and brass of such ships as were most seriously damaged for repairing the rest, and ordered whatever things besides were necessary for this object to be brought to him from the continent. And thus, since that business was executed by the soldiers with the greatest energy, he effected that, after the loss of twelve ships, a voyage could be made well enough in the rest.

4.32 While these things are being transacted, one légion had been sent to forage, according to custom, and no suspicion of war had arisen as yet, and some of the people remained in the country parts, others went backward and forward to the camp, they who were on duty at the gates of the camp reported to Cæsar that a greater dust than was usual was seen in that direction in which the légion had marched. Cæsar, suspecting that which was [really the case]—that some new enterprise was undertaken by the barbarians—ordered the two cohorts which were on duty, to march into that quarter with him, and two other cohorts to relieve them on duty; the rest to be armed and follow him immediately. When he had advanced some little way from the camp, he saw that his men were overpowered by the enemy and scarcely able to stand their ground, and that, the légion being crowded together, weapons were being cast on them from all sides. For as all the corn was reaped in every part with the exception of one, the enemy, suspecting that our men would repair to that, had concealed themselves in the woods during the night. Then attacking them suddenly, scattered as they were, and when they had laid aside their arms, and were engaged in reaping, they killed a small number, threw the rest into confusion, and surrounded them with their cavalry and chariots.

4.33 Their mode of fighting with their chariots is this: firstly, they drive about in all directions and throw their weapons and generally break the ranks of the enemy with the very dread of their horses and the noise of their wheels; and when they have worked themselves in between the troops of horse, leap from their chariots and engage on foot. The charioteers in the mean time withdraw some little distance from the battle, and so place themselves with the chariots that, if their masters are overpowered by the number of the enemy, they may have a ready retreat to their own troops. Thus they display in battle the speed of horse, [together with] the firmness of infantry; and by daily practice and exercise attain to such expertness that they are accustomed, even on a declining and steep place, to check their horses at full speed, and manage and turn them in an instant and run along the pole, and stand on the yoke, and thence betake themselves with the greatest celerity to their chariots again.

4.34 Under these circumstances, our men being dismayed by the novelty of this mode of battle, Cæsar most seasonably brought assistance; for upon his arrival the enemy paused, and our men recovered from their fear; upon which thinking the time unfavorable for provoking the enemy and coming to an action, he kept himself in his own quarter, and, a short time having intervened, drew back the légions into the camp. While these things are going on, and all our men engaged, the rest of the Brítons, who were in the fields, departed. Storms then set in for several successive days, which both confined our men to the camp and hindered the enemy from attacking us. In the mean time the barbarians dispatched messengers to all parts, and reported to their people the small number of our soldiers, and how good an opportunity was given for obtaining spoil and for liberating themselves forever, if they should only drive the Rómans from their camp. Having by these means speedily got together a large force of infantry and of cavalry they came up to the camp.

4.35 Although Cæsar anticipated that the same thing which had happened on former occasions would then occur—that, if the enemy were routed, they would escape from danger by their speed; still, having got about thirty horse, which Cómmius the Atrebátian, of whom mention has been made, had brought over with him [from Gaul], he drew up the légions in order of battle before the camp. When the action commenced, the enemy were unable to sustain the attack of our men long, and turned their backs; our men pursued them as far as their speed and strength permitted, and slew a great number of them; then, having destroyed and burned every thing far and wide, they retreated to their camp.

4.36 The same day, ambassadors sent by the enemy came to Cæsar to negotiate a peace. Cæsar doubled the number of hostages which he had before demanded; and ordered that they should be brought over to the continent, because, since the time of the equinox was near, he did not consider that, with his ships out of repair, the voyage ought to be deferred till winter. Having met with favorable weather, he set sail a little after midnight, and all his fleet arrived safe at the continent, except two of the ships of burden which could not make the same port which the other ships did, and were carried a little lower down.

Gáius Július Cæsar, *Commentaries on the Gállic War*, 4.20-4.36
(translated by W.A. McDevitte and W.S. Bohn)

A Description of the Gauls

6.13 Throughout all Gaul there are two orders of those men who are of any rank and dignity: for the commonality is held almost in the condition of slaves, and dares to undertake nothing of itself, and is admitted to no deliberation. The greater part, when they are pressed either by debt, or the large amount of their tributes, or the oppression of the more powerful, give themselves up in vassalage to the nobles, who possess over them the same rights without exception as masters over their slaves. But of these two orders, one is that of the drúids, the other that of the knights. The former are engaged in things sacred, conduct the public and the private sacrifices, and interpret all matters of religion. To these a large number of the young men resort for the purpose of instruction, and [the drúids] are in great honor among them. For they determine respecting almost all controversies, public and private; and if any crime has been perpetrated, if murder has been committed, if there be any dispute about an inheritance, if any about boundaries, these same persons decide it; they decree rewards and punishments; if any one, either in a private or public capacity, has not submitted to their decision, they interdict him from the sacrifices. This among them is the most heavy punishment.

Those who have been thus interdicted are esteemed in the number of the impious and the criminal: all shun them, and avoid their society and conversation, lest they receive some evil from their contact; nor is justice administered to them when seeking it, nor is any dignity bestowed on them. Over all these drúids one presides, who possesses supreme authority among them. Upon his death, if any individual among the rest is pre-eminent in dignity, he succeeds; but, if there are many equal, the election is made by the suffrages of the drúids; sometimes they even contend for the presidency with arms. These assemble at a fixed period of the year in a consecrated place in the territories of the Carnútes, which is reckoned the central region of the whole of Gaul. Hither all, who have disputes, assemble from every part, and submit to their decrees and determinations. This institution is supposed to have been devised in Brítain, and to have been brought over from it into Gaul; and now those who desire to gain a more accurate knowledge of that system generally proceed thither for the purpose of studying it.

6.14 The drúids do not go to war, nor pay tribute together with the rest; they have an exemption from military service and a dispensation in all matters. Induced by such great advantages, many embrace this profession of their own accord, and [many] are sent to it by their parents and relations. They are said there to learn by heart a great number of verses; accordingly some remain in the course of training twenty years. Nor do they regard it lawful to commit these to writing, though in almost all other matters, in their public and private transactions, they use Greek characters. That practice they seem to me to have adopted for two reasons; because they neither desire their doctrines to be divulged among the mass of the people, nor those who learn, to devote themselves the less to the efforts of memory, relying on writing; since it generally occurs to most men, that, in their dependence on writing, they relax their diligence in learning thoroughly, and their employment of the memory. They wish to inculcate this as one of their leading tenets, that souls do not become extinct, but pass after death from one body to another, and they think that men by this tenet are in a great degree excited to valor, the fear of death being disregarded. They likewise discuss and impart to the youth many things respecting the stars and their motion, respecting the extent of the world and of our earth, respecting the nature of things, respecting the power and the majesty of the immortal gods.

6.15 The other order is that of the knights. These, when there is occasion and any war occurs (which before Cæsar's arrival was for the most part wont to happen every year, as either they on their part were inflicting injuries or repelling those which others inflicted on them), are all engaged in war. And those of them most distinguished by birth and resources, have the greatest number of vassals and dependents about them. They acknowledge this sort of influence and power only.

6.16 The nation of all the Gauls is extremely devoted to superstitious rites; and on that account they who are troubled with unusually severe diseases, and they who are engaged in battles and dangers, either sacrifice men as victims, or vow that they will sacrifice them, and employ the drúids as the performers of those sacrifices; because they think that unless the life of a man be offered for the life of a man, the mind of the immortal gods can not be rendered propitious, and they have sacrifices of that kind ordained for national purposes. Others have figures of vast size, the limbs of which formed of osiers they fill with living men, which being set on fire, the men perish enveloped in the flames. They consider that the oblation of such as have been taken in theft, or in robbery, or any other offense, is more acceptable to the immortal gods; but when a supply of that class is wanting, they have recourse to the oblation of even the innocent.

6.17 They worship as their divinity, Mércury in particular, and have many images of him, and regard him as the inventor of all arts, they consider him the guide of their journeys and marches, and believe him to have great influence over the acquisition of gain and mercantile transactions. Next to him they worship Apóllo, and Mars, and Júpiter, and Minérva; respecting these deities they have for the most part the same belief as other nations: that Apóllo averts diseases, that Minérva imparts the invention of manufactures, that Júpiter possesses the sovereignty of the heavenly powers; that Mars presides over wars. To him, when they have determined to engage in battle, they commonly vow those things which they shall take in war. When they have conquered, they sacrifice whatever captured animals may have survived the conflict, and collect the other things into one place. In many states you may see piles of these things heaped up in their consecrated spots; nor does it often happen that any one, disregarding the sanctity of the case, dares either to secrete in his house things captured, or take away those deposited; and the most severe punishment, with torture, has been established for such a deed.

6.18 All the Gauls assert that they are descended from the god Dis, and say that this tradition has been handed down by the drúids. For that reason they compute the divisions of every season, not by the number of days, but of nights; they keep birthdays and the beginnings of months and years in such an order that the day follows the night. Among the other usages of their life, they differ in this from almost all other nations, that they do not permit their children to approach them openly until they are grown up so as to be able to bear the service of war; and they regard it as indecorous for a son of boyish age to stand in public in the presence of his father.

6.19 Whatever sums of money the husbands have received in the name of dowry from their wives, making an estimate of it, they add the same amount out of their own estates. An account is kept of all this money conjointly, and the profits are laid by: whichever of them shall have survived [the other], to that one the portion of both reverts together with the profits of the previous time. Husbands have power of life and death over their wives as well as over their children: and when the father of a family, born in a more than commonly distinguished rank, has died, his relations assemble, and, if the circumstances of his death are suspicious, hold an investigation upon the wives in the manner adopted toward slaves; and, if proof be obtained, put them to severe torture, and kill them. Their funerals, considering the state of civilization among the Gauls, are magnificent and costly; and they cast into the fire all things, including living creatures, which they suppose to have been dear to them when alive; and, a little before this period, slaves and dependents, who were ascertained to have been beloved by them, were, after the regular funeral rites were completed, burnt together with them.

6.20 Those states which are considered to conduct their commonwealth more judiciously, have it ordained by their laws, that, if any person shall have heard by rumor and report from his neighbors any thing concerning the commonwealth, he shall convey it to the magistrate, and not impart it to any other; because it has been discovered that inconsiderate and inexperienced men were often alarmed by false reports, and driven to some rash act, or else took hasty measures in affairs of the highest importance. The magistrates conceal those things which require to be kept unknown; and they disclose to the people whatever they determine to be expedient. It is not lawful to speak of the commonwealth, except in council.

Gáius Július Cǽsar, *Commentaries on the Gállic War*, 6.13-6.20
(translated by W.A. McDevitte and W.S. Bohn)

A Description of the Gérmans

6.21 The Gérmans differ much from these usages, for they have neither drúids to preside over sacred offices, nor do they pay great regard to sacrifices. They rank in the number of the gods those alone whom they behold, and by whose instrumentality they are obviously benefited, namely, the sun, fire, and the moon; they have not heard of the other deities even by report. Their whole life is occupied in hunting and in the pursuits of the military art; from childhood they devote themselves to fatigue and hardships. Those who have remained chaste for the longest time, receive the greatest commendation among their people; they think that by this the growth is promoted, by this the physical powers are increased and the sinews are strengthened. And to have had knowledge of a woman before the twentieth year they reckon among the most disgraceful acts; of which matter there is no concealment, because they bathe promiscuously in the rivers and [only] use skins or small cloaks of deer's hides, a large portion of the body being in consequence naked.

6.22 They do not pay much attention to agriculture, and a large portion of their food consists in milk, cheese, and flesh; nor has any one a fixed quantity of land or his own individual limits; but the magistrates and the leading men each year apportion to the tribes and families, who have united together, as much land as, and in the place in which, they think proper, and the year after compel them to remove elsewhere. For this enactment they advance many reasons—lest seduced by long-continued custom, they may exchange their ardor in the waging of war for agriculture; lest they may be anxious to acquire extensive estates, and the more powerful drive the weaker from their possessions; lest they construct their houses with too great a desire to avoid cold and heat; lest the desire of wealth spring up, from which cause divisions and discords arise; and that they may keep the common people in a contented state of mind, when each sees his own means placed on an equality with [those of] the most powerful.

6.23 It is the greatest glory to the several states to have as wide deserts as possible around them, their frontiers having been laid waste. They consider this the real evidence of their prowess, that their neighbors shall be driven out of their lands and abandon them, and that no one dare settle near them; at the same time they think that they shall be on that account the more secure, because they have removed the apprehension of a sudden incursion. When a state either repels war waged against it, or wages it against another, magistrates are chosen to preside over that war with such authority, that they have power of life and death. In peace there is no common magistrate, but the chiefs of provinces and cantons administer justice and determine controversies among their own people. Robberies which are committed beyond the boundaries of each state bear no infamy, and they avow that these are committed for the purpose of disciplining their youth and of preventing sloth. And when any of their chiefs has said in an assembly "that he will be their leader, let those who are willing to follow, give in their names;" they who approve of both the enterprise and the man arise and promise their assistance and are applauded by the people; such of them as have not followed him are accounted in the number of deserters and traitors, and confidence in all matters is afterward refused them. To injure guests they regard as impious; they defend from wrong those who have come to them for any purpose whatever, and esteem them inviolable; to them the houses of all are open and maintenance is freely supplied.

6.24 And there was formerly a time when the Gauls excelled the Gérmans in prowess, and waged war on them offensively, and, on account of the great number of their people and the insufficiency of their land, sent colonies over the Rhine. Accordingly, the Vólcæ Tectósages, seized on those parts of Gérmany which are the most fruitful [and lie] around the Hercýnian forest, (which, I perceive, was known by report to Eratósthenes and some other Greeks, and which they call Orcýnia), and settled there. Which nation to this time retains its position in those settlements, and has a very high character for justice and military merit; now also they continue in the same scarcity, indigence, hardihood, as the Gérmans, and use the same food and dress; but their proximity to the Province and knowledge of commodities from countries beyond the sea supplies to the Gauls many things tending to luxury as well as civilization. Accustomed by degrees to be overmatched and worsted in many engagements, they do not even compare themselves to the Gérmans in prowess.

Gáius Július Cǽsar, *Commentaries on the Gállic War*, 6.21-6.24
(translated by W.A. McDevitte and W.S. Bohn)

Crássus Defeated by the Párthians

All were well pleased with the chance, for the people were desirous that Pómpey should not go far from the city, and he, being extremely fond of his wife, was very glad to continue there; but Crássus was so transported with his fortune, that it was manifest he thought he had never had such good luck befall him as now, so that he had much to do to contain himself before company and strangers; but amongst his private friends he let fall many vain and childish words, which were unworthy of his age, and contrary to his usual character, for he had been very little given to boasting hitherto. But then being strangely puffed up, and his head heated, he would not limit his fortune with Párthia and Sýria; but looking on the actions of Lucúllus against Tigránes and the exploits of Pómpey against Mithridátes as but child's play, he proposed to himself in his hopes to pass as far as Báctria and Índia, and the utmost ocean. Not that he was called upon by the decree which appointed him to his office to undertake any expedition against the Párthians, but it was well known that he was eager for it, and Cǽsar wrote to him out of Gaul, commending his resolution, and inciting him to the war.

And when Atéius, the tríbune of the people, designed to stop his journey, and many others murmured that one man should undertake a war against a people that had done them no injury, and were at amity with them, he desired Pómpey to stand by him and accompany him out of the town, as he had a great name amongst the common people. And when several were prepared to interfere and raise an outcry, Pómpey appeared with a pleasing countenance, and so mollified the people, that they let Crássus pass quietly. Atéius, however, met him, and first by word of mouth warned and conjured him not to proceed, and then commanded his attendant officer to seize him and detain him; but the other tríbunes not permitting it, the officer released Crássus. Atéius, therefore, running to the gate, when Crássus was come thither, set down a chafing-dish with lighted fire in it, and burning incense and pouring libations on it, cursed him with dreadful imprecations, calling upon and naming several strange and horrible deities. In the Róman belief there is so much virtue in these sacred and ancient rites, that no man can escape the effects of them, and that the utterer himself seldom prospers; so that they are not often made use of, and but upon a great occasion. And Atéius was blamed at the time for resorting to them, as the city itself, in whose cause he used them, would be the first to feel the ill effects of these curses and supernatural terrors.

Crássus arrived at Brundísium, and though the sea was very rough, he had not patience to wait, but went on board, and lost many of his ships. With the remnant of his army he marched rapidly through Galátia, where meeting with king Deiótarus, who, though he was very old, was about building a new city, Crássus scoffingly told him, "Your majesty begins to build at the twelfth hour." "Neither do you," said he, "O general, undertake your Párthian expedition very early." For Crássus was then sixty years old, and he seemed older than he was. At his first coming, things went as he would have them, for he made a bridge over Euphrátes without much difficulty, and passed over his army in safety, and occupied many cities of Mesopotámia, which yielded voluntarily. But a hundred of his men were killed in one, in which Apollónius was tyrant; therefore, bringing his forces against it, he took it by storm, plundered the goods, and sold the inhabitants. The Greeks call this city Zenodótia, upon the taking of which, he permitted the army to salute him Imperátor, but this was very ill thought of, and it looked as if he despaired a nobler achievement, that he made so much of this little success.

Putting garrisons of seven thousand foot and one thousand horse in the new conquests, he returned to take up his winter quarters in Sýria, where his son was to meet him coming from Cǽsar out of Gaul, decorated with rewards for his valor, and bringing with him one thousand select horse. Here Crássus seemed to commit his first error, and except, indeed, the whole expedition, his greatest; for, whereas he ought to have gone forward and seized Bábylon and Seleúcia, cities that were ever at enmity with the Párthians, he gave the enemy time to provide against him. Besides, he spent his time in Sýria more like an usurer than a general, not in taking an account of the arms, and in improving the skill and discipline of his soldiers, but in computing the revenue of the cities, wasting many days in weighing by scale and balance the treasure that was in the temple of Hierápolis, issuing requisitions for levies of soldiers upon particular towns and kingdoms, and then again withdrawing them on payment of sums of money, by which he lost his credit and became despised. Here, too, he met with the first ill-omen from that goddess, whom some call Vénus, others Júno, others Nature, or the Cause that produces out of moisture the first principles and seeds of all things, and gives mankind their earliest knowledge of all that is good for them. For as they were going out of the temple, young Crássus stumbled, and his father fell upon him.

When he drew his army out of winter quarters, ambassadors came to him from Ársaces, with this short speech: If the army was sent by the people of Rome, he denounced mortal war, but if, as he understood was the case, against the consent of his country, Crássus for his own private profit had invaded his territory, then their king would be more merciful, and taking pity upon Crássus's dotage, would send those soldiers back, who had been left not so truly to keep guard on him as to be his prisoners. Crássus boastfully told them he would return his answer at Seleúcia, upon which Vagíses, the eldest of them, laughed and showed the palm of his hand, saying, "Hair will grow here before you will see Seleúcia;" so they returned to their king, Hyródes, telling him it was war. Several of the Rómans that were in garrison in Mesopotámia with great hazard made their escape, and brought word that the danger was worth consideration, urging their own eye-witness of the numbers of the enemy, and the manner of their fighting, when they assaulted their towns; and, as men's manner is, made all seem greater than really it was. By flight it was impossible to escape them, and as impossible to overtake them when they fled, and they had a new and strange sort of darts, as swift as sight, for they pierced whatever they met with, before you could see who threw; their men-at-arms were so provided that their weapons would cut through any thing, and their armor give way to nothing.

All which when the soldiers heard, their hearts failed them; for till now they thought there was no difference between the Párthians and the Arménians or Cappadócians, whom Lucúllus grew weary with plundering, and had been persuaded that the main difficulty of the war consisted only in the tediousness of the march, and the trouble of chasing men that durst not come to blows, so that the danger of a battle was beyond their expectation; accordingly, some of the officers advised Crássus to proceed no further at present, but reconsider the whole enterprise, amongst whom in particular was Cássius, the quæstor. The soothsayers, also, told him privately the signs found in the sacrifices were continually adverse and unfavorable. But he paid no heed to them, or to anybody who gave any other advice than to proceed.

Nor did Artabázes, king of Arménia, confirm him a little, who came to his aid with six thousand horse; who, however, were said to be only the king's life-guard and suite, for he promised ten thousand cuirassiers more, and thirty thousand foot, at his own charge. He urged Crássus to invade Párthia by the way of Arménia, for not only would he be able there to supply his army with abundant provision, which he would give him, but his passage would be more secure in the mountains and hills, with which the whole country was covered, making it almost impassable to horse, in which the main strength of the Párthians consisted. Crássus returned him but cold thanks for his readiness to serve him, and for the splendor of his assistance, and told him he was resolved to pass through Mesopotámia, where he had left a great many brave Róman soldiers; whereupon the Arménian went his way.

As Crássus was taking the army over the river at Zéugma, he encountered preternaturally violent thunder, and the lightning flashed in the faces of the troops, and during the storm a hurricane broke upon the bridge, and carried part of it away; two thunderbolts fell upon the very place where the army was going to encamp; and one of the general's horses, magnificently caparisoned, dragged away the groom into the river and was drowned. It is said, too, that when they went to take up the first standard, the eagle of itself turned its head backward; and after he had passed over his army, as they were distributing provisions, the first thing they gave was lentils and salt, which with the Rómans are the food proper to funerals, and are offered to the dead. And as Crássus was haranguing his soldiers, he let fall a word which was thought very ominous in the army; for "I am going," he said, "to break down the bridge, that none of you may return;" and whereas he ought, when he had perceived his blunder, to have corrected himself, and explained his meaning, seeing the men alarmed at the expression, he would not do it out of mere stubbornness. And when at the last general sacrifice the priest gave him the entrails, they slipped out of his hand, and when he saw the standers-by concerned at it, he laughed and said, "See what it is to be an old man; but I shall hold my sword fast enough."

So he marched his army along the river with seven légions, little less than four thousand horse, and as many light-armed soldiers, and the scouts returning declared that not one man appeared, but that they saw the footing of a great many horses which seemed to be retiring in flight, whereupon Crássus conceived great hopes, and the Rómans began to despise the Párthians, as men that would not come to combat, hand to hand. But Cássius spoke with him again, and advised him to refresh his army in some of the garrison towns, and remain there till they could get some certain intelligence of the enemy, or at least to make toward Seleúcia, and keep by the river, that so they might have the convenience of having provision constantly supplied by the boats, which might always accompany the army, and the river would secure them from being environed, and, if they should fight, it might be upon equal terms.

While Crássus was still considering, and as yet undetermined, there came to the camp an Árab chief named Ariámnes, a cunning and wily fellow, who, of all the evil chances which combined to lead them on to destruction, was the chief and the most fatal. Some of Pómpey's old soldiers knew him, and remembered him to have received some kindnesses of Pómpey, and to have been looked upon as a friend to the Rómans, but he was now suborned by the king's generals, and sent to Crássus to entice him if possible from the river and hills into the wide open plain, where he might be surrounded. For the Párthians desired anything, rather than to be obliged to meet the Rómans face to face. He, therefore, coming to Crássus, (and he had a persuasive tongue,) highly commended Pómpey as his benefactor, and admired the forces that Crássus had with him, but seemed to wonder why he delayed and made preparations, as if he should not use his feet more than any arms, against men that, taking with them their best goods and chattels, had designed long ago to fly for refuge to the Scýthians or Hyrcánians. "If you meant to fight, you should have made all possible haste, before the king should recover courage, and collect his forces together; at present you see Suréna and Silláces opposed to you, to draw you off in pursuit of them, while the king himself keeps out of the way."

But this was all a lie, for Hyródes had divided his army in two parts, with one he in person wasted Arménia, revenging himself upon Artavásdes, and sent Suréna against the Rómans, not out of contempt, as some pretend, for there is no likelihood that he should despise Crássus, one of the chiefest men of Rome, to go and fight with Artavásdes, and invade Arménia; but much more probably he really apprehended the danger, and therefore waited to see the event, intending that Suréna should first run the hazard of a battle, and draw the enemy on. Nor was this Suréna an ordinary person, but in wealth, family, and reputation, the second man in the kingdom, and in courage and prowess the first, and for bodily stature and beauty no man like him. Whenever he traveled privately, he had one thousand camels to carry his baggage, two hundred chariots for his concubines, one thousand completely armed men for his life-guards, and a great many more light-armed; and he had at least ten thousand horsemen altogether, of his servants and retinue. The honor had long belonged to his family, that at the king's coronation he put the crown upon his head, and when this very king Hyródes had been exiled, he brought him in; it was he, also, that took the great city of Seleúcia, was the first man that scaled the walls, and with his own hand beat off the defenders. And though at this time he was not above thirty years old, he had a great name for wisdom and sagacity, and, indeed, by these qualities chiefly, he overthrew Crássus, who first through his overweening confidence, and afterwards because he was cowed by his calamities, fell a ready victim to his subtlety.

When Ariámnes had thus worked upon him, he drew him from the river into vast plains, by a way that at first was pleasant and easy, but afterwards very troublesome by reason of the depth of the sand; no tree, nor any water, and no end of this to be seen; so that they were not only spent with thirst, and the difficulty of the passage, but were dismayed with the uncomfortable prospect of not a bough, not a stream, not a hillock, not a green herb, but in fact a sea of sand, which encompassed the army with its waves. They began to suspect some treachery, and at the same time came messengers from Artavásdes, that he was fiercely attacked by Hyródes, who had invaded his country, so that now it was impossible for him to send any succors, and that he therefore advised Crássus to turn back, and with joint forces to give Hyródes battle, or at least that he should march and encamp where horses could not easily come, and keep to the mountains. Crássus, out of anger and perverseness, wrote him no answer, but told them, at present he was not at leisure to mind the Arménians, but he would call upon them another time, and revenge himself upon Artavásdes for his treachery.

Cássius and his friends began again to complain, but when they perceived that it merely displeased Crássus, they gave over, but privately railed at the barbarian, "What evil genius, O thou worst of men, brought thee to our camp, and with what charms and potions hast thou bewitched Crássus, that he should march his army through a vast and deep desert, through ways which are rather fit for a captain of Arábian robbers, than for the general of a Róman army?" But the barbarian, being a wily fellow, very submissively exhorted them, and encouraged them to sustain it a little further, and ran about the camp, and, professing to cheer up the soldiers, asked them, jokingly, "What, do you think you march through Campánia, expecting everywhere to find springs, and shady trees, and baths, and inns of entertainment? Consider you now travel through the confines of Arábia and Assýria." Thus he managed them like children, and before the cheat was discovered, he rode away; not but that Crássus was aware of his going, but he had persuaded him that he would go and contrive how to disorder the affairs of the enemy.

It is related that Crássus came abroad that day not in his scarlet robe, which Róman generals usually wear, but in a black one, which, as soon as he perceived, he changed. And the standard-bearers had much ado to take up their eagles, which seemed to be fixed to the place. Crássus laughed at it, and hastened their march, and compelled his infantry to keep pace with his cavalry, till some few of the scouts returned and told them that their fellows were slain and they hardly escaped, that the enemy was at hand in full force, and resolved to give them battle. On this all was in an uproar; Crássus was struck with amazement, and for haste could scarcely put his army in good order. First, as Cássius advised, he opened their ranks and files that they might take up as much space as could be, to prevent their being surrounded, and distributed the horse upon the wings, but afterwards changing his mind, he drew up his army in a square, and made a front every way, each of which consisted of twelve cohorts, to every one of which he allotted a troop of horse, that no part might be destitute of the assistance that the horse might give, and that they might be ready to assist everywhere, as need should require. Cássius commanded one of the wings, young Crássus the other, and he himself was in the middle.

Thus they marched on till they came to a little river named Balíssus, a very inconsiderable one in itself, but very grateful to the soldiers, who had suffered so much by drought and heat all along their march. Most of the commanders were of the opinion that they ought to remain there that night, and to inform themselves as much as possible of the number of the enemies, and their order, and so march against them at break of day; but Crássus was so carried away by the eagerness of his son, and the horsemen that were with him, who desired and urged him to lead them on and engage, that he commanded those that had a mind to it to eat and drink as they stood in their ranks, and before they had all well done, he led them on, not leisurely and with halts to take breath, as if he was going to battle, but kept on his pace as if he had been in haste, till they saw the enemy, contrary to their expectation, neither so many nor so magnificently armed as the Rómans expected. For Suréna had hid his main force behind the first ranks, and ordered them to hide the glittering of their armor with coats and skins. But when they approached and the general gave the signal, immediately all the field rung with a hideous noise and terrible clamor. For the Párthians do not encourage themselves to war with cornets and trumpets, but with a kind of kettle-drum, which they strike all at once in various quarters. With these they make a dead hollow noise like the bellowing of beasts, mixed with sounds resembling thunder, having, it would seem, very correctly observed, that of all our senses hearing most confounds and disorders us, and that the feelings excited through it most quickly disturb, and most entirely overpower the understanding.

When they had sufficiently terrified the Rómans with their noise, they threw off the covering of their armor, and shone like lightning in their breastplates and helmets of polished Margiánian steel, and with their horses covered with brass and steel trappings. Suréna was the tallest and finest looking man himself, but the delicacy of his looks and effeminacy of his dress did not promise so much manhood as he really was master of; for his face was painted, and his hair parted after the fashion of the Medes, whereas the other Párthians made a more terrible appearance, with their shaggy hair gathered in a mass upon their foreheads after the Scýthian mode. Their first design was with their lances to beat down and force back the first ranks of the Rómans, but when they perceived the depth of their battle, and that the soldiers firmly kept their ground, they made a retreat, and pretending to break their order and disperse, they encompassed the Róman square before they were aware of it.

Crássus commanded his light-armed soldiers to charge, but they had not gone far before they were received with such a shower of arrows that they were glad to retire amongst the heavy-armed, with whom this was the first occasion of disorder and terror, when they perceived the strength and force of their darts, which pierced their arms, and passed through every kind of covering, hard and soft alike. The Párthians now placing themselves at distances began to shoot from all sides, not aiming at any particular mark, (for, indeed, the order of the Rómans was so close, that they could not miss if they would,) but simply sent their arrows with great force out of strong bent bows, the strokes from which came with extreme violence. The position of the Rómans was a very bad one from the first; for if they kept their ranks, they were wounded, and if they tried to charge, they hurt the enemy none the more, and themselves suffered none the less. For the Párthians threw their darts as they fled, an art in which none but the Scýthians excel them, and it is, indeed, a cunning practice, for while they thus fight to make their escape, they avoid the dishonor of a flight.

However, the Rómans had some comfort to think that when they had spent all their arrows, they would either give over or come to blows; but when they presently understood that there were numerous camels loaded with arrows, and that when the first ranks had discharged those they had, they wheeled off and took more, Crássus seeing no end of it, was out of all heart, and sent to his son that he should endeavor to fall in upon them before he was quite surrounded; for the enemy advanced most upon that quarter, and seemed to be trying to ride round and come upon the rear. Therefore the young man, taking with him thirteen hundred horse, one thousand of which he had from Cǽsar, five hundred archers, and eight cohorts of the full-armed soldiers that stood next him, led them up with design to charge the Párthians. Whether it was that they found themselves in a piece of marshy ground, as some think, or else designing to entice young Crássus as far as they could from his father, they turned and began to fly; whereupon he crying out that they durst not stand, pursued them, and with him Censorínus and Megabácchus, both famous, the latter for his courage and prowess, the other for being of a senator's family, and an excellent orator, both intimates of Crássus, and of about the same age. The horse thus pushing on, the infantry stayed little behind, being exalted with hopes and joy, for they supposed they had already conquered, and now were only pursuing; till when they were gone too far, they perceived the deceit, for they that seemed to fly, now turned again, and a great many fresh ones came on.

Upon this they made an halt, for they doubted not but now the enemy would attack them, because they were so few. But they merely placed their cuirassiers to face the Rómans, and with the rest of their horse rode about scouring the field, and thus stirring up the sand, they raised such a dust that the Rómans could neither see nor speak to one another, and being driven in upon one another in one close body, they were thus hit and killed, dying, not by a quick and easy death, but with miserable pains and convulsions; for writhing upon the darts in their bodies, they broke them in their wounds, and when they would by force pluck out the barbed points, they caught the nerves and veins, so that they tore and tortured themselves. Many of them died thus, and those that survived were disabled for any service, and when Públius exhorted them to charge the cuirassiers, they showed him their hands nailed to their shields, and their feet stuck to the ground, so that they could neither fly nor fight. He charged in himself boldly, however, with his horse, and came to close quarters with them, but was very unequal, whether as to the offensive or defensive part; for with his weak and little javelins, he struck against targets that were of tough raw hides and iron, whereas the lightly clad bodies of his Gáulish horsemen were exposed to the strong spears of the enemy. For upon these he mostly depended, and with them he wrought wonders; for they would catch hold of the great spears, and close upon the enemy, and so pull them off from their horses, where they could scarce stir by reason of the heaviness of their armor, and many of the Gauls quitting their own horses, would creep under those of the enemy, and stick them in the belly; which, growing unruly with the pain, trampled upon their riders and upon the enemies promiscuously. The Gauls were chiefly tormented by the heat and drought, being not accustomed to either, and most of their horses were slain by being spurred on against the spears, so that they were forced to retire among the foot, bearing off Públius grievously wounded.

Observing a sandy hillock not far off, they made to it, and tying their horses to one another, and placing them in the midst, and joining all their shields together before them, they thought they might make some defense against the barbarians. But it fell out quite contrary, for when they were drawn up in a plain, the front in some measure secured those that were behind; but when they were upon the hill, one being of necessity higher up than another, none were in shelter, but all alike stood equally exposed, bewailing their inglorious and useless fate. There were with Públius two Greeks that lived near there at Cárrhæ, Hierónymus and Nicómachus; these men urged him to retire with them and fly to Íchnæ, a town not far from thence, and friendly to the Rómans. "No," said he, "there is no death so terrible, for the fear of which Públius would leave his friends that die upon his account;" and bidding them to take care of themselves, he embraced them and sent them away, and, because he could not use his arm, for he was run through with a dart, he opened his side to his armor-bearer, and commanded him to run him through. It is said that Censorínus fell in the same manner. Megabácchus slew himself, as did also the rest of best note. The Párthians coming upon the rest with their lances, killed them fighting, nor were there above five hundred taken prisoners. Cutting off the head of Públius, they rode off directly towards Crássus.

His condition was thus. When he had commanded his son to fall upon the enemy, and word was brought him that they fled and that there was a distant pursuit, and perceiving also that the enemy did not press upon him so hard as formerly, for they were mostly gone to fall upon Públius, he began to take heart a little; and drawing his army towards some sloping ground, expected when his son would return from the pursuit. Of the messengers whom Públius sent to him, (as soon as he saw his danger,) the first were intercepted by the enemy, and slain; the last hardly escaping, came and declared that Públius was lost, unless he had speedy succors. Crássus was terribly distracted, not knowing what counsel to take, and indeed no longer capable of taking any; overpowered now by fear for the whole army, now by desire to help his son.

At last he resolved to move with his forces. Just upon this, up came the enemy with their shouts and noises more terrible than before, their drums sounding again in the ears of the Rómans, who now feared a fresh engagement. And they who brought Públius's head upon the point of a spear, riding up near enough that it could be known, scoffingly inquired where were his parents, and what family he was of, for it was impossible that so brave and gallant a warrior should be the son of so pitiful a coward as Crássus. This sight above all the rest dismayed the Rómans, for it did not incite them to anger as it might have done, but to horror and trembling, though they say Crássus outdid himself in this calamity, for he passed through the ranks and cried out to them, "This, O my countrymen, is my own peculiar loss, but the fortune and the glory of Rome is safe and untainted so long as you are safe. But if any one be concerned for my loss of the best of sons, let him show it in revenging him upon the enemy. Take away their joy, revenge their cruelty, nor be dismayed at what is past; for whoever tries for great objects must suffer something. Neither did Lucúllus overthrow Tigránes without bloodshed, nor Scípio Antíochus; our ancestors lost one thousand ships about Sícily, and how many generals and captains in Ítaly? no one of which losses hindered them from overthrowing their conquerors; for the State of Rome did not arrive to this height by fortune, but by perseverance and virtue in confronting danger."

While Crássus thus spoke exhorting them, he saw but few that gave much heed to him, and when he ordered them to shout for the battle, he could no longer mistake the despondency of his army, which made but a faint and unsteady noise, while the shout of the enemy was clear and bold.

And when they came to the business, the Párthian servants and dependents riding about shot their arrows, and the horsemen in the foremost ranks with their spears drove the Rómans close together, except those who rushed upon them for fear of being killed by their arrows. Neither did these do much execution, being quickly dispatched; for the strong thick spear made large and mortal wounds, and often run through two men at once. As they were thus fighting, the night coming on parted them, the Párthians boasting that they would indulge Crássus with one night to mourn his son, unless upon better consideration he would rather go to Ársaces, than be carried to him. These, therefore, took up their quarters near them, being flushed with their victory. But the Rómans had a sad night of it; for neither taking care for the burial of their dead, nor the cure of the wounded, nor the groans of the expiring, every one bewailed his own fate. For there was no means of escaping, whether they should stay for the light, or venture to retreat into the vast desert in the dark. And now the wounded men gave them new trouble, since to take them with them would retard their flight, and if they should leave them, they might serve as guides to the enemy by their cries.

However, they were all desirous to see and hear Crássus, though they were sensible that he was the cause of all their mischief. But he wrapped his cloak around him, and hid himself, where he lay as an example, to ordinary minds, of the caprice of fortune, but to the wise, of inconsiderateness and ambition; who, not content to be superior to so many millions of men, being inferior to two, esteemed himself as the lowest of all. Then came Octávius, his lieutenant, and Cássius, to comfort him, but he being altogether past helping, they themselves called together the centúrions and tríbunes, and agreeing that the best way was to fly, they ordered the army out, without sound of trumpet, and at first with silence. But before long, when the disabled men found they were left behind, strange confusion and disorder, with an outcry and lamentation, seized the camp, and a trembling and dread presently fell upon them, as if the enemy were at their heels.

By which means, now and then turning out of their way, now and then standing to their ranks, sometimes taking up the wounded that followed, sometimes laying them down, they wasted the time, except three hundred horse, whom Egnátius brought safe to Cárrhæ about midnight; where calling, in the Róman tongue, to the watch, as soon as they heard him, he bade them tell Copónius, the governor, that Crássus had fought a very great battle with the Párthians; and having said but this, and not so much as telling his name, he rode away at full speed to Zéugma. And by this means he saved himself and his men, but lost his reputation by deserting his general. However, his message to Copónius was for the advantage of Crássus; for he, suspecting by this hasty and confused delivery of the message that all was not well, immediately ordered the garrison to be in arms, and as soon as he understood that Crássus was upon the way towards him, he went out to meet him, and received him with his army into town.

The Párthians, although they perceived their dislodgement in the night, yet did not pursue them, but as soon as it was day, they came upon those that were left in the camp, and put no less than four thousand to the sword, and with their light-horse picked up a great many stragglers. Varguntínus, the lieutenant, while it was yet dark, had broken off from the main body with four cohorts which had strayed out of the way; and the Párthians encompassing these on a small hill, slew every man of them excepting twenty, who with their drawn swords forced their way through the thickest, and they admiring their courage, opened their ranks to the right and left, and let them pass without molestation to Cárrhæ.

Soon after a false report was brought to Suréna, that Crássus, with his principal officers, had escaped, and that those who were got into Cárrhæ were but a confused rout of insignificant people, not worth further pursuit. Supposing, therefore, that he had lost the very crown and glory of his victory, and yet being uncertain whether it were so or not, and anxious to ascertain the fact, that so he should either stay and besiege Cárrhæ or follow Crássus, he sent one of his interpreters to the walls, commanding him in Látin to call for Crássus or Cássius, for that the general, Suréna, desired a conference. As soon as Crássus heard this, he embraced the proposal, and soon after there came up a band of Arábians, who very well knew the faces of Crássus and Cássius, as having been frequently in the Róman camp before the battle. They having espied Cássius from the wall, told him that Suréna desired a peace, and would give them safe convoy, if they would make a treaty with the king his master, and withdraw all their troops out of Mesopotámia; and this he thought most advisable for them both, before things came to the last extremity; Cássius, embracing the proposal, desired that a time and place might be appointed where Crássus and Suréna might have an interview. The Arábians, having charged themselves with the message, went back to Suréna, who was not a little rejoiced that Crássus was there to be besieged.

Next day, therefore, he came up with his army, insulting over the Rómans, and haughtily demanding of them Crássus and Cássius bound, if they expected any mercy. The Rómans, seeing themselves deluded and mocked, were much troubled at it, but advising Crássus to lay aside his distant and empty hopes of aid from the Arménians, resolved to fly for it; and this design ought to have been kept private, till they were upon their way, and not have been told to any of the people of Cárrhæ. But Crássus let this also be known to Andrómachus, the most faithless of men, nay he was so infatuated as to choose him for his guide. The Párthians then, to be sure, had punctual intelligence of all that passed; but it being contrary to their usage, and also difficult for them to fight by night, and Crássus having chosen that time to set out, Andrómachus, lest he should get the start too far of his pursuers, led him hither and thither, and at last conveyed him into the midst of morasses and places full of ditches, so that the Rómans had a troublesome and perplexing journey of it, and some there were who, supposing by these windings and turnings of Andrómachus that no good was intended, resolved to follow him no further.

And at last Cássius himself returned to Cárrhæ, and his guides, the Arábians, advising him to tarry there till the moon was got out of Scórpio, he told them that he was most afraid of Sagittárius, and so with five hundred horse went off to Sýria. Others there were, who having got honest guides, took their way by the mountains called Sínnaca, and got into places of security by daybreak; these were five thousand under the command of Octávius, a very gallant man. But Crássus fared worse; day overtook him still deceived by Andrómachus, and entangled in the fens and the difficult country. There were with him four cohorts of légionary soldiers, a very few horsemen, and five líctors, with whom having with great difficulty got into the way, and not being a mile and a half from Octávius, instead of going to join him, although the enemy were already upon him, he retreated to another hill, neither so defensible nor impassable for the horse, but lying under the hills of Sínnaca, and continued so as to join them in a long ridge through the plain. Octávius could see in what danger the general was, and himself, at first but slenderly followed, hurried to the rescue. Soon after, the rest, upbraiding one another with baseness in forsaking their officers, marched down, and falling upon the Párthians, drove them from the hill, and compassing Crássus about, and fencing him with their shields, declared proudly, that no arrow in Párthia should ever touch their general, so long as there was a man of them left alive to protect him.

Suréna, therefore, perceiving his soldiers less inclined to expose themselves, and knowing that if the Rómans should prolong the battle till night, they might then gain the mountains and be out of his reach, betook himself to his usual craft. Some of the prisoners were set free, who had, as it was contrived, been in hearing, while some of the barbarians spoke of a set purpose in the camp to the effect that the king did not design the war to be pursued to extremity against the Rómans, but rather desired, by his gentle treatment of Crássus, to make a step towards reconciliation. And the barbarians desisted from fighting, and Suréna himself, with his chief officers, riding gently to the hill, unbent his bow and held out his hand, inviting Crássus to an agreement, and saying that it was beside the king's intentions, that they had thus had experience of the courage and the strength of his soldiers; that now he desired no other contention but that of kindness and friendship, by making a truce, and permitting them to go away in safety.

These words of Suréna the rest received joyfully, and were eager to accept the offer; but Crássus, who had had sufficient experience of their perfidiousness, and was unable to see any reason for the sudden change, would give no ear to them, and only took time to consider. But the soldiers cried out and advised him to treat, and then went on to upbraid and affront him, saying that it was very unreasonable that he should bring them to fight with such men armed, whom himself, without their arms, durst not look in the face. He tried first to prevail with them by entreaties, and told them that if they would have patience till evening, they might get into the mountains and passes, inaccessible for horse, and be out of danger, and withal he pointed out the way with his hand, entreating them not to abandon their preservation, now close before them. But when they mutinied and clashed their targets in a threatening manner, he was overpowered and forced to go, and only turning about at parting, said, "You, Octávius and Petrónius, and the rest of the officers who are present, see the necessity of going which I lie under, and cannot but be sensible of the indignities and violence offered to me. Tell all men when you have escaped, that Crássus perished rather by the subtlety of his enemies, than by the disobedience of his countrymen."

Octávius, however, would not stay there, but with Petrónius went down from the hill; as for the líctors, Crássus bade them be gone. The first that met him were two half-blood Greeks, who, leaping from their horses, made a profound reverence to Crássus, and desired him, in Greek, to send some before him, who might see that Suréna himself was coming towards them, his retinue disarmed, and not having so much as their wearing swords along with them. But Crássus answered, that if he had the least concern for his life, he would never have entrusted himself in their hands, but sent two brothers of the name of Róscius, to inquire on what terms, and in what numbers they should meet. These Suréna ordered immediately to be seized, and himself with his principal officers came up on horseback, and greeting him, said, "How is this, then? A Róman commander is on foot, whilst I and my train are mounted." But Crássus replied, that there was no error committed on either side, for they both met according to the custom of their own country. Suréna told him that from that time there was a league between the king his master and the Rómans, but that Crássus must go with him to the river to sign it, "for you Rómans," said he, "have not good memories for conditions," and so saying, reached out his hand to him.

Crássus, therefore, gave order that one of his horses should be brought; but Suréna told him there was no need, "the king, my master, presents you with this;" and immediately a horse with a golden bit was brought up to him, and himself was forcibly put into the saddle by the grooms, who ran by the side and struck the horse to make the more haste. But Octávius running up, got hold of the bridle, and soon after one of the officers, Petrónius, and the rest of the company came up, striving to stop the horse, and pulling back those who on both sides of him forced Crássus forward. Thus from pulling and thrusting one another, they came to a tumult, and soon after to blows. Octávius, drawing his sword, killed a groom of one of the barbarians, and one of them, getting behind Octávius, killed him. Petrónius was not armed, but being struck on the breastplate, fell down from his horse, though without hurt. Crássus was killed by a Párthian, called Pomáxathres; others say, by a different man, and that Pomáxathres only cut off his head and right hand after he had fallen. But this is conjecture rather than certain knowledge, for those that were by had not leisure to observe particulars, and were either killed fighting about Crássus, or ran off at once to get to their comrades on the hill. But the Párthians coming up to them, and saying that Crássus had the punishment he justly deserved, and that Suréna bade the rest come down from the hill without fear, some of them came down and surrendered themselves, others were scattered up and down in the night, a very few of whom got safe home, and others the Arábians, beating through the country, hunted down and put to death. It is generally said, that in all twenty thousand men were slain, and ten thousand taken prisoners.

Suréna sent the head and hand of Crássus to Hyródes, the king, into Arménia, but himself by his messengers scattering a report that he was bringing Crássus alive to Seleúcia, made a ridiculous procession, which by way of scorn, he called a triumph. For one Gáius Pacciánus, who of all the prisoners was most like Crássus, being put into a woman's dress of the fashion of the barbarians, and instructed to answer to the title of Crássus and Imperátor, was brought sitting upon his horse, while before him went a parcel of trumpeters and líctors upon camels. Purses were hung at the end of the bundles of rods, and the heads of the slain fresh bleeding at the end of their axes. After them followed the Seleúcian singing women, repeating scurrilous and abusive songs upon the effeminacy and cowardliness of Crássus.

Plútarch, Life of Crássus (translated by John Dryden)

Július Cæsar Crosses the Rúbicon

27 Moreover, to retain his relationship and friendship with Pómpey, Cæsar offered him his sister's granddaughter Octávia in marriage, although she was already the wife of Gáius Marcéllus, and asked for the hand of Pómpey's daughter, who was promised to Fáustus Súlla. When he had put all Pómpey's friends under obligation, as well as the greater part of the senate, through loans made without interest or at a low rate, he lavished gifts on men of all other classes, both those whom he invited to accept his bounty and those who applied to him unasked, including even freedmen and slaves who were special favorites of their masters or patrons. In short, he was the sole and ever ready help of all who were in legal difficulties or in debt and of young spendthrifts, excepting only those whose burden of guilt or poverty was so heavy, or who were so given up to riotous living, that even he could not save them; and to these he declared in the plainest terms that what they needed was a civil war.

28 He took no less pains to win the devotion of princes and provinces all over the world, offering prisoners to some by the thousand as a gift, and sending auxiliary troops to the aid of others whenever they wished, and as often as they wished, without the sanction of the senate or people, besides adorning the principal cities of Ásia and Greece with magnificent public works, as well as those of Ítaly and the provinces of Gaul and Spain. At last, when all were thunder-struck at his actions and wondered what their purpose could be, the cónsul Márcus Cláudius Marcéllus, after first making proclamation that he purposed to bring before the senate a matter of the highest public moment, proposed that a successor to Cæsar be appointed before the end of his term, on the ground that the war was ended, peace was established, and the victorious army ought to be disbanded; also that no account be taken of Cæsar at the elections, unless he were present, since Pómpey's subsequent action had not annulled the decree of the people. And it was true that when Pómpey proposed a bill touching the privileges of officials, in the clause whereby he debarred absentees from candidacy for office he forgot to make a special exception in Cæsar's case, and did not correct the oversight until the law had been inscribed on a tablet of bronze and deposited in the treasury. Not content with depriving Cæsar of his provinces and his privilege, Marcéllus also moved that the colonists whom Cæsar had settled in Nóvum Cómum by the bill of Vatínius should lose their citizenship, on the ground that it had been given from political motives and was not authorized by the law.

29 Greatly troubled by these measures, and thinking, as they say he was often heard to remark, that now that he was the leading man of the state, it was harder to push him down from the first place to the second than it would be from the second to the lowest, Cæsar stoutly resisted Marcéllus, partly through vetoes of the tríbunes and partly through the other cónsul, Sérvius Sulpícius. When next year Gáius Marcéllus, who had succeeded his cousin Márcus as cónsul, tried the same thing, Cæsar by a heavy bribe secured the support of the other cónsul, Æmílius Páullus, and of Gáius Cúrio, the most reckless of the tríbunes. But seeing that everything was being pushed most persistently, and that even the cónsuls elect were among the opposition, he sent a written appeal to the senate, not to take from him the privilege which the people had granted, or else to compel the others in command of armies to resign also; feeling sure, it was thought, that he could more readily muster his veterans as soon as he wished, than Pómpey his newly levied troops. He further proposed a compromise to his opponents, that after giving up eight légions and Transálpine Gaul, he be allowed to keep two légions and Cisálpine Gaul, or at least one légion and Illýricum, until he was elected cónsul.

30 But when the senate declined to interfere, and his opponents declared that they would accept no compromise in a matter affecting the public welfare, he crossed to Hither Gaul, and after holding all the assizes, halted at Ravénna, intending to resort to war if the senate took any drastic action against the tríbunes of the commons who interposed vetoes in his behalf. Now this was his excuse for the civil war, but it is believed that he had other motives. Gnǽus Pompéius used to declare that since Cǽsar's own means were not sufficient to complete the works which he had planned, nor to do all that he had led the people to expect on his return, he desired a state of general unrest and turmoil. Others say that he dreaded the necessity of rendering an account for what he had done in his first cónsulship contrary to the auspices and the laws, and regardless of vetoes; for Márcus Cáto often declared, and took oath too, that he would impeach Cǽsar the moment he had disbanded his army. It was openly said too that if he was out of office on his return, he would be obliged, like Mílo, to make his defense in a court hedged about by armed men. The latter opinion is the more credible one in view of the assertion of Asínius Póllio, that when Cǽsar at the battle of Pharsálus saw his enemies slain or in flight, he said, word for word: "They would have it so. Even I, Gáius Cǽsar, after so many great deeds, should have been found guilty, if I had not turned to my army for help." Some think that habit had given him a love of power, and that weighing the strength of his adversaries against his own, he grasped the opportunity of usurping the despotism which had been his heart's desire from early youth. Cícero too was seemingly of this opinion, when he wrote in the third book of his *De Officiis* that Cǽsar ever had upon his lips these lines of Eurípides, of which Cícero himself adds a version:

> If wrong may e'er be right, for a throne's sake
> Were wrong most right—be God in all else feared.

31 Accordingly, when word came that the veto of the tríbunes had been set aside and they themselves had left the city, he at once sent on a few cohorts with all secrecy, and then, to disarm suspicion, concealed his purpose by appearing at a public show inspecting the plans of a gladiatorial school which he intended building, and joining as usual in a banquet with a large company. It was not until after sunset that he set out very privately with a small company, taking the mules from a bakeshop hard by and harnessing them to a carriage; and when his lights went out and he lost his way, he was astray for some time, but at last found a guide at dawn and got back to the road on foot by narrow by-paths. Then, overtaking his cohorts at the river Rúbicon, which was the boundary of his province, he paused for a while, and realizing what a step he was taking, he turned to those about him and said: "Even yet we may draw back; but once cross yon little bridge, and the whole issue is with the sword."

32 As he stood in doubt, this sign was given him. On a sudden there appeared hard by a being of wondrous stature and beauty, who sat and played upon a reed; and when not only the shepherds flocked to hear him, but many of the soldiers left their posts, and among them some of the trumpeters, the apparition snatched a trumpet from one of them, rushed to the river, and sounding the war-note with mighty blast, strode to the opposite bank. Then Cǽsar cried: "Take we the course which the signs of the gods and the false dealing of our foes point out. The die is cast," said he.

33 Accordingly, crossing with his army, and welcoming the tríbunes of the commons, who had come to him after being driven from Rome, he harangued the soldiers with tears, and rending his robe from his breast besought their faithful service. It is even thought that he promised every man a knight's estate, but that came of a misunderstanding: for since he often pointed to the finger of his left hand as he addressed them and urged them on, declaring that to satisfy all those who helped him to defend his honor he would gladly tear this very ring from his hand, those on the edge of the assembly, who could see him better than they could hear his words, assumed that he said what his gesture seemed to mean; and so the report went about that he had promised them the right of the ring and four hundred thousand sésterces as well.

Suetónius, *Lives of the Twelve Cǽsars*, Július Cǽsar 27-33 (translated by J. C. Rolfe)

The Assassination of Július Cǽsar

76 Yet after all, his other actions and word so turn the scale, that it is thought that he abused his power and was justly slain. For not only did he accept excessive honors, such as an uninterrupted cónsulship, the dictatorship for life, and the cénsorship of public morals, as well as the forename Imperátor, the surname of Father of his Country, a statue among those of the kings, and a raised couch in the orchestra; but he also allowed honors to be bestowed on him which were too great for mortal man: a golden throne in the House and on the judgment seat; a chariot and litter in the procession at the círcus; temples, altars, and statues beside those of the gods; a special priest, an additional college of the Lúperci, and the calling of one of the months by his name. In fact, there were no honors which he did not receive or confer at pleasure.

He held his third and fourth cónsulships in name only, content with the power of the dictatorship conferred on him at the same time as the cónsulships. Moreover, in both years he substituted two cónsuls for himself for the last three months, in the meantime holding no elections except for tríbunes and plebéian ǽdiles, and appointing prefects instead of the prǽtors, to manage the affairs of the city during his absence. When one of the cónsuls suddenly died the day before the Kálends [First] of January, he gave the vacant office for a few hours to a man who asked for it. With the same disregard of law and precedent he named magistrates for several years to come, bestowed the emblems of cónsular rank on ten ex-prǽtors, and admitted to the House men who had been given citizenship, and in some cases half-civilized Gauls. He assigned the charge of the mint and of the public revenues to his own slaves, and gave the oversight and command of the three légions which he had left at Alexándria to a favorite of his called Rúfio, son of one of his freedmen.

77 No less arrogant were his public utterances, which Títus Ámpius records: that the state was nothing, a mere name without body or form; that Súlla did not know his A. B. C. when he laid down his dictatorship; that men ought now to be more circumspect in addressing him, and to regard his word as law. So far did he go in his presumption, that when a soothsayer once reported direful inwards without a heart, he said: "They will be more favorable when I wish it; it should not be regarded as a portent, if a beast has no heart."

78 But it was the following action in particular that roused deadly hatred against him. When the Senate approached him in a body with many highly honorary decrees, he received them before the temple of Vénus Génetrix without rising. Some think that when he attempted to get up, he was held back by Cornélius Bálbus; others, that he made no such move at all, but on the contrary frowned angrily on Gáius Trebátius when he suggested that he should rise. And this action of his seemed the more intolerable, because when he himself in one of his triumphal processions rode past the benches of the tríbunes, he was so incensed because a member of the college, Póntius Áquila, did not rise, that he cried: "Come then, Áquila, take back the republic from me, you tríbune"; and for several days he would not make a promise to any one without adding, "That is, if Póntius Áquila will allow me."

79 To an insult which so plainly showed his contempt for the Senate he added an act of even greater insolence; for at the Látin Festival, as he was returning to the city, amid the extravagant and unprecedented demonstrations of the populace, someone in the press placed on his statue a laurel wreath with a white fillet tied to it; and when Epídius Marúllus and Cæsétius Flávius, tríbunes of the commons, gave orders that the ribbon be removed from the wreath and the man taken off to prison, Cǽsar sharply rebuked and deposed them, either offended that the hint at regal

91

power had been received with so little favor, or, as he asserted, that he had been robbed of the glory of refusing it. But from that time on he could not rid himself of the odium of having aspired to the title of monarch, although he replied to the commons, when they hailed him as king, "I am Cæsar and no king," and at the Lupercália, when the cónsul Ántony several times attempted to place a crown upon his head as he spoke from the róstra, he put it aside and at last sent it to the Cápitol, to be offered to Júpiter Óptimus Máximus. Nay, more, the report had spread in various quarters that he intended to move to Ílium or Alexándria, taking with him the resources of the state, draining Ítaly by levies, and leaving the charge of the city to his friends; also that at the next meeting of the Senate Lúcius Cótta would announce as the decision of Fifteen, that inasmuch as it was written in the books of fate that the Párthians could be conquered only by a king, Cæsar should be given that title.

80 It was this that led the conspirators to hasten in carrying out their designs, in order to avoid giving their assent to this proposal. Therefore the plots which had previously been formed separately, often by groups of two or three, were united in a general conspiracy, since even the populace no longer were pleased with present conditions, but both secretly and openly rebelled at his tyranny and cried out for defenders of their liberty. On the admission of foreigners to the Senate, a placard was posted: "God bless the Commonwealth! let no one consent to point out the House to a newly made senator." The following verses too were sung everywhere:

> Cæsar led the Gauls in triumph, led them to the senate house;
> Then the Gauls put off their breeches, and put on the laticlave.

When Quíntus Máximus, whom he had appointed cónsul in his place for three months, was entering the theatre, and his líctor called attention to his arrival in the usual manner, a general shout was raised: "He's no cónsul!" At the first election after the deposing of Cæsétius and Marúllus, the tríbunes, several votes were found for their appointment as cónsuls. Some wrote on the base of Lúcius Brútus' statue: "Oh, that you were still alive"; and on that of Cæsar himself:

> First of all was Brútus cónsul, since he drove the kings from Rome;
> Since this man drove out the cónsuls, he at last is made our king.

More than sixty joined the conspiracy against him, led by Gáius Cássius and Márcus and Décimus Brútus. At first they hesitated whether to form two divisions at the elections in the Cámpus Mártius, so that while some hurled him from the bridge as he summoned the tribes to vote, the rest might wait below and slay him; or to set upon him in the Sacred Way or at the entrance to the theatre. When, however, a meeting of the Senate was called for the Ides of March in the Hall of Pómpey, they readily gave that time and place the preference.

81 Now Cæsar's approaching murder was foretold to him by unmistakable signs. A few months before, when the settlers assigned to the colony at Cápua by the Júlian Law were demolishing some tombs of great antiquity, to build country houses, and plied their work with the greater vigor because as they rummaged about they found a quantity of vases of ancient workmanship, there was discovered in a tomb, which was said to be that of Cápys, the founder of Cápua, a bronze tablet, inscribed with Greek words and characters to this purport: "Whenever the bones of Cápys shall be moved, it will come to pass that a son of Ilium shall be slain at the hands of his kindred, and presently avenged at heavy cost to Ítaly." And let no one think this tale a myth or a lie, for it is vouched for by Cornélius Bálbus, an intimate friend of Cæsar. Shortly before his death, as he was told, the herds of horses which he had dedicated to the river Rúbicon when he crossed it, and had let loose without a keeper, stubbornly refused to graze and wept copiously. Again, when he was offering sacrifice, the soothsayer Spurínna warned him to beware of danger, which would come not later than the Ides of March; and on the day before the Ides of that month a little bird called the king-bird flew into the Hall of Pómpey with a sprig of laurel, pursued by others of various kinds from the grove hard by, which tore it to pieces in the hall. In fact the very night before his murder he dreamt now that he was flying above the clouds, and now that he was clasping the hand of Júpiter; and his wife Calpúrnia thought that the pediment of their house fell, and that her husband was stabbed in her arms; and on a sudden the door of the room flew open of its own accord.

Both for these reasons and because of poor health he hesitated for a long time whether to stay at home and put off what he had planned to do in the senate; but at last, urged by Décimus Brútus not to disappoint the full meeting which had for some time been waiting for him, he went forth almost at the end of the fifth hour; and when a note revealing the plot was handed him by someone on the way, he put it with others which he held in his left hand, intending to read them presently. Then, after several victims had been slain, and he could not get favorable omens, he entered the House in defiance of portents, laughing at Spurínna and calling him a false prophet, because the Ides of March were come without bringing him harm; though Spurínna replied that they had of a truth come, but they had not gone.

82 As he took his seat, the conspirators gathered about him as if to pay their respects, and straightway Tíllius Címber, who had assumed the lead, came nearer as though to ask something; and when Cæsar with a gesture put him off to another time, Címber caught his tóga by both shoulders; then as Cæsar cried, "Why, this is violence!" one of the Cáscas stabbed him from one side just below the throat. Cæsar caught Cásca's arm and ran it through with his stylus, but as he tried to leap to his feet, he was stopped by another wound. When he saw that he was beset on every side by drawn daggers, he muffled his head in his robe, and at the same time drew down its lap to his feet with his left hand, in order to fall more decently, with the lower part of his body also covered. And in this wise he was stabbed with three and twenty wounds, uttering not a word, but merely a groan at the first stroke, though some have written that when Márcus Brútus rushed at him, he said in Greek, "You too, my child?" All the conspirators made off, and he lay there lifeless for some time, and finally three common slaves put him on a litter and carried him home, with one arm hanging down. And of so many wounds none was mortal, in the opinion of the physician Antístius, except the second one in the breast. The conspirators had intended after slaying him to drag his body to the Tíber, confiscate his property, and revoke his decrees; but they forbore through fear of Márcus Antónius the cónsul, and Lépidus, the master of horse.

Suetónius, *Lives of the Twelve Cæsars*, Július Cæsar 76-82 (translated by J. C. Rolfe)

The Character and Reputation of Márcus Brútus

Márcus Brútus was descended from that Június Brútus to whom the ancient Rómans erected a statue of brass in the Cápitol among the images of their kings with a drawn sword in his hand, in remembrance of his courage and resolution in expelling the Tárquins and destroying the monarchy. But that ancient Brútus was of a severe and inflexible nature, like steel of too hard a temper, and having never had his character softened by study and thought, he let himself be so far transported with his rage and hatred against tyrants, that, for conspiring with them, he proceeded to the execution even of his own sons. But this Brútus, whose life we now write, having to the goodness of his disposition added the improvements of learning and the study of philosophy, and having stirred up his natural parts, of themselves grave and gentle, by applying himself to business and public affairs, seems to have been of a temper exactly framed for virtue; insomuch that they who were most his enemies upon account of his conspiracy against Cæsar, if in that whole affair there was any honorable or generous part, referred it wholly to Brútus, and laid whatever was barbarous and cruel to the charge of Cássius, Brútus's connection and familiar friend, but not his equal in honesty and pureness of purpose. His mother, Servília, was of the family of Servílius Ahála, who, when Spúrius Mælius worked the people into a rebellion and designed to make himself king, taking a dagger under his arm, went forth into the market-place, and, upon pretense of having some private business with him, came up close to him, and, as he bent his head to hear what he had to say, struck him with his dagger and slew him. And thus much, as concerns his descent by the mother's side, is confessed by all; but as for his father's family, they who for Cæsar's murder bore any hatred or ill-will to Brútus say that he came not from that Brútus who expelled the Tárquins, there being none of his race left after the execution of his two sons; but that his ancestor was a plebéian, son of one Brútus, a steward, and only rose in the latest times to office or dignity in the commonwealth. But Posidónius the philosopher writes that it is true indeed what the history relates, that two of the sons of Brútus who were of men's estate were put to death, but that a third, yet an infant, was left alive, from whom the family was propagated down to Márcus Brútus; and further, that there were several famous persons of this house in his time whose looks very much resembled the statue of Június Brútus.

Cáto the philosopher was brother to Servília, the mother of Brútus, and he it was whom of all the Rómans his nephew most admired and studied to imitate, and he afterwards married his daughter Pórcia. Of all the sects of the Greek philosophers, though there was none of which he had not been a hearer and in which he had not made some proficiency, yet he chiefly esteemed the Plátonists; and, not much approving of the modern and middle Acádemy, as it is called, he applied himself to the study of the ancient. He was all his lifetime a great admirer of Antíochus of the city of Áscalon, and took his brother Arístus into his own house for his friend and companion, a man for his learning inferior indeed to many of the philosophers, but for the evenness of his temper and steadiness of his conduct equal to the best. As for Émpylus, of whom he himself and his friends often make mention in their epistles, as one that lived with Brútus, he was a rhetorician, and has left behind him a short but well-written history of the death of Cæsar, entitled Brútus.

In Látin, he had by exercise attained a sufficient skill to be able to make public addresses and to plead a cause; but in Greek, he must be noted for affecting the sententious and short Lacónic way of speaking in sundry passages of his epistles; as when, in the beginning of the war, he wrote thus to the Pergaménians: "I hear you have given Dolabélla money; if willingly, you must own you have injured me; if unwillingly, show it by giving willingly to me." And another time to the Sámians: "Your counsels are remiss and your performances slow: what think ye will be the end?" And of the Patáreans thus: "The Xánthians, suspecting my kindness, have made their country the grave of their despair; the Patáreans, trusting themselves to me, enjoy in all points their former liberty; it is in your power to choose the judgment of the Patáreans or the fortune of the Xánthians." And this is the style for which some of his letters are to be noted.

When he was but a very young man, he accompanied his uncle Cáto, to Cýprus, when he was sent there against Ptólemy. But when Ptólemy killed himself, Cáto, being by some necessary business detained in the isle of Rhodes, had already sent one of his friends, named Canídius, to take into his care and keeping the treasure of the king; but presently, not feeling sure of his honesty, he wrote to Brútus to sail immediately for Cýprus out of Pamphýlia, where he then was staying to refresh himself, being but just recovered of a fit of sickness. He obeyed his orders, but with a great deal of unwillingness, as well out of respect to Canídius, who was thrown out of this employment by Cáto with so much disgrace, as also because he esteemed such a commission mean, and unsuitable to him, who was in the prime of his youth, and given to books and study. Nevertheless, applying himself to the business, he behaved himself so well in it that he was highly commended by Cáto, and, having turned all the goods of Ptólemy into ready money, he sailed with the greatest part of it in his own ship to Rome.

But upon the general separation into two factions, when, Pómpey and Cæsar taking up arms against one another, the whole empire was turned into confusion, it was commonly believed that he would take Cæsar's side; for his father in past time had been put to death by Pómpey. But he, thinking it his duty to prefer the interest of the public to his own private feelings, and judging Pómpey's to be the better cause, took part with him; though formerly he used not so much as to salute or take any notice of Pómpey, if he happened to meet him, esteeming it a pollution to have the least conversation with the murderer of his father. But now, looking upon him as the general of his country, he placed himself under his command, and set sail for Cilícia in quality of lieutenant to Séstius, who had the government of that province. But finding no opportunity there of doing any great service, and hearing that Pómpey and Cæsar were now near one another and preparing for the battle upon which all depended, he came of his own accord to Macedónia to partake in the danger. At his coming it is said that Pómpey was so surprised and so pleased, that, rising from his chair in the sight of all who were about him, he saluted and embraced him, as one of the chiefest of his party. All the time that he was in the camp, excepting that which he spent in Pómpey's company, he employed in reading and in study, which he did not neglect even the day before the great battle. It was the middle of summer, and the heat was very great, the camp having been pitched near some marshy ground, and the people that carried Brútus's tent were a long while before they came. Yet though upon these accounts he was extremely harassed and out of order, having scarcely by the middle of the day anointed himself and eaten a sparing meal, whilst most others were either asleep or taken up with the thoughts and apprehensions of what would be the issue of the fight, he spent his time until evening in writing an epitome of Polýbius.

It is said that Cæsar had so great a regard for him that he ordered his commanders by no means to kill Brútus in the battle, but to spare him, if possible, and bring him safe to him, if he would willingly surrender himself; but if he made any resistance, to suffer him to escape rather than do him any violence. And this he is believed to have done out of a tenderness to Servília, the mother of Brútus; for Cæsar had, it seems, in his youth been very intimate with her, and she passionately in love with him; and, considering that Brútus was born about that time in which their loves were at the highest, Cæsar had a belief that he was his own child. The story is told, that when the great question of the conspiracy of Cátiline, which had like to have been the destruction of the commonwealth, was debated in the senate, Cáto and Cæsar were both standing up, contending together on the decision to be come to; at which time a little note was delivered to Cæsar from without, which he took and read silently to himself. Upon this, Cáto cried out aloud, and accused Cæsar of holding correspondence with and receiving letters from the enemies of the commonwealth; and when many other senators exclaimed against it, Cæsar delivered the note as he had received it to Cáto, who reading it found it to be a love-letter from his own sister Servília, and threw it back again to Cæsar with the words, "Keep it, you drunkard," and returned to the subject of the debate. So public and notorious was Servília's love to Cæsar.

After the great overthrow at Pharsália, Pómpey himself having made his escape to the sea, and Cæsar's army storming the camp, Brútus stole privately out by one of the gates leading to marshy ground full of water and covered with reeds, and, traveling through the night, got safe to Laríssa. From Laríssa he wrote to Cæsar, who expressed a great deal of joy to hear that he was safe, and, bidding him come, not only forgave him freely, but honored and esteemed him among his chiefest friends. Now when nobody could give any certain account which way Pómpey had fled, Cæsar took a little journey alone with Brútus, and tried what was his opinion herein, and after some discussion which passed between them, believing that Brútus's conjecture was the right one, laying aside all other thoughts, he set out directly to pursue him towards Égypt. But Pómpey, having reached Égypt, as Brútus guessed his design was to do, there met his fate.

Plútarch, *Life of Brútus* (translated by John Dryden)

The Conspiracy Against Cæsar

Brútus in the mean time gained Cæsar's forgiveness for his friend Cássius; and pleading also in defense of the king of the Lýbians, though he was overwhelmed with the greatness of the crimes alleged against him, yet by his entreaties and deprecations to Cæsar in his behalf, he preserved to him a great part of his kingdom. It is reported that Cæsar, when he first heard Brútus speak in public, said to his friends, "I know not what this young man intends, but, whatever he intends, he intends vehemently." For his natural firmness of mind, not easily yielding, or complying in favor of every one that entreated his kindness, once set into action upon motives of right reason and deliberate moral choice, whatever direction it thus took, it was pretty sure to take effectively, and to work in such a way as not to fail in its object. No flattery could ever prevail with him to listen to unjust petitions; and he held that to be overcome by the importunities of shameless and fawning entreaties, though some compliment it with the name of modesty and bashfulness, was the worst disgrace a great man could suffer. And he used to say, that he always felt as if they who could deny nothing could not have behaved well in the flower of their youth.

Cæsar, being about to make his expedition into África against Cáto and Scípio, committed to Brútus the government of Cisálpine Gaul, to the great happiness and advantage of that province. For while people in other provinces were in distress with the violence and avarice of their governors, and suffered as much oppression as if they had been slaves and captives of war, Brútus, by his easy government, actually made them amends for their calamities under former rulers, directing moreover all their gratitude for his good deeds to Cæsar himself; insomuch that it was a most welcome and pleasant spectacle to Cæsar, when in his return he passed through Ítaly, to see the cities that were under Brútus's command and Brútus himself increasing his honor and joining agreeably in his progress.

Now several prætorships being vacant, it was all men's opinion, that that of the chiefest dignity, which is called the prætorship of the city, would be conferred either upon Brútus or Cássius; and some say that, there having been some little difference upon former accounts between them, this competition set them much more at variance, though they were connected in their families, Cássius having married Júnia, the sister of Brútus. Others say that the contention was raised between them by Cæsar's doing, who had privately given each of them such hopes of his favor as led them on, and provoked them at last into this open competition and trial of their interest. Brútus had only the reputation of his honor and virtue to oppose to the many and gallant actions performed by Cássius against the Párthians. But Cæsar, having heard each side, and deliberating about the matter among his friends, said, "Cássius has the stronger plea, but we must let Brútus be first prætor." So another prætorship was given to Cássius; the gaining of which could not so much oblige him, as he was incensed for the loss of the other. And in all other things Brútus was partaker of Cæsar's power as much as he desired; for he might, if he had pleased, have been the chief of all his friends, and had authority and command beyond them all, but Cássius and the company he met with him drew him off from Cæsar. Indeed, he was not yet wholly reconciled to Cássius, since that competition which was between them; but yet he gave ear to Cássius's friends, who were perpetually advising him not to be so blind as to suffer himself to be softened and won upon by Cæsar, but to shun the kindness and favors of a tyrant, which they intimated that Cæsar showed him, not to express any honor to his merit or virtue, but to unbend his strength, and undermine his vigor of purpose.

Neither was Cæsar wholly without suspicion of him, nor wanted informers that accused Brútus to him; but he feared, indeed, the high spirit and the great character and the friends that he had, but thought himself secure in his moral disposition. When it was told him that Ántony and Dolabélla designed some disturbance, "It is not," said he, "the fat and the long-haired men that I fear, but the pale and the lean," meaning Brútus and Cássius. And when some maligned Brútus to him, and advised him to beware of him, taking hold of his flesh with his hand, "What," he said, "do you think that Brútus will not wait out the time of this little body?" as if he thought none so fit to succeed him in his power as Brútus. And indeed it seems to be without doubt that Brútus might have been the first man in the commonwealth, if he had had patience but a little time to be second to Cæsar, and would have suffered his power to decline after it was come to its highest pitch, and the fame of his great actions to die away by degrees. But Cássius, a man of a fierce disposition, and one that out of private malice, rather than love of the public, hated Cæsar, not the tyrant, continually fired and stirred him up. Brútus felt the rule an oppression, but Cássius hated the ruler; and, among other reasons on which he grounded his quarrel against Cæsar, the loss of his lions which he had procured when he was ædile elect was one: for Cæsar, finding these in Mégara, when that city was taken by Calénus, seized them to himself. These beasts, they say, were a great calamity to the Megárians; for, when their city was just taken, they broke open the lions' dens, and pulled off their chains and let them loose, that they might run upon the enemy that was entering the city; but the lions turned upon them themselves, and tore to pieces a great many unarmed persons running about, so that it was a miserable spectacle even to their enemies to behold.

And this, some say, was the chief provocation that stirred up Cássius to conspire against Cǽsar; but they are much in the wrong. For Cássius had from his youth a natural hatred and rancor against the whole race of tyrants, which he showed when he was but a boy, and went to the same school with Fáustus, the son of Súlla; for, on his boasting himself amongst the boys, and extolling the sovereign power of his father, Cássius rose up and struck him two or three boxes on the ear; which when the guardians and relations of Fáustus designed to inquire into and to prosecute, Pómpey forbade them, and, sending for both the boys together, examined the matter himself. And Cássius then is reported to have said thus, "Come, then, Fáustus, dare to speak here those words that provoked me, that I may strike you again as I did before." Such was the disposition of Cássius.

But Brútus was roused up and pushed on to the undertaking by many persuasions of his familiar friends, and letters and invitations from unknown citizens. For under the statue of his ancestor Brútus, that overthrew the kingly government, they wrote the words, "O that we had a Brútus now!" and, "O that Brútus were alive!" And Brútus's own tribunal, on which he sate as prætor, was filled each morning with writings such as these: "You are asleep, Brútus," and, "You are not a true Brútus." Now the flatterers of Cǽsar were the occasion of all this, who, among other invidious honors which they strove to fasten upon Cǽsar, crowned his statues by night with diadems, wishing to incite the people to salute him king instead of dictator. But quite the contrary came to pass, as I have more particularly related in the life of Cǽsar.

When Cássius went about soliciting friends to engage in this design against Cǽsar, all whom he tried readily consented, if Brútus would be head of it; for their opinion was that the enterprise wanted not hands or resolution, but the reputation and authority of a man such as he was, to give as it were the first religious sanction, and by his presence, if by nothing else, to justify the undertaking; that without him they should go about this action with less heart, and should lie under greater suspicions when they had done it, for, if their cause had been just and honorable, people would be sure that Brútus would not have refused it. Cássius, having considered these things with himself, went to Brútus, and made him the first visit after their falling out; and after the compliments of reconciliation had passed, and former kindnesses were renewed between them, he asked him if he designed to be present in the senate on the Kálends of March, for it was discoursed, he said, that Cǽsar's friends intended then to move that he might be made king.

When Brútus answered, that he would not be there, "But what," says Cássius, "if they should send for us?" "It will be my business then," replied Brútus, "not to hold my peace, but to stand up boldly, and die for the liberty of my country." To which Cássius with some emotion answered, "But what Róman will suffer you to die? What, do you not know yourself, Brútus? Or do you think that those writings that you find upon your prætor's seat were put there by weavers and shopkeepers, and not by the first and most powerful men of Rome? From other prætors, indeed, they expect largesses and shows and gladiators, but from you they claim, as an hereditary debt, the extirpation of tyranny; they are all ready to suffer any thing on your account, if you will but show yourself such as they think you are and expect you should be." Which said, he fell upon Brútus, and embraced him; and after this, they parted each to try their several friends.

Among the friends of Pómpey there was one Gáius Ligárius, whom Cǽsar had pardoned, though accused for having been in arms against him. This man, not feeling so thankful for having been forgiven as he felt oppressed by that power which made him need a pardon, hated Cǽsar, and was one of Brútus's most intimate friends. Him Brútus visited, and, finding him sick, "O Ligárius," says he, "what a time have you found out to be sick in!" At which words Ligárius, raising himself and leaning on his elbow, took Brútus by the hand, and said, "But, O Brútus, if you are on any design worthy of yourself, I am well."

From this time, they tried the inclinations of all their acquaintance that they durst trust, and communicated the secret to them, and took into the design not only their familiar friends, but as many as they believed bold and brave and despisers of death. For which reason they concealed the plot from Cícero, though he was very much trusted and as well beloved by them all, lest, to his own disposition, which was naturally timorous, adding now the wariness and caution of old age, by his weighing, as he would do, every particular, that he might not make one step without the greatest security, he should blunt the edge of their forwardness and resolution in a business which required all the dispatch imaginable. As indeed there were also two others that were companions of Brútus, Statílius the Epicuréan, and Favónius the admirer of Cáto, whom he left out for this reason: as he was conversing one day with them, trying them at a distance, and proposing some such question to be disputed of as among philosophers, to see what opinion they were of, Favónius declared his judgment to be that a civil war was worse than the most illegal monarchy; and Statílius held, that, to bring himself into troubles and danger upon the account of evil or foolish men, did not become a man that had any wisdom or discretion. But Lábeo, who was present, contradicted them both; and Brútus, as if it had been an intricate dispute, and difficult to be decided, held his peace for that time, but afterwards discovered the whole design to Lábeo, who readily undertook it.

The next thing that was thought convenient, was to gain the other Brútus, surnamed Albínus, a man of himself of no great bravery or courage, but considerable for the number of gladiators that he was maintaining for a public show, and the great confidence that Cæsar put in him. When Cássius and Lábeo spoke with him concerning the matter, he gave them no answer; but, seeking an interview with Brútus himself alone, and finding that he was their captain, he readily consented to partake in the action. And among the others, also, the most and best were gained by the name of Brútus. And, though they neither gave nor took any oath of secrecy, nor used any other sacred rite to assure their fidelity to each other, yet all kept their design so close, were so wary, and held it so silently among themselves, that, though by prophecies and apparitions and signs in the sacrifices the gods gave warning of it, yet could it not be believed.

Plútarch, *Life of Brútus* (translated by John Dryden)

Brútus and Pórcia

Now Brútus, feeling that the noblest spirits of Rome for virtue, birth, or courage were depending upon him, and surveying with himself all the circumstances of the dangers they were to encounter, strove indeed as much as possible, when abroad, to keep his uneasiness of mind to himself, and to compose his thoughts; but at home, and especially at night, he was not the same man, but sometimes against his will his working care would make him start out of his sleep, and other times he was taken up with further reflection and consideration of his difficulties, so that his wife that lay with him could not choose but take notice that he was full of unusual trouble, and had in agitation some dangerous and perplexing question. Pórcia, as was said before, was the daughter of Cáto, and Brútus, her cousin-german, had married her very young, though not a maid, but after the death of her former husband, by whom she had one son, that was named Bíbulus; and there is a little book, called Memoirs of Brútus, written by him, yet extant. This Pórcia, being addicted to philosophy, a great lover of her husband, and full of an understanding courage, resolved not to inquire into Brútus's secrets before she had made this trial of herself. She turned all her attendants out of her chamber, and, taking a little knife, such as they use to cut nails with, she gave herself a deep gash in the thigh; upon which followed a great flow of blood, and, soon after, violent pains and a shivering fever, occasioned by the wound. Now when Brútus was extremely anxious and afflicted for her, she, in the height of all her pain, spoke thus to him: "I, Brútus, being the daughter of Cáto, was given to you in marriage, not like a concubine, to partake only in the common intercourse of bed and board, but to bear a part in all your good and all your evil fortunes; and for your part, as regards your care for me, I find no reason to complain; but from me, what evidence of my love, what satisfaction can you receive, if I may not share with you in bearing your hidden griefs, nor be admitted to any of your counsels that require secrecy and trust? I know very well that women seem to be of too weak a nature to be trusted with secrets; but certainly, Brútus, a virtuous birth and education, and the company of the good and honorable, are of some force to the forming our manners; and I can boast that I am the daughter of Cáto and the wife of Brútus, in which two titles though before I put less confidence, yet now I have tried myself, and find that I can bid defiance to pain." Which words having spoken, she showed him her wound, and related to him the trial that she had made of her constancy; at which he being astonished, lifted up his hands to heaven, and begged the assistance of the gods in his enterprise, that he might show himself a husband worthy of such a wife as Pórcia. So then he comforted his wife.

Plútarch, Life of Brútus (translated by John Dryden)

The Ides of March

But a meeting of the senate being appointed, at which it was believed that Cæsar would be present, they agreed to make use of that opportunity: for then they might appear all together without suspicion; and, besides, they hoped that all the noblest and leading men of the commonwealth, being then assembled, as soon as the great deed was done, would immediately stand forward, and assert the common liberty. The very place, too, where the senate was to meet, seemed to be by divine appointment favorable to their purpose. It was a portico, one of those joining the theatre, with a large recess, in which there stood a statue of Pómpey, erected to him by the commonwealth, when he adorned that part of the city with the porticos and the theatre. To this place it was that the senate was summoned for the middle of March (the Ides of March is the Róman name for the day); as if some more than human power were leading the man thither, there to meet his punishment for the death of Pómpey.

As soon as it was day, Brútus, taking with him a dagger, which none but his wife knew of, went out. The rest met together at Cássius's house, and brought forth his son, that was that day to put on the manly gown, as it is called, into the fórum; and from thence, going all to Pómpey's porch, stayed there, expecting Cæsar to come without delay to the senate. Here it was chiefly that any one who had known what they had purposed, would have admired the unconcerned temper and the steady resolution of these men in their most dangerous undertaking; for many of them, being prætors, and called upon by their office to judge and determine causes, did not only hear calmly all that made application to them and pleaded against each other before them, as if they were free from all other thoughts, but decided causes with as much accuracy and judgment as they had heard them with attention and patience. And when one person refused to stand to the award of Brútus, and with great clamor and many attestations appealed to Cæsar, Brútus, looking round about him upon those that were present, said, "Cæsar does not hinder me, nor will he hinder me, from doing according to the laws."

Yet there were many unusual accidents that disturbed them and by mere chance were thrown in their way. The first and chiefest was the long stay of Cæsar, though the day was far spent, and his being detained at home by his wife, and forbidden by the soothsayers to go forth, upon some defect that appeared in his sacrifice. Another was this: There came a man up to Cásca, one of the company, and, taking him by the hand, "You concealed," said he, "the secret from us, but Brútus has told me all." At which words when Cásca was surprised, the other said laughing, "How come you to be so rich of a sudden, that you should stand to be chosen ædile?" So near was Cásca to let out the secret, upon the mere ambiguity of the other's expression. Then Popílius Lænas, a senator, having saluted Brútus and Cássius more earnestly than usual, whispered them softly in the ear and said, "My wishes are with you, that you may accomplish what you design, and I advise you to make no delay, for the thing is now no secret." This said, he departed, and left them in great suspicion that the design had taken wind.

In the mean while, there came one in all haste from Brútus's house, and brought him news that his wife was dying. For Pórcia, being extremely disturbed with expectation of the event, and not able to bear the greatness of her anxiety, could scarce keep herself within doors; and at every little noise or voice she heard, starting up suddenly, like those possessed with the bácchic frenzy, she asked every one that came in from the fórum what Brútus was doing, and sent one messenger after another to inquire. At last, after long expectation, the strength of her body could hold out no longer; her mind was overcome with her doubts and fears, and she lost the control of herself, and began to faint away. She had not time to betake herself to her chamber, but, sitting as she was amongst her women, a sudden swoon and a great stupor seized her, and her color changed, and her speech was quite lost. At this sight, her women made a loud cry, and many of the neighbors running to Brútus's door to know what was the matter, the report was soon spread abroad that Pórcia was dead; though with her women's help she recovered in a little while, and came to herself again. When Brútus received this news, he was extremely troubled, nor without reason, yet was not so carried away by his private grief as to quit his public purpose.

For now news was brought that Cǽsar was coming, carried in a litter. For, being discouraged by the ill omens that attended his sacrifice, he had determined to undertake no affairs of any great importance that day, but to defer them till another time, excusing himself that he was sick. As soon as he came out of his litter, Popílius Lǽnas, he who but a little before had wished Brútus good success in his undertaking, coming up to him, conversed a great while with him, Cǽsar standing still all the while, and seeming to be very attentive. The conspirators, (to give them this name,) not being able to hear what he said, but guessing by what themselves were conscious of that this conference was the discovery of their treason, were again disheartened, and, looking upon one another, agreed from each other's countenances that they should not stay to be taken, but should all kill themselves. And now when Cássius and some others were laying hands upon their daggers under their robes, and were drawing them out, Brútus, viewing narrowly the looks and gesture of Lǽnas, and finding that he was earnestly petitioning and not accusing, said nothing, because there were many strangers to the conspiracy mingled amongst them, but by a cheerful countenance encouraged Cássius. And after a little while, Lǽnas, having kissed Cǽsar's hand, went away, showing plainly that all his discourse was about some particular business relating to himself.

Now when the senate was gone in before to the chamber where they were to sit, the rest of the company placed themselves close about Cǽsar's chair, as if they had some suit to make to him, and Cássius, turning his face to Pómpey's statue, is said to have invoked it, as if it had been sensible of his prayers. Trebónius, in the meanwhile, engaged Ántony's attention at the door, and kept him in talk outside. When Cǽsar entered, the whole senate rose up to him. As soon as he was set down, the men all crowded round about him, and set Tíllius Címber, one of their own number, to intercede in behalf of his brother, that was banished; they all joined their prayers with his, and took Cǽsar by the hand, and kissed his head and his breast. But he putting aside at first their supplications, and afterwards, when he saw they would not desist, violently rising up, Tíllius with both hands caught hold of his robe and pulled it off from his shoulders, and Cásca, that stood behind him, drawing his dagger, gave him the first, but a slight wound, about the shoulder. Cǽsar snatching hold of the handle of the dagger, and crying out aloud in Látin, "Villain Cásca, what do you?" he, calling in Greek to his brother, bade him come and help. And by this time, finding himself struck by a great many hands, and looking round about him to see if he could force his way out, when he saw Brútus with his dagger drawn against him, he let go Cásca's hand, that he had hold of, and, covering his head with his robe, gave up his body to their blows. And they so eagerly pressed towards the body, and so many daggers were hacking together, that they cut one another; Brútus, particularly, received a wound in his hand, and all of them were besmeared with the blood.

Cæsar being thus slain, Brútus, stepping forth into the midst, intended to have made a speech, and called back and encouraged the senators to stay; but they all affrighted ran away in great disorder, and there was a great confusion and press at the door, though none pursued or followed. For they had come to an express resolution to kill nobody besides Cæsar, but to call and invite all the rest to liberty. It was indeed the opinion of all the others, when they consulted about the execution of their design, that it was necessary to cut off Ántony with Cæsar, looking upon him as an insolent man, an affecter of monarchy, and one that, by his familiar intercourse, had gained a powerful interest with the soldiers. And this they urged the rather, because at that time to the natural loftiness and ambition of his temper there was added the dignity of being cónsul and colleague to Cæsar. But Brútus opposed this counsel, insisting first upon the injustice of it, and afterwards giving them hopes that a change might be worked in Ántony. For he did not despair but that so highly gifted and honorable a man, and such a lover of glory as Ántony, stirred up with emulation of their great attempt, might, if Cæsar were once removed, lay hold of the occasion to be joint restorer with them of the liberty of his country.

Thus did Brútus save Ántony's life. But he, in the general consternation, put himself into a plebéian habit, and fled. But Brútus and his party marched up to the Cápitol, in their way showing their hands all bloody, and their naked swords, and proclaiming liberty to the people. At first all places were filled with cries and shouts; and the wild running to and fro, occasioned by the sudden surprise and passion that every one was in, increased the tumult in the city. But no other bloodshed following, and no plundering of the goods in the streets, the senators and many of the people took courage and went up to the men in the Cápitol; and, a multitude being gathered together, Brútus made an oration to them, very popular, and proper for the state that affairs were then in. Therefore, when they applauded his speech, and cried out to him to come down, they all took confidence and descended into the fórum; the rest promiscuously mingled with one another, but many of the most eminent persons, attending Brútus, conducted him in the midst of them with great honor from the Cápitol, and placed him in the róstra. At the sight of Brútus, the crowd, though consisting of a confused mixture and all disposed to make a tumult, were struck with reverence, and expected what he would say with order and with silence, and, when he began to speak, heard him with quiet and attention. But that all were not pleased with this action they plainly showed when, Cínna beginning to speak and accuse Cæsar, they broke out into a sudden rage, and railed at him in such language, that the whole party thought fit again to withdraw to the Cápitol. And there Brútus, expecting to be besieged, dismissed the most eminent of those that had accompanied them thither, not thinking it just that they who were not partakers of the fact should share in the danger.

Plútarch, Life of Brútus (translated by John Dryden)

Cæsar's Funeral

But the next day, the senate being assembled in the temple of the Earth, and Ántony and Pláncus and Cícero having made orations recommending concord in general and an act of oblivion, it was decreed, that the men should not only be put out of all fear or danger, but that the cónsuls should see what honors and dignities were proper to be conferred upon them. After which done, the senate broke up; and, Ántony having sent his son as an hostage to the Cápitol, Brútus and his company came down, and mutual salutes and invitations passed amongst them, the whole of them being gathered together. Ántony invited and entertained Cássius, Lépidus did the same to Brútus, and the rest were invited and entertained by others, as each of them had acquaintance or friends. And as soon as it was day, the senate met again and voted thanks to Ántony for having stifled the beginning of a civil war; afterwards Brútus and his associates that were present received encomiums, and had provinces assigned and distributed among them. Crete was allotted to Brútus, África to Cássius, Ásia to Trebónius, Bithýnia to Címber, and to the other Brútus Gaul about the Po.

After these things, they began to consider of Cæsar's will, and the ordering of his funeral. Ántony desired that the will might be read, and that the body should not have a private or dishonorable interment, lest that should further exasperate the people. This Cássius violently opposed, but Brútus yielded to it, and gave leave; in which he seems to have a second time committed a fault. For as before in sparing the life of Ántony he could not be without some blame from his party, as thereby setting up against the conspiracy a dangerous and difficult enemy, so now, in suffering him to have the ordering of the funeral, he fell into a total and irrecoverable error. For first, it appearing by the will that Cæsar had bequeathed to the Róman people seventy-five dráchmas a man, and given to the public his gardens beyond Tíber (where now the temple of Fortune stands), the whole city was fired with a wonderful affection for him, and a passionate sense of the loss of him.

And when the body was brought forth into the fórum, Ántony, as the custom was, making a funeral oration in the praise of Cæsar, and finding the multitude moved with his speech, passing into the pathetic tone, unfolded the bloody garment of Cæsar, showed them in how many places it was pierced, and the number of his wounds. Now there was nothing to be seen but confusion; some cried out to kill the murderers, others (as was formerly done when Clódius led the people) tore away the benches and tables out of the shops round about, and, heaping them all together, built a great funeral pile, and, having put the body of Cæsar upon it, set it on fire, the spot where this was done being moreover surrounded with a great many temples and other consecrated places, so that they seemed to burn the body in a kind of sacred solemnity. As soon as the fire flamed out, the multitude, flocking in some from one part and some from another, snatched the brands that were half burnt out of the pile, and ran about the city to fire the houses of the murderers of Cæsar. But they, having beforehand well fortified themselves, repelled this danger.

Plútarch, *Life of Brútus* (translated by John Dryden)

The Deification of Július Cæsar

88 He died in the fifty-sixth year of his age, and was numbered among the gods, not only by a formal decree, but also in the conviction of the common people. For at the first of the games which his heir Augústus gave in honor of his apotheósis, a comet shone for seven successive days, rising about the eleventh hour, and was believed to be the soul of Cæsar, who had been taken to heaven; and this is why a star is set upon the crown of his head in his statue. It was voted that the hall in which he was slain be walled up, that the Ides of March be called the Day of Párricide, and that a meeting of the senate should never be called on that day.

Suetónius, *Lives of the Twelve Cæsars*, Július Cæsar 88 (translated by J.C. Rolfe)

The Battle of Philíppi

128 The day was consumed in preparations till the ninth hour, when two eagles fell upon each other and fought in the space between the armies, amid the profoundest silence. When the one on the side of Brútus took flight his enemies raised a great shout and battle was joined. The onset was superb and terrible. They had little need of arrows, stones, or javelins, which are customary in war, for they did not resort to the usual maneuvers and tactics of battles, but, coming to close combat with naked swords, they slew and were slain, seeking to break each other's ranks. On the one side it was a fight for self-preservation rather than victory: on the other for victory and for the satisfaction of the general who had been forced to fight against his will. The slaughter and the groans were terrible. The bodies of the fallen were carried back and others stepped into their places from the reserves. The generals flew hither and thither overlooking everything, exciting the men by their ardor, exhorting the toilers to toil on, and relieving those who were exhausted so that there was always fresh courage at the front.

Finally, the soldiers of Octávian, either from fear of famine, or by the good fortune of Octávian himself (for certainly the soldiers of Brútus were not blameworthy), pushed back the enemy's line as though they were turning round a very heavy machine. The latter were driven back step by step, slowly at first and without loss of courage. Presently their ranks broke and they retreated more rapidly, and then the second and third ranks in the rear retreated with them, all mingled together in disorder, crowded by each other and by the enemy, who pressed upon them without ceasing until it became plainly a flight. The soldiers of Octávian, then especially mindful of the order they had received, seized the gates of the enemy's fortification at great risk to themselves because they were exposed to missiles from above and in front, but they prevented a great many of the enemy from gaining entrance. These fled, some to the sea, and some through the river Zygáctes to the mountains.

129 The enemy having been routed, the generals divided the remainder of the work between themselves, Octávian to capture those who should break out of the camp and to watch the main camp, while Ántony was everything, and attacked everywhere, falling upon the fugitives and those who still held together, and upon their other camping-places, crushing all alike with vehement impetuosity. Fearing lest the leaders should escape him and collect another army, he dispatched cavalry upon the roads and outlets of the field of battle to capture those who were trying to escape. These divided their work; some of them hurried up the mountain with Rháscus, the Thrácian, who was sent with them on account of his knowledge of the roads. They surrounded the fortified positions and escarpments, hunted down the fugitives, and kept watch upon those inside. Others pursued Brútus himself. Lucílius seeing them rushing on furiously surrendered himself, pretending to be Brútus, and asked them to take him to Ántony instead of Octávian; for which reason chiefly he was believed to be Brútus trying to avoid his implacable enemy.

When Ántony heard that they were bringing him, he went to meet him, with a pause to reflect on the fortune, the dignity, and the virtue of the man, and thinking how he should receive Brútus. As he was approaching, Lucílius presented himself, and said with perfect boldness, "You have not captured Brútus, nor will virtue ever be taken prisoner by baseness. I deceived these men and so here I am." Ántony, observing that the horsemen were ashamed of their mistake, consoled them, saying, "The game you have caught for me is not worse, but better than you think, as much better as a friend is than an enemy." Then he committed Lucílius to the care of one of his friends, and later took him into his own service and employed him in a confidential capacity.

130 Brútus fled to the mountains with a considerable force, intending to return to his camp by night, or to move down to the sea. But since all the roads were encompassed by guards he passed the night under arms with all his party, and it is said that, looking up to the stars, he exclaimed, "Forget not, Zeus, the author of these ills," referring to Ántony. It is said that Ántony himself repeated this saying at a later period in the midst of his own dangers, regretting that when he might have associated himself with Cássius and Brútus, he had become the tool of Octávian. At the present time, however, Ántony passed the night under arms with his outposts over against Brútus, fortifying himself with a breastwork of dead bodies and spoils collected together. Octávius toiled until midnight and then retired on account of his illness, leaving Norbánus to watch the enemy's camp.

131 On the following day Brútus, seeing the enemy still lying in wait for him, and having fewer than four full légions, which had ascended the mountain with him, thought it best not to address himself to his troops, but to their officers, who were ashamed and repentant of their fault. To them he sent to put them to the test and to learn whether they were willing to break through the enemy's lines and regain their own camp, which was still held by their troops who had been left there. These officers, though they had rushed to battle unadvisedly, had been of good courage for the most part, but now, for some divine infatuation was already upon them, gave to their general the undeserved answer that he should look out for himself, that they had tempted fortune many times, and that

103

they would not throw away the last remaining hope of accommodation. Then Brútus said to his friends, "I am no longer useful to my country if such is the temper of these men," and calling Stráto, the Épirote, who was one of his friends, gave him the order to stab him. While Stráto still urged him to deliberate, Brútus called one of his servants. Then Stráto said, "Your friend shall not come short of your servants in executing your last commands, if the decision is actually reached." With these words he thrust his sword into the side of Brútus, who did not shrink or turn away.

132 So died Cássius and Brútus, two most noble and illustrious Rómans, and of incomparable virtue, but for one crime; for although they belonged to the party of Pómpey the Great, and had been the enemies, in peace and in war, of Gáius Cæsar, he made them his friends, and from being friends he was treating them as sons. The Senate at all times had a peculiar attachment to them, and commiseration for them when they fell into misfortune. On account of those two it granted amnesty to all the assassins, and when they took flight it bestowed governorships on them in order that they should not be exiles; not that it was disregardful of Gáius Cæsar or rejoiced at what had happened to him, for it admired his bravery and good fortune, gave him a public funeral at his death, ratified his acts, and had for a long time awarded the magistracies and governorships to his nominees, considering that nothing better could be devised than what he proposed. But its zeal for these two men and its solicitude for them brought it under suspicion of complicity in the assassination—so much were those two held in honor by all. By the most illustrious of the exiles they were more honored than Séxtus Pompéius, although he was nearer and not irreconcilable to the triúmvirs, while they were farther away and irreconcilable.

Áppian, *Civil Wars*, 4.128-4.132 (translated by Horace White)

CHAPTER XXII

THE TIMES OF ÁNTONY AND OCTÁVIUS

The Rise of Ántony and Octávius, I.—Civil War between Ántony and Octávius, II.
Review of the Period of the Civil Wars, III.

The Political Position of Cícero

He [Cícero] had no concern in the design that was now forming against Cǽsar, although, in general, he was Brútus's most principal confidant, and one who was as aggrieved at the present, and as desirous of the former state of public affairs, as any other whatsoever. But they feared his temper, as wanting courage, and his old age, in which the most daring dispositions are apt to be timorous.

As soon, therefore, as the act was committed by Brútus and Cássius, and the friends of Cǽsar were got together, so that there was fear the city would again be involved in a civil war, Ántony, being cónsul, convened the senate, and made a short address recommending concord. And Cícero, following with various remarks such as the occasion called for, persuaded the senate to imitate the Athénians, and decree an amnesty for what had been done in Cǽsar's case, and to bestow provinces on Brútus and Cássius. But neither of these things took effect. For as soon as the common people, of themselves inclined to pity, saw the dead body of Cǽsar borne through the market-place, and Ántony showing his clothes filled with blood, and pierced through in every part with swords, enraged to a degree of frenzy, they made a search for the murderers, and with firebrands in their hands ran to their houses to burn them. They, however, being forewarned, avoided this danger; and expecting many more and greater to come, they left the city.

Ántony on this was at once in exultation, and every one was in alarm with the prospect that he would make himself sole ruler, and Cícero in more alarm than any one. For Ántony, seeing his influence reviving in the commonwealth, and knowing how closely he was connected with Brútus, was ill-pleased to have him in the city. Besides, there had been some former jealousy between them, occasioned by the difference of their manners. Cícero, fearing the event, was inclined to go as lieutenant with Dolabélla into Sýria. But Hírtius and Pánsa, cónsuls elect as successors of Ántony, good men and lovers of Cícero, entreated him not to leave them, undertaking to put down Ántony if he would stay in Rome. And he, neither distrusting wholly, nor trusting them, let Dolabélla go without him, promising Hírtius that he would go and spend his summer at Áthens, and return again when he entered upon his office. So he set out on his journey; but some delay occurring in his passage, new intelligence, as often happens, came suddenly from Rome, that Ántony had made an astonishing change, and was doing all things and managing all public affairs at the will of the senate, and that there wanted nothing but his presence to bring things to a happy settlement. And therefore, blaming himself for his cowardice, he returned again to Rome, and was not deceived in his hopes at the beginning. For such multitudes flocked out to meet him, that the compliments and civilities which were paid him at the gates, and at his entrance into the city, took up almost one whole day's time.

On the morrow, Ántony convened the senate, and summoned Cícero thither. He came not, but kept his bed, pretending to be ill with his journey; but the true reason seemed the fear of some design against him, upon a suspicion and intimation given him on his way to Rome. Ántony, however, showed great offence at the affront, and sent soldiers, commanding them to bring him or burn his house; but many interceding and supplicating for him, he was contented to accept sureties. Ever after, when they met, they passed one another with silence, and continued on their guard, till Cǽsar, the younger, coming from Apollónia, entered on the first Cǽsar's inheritance, and was engaged in a dispute with Ántony about two thousand five hundred myriads of money, which Ántony detained from the estate.

Upon this, Philíppus, who married the mother, and Marcéllus, who married the sister of young Cǽsar, came with the young man to Cícero, and agreed with him that Cícero should give them the aid of his eloquence and political influence with the senate and people, and Cǽsar give Cícero the defense of his riches and arms. For the young man had already a great party of the soldiers of Cǽsar about him. And Cícero's readiness to join him was founded, it is said, on some yet stronger motives; for it seems, while Pómpey and Cǽsar were yet alive, Cícero, in his sleep, had fancied himself engaged in calling some of the sons of the senators into the Cápitol, Júpiter being about, according to the dream, to declare one of them the chief ruler of Rome. The citizens, running up with curiosity, stood about the temple, and the youths, sitting in their purple-bordered robes, kept silence.

On a sudden the doors opened, and the youths, arising one by one in order, passed round the god, who reviewed them all, and, to their sorrow, dismissed them; but when this one was passing by, the god stretched forth his right hand and said, "O ye Rómans, this young man, when he shall be lord of Rome, shall put an end to all your civil wars." It is said that Cícero formed from his dream a distinct image of the youth, and retained it afterwards perfectly, but did not know who it was. The next day, going down into the Cámpus Mártius, he met the boys returning from their gymnastic exercises, and the first was he, just as he had appeared to him in his dream. Being astonished at it, he asked him who were his parents. And it proved to be this young Cǽsar, whose father was a man of no great eminence, Octávius, and his mother, Áttia, Cǽsar's sister's daughter; for which reason, Cǽsar, who had no children, made him by will the heir of his house and property. From that time, it is said that Cícero studiously noticed the youth whenever he met him, and he as kindly received the civility; and by fortune he happened to be born when Cícero was cónsul.

These were the reasons spoken of; but it was principally Cícero's hatred of Ántony, and a temper unable to resist honor, which fastened him to Cǽsar, with the purpose of getting the support of Cǽsar's power for his own public designs. For the young man went so far in his court to him, that he called him Father; at which Brútus was so highly displeased, that, in his epistles to Átticus he reflected on Cícero saying, it was manifest, by his courting Cǽsar for fear of Ántony, he did not intend liberty to his country, but an indulgent master to himself. Notwithstanding, Brútus took Cícero's son, then studying philosophy at Áthens, gave him a command, and employed him in various ways, with a good result. Cícero's own power at this time was at the greatest height in the city, and he did whatsoever he pleased; he completely overpowered and drove out Ántony, and sent the two cónsuls, Hírtius and Pánsa, with an army, to reduce him; and, on the other hand, persuaded the senate to allow Cǽsar the líctors and ensigns of a prǽtor, as though he were his country's defender. But after Ántony was defeated in battle, and the two cónsuls slain, the armies united, and ranged themselves with Cǽsar. And the senate, fearing the young man, and his extraordinary fortune, endeavored, by honors and gifts, to call off the soldiers from him, and to lessen his power; professing there was no further need of arms, now Ántony was put to flight.

This giving Cǽsar an affright, he privately sends some friends to entreat and persuade Cícero to procure the cónsular dignity for them both together; saying he should manage the affairs as he pleased, should have the supreme power, and govern the young man who was only desirous of name and glory. And Cǽsar himself confessed, that in fear of ruin, and in danger of being deserted, he had seasonably made use of Cícero's ambition, persuading him to stand with him, and to accept the offer of his aid and interest for the cónsulship.

Plútarch, *Life of Cícero* (translated by John Dryden)

The Murder of Cícero

And now, more than at any other time, Cícero let himself be carried away and deceived, though an old man, by the persuasions of a boy. He joined him in soliciting votes, and procured the good-will of the senate, not without blame at the time on the part of his friends; and he, too, soon enough after, saw that he had ruined himself, and betrayed the liberty of his country. For the young man, once established, and possessed of the office of cónsul, bade Cícero farewell; and, reconciling himself to Ántony and Lépidus, joined his power with theirs, and divided the government, like a piece of property, with them.

Thus united, they made a schedule of above two hundred persons who were to be put to death. But the greatest contention in all their debates was on the question of Cícero's case. Ántony would come to no conditions, unless he should be the first man to be killed. Lépidus held with Ántony, and Cǽsar opposed them both. They met secretly and by themselves, for three days together, near the town of Bonónia. The spot was not far from the camp, with a river surrounding it. Cǽsar, it is said, contended earnestly for Cícero the first two days; but on the third day he yielded, and gave him up. The terms of their mutual concessions were these: that Cǽsar should desert Cícero, Lépidus his brother Páullus, and Ántony, Lúcius Cǽsar, his uncle by his mother's side. Thus they let their anger and fury take from them the sense of humanity, and demonstrated that no beast is more savage than man, when possessed with power answerable to his rage.

Whilst these things were contriving, Cícero was with his brother at his country-house near Túsculum; whence, hearing of the proscriptions, they determined to pass to Ástura, a villa of Cícero's near the sea, and to take shipping from thence for Macedónia to Brútus, of whose strength in that province news had already been heard. They traveled together in their separate litters, overwhelmed with sorrow; and often stopping on the way till their litters came together, condoled with one another. But Quíntus was the more disheartened, when he reflected on his want of means for his journey; for, as he said, he had brought nothing with him from home. And even Cícero himself had but a slender provision. It was judged, therefore, most expedient that Cícero should make what haste he could to fly, and Quíntus return home to provide necessaries, and thus resolved, they mutually embraced, and parted with many tears.

Quíntus, within a few days after, betrayed by his servants to those who came to search for him, was slain, together with his young son. But Cícero was carried to Ástura, where, finding a vessel, he immediately went on board her, and sailed as far as Circǽum with a prosperous gale; but when the pilots resolved immediately to set sail from thence, whether fearing the sea, or not wholly distrusting the faith of Cǽsar, he went on shore, and passed by land a hundred furlongs, as if he was going for Rome. But losing resolution and changing his mind, he again returned to the sea, and there spent the night in fearful and perplexed thoughts. Sometimes he resolved to go into Cǽsar's house privately, and there kill himself upon the altar of his household gods, to bring divine vengeance upon him; but the fear of torture put him off this course. And after passing through a variety of confused and uncertain counsels, at last he let his servants carry him by sea to Cápitæ, where he had a house, an agreeable place to retire to in the heat of summer, when the Etésian winds are so pleasant.

There was at that place a chapel of Apóllo, not far from the sea-side, from which a flight of crows rose with a great noise, and made towards Cícero's vessel as it rowed to land, and lighting on both sides of the yard, some croaked, others pecked the ends of the ropes. This was looked upon by all as an ill omen; and, therefore, Cícero went again ashore, and entering his house, lay down upon his bed to compose himself to rest. Many of the crows settled about the window, making a dismal cawing; but one of them alighted upon the bed where Cícero lay covered up, and with its bill by little and little pecked off the clothes from his face. His servants, seeing this, blamed themselves that they should stay to be spectators of their master's murder, and do nothing in his defense, whilst the brute creatures came to assist and take care of him in his undeserved affliction;

and, therefore, partly by entreaty, partly by force, they took him up, and carried him in his litter towards the sea-side.

But in the mean time the assassins were come with a band of soldiers, Herénnius, a centúrion, and Popílius, a tríbune, whom Cícero had formerly defended when prosecuted for the murder of his father. Finding the doors shut, they broke them open, and Cícero not appearing, and those within saying they knew not where he was, it is stated that a youth, who had been educated by Cícero in the liberal arts and sciences, an emancipated slave of his brother Quíntus, Philólogus by name, informed the tríbune that the litter was on its way to the sea through the close and shady walks. The tríbune, taking a few with him, ran to the place where he was to come out. And Cícero, perceiving Herénnius running in the walks, commanded his servants to set down the litter; and stroking his chin, as he used to do, with his left hand, he looked steadfastly upon his murderers, his person covered with dust, his beard and hair untrimmed, and his face worn with his troubles. So that the greatest part of those that stood by covered their faces whilst Herénnius slew him. And thus was he murdered, stretching forth his neck out of the litter, being now in his sixty-fourth year. Herénnius cut off his head, and, by Ántony's command, his hands also, by which his Philíppics were written; for so Cícero styled those orations he wrote against Ántony....

When these members of Cícero were brought to Rome, Ántony was holding an assembly for the choice of public officers; and when he heard it, and saw them, he cried out, "Now let there be an end of our proscriptions." He commanded his head and hands to be fastened up over the Róstra, where the orators spoke; a sight which the Róman people shuddered to behold, and they believed they saw there not the face of Cícero, but the image of Ántony's own soul. And yet amidst these actions he did justice in one thing, by delivering up Philólogus to Pompónia, the wife of Quíntus; who, having got his body into her power, besides other grievous punishments, made him cut off his own flesh by pieces, and roast and eat it; for so some writers have related. But Tíro, Cícero's emancipated slave, has not so much as mentioned the treachery of Philólogus.

Some long time after, Cæsar, I have been told, visiting one of his daughter's sons, found him with a book of Cícero's in his hand. The boy for fear endeavored to hide it under his gown; which Cæsar perceiving, took it from him, and turning over a great part of the book standing, gave it him again, and said, "My child, this was a learned man, and a lover of his country." And immediately after he had vanquished Ántony, being then cónsul, he made Cícero's son his colleague in the office; and under that cónsulship, the senate took down all the statues of Ántony, and abolished all the other honors that had been given him, and decreed that none of that family should thereafter bear the name of Márcus; and thus the final acts of the punishment of Ántony were, by the divine powers, devolved upon the family of Cícero.

Plútarch, Life of Cícero (translated by John Dryden)

Preparations for the Battle of Áctium

When the armaments gathered for the war, Ántony had no less than five hundred ships of war, including numerous galleys of eight and ten banks of oars, as richly ornamented as if they were meant for a triumph. He had a hundred thousand foot and twelve thousand horse. He had vassal kings attending, Bócchus of Líbya, Tarcondémus of the Upper Cilícia, Archeláus of Cappadócia, Philadélphus of Paphlagónia, Mithridátes of Commagéne, and Sadálas of Thrace; all these were with him in person. Out of Póntus Pólemon sent him considerable forces, as did also Málchus from Arábia, Hérod the Jew, and Amýntas, king of Lycaónia and Galátia; also the Médian king sent some troops to join him. Cæsar had two hundred and fifty galleys of war, eighty thousand foot, and horse about equal to the enemy. Ántony's empire extended from Euphrátes and Arménia to the Iónian sea and the Illýrians; Cæsar's, from Illýria to the westward ocean, and from the ocean all along the Túscan and Sicílian sea. Of África, Cæsar had all the coast opposite to Ítaly, Gaul, and Spain, as far as the Pillars of Hércules, and Ántony the provinces from Cyréne to Ethiópia.

But so wholly was he now the mere appendage to the person of Cleopátra, that, although he was much superior to the enemy in land-forces, yet, out of complaisance to his mistress, he wished the victory to be gained by sea, and that, too, when he could not but see how, for want of sailors, his captains, all through unhappy Greece, were pressing every description of men, common travelers and ass-drivers, harvest laborers and boys, and for all this the vessels had not their complements, but remained, most of them, ill-manned and badly rowed. Cæsar, on the other side, had ships that were built not for size or show, but for service, not pompous galleys, but light, swift, and perfectly manned; and from his head-quarters at Taréntum and Brundísium he sent messages to Ántony not to protract the war, but come out with his forces; he would give him secure roadsteads and ports for his fleet, and, for his land army to disembark and pitch their camp, he would leave him as much ground in Ítaly, inland from the sea, as a horse could traverse in a single course. Ántony, on the other side, with the like bold language, challenged him to a single combat, though he were much the older; and, that being refused, proposed to meet him in the Pharsálian fields, where Cæsar and Pómpey had fought before. But whilst Ántony lay with his fleet near Áctium, where now stands Nicópolis, Cæsar seized his opportunity, and crossed the Ionian sea, securing himself at a place in Epírus called the Ladle. And when those about Ántony were much disturbed, their land-forces being a good way off, "Indeed," said Cleopátra, in mockery, "we may well be frightened if Cæsar has got hold of the Ladle!"

On the morrow, Ántony, seeing the enemy sailing up, and fearing lest his ships might be taken for want of the soldiers to go on board of them, armed all the rowers, and made a show upon the decks of being in readiness to fight; the oars were mounted as if waiting to be put in motion, and the vessels themselves drawn up to face the enemy on either side of the channel of Áctium, as though they were properly manned, and ready for an engagement. And Cæsar, deceived by this stratagem, retired. He was also thought to have shown considerable skill in cutting off the water from the enemy by some lines of trenches and forts, water not being plentiful anywhere else, nor very good. And again, his conduct to Domítius was generous, much against the will of Cleopátra. For when he had made his escape in a little boat to Cæsar, having then a fever upon him, although Ántony could not but resent it highly, yet he sent after him his whole equipage, with his friends and servants; and Domítius, as if he would give a testimony to the world how repentant he had become on his desertion and treachery being thus manifest, died soon after.

Among the kings, also, Amýntas and Deiótarus went over to Cæsar. And the fleet was so unfortunate in every thing that was undertaken, and so unready on every occasion, that Ántony was driven again to put his confidence in the land-forces. Canídius, too, who commanded the légions, when he saw how things stood, changed his opinion, and now was of advice that Cleopátra should be sent back, and that, retiring into Thrace or Macedónia, the quarrel should be decided in a land fight. For Dícomes, also, the king of the Gétæ, promised to come and join him with a great army, and it would not be any kind of disparagement to him to yield the sea to Cæsar, who, in the Sicílian wars, had had such long practice in ship-fighting; on the contrary, it would be simply ridiculous for Ántony, who was by land the most experienced commander living, to make no use of his well-disciplined and numerous infantry, scattering and wasting his forces by parceling them out in the ships. But for all this, Cleopátra prevailed that a sea-fight should determine all, having already an eye to flight, and ordering all her affairs, not so as to assist in gaining a victory, but to escape with the greatest safety from the first commencement of a defeat. There were two long walls, extending from the camp to the station of the ships, between which Ántony used to pass to and fro without suspecting any danger. But Cæsar, upon the suggestion of a servant that it would not be difficult to surprise him, laid an ambush, which, rising up somewhat too hastily, seized the man that came just before him, he himself escaping narrowly by flight.

Plútarch, *Life of Ántony* (translated by John Dryden)

The Battle of Áctium

When it was resolved to stand to a fight at sea, they set fire to all the Egýptian ships except sixty; and of these the best and largest, from ten banks down to three, he manned with twenty thousand full-armed men, and two thousand archers. Here it is related that a foot captain, one that had fought often under Ántony, and had his body all mangled with wounds, exclaimed, "O, my general, what have our wounds and swords done to displease you, that you should give your confidence to rotten timbers? Let Egýptians and Phœnícians contend at sea, give us the land, where we know well how to die upon the spot or gain the victory." To which he answered nothing, but, by his look and motion of his hand seeming to bid him be of good courage, passed forwards, having already, it would seem, no very sure hopes, since when the masters proposed leaving the sails behind them, he commanded they should be put aboard, "For we must not," said he, "let one enemy escape."

That day and the three following the sea was so rough they could not engage. But on the fifth there was a calm, and they fought; Ántony commanding with Publícola the right, and Cǽlius the left squadron, Márcus Octávius and Márcus Instéius the center. Cǽsar gave the charge of the left to Agríppa, commanding in person on the right. As for the land-forces, Canídius was general for Ántony, Táurus for Cǽsar; both armies remaining drawn up in order along the shore. Ántony in a small boat went from one ship to another, encouraging his soldiers, and bidding them stand firm, and fight as steadily on their large ships as if they were on land. The masters he ordered that they should receive the enemy lying still as if they were at anchor, and maintain the entrance of the port, which was a narrow and difficult passage.

Of Cǽsar they relate, that, leaving his tent and going round, while it was yet dark, to visit the ships, he met a man driving a donkey, and asked him his name. He answered him that his own name was "Fortunate, and my donkey," says he, "is called Conqueror." And afterwards, when he disposed the beaks of the ships in that place in token of his victory, the statue of this man and his ass in bronze were placed amongst them. After examining the rest of his fleet, he went in a boat to the right wing, and looked with much admiration at the enemy lying perfectly still in the straits, in all appearance as if they had been at anchor. For some considerable length of time he actually thought they were so, and kept his own ships at rest, at a distance of about eight furlongs from them. But about noon a breeze sprang up from the sea, and Ántony's men, weary of expecting the enemy so long, and trusting to their large tall vessels, as if they had been invincible, began to advance the left squadron. Cǽsar was overjoyed to see them move, and ordered his own right squadron to retire, that he might entice them out to sea as far as he could, his design being to sail round and round, and so with his light and well-manned galleys to attack these huge vessels, which their size and their want of men made slow to move and difficult to manage.

When they engaged, there was no charging or striking of one ship by another, because Ántony's, by reason of their great bulk, were incapable of the rapidity required to make the stroke effectual, and, on the other side, Cǽsar's durst not charge head to head on Ántony's, which were all armed with solid masses and spikes of brass; nor did they like even to run in on their sides, which were so strongly built with great squared pieces of timber, fastened together with iron bolts, that their vessels' beaks would easily have been shattered upon them. So that the engagement resembled a land fight, or, to speak yet more properly, the attack and defense of a fortified place; for there were always three or four vessels of Cǽsar's about one of Ántony's, pressing them with spears, javelins, poles, and several inventions of fire, which they flung among them, Ántony's men using catapults also, to pour down missiles from wooden towers. Agríppa drawing out the squadron under his command to outflank the enemy, Publícola was obliged to observe his motions, and gradually to break off from the middle squadron, where some confusion and alarm ensued, while Arrúntius engaged them.

But the fortune of the day was still undecided, and the battle equal, when on a sudden Cleopátra's sixty ships were seen hoisting sail and making out to sea in full flight, right through the ships that were engaged. For they were placed behind the great ships, which, in breaking through, they put into disorder. The enemy was astonished to see them sailing off with a fair wind towards Peloponnésus. Here it was that Ántony showed to all the world that he was no longer actuated by the thoughts and motives of a commander or a man, or indeed by his own judgment at all, and what was once said as a jest, that the soul of a lover lives in some one else's body, he proved to be a serious truth. For, as if he had been born part of her, and must move with her wheresoever she went, as soon as he saw her ship sailing away, he abandoned all that were fighting and spending their lives for him, and put himself aboard a galley of five ranks of oars, taking with him only Alexánder of Sýria and Scéllias, to follow her that had so well begun his ruin and would hereafter accomplish it.

She, perceiving him to follow, gave the signal to come aboard. So, as soon as he came up with them, he was taken into the ship. But without seeing her or letting himself be seen by her, he went forward by himself, and sat alone, without a word, in the ship's prow, covering his face with his two hands. In the meanwhile, some of Cǽsar's light Libúrnian ships, that were in pursuit, came in sight. But on Ántony's commanding to face about, they all gave back except Éurycles the Lacónian, who pressed on, shaking a lance from the deck, as if he meant to hurl it at him. Ántony, standing at the prow, demanded of him, "Who is this that pursues Ántony?" "I am," said he, "Éurycles, the son of Láchares, armed with Cǽsar's fortune to revenge my father's death." Láchares had been condemned for a robbery, and beheaded by Ántony's orders. However, Éurycles did not attack Ántony, but ran with his full force upon the other admiral-galley (for there were two of them), and with the blow turned her round, and took both her and another ship, in which was a quantity of rich plate and furniture.

So soon as Éurycles was gone, Ántony returned to his posture, and sat silent, and thus he remained for three days, either in anger with Cleopátra, or wishing not to upbraid her, at the end of which they touched at Tænárus. Here the women of their company succeeded first in bringing them to speak, and afterwards to eat and sleep together. And, by this time, several of the ships of burden and some of his friends began to come in to him from the rout, bringing news of his fleet's being quite destroyed, but that the land-forces, they thought, still stood firm. So that he sent messengers to Canídius to march the army with all speed through Macedónia into Ásia. And, designing himself to go from Tænarus into África, he gave one of the merchant ships, laden with a large sum of money, and vessels of silver and gold of great value, belonging to the royal collections, to his friends, desiring them to share it amongst them, and provide for their own safety. They refusing his kindness with tears in their eyes, he comforted them with all the goodness and humanity imaginable, entreating them to leave him, and wrote letters in their behalf to Theóphilus, his steward, at Córinth, that he would provide for their security, and keep them concealed till such time as they could make their peace with Cǽsar. This Theóphilus was the father of Hippárchus, who had such interest with Ántony, who was the first of all his freedmen that went over to Cǽsar, and who settled afterwards at Córinth. In this posture were affairs with Ántony.

But at Áctium, his fleet, after a long resistance to Cǽsar, and suffering the most damage from a heavy sea that set in right ahead, scarcely, at four in the afternoon, gave up the contest, with the loss of not more than five thousand men killed, but of three hundred ships taken, as Cǽsar himself has recorded. Only few had known of Ántony's flight; and those who were told of it could not at first give any belief to so incredible a thing, as that a general who had nineteen entire légions and twelve thousand horse upon the sea-shore, could abandon all and fly away; and he, above all, who had so often experienced both good and evil fortune, and had in a thousand wars and battles been inured to changes.

His soldiers, however, would not give up their desires and expectations, still fancying he would appear from some part or other, and showed such a generous fidelity to his service, that, when they were thoroughly assured that he was fled in earnest, they kept themselves in a body seven days, making no account of the messages that Cæsar sent to them. But at last, seeing that Canídius himself, who commanded them, was fled from the camp by night, and that all their officers had quite abandoned them, they gave way, and made their submission to the conqueror. After this, Cæsar set sail for Áthens, where he made a settlement with Greece, and distributed what remained of the provision of corn that Ántony had made for his army among the cities, which were in a miserable condition, despoiled of their money, their slaves, their horses, and beasts of service. My great-grandfather Nicárchus used to relate, that the whole body of the people of our city were put in requisition to carry each one a certain measure of corn upon their shoulders to the sea-side near Antícyra, men standing by to quicken them with the lash. They had made one journey of the kind, but when they had just measured out the corn and were putting it on their backs for a second, news came of Ántony's defeat, and so saved Chæronéa, for all Ántony's purveyors and soldiers fled upon the news, and left them to divide the corn among themselves.

Plútarch, *Life of Ántony* (translated by John Dryden)

The Deaths of Ántony and Cleopátra

As soon as it was light, he marched his infantry out of the city, and posted them upon a rising ground, from whence he saw his fleet make up to the enemy. There he stood in expectation of the event; but, as soon as the fleets came near to one another, his men saluted Cæsar's with their oars; and, on their responding, the whole body of the ships, forming into a single fleet, rowed up direct to the city. Ántony had no sooner seen this, but the horse deserted him, and went over to Cæsar; and his foot being defeated, he retired into the city, crying out that Cleopátra had betrayed him to the enemies he had made for her sake. She, being afraid lest in his fury and despair he might do her a mischief, fled to her monument, and letting down the falling doors, which were strong with bars and bolts, she sent messengers who should tell Ántony she was dead. He, believing it, cried out, "Now, Ántony, why delay longer? Fate has snatched away the only pretext for which you could say you desired yet to live." Going into his chamber, and there loosening and opening his coat of armor, "I am not," said he, "troubled, Cleopátra, to be at present bereaved of you, for I shall soon be with you; but it distresses me that so great a general should be found of a tardier courage than a woman."

He had a faithful servant, whose name was Éros; he had engaged him formerly to kill him when he should think it necessary, and now he put him to his promise. Éros drew his sword, as designing to kill him, but, suddenly turning round, he slew himself. And as he fell dead at his feet, "It is well done, Éros," said Ántony; "you show your master how to do what you had not the heart to do yourself;" and so he ran himself into the belly, and laid himself upon the couch. The wound, however, was not immediately mortal; and the flow of blood ceasing when he lay down, presently he came to himself, and entreated those that were about him to put him out of his pain; but they all fled out of the chamber, and left him crying out and struggling, until Díomede, Cleopátra's secretary, came to him, having orders from her to bring him into the monument.

When he understood she was alive, he eagerly gave order to the servants to take him up, and in their arms was carried to the door of the building. Cleopátra would not open the door, but, looking from a sort of window, she let down ropes and cords, to which Ántony was fastened; and she and her two women, the only persons she had allowed to enter the monument, drew him up. Those that were present say that nothing was ever more sad than this spectacle, to see Ántony, covered all over with blood and just expiring, thus drawn up, still holding up his hands to her, and lifting up his body with the little force he had left. As, indeed, it was no easy task for the women; and Cleopátra, with all her force, clinging to the rope, and straining with her head to the ground, with difficulty pulled him up, while those below encouraged her with their cries, and joined in all her effort and anxiety.

When she had got him up, she laid him on the bed, tearing all her clothes, which she spread upon him; and, beating her breasts with her hands, lacerating herself, and disfiguring her own face with the blood from his wounds, she called him her lord, her husband, her emperor, and seemed to have pretty nearly forgotten all her own evils, she was so intent upon his misfortunes. Ántony, stopping her lamentations as well as he could, called for wine to drink, either that he was thirsty, or that he imagined that it might put him the sooner out of pain. When he had drunk, he advised her to bring her own affairs, so far as might be honorably done, to a safe conclusion, and that, among all the friends of Cæsar, she should rely on Proculéius; that she should not pity him in this last turn of fate, but rather rejoice for him in remembrance of his past happiness, who had been of all men the most illustrious and powerful, and, in the end, had fallen not ignobly, a Róman by a Róman overcome.

Just as he breathed his last, Proculéius arrived from Cæsar; for when Ántony gave himself his wound, and was carried in to Cleopátra, one of his guards, Dercetæus, took up Ántony's sword and hid it; and, when he saw his opportunity, stole away to Cæsar, and brought him the first news of Ántony's death, and withal showed him the bloody sword. Cæsar, upon this, retired into the inner part of his tent, and, giving some tears to the death of one that had been nearly allied to him in marriage, his colleague in empire, and companion in so many wars and dangers, he came out to his friends, and, bringing with him many letters, he read to them with how much reason and moderation he had always addressed himself to Ántony, and in return what overbearing and arrogant answers he received. Then he sent Proculéius to use his utmost endeavors to get Cleopátra alive into his power; for he was afraid of losing a great treasure, and, besides, she would be no small addition to the glory of his triumph. She, however, was careful not to put herself in Proculéius's power; but from within her monument, he standing on the outside of a door, on the level of the ground, which was strongly barred, but so that they might well enough hear one another's voice, she held a conference with him; she demanding that her kingdom might be given to her children, and he bidding her be of good courage, and trust Cæsar for every thing.

Having taken particular notice of the place, he returned to Cæsar, and Gállus was sent to parley with her the second time; who, being come to the door, on purpose prolonged the conference, while Proculéius fixed his scaling-ladders in the window through which the women had pulled up Ántony. And so entering, with two men to follow him, he went straight down to the door where Cleopátra was discoursing with Gállus. One of the two women who were shut up in the monument with her cried out, "Miserable Cleopátra, you are taken prisoner!" Upon which she turned quick, and, looking at Proculeius, drew out her dagger, which she had with her to stab herself. But Proculéius ran up quickly, and, seizing her with both his hands, "For shame," said he, "Cleopátra; you wrong yourself and Cæsar much, who would rob him of so fair an occasion of showing his clemency, and would make the world believe the most gentle of commanders to be a faithless and implacable enemy." And so, taking the dagger out of her hand, he also shook her dress to see if there were any poison hid in it. After this, Cæsar sent Epaphrodítus, one of his freedmen, with orders to treat her with all the gentleness and civility possible, but to take the strictest precautions to keep her alive...

There was a young man of distinction among Cæsar's companions, named Cornélius Dolabélla. He was not without a certain tenderness for Cleopátra, and sent her word privately, as she had besought him to do, that Cæsar was about to return through Sýria, and that she and her children were to be sent on within three days. When she understood this, she made her request to Cæsar that he would be pleased to permit her to make oblations to the departed Ántony; which being granted, she ordered herself to be carried to the place where he was buried, and there, accompanied by her women, she embraced his tomb with tears in her eyes, and spoke in this manner: "O, dearest Ántony," said she, "it is not long since that with these hands I buried you; then they were free, now I am a captive, and pay these last duties to you with a guard upon me, for fear that my just griefs and sorrows should impair my servile body, and make it less fit to appear in their triumph over you. No further offerings or libations expect from me; these are the last honors that Cleopátra can pay your memory, for she is to be hurried away far from you. Nothing could part us whilst we lived, but death seems to threaten to divide us. You, a Róman born, have found a grave in Égypt; I, an Egýptian, am to seek that favor, and none but that, in your country. But if the gods below, with whom you now are, either can or will do any thing (since those above have betrayed us), suffer not your living wife to be abandoned; let me not be led in triumph to your shame, but hide me and bury me here with you, since, amongst all my bitter misfortunes, nothing has afflicted me like this brief time that I have lived away from you."

Having made these lamentations, crowning the tomb with garlands and kissing it, she gave orders to prepare her a bath, and, coming out of the bath, she lay down and made a sumptuous meal. And a country fellow brought her a little basket, which the guards intercepting and asking what it was, the fellow put the leaves which lay uppermost aside, and showed them it was full of figs; and on their admiring the largeness and beauty of the figs, he laughed, and invited them to take some, which they refused, and, suspecting nothing, bade him carry them in. After her repast, Cleopátra sent to Cæsar a letter which she had written and sealed; and, putting everybody out of the monument but her two women, she shut the doors. Cæsar, opening her letter, and finding pathetic prayers and entreaties that she might be buried in the same tomb with Ántony, soon guessed what she was doing. At first he was going himself in all haste, but, changing his mind, he sent others to see. The thing had been quickly done. The messengers came at full speed, and found the guards apprehensive of nothing; but on opening the doors, they saw her stone-dead, lying upon a bed of gold, set out in all her royal ornaments. Íras, one of her women, lay dying at her feet, and Chármion, just ready to fall, scarce able to hold up her head, was adjusting her mistress's diadem. And when one that came in said angrily, "Was this well done of your lady, Chármion?" "Extremely well," she answered, "and as became the descendant of so many kings"; and as she said this, she fell down dead by the bedside.

Some relate that an asp was brought in amongst those figs and covered with the leaves, and that Cleopátra had arranged that it might settle on her before she knew, but, when she took away some of the figs and saw it, she said, "So here it is," and held out her bare arm to be bitten. Others say that it was kept in a vase, and that she vexed and pricked it with a golden spindle till it seized her arm. But what really took place is known to no one. Since it was also said that she carried poison in a hollow bodkin, about which she wound her hair; yet there was not so much as a spot found, or any symptom of poison upon her body, nor was the asp seen within the monument; only something like the trail of it was said to have been noticed on the sand by the sea, on the part towards which the building faced and where the windows were. Some relate that two faint puncture-marks were found on Cleopátra's arm, and to this account Cæsar seems to have given credit; for in his triumph there was carried a figure of Cleopátra, with an asp clinging to her. Such are the various accounts. But Cæsar, though much disappointed by her death, yet could not but admire the greatness of her spirit, and gave order that her body should be buried by Ántony with royal splendor and magnificence.

Plútarch, Life of Ántony (translated by John Dryden)

CHAPTER XXIII

THE REIGN OF AUGÚSTUS (31 B.C. - A.D. 14)

The New Imperial Government, I.—Augústus and the Róman World, II.—The Age of Augústus, III.

The Rule of Emperors

53.17 In this way the power of both people and senate passed entirely into the hands of Augústus, and from his time there was, strictly speaking, a monarch; for monarchy would be the truest name for it, no matter if two or three men did later hold the power at the same time. The name of monarchy, to be sure, the Rómans so detested that they called their emperors neither dictators nor kings nor anything of the sort; yet since the final authority for the government devolves upon them, they must needs be kings. The offices established by the laws, it is true, are maintained even now, except that of cénsor; but the entire direction and administration is absolutely in accordance with the wishes of the one in power at the time. And yet, in order to preserve the appearance of having this power by virtue of the laws and not because of their own domination, the emperors have taken to themselves all the functions, including the titles, of the offices which under the republic and by the free gift of the people were powerful, with the single exception of the dictatorship. Thus, they very often became cónsuls, and they are always styled procónsuls whenever they are outside the pomérium. The name of "imperátor" is held by them all for life, not only by those who have won victories in battle, but also by those who have not, in token of their independent authority, and this has displaced the titles of "king" and "dictator." These last titles they have never assumed since the time they first fell out of use in the conduct of the government, but the functions of these offices are secured to them under the appellation of "imperátor."

By virtue of the titles named they secure the right to make levies, to collect funds, declare war, make peace, rule foreigners and citizens alike everywhere and always—even to the extent of being able to put to death both knights and senators inside the pomérium—and all the other privileges once granted to the cónsuls and other officials possessing independent authority; and by virtue of holding the cénsorship they investigate our lives and morals as well as take the census, enrolling some in the equestrian and senatorial classes and erasing the names of others from these classes, according to their will. By virtue of being consecrated in all the priesthoods and of their right to bestow most of these positions upon others, as well as from the fact that, even if two or three persons hold the imperial office at the same time, one of them is high priest, they hold in their own hands supreme authority over all matters both profane and sacred. The tribunícian power, as it is called, which used to be conferred only upon men of the greatest influence, gives them the right to nullify the effects of measures taken by any other official, in case they do not approve it, and makes them immune from scurrilous abuse; and, if they appear to be wronged in even the slightest degree, not merely by deed, but even by word, they may destroy the guilty party, as one accursed, without a trial. The emperors, it should be explained, do not think it right to be tríbunes, inasmuch as they belong altogether to the patrícian class, but they assume the power of the tríbunes to its full extent, as it was when it was greatest; and in numbering the years they have held the imperial office they use the tribunícian power to mark the stages, the theory being that they receive it year by year along with those who are regularly made tríbunes. These are the institutions which they have taken over from the republic, essentially in the form in which they severally existed then, and also making use of these same names, their purpose being to create the impression that they possess no power that has not been granted them.

53.18 And further, they have acquired also another prerogative which was given to none of the ancient Rómans outright and unreservedly, and the possession of this alone would enable them to exercise the powers above named and the others besides. For they have been released from the laws, as the very words in Látin declare; that is, they are free from all compulsion of the laws and are bound by none of the written ordinances. Thus by virtue of these democratic names they have clothed themselves with all the powers of the government, to such an extent that they actually possess all the prerogatives of kings except their paltry title. For the appellation "Cǽsar" or "Augústus" confers upon them no peculiar power, but merely shows in the one case that they are heirs of the family to which they belong, and in the other the splendor of their official position. The term "Father" perhaps gives them a certain authority over us all—the authority which fathers once had over their children; yet it did not signify this at first, but betokened honor, and served as an admonition both to them, that they should love their subjects as they would their children, and to their subjects, that they should revere them as they would their fathers.

Cássius Dío, Róman History, 53.17-53.18 (translated by Earnest Carey)

Augústus to Restore the Republic?

28 [Augústus] twice thought of restoring the republic; first immediately after the overthrow of Ántony, remembering that his rival had often made the charge that it was his fault that it was not restored; and again in the weariness of a lingering illness, when he went so far as to summon the magistrates and the senate to his house, and submit an account of the general condition of the empire. Reflecting, however, that as he himself would not be free from danger if he should retire, so too it would be hazardous to trust the State to the control of more than one, he continued to keep it in his hands; and it is not easy to say whether his intentions or their results were the better. His good intentions he not only expressed from time to time, but put them on record as well in an edict in the following words: "May it be my privilege to establish the State in a firm and secure position, and reap from that act the fruit that I desire; but only if I may be called the author of the best possible government, and bear with me the hope when I die that the foundations which I have laid for the State will remain unshaken." And he realized his hope by making every effort to prevent any dissatisfaction with the new regime. Since the city was not adorned as the dignity of the empire demanded, and was exposed to flood and fire, he so beautified it that he could justly boast that he had found it built of brick and left it in marble. He made it safe too for the future, so far as human foresight could provide for this.

Suetónius, Lives of the Twelve Cǽsars, Augústus, 28 (translated by J. C. Rolfe)

Res Géstæ Dívi Augústi

1 Below is a copy of the acts of the Deified Augústus by which he placed the whole world under the sovereignty of the Róman people, and of the amounts which he expended upon the state and the Róman people, as engraved upon two bronze columns which have been set up in Rome.

At the age of nineteen, on my own initiative and at my own expense, I raised an army by means of which I restored liberty to the republic, which had been oppressed by the tyranny of a faction. For which service the senate, with complimentary resolutions, enrolled me in its order, in the cónsulship of Gáius Pánsa and Áulus Hírtius, giving me at the same time cónsular precedence in voting; it also gave me the impérium. As proprǽtor it ordered me, along with the cónsuls, "to see that the republic suffered no harm." In the same year, moreover, as both cónsuls had fallen in war, the people elected me cónsul and a triúmvir for settling the constitution.

2 Those who slew my father I drove into exile, punishing their deed by due process of law, and afterwards when they waged war upon the republic I twice defeated them in battle.

3 Wars, both civil and foreign, I undertook throughout the world, and when victorious I spared all citizens who sued for pardon. The foreign nations which could with safety be pardoned I preferred to save rather than to destroy. The number of Róman citizens who bound themselves to me by military oath was about 500,000. Of these I settled in colonies or sent back into their own towns, after their term of service, something more than 300,000, and to all I assigned lands, or gave money as a reward for military service. I captured six hundred ships, over and above those which were smaller than tríremes.

4 Twice I triumphed with an ovation, thrice I celebrated curule triumphs, and was saluted as imperátor twenty-one times. Although the Senate decreed me additional triumphs I set them aside. When I had performed the vows which I had undertaken in each war I deposited upon the Cápitol the laurels which adorned my fasces. For successful operations on land and sea, conducted either by myself or by my lieutenants under my auspices, the senate on fifty-five occasions decreed that thanks should be rendered to the immortal gods. The days on which such thanks were rendered by decree of the senate numbered 890. In my triumphs there were led before my chariot nine kings or children of kings. At the time of writing these words I had been thirteen times cónsul, and was in the thirty-seventh year of my tribunícian power.

5 The dictatorship offered me by the people and the Róman Senate, in my absence and later when present, in the cónsulship of Márcus Marcéllus and Lúcius Arrúntius I did not accept. I did not decline at a time of the greatest scarcity of grain the charge of the grain-supply, which I so administered that, within a few days, I freed the entire people, at my own expense, from the fear and danger in which they were. The cónsulship, either yearly or for life, then offered me I did not accept.

6 In the cónsulship of Márcus Vinúcius and Quíntus Lucrétius, and afterwards in that of Públius and Gnǽus Léntulus, and a third time in that of Páullus Fábius Máximus and Quíntus Túbero, when the Senate and the Róman people unanimously agreed that I should be elected overseer of laws and morals, without a colleague and with the fullest power, I refused to accept any power offered me which was contrary to the traditions of our ancestors. Those things which at that time the senate wished me to administer I carried out by virtue of my tribunícian power. And even in this office I five times received from the senate a colleague at my own request.

7 For ten years in succession I was one of the triúmvirs for the re-establishment of the constitution. To the day of writing this I have been prínceps senátus for forty years. I have been póntifex máximus, áugur, a member of the fifteen commissioners for performing sacred rites, one of the seven for sacred feasts, an árval brother, a sodális Títius, a fétial priest.

8 As cónsul for the fifth time, by order of the people and the senate I increased the number of the patrícians. Three times I revised the roll of the senate. In my sixth cónsulship, with Márcus Agríppa as my colleague, I made a census of the people. I performed the lústrum after an interval of forty-one years. In this lustration 4,063,000 Róman citizens were entered on the census roll. A second time, in the cónsulship of Gáius Censorínus and Gáius Asínius, I again performed the lústrum alone, with the cónsular impérium. In this lústrum 4,233,000 Róman citizens were entered on the census roll. A third time, with the cónsular impérium, and with my son Tibérius Cǽsar as my colleague, I performed the lústrum in the cónsulship of Séxtus Pompéius and Séxtus Apuléius. In this lústrum 4,937,000 Róman citizens were entered on the census roll. By the passage of new laws I restored many traditions of our ancestors which were then falling into disuse, and I myself set precedents in many things for posterity to imitate.

9 The senate decreed that every fifth year vows should be undertaken for my health by the cónsuls and the priests. In fulfillment of these vows games were often held in my lifetime, sometimes by the four chief colleges of priests, sometimes by the cónsuls. In addition the entire body of citizens with one accord, both individually and by municipalities, performed continued sacrifices for my health at all the couches of the gods.

10 By decree of the senate my name was included in the Sálian hymn, and it was enacted by law that my person should be sacred in perpetuity and that so long as I lived I should hold the tribunícian power. I declined to be made Póntifex Máximus in succession to a colleague still living, when the people tendered me that priesthood which my father had held. Several years later I accepted that sacred office when he at last was dead who, taking advantage of a time of civil disturbance, had seized it for himself, such a multitude from all Ítaly assembling for my election, in the cónsulship of Públius Sulpícius and Gáius Válgius, as is never recorded to have been in Rome before.

11 The Senate consecrated in honor of my return an altar to Fortúna Rédux at the Pórta Capéna, near the temple of Honor and Virtue, on which it ordered the pontiffs and the Véstal virgins to perform a yearly sacrifice on the anniversary of the day on which I returned to the city from Sýria, in the cónsulship of Quíntus Lucrétius and Márcus Vinúcius, and named the day, after my cognomen, the Augustália.

12 At the same time, by decree of the senate, part of the prǽtors and of the tríbunes of the people, together with the cónsul Quíntus Lucrétius and the leading men of the state, were sent to Campánia to meet me, an honor which up to the present time has been decreed to no one except myself. When I returned from Spain and Gaul, in the cónsulship of Tibérius Néro and Públius Quintílius, after successful operations in those provinces, the senate voted in honor of my return the consecration of an altar to Pax Augústa in the Cámpus Mártius, and on this altar it ordered the magistrates and priests and virgins to make annual sacrifice.

13 Jánus Quirínus, which our ancestors ordered to be closed whenever there was peace, secured by victory, throughout the whole domain of the Róman people on land and sea, and which, before my birth is recorded to have been closed but twice in all since the foundation of the city, the senate ordered to be closed thrice while I was princeps.

14 My sons Gáius and Lúcius Cǽsar, whom fortune snatched away from me in their youth, the senate and the Róman people to do me honor made cónsuls designate, each in his fifteenth year, providing that each should enter upon that office after a period of five years. The senate decreed that from the day on which they were introduced to the fórum they should take part in the counsels of state. Moreover, the entire body of Róman knights gave each of them the title of prínceps iuventútis and presented them with silver shields and spears.

15 To the Róman plebs I paid out three hundred sésterces per man in accordance with the will of my father, and in my own name in my fifth cónsulship I gave four hundred sésterces apiece from the spoils of war; a second time, moreover, in my tenth cónsulship I paid out of my own patrimony four hundred sésterces per man by way of bounty, and in my eleventh cónsulship I made twelve distributions of food from grain bought at my own expense, and in the twelfth year of my tribunícian power I gave for the third time four hundred sésterces to each man. These largesses of mine reached a number of persons never less than two hundred and fifty thousand. In the eighteenth year of my tribunícian power, as cónsul for the twelfth time, I gave to three hundred and twenty thousand of the city plebs sixty denárii apiece. In the colonies of my soldiers, as cónsul for the fifth time, I gave one thousand sésterces to each man from the spoils of war; about one hundred and twenty thousand men in the colonies received this triumphal largesse. When cónsul for the thirteenth time I gave sixty denárii apiece to the plebs who were then receiving public grain; these were a little more than two hundred thousand persons.

16 To the municipal towns I paid money for the lands which I assigned to soldiers in my own fourth cónsulship and afterwards in the cónsulship of Márcus Crássus and Gnǽus Léntulus the áugur. The sum which I paid for estates in Ítaly was about six hundred million sésterces, and the amount which I paid for lands in the provinces was about two hundred and sixty million. I was the first and only one to do this of all those who up to my time settled colonies of soldiers in Ítaly or in the provinces. And later, in the cónsulship of Tibérius Néro and Gnǽus Píso, likewise in the cónsulship of Gáius Antístius and Décimus Lǽlius, and of Gáius Calvísius and Lúcius Pasiénus, and of Lúcius Léntulus and Márcus Messálla, and of Lúcius Canínius and Quíntus Fabrícius, I paid cash gratuities to the soldiers whom I settled in their own towns at the expiration of their service, and for this purpose I expended four hundred million sésterces as an act of grace.

17 Four times I aided the public treasury with my own money, paying out in this manner to those in charge of the treasury one hundred and fifty million sésterces. And in the cónsulship of Márcus Lépidus and Lúcius Arrúntius I contributed one hundred and seventy million sésterces out of my own patrimony to the military treasury, which was established on my advice that from it gratuities might be paid to soldiers who had seen twenty or more years of service.

18 Beginning with the year in which Gnǽus and Públius Léntulus were cónsuls, whenever taxes were in arrears, I furnished from my own purse and my own patrimony tickets for grain and money, sometimes to a hundred thousand persons, sometimes to many more.

19 I built the cúria and the Chalcídicum adjoining it, the temple of Apóllo on the Pálatine with its porticoes, the temple of the deified Július, the Lúpercal, the pórtico at the Círcus Flamínius which I allowed to be called Octávia after the name of him who had constructed an earlier one on the same site, the state box at the Círcus Máximus, the temples on the Cápitol of Júpiter Ferétrius and Júpiter Tónans, the temple of Quirínus, the temples of Minérva, of Júno the Queen, and of Júpiter Líbertas, on the Áventine, the temple of the Láres at the highest point of the Sácra Vía, the temple of the Di Penátes on the Vélia, the temple of Youth, and the temple of the Great Mother on the Pálatine.

20 The Capitólium and the theatre of Pómpey, both works involving great expense, I rebuilt without any inscription of my own name. I restored the channels of the aqueducts which in several places were falling into disrepair through age, and doubled the capacity of the aqueduct called the Márcia by turning a new spring into its channel. I completed the Júlian Fórum and the basílica which was between the temple of Cástor and the temple of Sáturn, works begun and far advanced by my father, and when the same basílica was destroyed by fire I began its reconstruction on an enlarged site, to be inscribed with the names of my sons, and ordered that in case I should not live to complete it, it should be completed by my heirs. In my sixth cónsulship, in accordance with a decree of the senate, I rebuilt in the city eighty-two temples of the gods, omitting none which at that time stood in need of repair. As cónsul for the seventh time I constructed the Vía Flamínia from the city to Arímimum, and all the bridges except the Mílvian and the Minúcian.

21 On my own ground I built the temple of Mars Últor and the Augústan Fórum from the spoils of war. On ground purchased for the most part from private owners I built the theatre near the temple of Apóllo which was to bear the name of my son-in-law Márcus Marcéllus. From the spoils of war I consecrated offerings on the Cápitol, and in the temple of the divine Július, and in the temple of Apóllo, and in the temple of Vésta, and in the temple of Mars Últor, which cost me about one hundred million sésterces. In my fifth cónsulship I remitted thirty-five thousand pounds weight of coronary gold contributed by the municípia and the colonies of Italy, and thereafter, whenever I was saluted as imperátor, I did not accept the coronary gold, although the municípia and colonies voted it in the same kindly spirit as before.

22 Three times in my own name I gave a show of gladiators, and five times in the name of my sons or grandsons; in these shows there fought about ten thousand men. Twice in my own name I furnished for the people an exhibition of athletes gathered from all parts of the world, and a third time in the name of my grandson. Four times I gave games in my own name; as representing other magistrates twenty-three times. For the college of quindecémvirs, as master of that college and with Márcus Agríppa as my colleague, I conducted the Sécular Games in the cónsulship of Gáius Fúrnius and Márcus Silánus. In my thirteenth cónsulship I gave, for the first time, the games of Mars, which, since that time, the cónsuls by decree of the senate have given in successive years in conjunction with me. In my own name, or that of my sons or grandsons, on twenty-six occasions I gave to the people, in the círcus, in the fórum, or in the amphitheater, hunts of Áfrican wild beasts, in which about three thousand five hundred beasts were slain.

23 I gave the people the spectacle of a naval battle beyond the Tíber, at the place where now stands the grove of the Cǽsars, the ground having been excavated for a length of eighteen hundred and a breadth of twelve hundred feet. In this spectacle thirty beaked ships, tríremes or bíremes, and a large number of smaller vessels met in conflict. In these fleets there fought about three thousand men exclusive of the rowers.

24 After my victory I replaced in the temples in all the cities of the province of Ásia the ornaments which my antagonist in the war, when he despoiled the temples, had appropriated to his private use. Silver statues of me, on foot, on horseback, and in chariots were erected in the city to the number of about eighty; these I myself removed, and from the money thus obtained I placed in the temple of Apóllo golden offerings in my own name and in the name of those who had paid me the honor of a statue.

25 I freed the sea from pirates. About thirty thousand slaves, captured in that war, who had run away from their masters and had taken up arms against the republic, I delivered to their masters for punishment. The whole of Ítaly voluntarily took oath of allegiance to me and demanded me as its leader in the war in which I was victorious at Áctium. The provinces of the Spains, the Gauls, África, Sícily, and Sardínia took the same oath of allegiance. Those who served under my standards at that time included more than 700 senators, and among them eighty-three who had previously or have since been cónsuls up to the day on which these words were written, and about 170 have been priests.

26 I extended the boundaries of all the provinces which were bordered by races not yet subject to our empire. The provinces of the Gauls, the Spains, and Gérmany, bounded by the ocean from Gádes to the mouth of the Elbe, I reduced to a state of peace. The Alps, from the region which lies nearest to the Adriátic as far as the Túscan Sea, I brought to a state of peace without waging on any tribe an unjust war. My fleet sailed from the mouth of the Rhine eastward as far as the lands of the Címbri to which, up to that time, no Róman had ever penetrated either by land or by sea, and the Címbri and Chárydes and Sémnones and other peoples of the Gérmans of that same region through their envoys sought my friendship and that of the Róman people. On my order and under my auspices two armies were led, at almost the same time, into Ethiópia and into Arábia which is called the "Happy," and very large forces of the enemy of both races were cut to pieces in battle and many towns were captured. Ethiópia was penetrated as far as the town of Nábata, which is next to Méroë. In Arábia the army advanced into the territories of the Sabǽi to the town of Máriba.

27 Égypt I added to the empire of the Róman people. In the case of Greater Arménia, though I might have made it a province after the assassination of its King Artáxes, I preferred, following the precedent of our fathers, to hand that kingdom over to Tigránes, the son of King Artavásdes, and grandson of King Tigránes, through Tibérius Néro who was then my stepson. And later, when the same people revolted and rebelled, and was subdued by my son Gáius, I gave it over to King Ariobarzánes the son of Artabázus, King of the Medes, to rule, and after his death to his son Artavásdes. When he was murdered I sent into that kingdom Tigránes, who was sprung from the royal family of the Arménians. I recovered all the provinces extending eastward beyond the Adriátic Sea, and Cyréne, which were then for the most part in possession of kings, and, at an earlier time, Sícily and Sardínia, which had been seized in the servile war.

28 I settled colonies of soldiers in África, Sícily, Macedónia, both Spains, Achǽa, Ásia, Sýria, Gállia Narbonénsis, Pisídia. Moreover, Italy has twenty-eight colonies founded under my auspices which have grown to be famous and populous during my lifetime.

29 From Spain, Gaul, and the Dalmátians, I recovered, after conquering the enemy, many military standards which had been lost by other generals. The Párthians I compelled to restore to me the spoils and standards of three Róman armies, and to seek as suppliants the friendship of the Róman people. These standards I deposited in the inner shrine which is in the Temple of Mars Últor.

30 The tribes of the Pannónians, to which no army of the Róman people had ever penetrated before my principate, having been subdued by Tibérius Néro who was then my stepson and my legate, I brought under the sovereignty of the Róman people, and I pushed forward the frontier of Illýricum as far as the bank of the river Dánube. An army of Dácians which crossed to the south of that river was, under my auspices, defeated and crushed, and afterwards my own army was led across the Dánube and compelled the tribes of the Dácians to submit to the orders of the Róman people.

31 Embassies were often sent to me from the kings of Índia, a thing never seen before in the camp of any general of the Rómans. Our friendship was sought, through ambassadors, by the Bastárnæ and Scýthians, and by the kings of the Sarmátians who live on either side of the river Tánais, and by the king of the Albáni and of the Híberi and of the Medes.

32 Kings of the Párthians, Tiridátes, and later Phrátes, the son of King Phrátes, took refuge with me as suppliants; of the Medes, Artavásdes; of the Adiabeni, Artáxares; of the Brítons, Dumnobelláunus and Tim ...; of the Sugámbri, Mǽlo; of the Marcománni and Suévi ... Phrátes, son of Oródes, king of the Párthians, sent all his sons and grandsons to me in Italy, not because he had been conquered in war, but rather seeking our friendship by means of his own children as pledges. And a large number of other nations experienced the good faith of the Róman people during my principate who never before had had any interchange of embassies or of friendship with the Róman people.

33 From me the peoples of the Párthians and of the Medes received the kings for whom they asked through ambassadors, the chief men of those peoples; the Párthians Vonónes, son of King Phrátes, grandson of King Oródes; the Medes Ariobarzánes, the son of King Atavázdes, grandson of King Ariobarzánes.

34 In my sixth and seventh cónsulships, when I had extinguished the flames of civil war, after receiving by universal consent the absolute control of affairs, I transferred the republic from my own control to the will of the senate and the Róman people. For this service on my part I was given the title of Augústus by decree of the senate, and the doorposts of my house were covered with laurels by public act, and a civic crown was fixed above my door, and a golden shield was placed in the Cúria Júlia whose inscription testified that the senate and the Róman people gave me this in recognition of my valor, my clemency, my justice, and my piety. After that time I took precedence of all in rank, but of power I possessed no more than those who were my colleagues in any magistracy.

35 While I was administering my thirteenth cónsulship the senate and the equestrian order and the entire Róman people gave me the title of Father of my Country, and decreed that this title should be inscribed upon the vestibule of my house and in the senate-house and in the Fórum Augústum beneath the quadriga erected in my honor by decree of the senate. At the time of writing this I was in my seventy-sixth year.

1 The sum total of the money which he contributed to the treasury or to the Róman plebs or to discharged soldiers was 600,000,000 denárii.

2 The new works which he built were: the temple of Mars, of Júpiter Tónans and Ferétrius, of Apóllo, of the Deified Július, of Quirínus, of Minérva, of Júno the queen, of Júpiter Líbertas, of the Láres, of the Di Penátes, of Youth, of the Mother of the gods, the Lúpercal, the state box at the círcus, the senate-house with the Chalcídicum, the Augústan Fórum, the Basílica Júlia, the theatre of Marcéllus, ... the grove of the Cǽsars beyond the Tíber.

3 He restored the Cápitol and sacred buildings to the number of eighty-two, the theatre of Pómpey, the aqueducts, the Flamínian Way.

4 The expenditures provided for theatrical shows, gladiatorial sports, for exhibitions of athletes, for hunts of wild beasts, and the naval combat, and his gifts to colonies in Ítaly, to cities in the provinces which had been destroyed by earthquake or conflagration, or to individual friends and senators, whose property he raised to the required rating, are too numerous to be reckoned.

Augústus Cǽsar, Res Géstæ Dívi Augústi (translated by Frederick W. Shipley)

The Ambush of Quintílius Várus

2.117 Scarcely had Cǽsar put the finishing touch upon the Pannónian and Dalmátian war, when, within five days of the completion of this task, dispatches from Gérmany brought the baleful news of the death of Várus, and of the slaughter of three légions, of as many divisions of cavalry, and of six cohorts—as though fortune were granting us this indulgence at least, that such a disaster should not be brought upon us when our commander was occupied by other wars. The cause of this defeat and the personality of the general require of me a brief digression.

Várus Quintílius, descended from a famous rather than a high-born family, was a man of mild character and of a quiet disposition, somewhat slow in mind as he was in body, and more accustomed to the leisure of the camp than to actual service in war. That he was no despiser of money is demonstrated by his governorship of Sýria: he entered the rich province a poor man, but left it a rich man and the province poor. When placed in charge of the army in Gérmany, he entertained the notion that the Gérmans were a people who were men only in limbs and voice, and that they, who could not be subdued by the sword, could be soothed by the law. With this purpose in mind he entered the heart of Gérmany as though he were going among a people enjoying the blessings of peace, and sitting on his tribunal he wasted the time of a summer campaign in holding court and observing the proper details of legal procedure.

2.118 But the Gérmans, who with their great ferocity combine great craft, to an extent scarcely credible to one who has had no experience with them, and are a race to lying born, by trumping up a series of fictitious lawsuits, now provoking one another to disputes, and now expressing their gratitude that Róman justice was settling these disputes, that their own barbarous nature was being softened down by this new and hitherto unknown method, and that quarrels which were usually settled by arms were now being ended by law, brought Quintílius to such a complete degree of negligence, that he came to look upon himself as a city prǽtor administering justice in the fórum, and not a general in command of an army in the heart of Gérmany. Thereupon appeared a young man of noble birth, brave in action and alert in mind, possessing an intelligence quite beyond the ordinary barbarian; he was, namely, Armínius, the son of Sígimer, a prince of that nation, and he showed in his countenance and in his eyes the fire of the mind within. He had been associated with us constantly on private campaigns, and had even attained the dignity of equestrian rank. This young man made use of the negligence of the general as an opportunity for treachery, sagaciously seeing that no one could be more quickly overpowered than the man who feared nothing, and that the most common beginning of disaster was a sense of security.

At first, then, he admitted but a few, later a large number, to a share in his design; he told them, and convinced them too, that the Rómans could be crushed, added execution to resolve, and named a day for carrying out the plot. This was disclosed to Várus through Segéstes, a loyal man of that race and of illustrious name, who also demanded that the conspirators be put in chains. But fate now dominated the plans of Várus and had blindfolded the eyes of his mind. Indeed, it is usually the case that heaven perverts the judgment of the man whose fortune it means to reverse, and brings it to pass—and this is the wretched part of it—that that which happens by chance seems to be deserved, and accident passes over into culpability. And so Quintílius refused to believe the story, and insisted upon judging the apparent friendship of the Gérmans toward him by the standard of his merit. And, after this first warning, there was no time left for a second.

2.119 The details of this terrible calamity, the heaviest that had befallen the Rómans on foreign soil since the disaster of Crássus in Párthia, I shall endeavor to set forth, as others have done, in my larger work. Here I can merely lament the disaster as a whole. An army unexcelled in bravery, the first of Róman armies in discipline, in energy, and in experience in the field, through the negligence of its general, the perfidy of the enemy, and the unkindness of fortune was surrounded, nor was as much opportunity as they had wished given to the soldiers either of fighting or of extricating themselves, except against heavy odds; nay, some were even heavily chastised for using the arms and showing the spirit of Rómans. Hemmed in by forests and marshes and ambuscades, it was exterminated almost to a man by the very enemy whom it had always slaughtered like cattle, whose life or death had depended solely upon the wrath or the pity of the Rómans.

The general had more courage to die than to fight, for, following the example of his father and grandfather, he ran himself through with his sword. Of the two prefects of the camp, Lúcius Éggius furnished a precedent as noble as that of Ceiónius was base, who, after the greater part of the army had perished, proposed its surrender, preferring to die by torture at the hands of the enemy than in battle. Vála Numónius, lieutenant of Várus, who, in the rest of his life, had been an inoffensive and an honorable man, also set a fearful example in that he left the infantry unprotected by the cavalry and in flight tried to reach the Rhine with his squadrons of horse. But fortune avenged his act, for he did not survive those whom he had abandoned, but died in the act of deserting them. The body of Várus, partially burned, was mangled by the enemy in their barbarity; his head was cut off and taken to Marobóduus and was sent by him to Cæsar; but in spite of the disaster it was honored by burial in the tomb of his family.

Gáius Velléius Patérculus, *The Róman History*, 2.117-2.119
(translated by Frederick W. Shipley)

CHAPTER XXIV

THE JÚLIAN EMPERORS: TIBÉRIUS TO NÉRO

The Reign of Tibérius (A.D. 14-37), I.—The Reign of Calígula (A.D. 37-41), II.
The Reign of Cláudius (A.D. 41-54), III.—The Reign of Néro (A.D. 54-68), III.

Ǽlius Sejánus

4.1 The year when Gáius Asínius and Gáius Antístius were cónsuls was the ninth of Tibérius's reign, a period of tranquillity for the State and prosperity for his own house, for he counted Germánicus's death a happy incident. Suddenly fortune deranged everything; the emperor became a cruel tyrant, as well as an abettor of cruelty in others. Of this the cause and origin was Ǽlius Sejánus, commander of the prætórian cohorts, of whose influence I have already spoken. I will now fully describe his extraction, his character, and the daring wickedness by which he grasped at power.

Born at Vulsínii, the son of Séius Strábo, a Róman knight, he attached himself in his early youth to Gáius Cǽsar, grandson of the Divine Augústus, and the story went that he had sold his person to Apícius, a rich debauchee. Soon afterwards he won the heart of Tibérius so effectually by various artifices that the emperor, ever dark and mysterious towards others, was with Sejánus alone careless and free-spoken. It was not through his craft, for it was by this very weapon that he was overthrown; it was rather from heaven's wrath against Rome, to whose welfare his elevation and his fall were alike disastrous. He had a body which could endure hardships, and a daring spirit. He was one who screened himself, while he was attacking others; he was as cringing as he was imperious; before the world he affected humility; in his heart he lusted after supremacy, for the sake of which he sometimes lavish and luxurious, but oftener energetic and watchful, qualities quite as mischievous when hypocritically assumed for the attainment of sovereignty.

4.2 He strengthened the hitherto moderate powers of his office by concentrating the cohorts scattered throughout the capital into one camp, so that they might all receive orders at the same moment, and that the sight of their numbers and strength might give confidence to themselves, while it would strike terror into the citizens. His pretexts were the demoralization incident to a dispersed soldiery, the greater effectiveness of simultaneous action in the event of a sudden peril, and the stricter discipline which would be insured by the establishment of an encampment at a distance from the temptations of the city. As soon as the camp was completed, he crept gradually into the affections of the soldiers by mixing with them and addressing them by name, himself selecting the centúrions and tríbunes. With the Senate too he sought to ingratiate himself, distinguishing his partisans with offices and provinces, Tibérius readily yielding, and being so biased that not only in private conversation but before the senators and the people he spoke highly of him as the partner of his toils, and allowed his statues to be honored in theatres, in fórums, and at the head-quarters of our légions.

Tácitus, *Annals*, 4.1-4.2
(translated by Alfred John Church and William Jackson Brodribb)

Gáius (Calígula) Builds a Sea Bridge

19 Besides this, he devised a novel and unheard of kind of pageant; for he bridged the gap between Báiæ and the mole at Putéoli, a distance of about thirty-six hundred paces, by bringing together merchant ships from all sides and anchoring them in a double line, afterwards a mound of earth was heaped upon them and fashioned in the manner of the Áppian Way. Over this bridge he rode back and forth for two successive days, the first day on a caparisoned horse, himself resplendent in a crown of oak leaves, a buckler, a sword, and a cloak of cloth of gold; on the second, in the dress of a charioteer in a car drawn by a pair of famous horses, carrying before him a boy named Daréus, one of the hostages from Párthia, and attended by the entire prætórian guard and a company of his friends in Gállic chariots. I know that many have supposed that Gáius devised this kind of bridge in rivalry of Xérxes, who excited no little admiration by bridging the much narrower Héllespont; others, that it was to inspire fear in Gérmany and Brítain, on which he had gardens, by the fame of some stupendous work. But when I was a boy, I used to hear my grandfather say that the reason for the work, as revealed by the emperor's confidential courtiers, was that Thrasýllus the astrologer had declared to Tibérius, when he was worried about his successor and inclined towards his natural grandson, that Gáius had no more chance of becoming emperor than of riding about over the gulf of Báiæ with horses.

Suetónius, Lives of the Twelve Cæsars, Gáius 19 (translated by J. C. Rolfe)

Calígula, the Monster

22 So much for Calígula as emperor; we must now tell of his career as a monster. After he had assumed various surnames (for he was called "Pious," "Child of the Camp," "Father of the Armies," and "Greatest and Best of Cæsars"), chancing to overhear some kings, who had come to Rome to pay their respects to him, disputing at dinner about the nobility of their descent, he cried:

> Let there be one Lord, one King.

And he came near assuming a crown at once and changing the semblance of a principate into the form of a monarchy. But on being reminded that he had risen above the elevation both of princes and kings, he began from that time on to lay claim to divine majesty; for after giving orders that such statues of the gods as were especially famous for their sanctity or their artistic merit, including that of Júpiter of Olýmpia, should be brought from Greece, in order to remove their heads and put his own in their place, he built out a part of the Palace as far as the Fórum, and making the temple of Cástor and Póllux its vestibule, he often took his place between the divine brethren, and exhibited himself there to be worshipped by those who presented themselves; and some hailed him as Júpiter Latiáris. He also set up a special temple to his own godhead, with priests and with victims of the choicest kind. In this temple was a life-sized statue of the emperor in gold, which was dressed each day in clothing such as he wore himself.

The richest citizens used all their influence to secure the priesthoods of his cult and bid high for the honor. The victims were flamingoes, peacocks, black grouse, guinea-hens and pheasants, offered day by day each after its own kind. At night he used constantly to invite the full and radiant moon to his embraces and his bed, while in the daytime he would talk confidentially with Júpiter Capitolínus, now whispering and then in turn his ear to the mouth of the god, now in louder and even angry language; for he was heard to make the threat: "Lift me up, or I'll lift thee." But finally won by entreaties, as he reported, and even invited to live with the god, he built a bridge over the temple to the Deified Augústus, and thus joined his Palace to the Cápitol. Presently, to be nearer yet, he laid the foundations of a new house in the court of the Cápitol.

26 It would be trivial and pointless to add to this an account of his treatment of his relatives and friends, Ptólemy, son of king Júba, his cousin (for he was the grandson of Mark Ántony by Ántony's daughter Seléne), and in particular Mácro himself and even Énnia, who helped him to the throne; all these were rewarded for their kinship and their faithful services by a bloody death. He was no whit more respectful or mild towards the senate, allowing some who had held the highest offices to run in their tógas for several miles beside his chariot and to wait on him at table, standing napkin in hand either at the head of his couch, or at his feet. Others he secretly put to death, yet continued to send for them as if they were alive, after a few days falsely asserting that they had committed suicide. When the cónsuls forgot to make proclamation of his birthday, he deposed them, and left the state for three days without its highest magistrates. He flogged his quǽstor, who was charged with conspiracy, stripping off the man's clothes and spreading them under the soldiers' feet, to give them a firm footing as they beat him.

He treated the other orders with like insolence and cruelty. Being disturbed by the noise made by those who came in the middle of the night to secure the free seats in the Círcus, he drove them all out with cudgels; in the confusion more than twenty Róman knights were crushed to death, with as many matrons and a countless number of others. At the plays in the theatre, sowing discord between the commons and the knights, he scattered the gift tickets ahead of time, to induce the rabble to take the seats reserved for the equestrian order. At a gladiatorial show he would sometimes draw back the awnings when the sun was hottest and give orders that no one be allowed to leave; then removing the usual equipment, he would match worthless decrepit gladiators against mangy wild beasts, and have sham fights between householders who were of good repute, but conspicuous for some bodily infirmity. Sometimes too he would shut up the granaries and condemn the people to hunger.

27 The following are special instances of his innate brutality. When cattle to feed the wild beasts which he had provided for a gladiatorial show were rather costly, he selected criminals to be devoured, and reviewing the line of prisoners without examining the charges, but merely taking his place in the middle of a colonnade, he bade them be led away "from baldhead to baldhead." A man who had made a vow to fight in the arena, if the emperor recovered, he compelled to keep his word, watched him as he fought sword in hand, and would not let him go until he was victorious, and then only after many entreaties. Another who had offered his life for the same reason, but delayed to kill himself, he turned over to his slaves, with orders to drive him through the streets decked with sacred boughs and fillets, calling for the fulfillment of his vow, and finally hurl him from the embankment.

Many men of honorable rank were first disfigured with the marks of branding-irons and then condemned to the mines, to work at building roads, or to be thrown to the wild beasts; or else he shut them up in cages on all fours, like animals, or had them sawn asunder. Not all these punishments were for serious offences, but merely for criticizing one of his shows, or for never having sworn by his Genius. He forced parents to attend the executions of their sons, sending a litter for one man who pleaded ill health, and inviting another to dinner immediately after witnessing the death, and trying to rouse him to gaiety and jesting by a great show of affability. He had the manager of his gladiatorial shows and beast-baitings beaten with chains in his presence for several successive days, and would not kill him until he was disgusted at the stench of his putrefied brain. He burned a writer of Atéllan farces alive in the middle of the arena of the amphitheater, because of a humorous line of double meaning. When a Róman knight on being thrown to the wild beasts loudly protested his innocence, he took him out, cut off his tongue, and put him back again.

28 Having asked a man who had been recalled from an exile of long standing, how in the world he spent his time there, the man replied by way of flattery: "I constantly prayed the gods for what has come to pass, that Tibérius might die and you become emperor." Thereupon Calígula, thinking that his exiles were likewise praying for his death, sent emissaries from island to island to butcher them all. Wishing to have one of the senators torn to pieces, he induced some of the members to assail him suddenly, on his entrance into the House, with the charge of being a public enemy, to stab him with their styles, and turn him over to the rest to be mangled; and his cruelty was not sated until he saw the man's limbs, members, and bowels dragged through the streets and heaped up before him.

29 He added to the enormity of his crimes by the brutality of his language. He used to say that there was nothing in his own character which he admired and approved more highly than what he called his ἀδιατρεψία, that is to say, his shameless impudence. When his grandmother Antónia gave him some advice, he was not satisfied merely to listen but replied: "Remember that I have the right to do anything to anybody." When he was on the point of killing his brother, and suspected that he had taken drugs as a precaution against poison, he cried: "What! an antidote against Cæsar?" After banishing his sisters, he made the threat that he not only had islands, but swords as well. An ex-prætor who had retired to Antícyra for his health, sent frequent requests for an extension of his leave, but Calígula had him put to death, adding that a man who had not been helped by so long a course of hellebore needed to be bled. On signing the list of prisoners who were to be put to death later, he said that he was clearing his accounts. Having condemned several Gauls and Greeks to death in a body, he boasted that he had subdued Gallogræcia.

30 He seldom had anyone put to death except by numerous slight wounds, his constant order, which soon became well-known, being: "Strike so that he may feel that he is dying." When a different man than he had intended had been killed, through a mistake in the names, he said that the victim too had deserved the same fate. He often uttered the familiar line of the tragic poet:

> Let them hate me, so they but fear me.

He often inveighed against all the senators alike, as adherents of Sejánus and informers against his mother and brothers, producing the documents which he pretended to have burned, and upholding the cruelty of Tibérius as forced upon him, since he could not but believe so many accusers. He constantly tongue-lashed the equestrian order as devotees of the stage and the arena. Angered at the rabble for applauding a faction which he opposed, he cried: "I wish the Róman people had but a single neck," and when the brigand Tetrínius was demanded, he said that those who asked for him were Tetríniuses also. Once a band of five retiárii in tunics, matched against the same number of secutóres, yielded without a struggle; but when their death was ordered, one of them caught up his trident and slew all the victors. Calígula bewailed this in a public proclamation as a most cruel murder, and expressed his horror of those who had had the heart to witness it.

31 He even used openly to deplore the state of his times, because they had been marked by no public disasters, saying that the rule of Augústus had been made famous by the Várus massacre, and that of Tibérius by the collapse of the amphitheater at Fidénæ, while his own was threatened with oblivion because of its prosperity; and every now and then he wished for the destruction of his armies, for famine, pestilence, fires, or a great earthquake.

32 His acts and words were equally cruel, even when he was indulging in relaxation and given up to amusement and feasting. While he was lunching or reveling capital examinations by torture were often made in his presence, and a soldier who was adept at decapitation cut off the heads of those who were brought from prison. At Putéoli, at the dedication of the bridge that he contrived, as has been said, after inviting a number to come to him from the shore, on a sudden he had them all thrown overboard; and when some caught hold of the rudders of the ships, he pushed them off into the sea with boathooks and oars. At a public banquet in Rome he immediately handed a slave over to the executioners for stealing a strip of silver from the couches, with orders that his hands be cut off and hung from his neck upon his breast, and that he then be led about among the guests, preceded by a placard giving the reason for his punishment. When a murmíllo from the gladiatorial school fought with him with wooden swords and fell on purpose, he stabbed him a real dagger and then ran about with a palm-branch, as victors do. Once when he stood by the altar dressed as a pópa, and a victim was brought up, he raised his mallet on high and slew the cultrárius. At one of his more sumptuous banquets he suddenly burst into a fit of laughter, and when the cónsuls, who were reclining next him, politely inquired at what he was laughing, he replied; "What do you suppose, except that a single nod of mine both of you could have your throats cut on the spot?"

33 As a sample of his humor, he took his place beside a statue of Júpiter, and asked the tragic actor Apélles which of the two seemed to him the greater, and when he hesitated, Calígula had him flayed with whips, extolling his voice from time to time, when the wretch begged for mercy, as passing sweet even in his groans. Whenever he kissed the neck of his wife or sweetheart, he would say: "Off comes this beautiful head whenever I give the word." He even used to threaten now and then that he would resort to torture if necessary, to find out from his dear Cæsónia why he loved her so passionately.

Suetónius, Lives of the Twelve Cæsars, Gáius 22, 26-33 (translated by J. C. Rolfe)

Calígula, the Military Failure

44 On reaching his camp, to show his vigilance and strictness as a commander, he dismissed in disgrace the generals who were late in bringing in the auxiliaries from various places, and in reviewing his troops he deprived many of the chief centúrions who were well on in years of their rank, in some cases only a few days before they would have served their time, giving as a reason their age and infirmity; then railing at the rest for their avarice, he reduced the rewards given on completion of full military service to six thousand sésterces.

All that he accomplished was to receive the surrender of Admínius, son of Cynobellínus king of the Brítons, who had been banished by his father and had deserted to the Rómans with a small force; yet as if the entire island had submitted to him, he sent a grandiloquent letter to Rome, commanding the couriers who carried it to ride in their post-chaise all the way to the Fórum and the House, and not to deliver it to anyone except the cónsuls, in the temple of Mars the Avenger, before a full meeting of the senate.

45 Presently, finding no one to fight with, he had a few Gérmans of his body-guard taken across the river and concealed there, and word brought him after luncheon with great bustle and confusion that the enemy were close at hand. Upon this he rushed out with his friends and a part of the prætórian cavalry to the woods close by, and after cutting the branches from some trees and adorning them like trophies, he returned by torchlight, taunting those who had not followed him as timorous and cowardly, and presenting his companions and the partners in his victory with crowns of a new kind and of a new name, ornamented with figures of the sun, moon and stars, and called exploratóriæ. Another time some hostages were taken from a common school and secretly sent on ahead of him, when he suddenly left a banquet and pursued them with the cavalry as if they were runaways, caught them, and brought them back in fetters, in this farce too showing immoderate extravagance. On coming back to the table, when some announced that the army was assembled, he urged them to take their places just as they were, in their coats of mail. He also admonished them in the familiar line of Vérgil to "bear up and save themselves for better days."

Meanwhile he rebuked the absent senate and people in a stern edict because "while Cæsar was fighting and exposed to such dangers they were indulging in revels and frequenting the theatres and their pleasant villas."

46 Finally, as if he intended to bring the war to an end, he drew up a line of battle on the shore of the Ocean, arranging his ballístas and other artillery; and when no one knew or could imagine what he was going to do, he suddenly bade them gather shells and fill their helmets and the folds of their gowns, calling them "spoils from the Ocean, due to the Cápitol and Pálatine." As a monument of his victory he erected a lofty tower, from which lights were to shine at night to guide the course of ships, as from the Pháros. Then promising the soldiers a gratuity of a hundred denárii each, as if he had shown unprecedented liberality, he said, "Go your way happy; go your way rich."

47 Then turning his attention to his triumph, in addition to a few captives and deserters from the barbarians he chose all the tallest of the Gauls, and as he expressed it, those who were "worthy of a triumph," as well as some of the chiefs. These he reserved for his parade, compelling them not only to dye their hair red and to let it grow long, but also to learn the language of the Gérmans and assume barbarian names. He also had the tríremes in which he had entered the Ocean carried overland to Rome for the greater part of the way. He wrote besides to his financial agents to prepare for a triumph at the smallest possible cost, but on a grander scale than had ever before been known, since the goods of all were at their disposal.

48 Before leaving the province he formed a design of unspeakable cruelty, that of butchering the légions that had begun the mutiny years before just after the death of Augústus, because they had beleaguered his father Germánicus, their leader, and himself, at the time an infant; and though he was with difficulty turned from this mad purpose, he could by no means be prevented from persisting in his desire to decimate them. Accordingly he summoned them to an assembly without their arms, not even wearing their swords, and surrounded them with armed horsemen. But seeing that some of the légionaries, suspecting his purpose, were stealing off to resume their arms, in case any violence should be offered them, he fled from the assembly and set out for the city in a hurry, turning all his ferocity upon senate, against which he uttered open threats, in order to divert the gossip about his own dishonor. He complained among other things that he had been cheated of his fairly earned triumph; whereas a short time before he had himself given orders that on pain of death no action should be taken about his honors.

49 Therefore when he was met on the road by envoys from that distinguished body, begging him to hasten his return, he roared, "I will come, and this will be with me," frequently smiting the hilt of the sword which he wore at his side. He also made proclamation that he was returning, not only to those who desired his presence, the equestrian order and the people, for to the senate he would never more be fellow-citizen nor prince. He even forbade anyone of the senators to meet him. Then giving up or postponing his triumph, he entered the city on his birthday in an ovation; and within four months he perished, having dared great crimes and meditating still greater ones. For he had made up his mind to move to Ántium, and later to Alexándria, after first slaying the noblest members of the two orders. That no one may doubt this, let me say that among his private papers two notebooks were found with different titles, one called "The Sword" and the other "The Dagger," and both containing the names and marks of identification of those whom he had doomed to death. There was found besides a great chest full of divers kinds of poisons, which they say were later thrown into the sea by Cláudius and so infected it as to kill the fish, which were thrown up by the tide upon the neighboring shores.

Suetónius, Lives of the Twelve Cǽsars, Gáius 44-49 (translated by J. C. Rolfe)

The Mental and Physical Incapacities of Calígula

50 He was very tall and extremely pale, with an unshapely body, but very thin neck and legs. His eyes and temples were hollow, his forehead broad and grim, his hair thin and entirely gone on the top of his head, though his body was hairy. Because of this to look upon him from a higher place as he passed by, or for any reason whatever to mention a goat, was treated as a capital offence. While his face was naturally forbidding and ugly, he purposely made it even more savage, practicing all kinds of terrible and fearsome expressions before a mirror.

He was sound neither of body nor mind. As a boy he was troubled with the falling sickness, and while in his youth he had some endurance, yet at times because of sudden faintness he was hardly able to walk, to stand up, to collect his thoughts, or to hold up his head. He himself realized his mental infirmity, and thought at times of going into retirement and clearing his brain. It is thought that his wife Cæsónia gave him a drug intended for a love potion, which however had the effect of driving him mad. He was especially tormented with sleeplessness; for he never rested more than three hours at night, and even for that length of time he did not sleep quietly, but was terrified by strange apparitions, once for example dreaming that the spirit of the Ocean talked with him. Therefore weary of lying in bed wide awake during the greater part of the night, he would now sit upon his couch, and now wander through the long colonnades, crying out from time to time for daylight and longing for its coming.

51 I think I may fairly attribute to mental weakness the existence of two exactly opposite faults in the same person, extreme assurance and, on the other hand, excessive timorousness. For this man, who so utterly despised the gods, was wont at the slightest thunder and lightning to shut his eyes, to muffle up his head, and if they increased, to leap from his bed and hide under it. In his journey through Sícily, though he made all manner of fun of the miracles in various places, he suddenly fled from Messána by night, panic-stricken by the smoke and roaring from Ætna's crater. Full of threats as he was also against the barbarians, when he was riding in a chariot through a narrow defile on the far side of the Rhine, and someone said that there would be no slight panic if the enemy should appear anywhere, he immediately mounted a horse and hastily returned to the bridges. Finding them crowded with camp servants and baggage, in his impatience of any delay he was passed along from hand to hand over the men's heads. Soon after, hearing of an uprising in Gérmany, he made preparations to flee from the city and equipped fleets for the purpose, finding comfort only in the thought that the provinces across the sea would at any rate be left him, in case the enemy should be victorious and take possession of the summits of the Alps, as the Címbri, or even of the city, as the Sénones had once done. And it was this, I think, that later inspired his assassins with the idea of pretending to the riotous soldiers that he had laid hands on himself in terror at the report of a defeat.

Suetónius, Lives of the Twelve Cǽsars, Gáius 50-51 (translated by J. C. Rolfe)

Cláudius is Made Emperor

10 Having spent the greater part of his life under these and like circumstances, he became emperor in his fiftieth year by a remarkable freak of fortune. When the assassins of Gáius shut out the crowd under pretense that the emperor wished to be alone, Cláudius was ousted with the rest and withdrew to an apartment called the Hermǽum; and a little later, in great terror at the news of the murder, he stole away to a balcony hard by and hid among the curtains which hung before the door. As he cowered there, a common soldier, who was prowling about at random, saw his feet, intending to ask who he was, pulled him out and recognized him; and when Cláudius fell at his feet in terror, he hailed him as emperor. Then he took him to the rest of his comrades, who were as yet in a condition of uncertainty and purposeless rage. These placed him in a litter, took turns in carrying it, since his own bearers had made off, and bore him to the Camp in a state of despair and terror, while the throng that met him pitied him, as an innocent man who was being hurried off to execution. Received within the rampart, he spent the night among the sentries with much less hope than confidence; for the cónsuls with the senate and the city cohorts had taken possession of the Fórum and the Cápitol, resolved on maintaining the public liberty.

When he too was summoned to the House by the tríbunes of the commons, to give his advice on the situation, he sent word that "he was detained by force and compulsion." But the next day, since the senate was dilatory in putting through its plans because of the tiresome bickering of those who held divergent views, while the populace, who stood about the hall, called for one ruler and expressly named Cláudius, he allowed the armed assembly of the soldiers to swear allegiance to him, and promised each man fifteen thousand sésterces; being the first of the Cǽsars who resorted to bribery to secure the fidelity of the troops.

Suetónius, Lives of the Twelve Cǽsars, Cláudius 10 (translated by J. C. Rolfe)

Agrippína Poisons Cláudius with Mushrooms

34 Cláudius was angered by Agrippína's actions, of which he was now becoming aware, and sought for his son Británnicus, who had purposely been kept out of his sight by her most of the time (for she was doing everything she could to secure the throne for Néro, inasmuch as he was her own son by her former husband Domítius); and he displayed his affection whenever he met the boy. He would not endure her behavior, but was preparing to put an end to her power, to cause his son to assume the tóga virílis, and to declare him heir to the throne. Agrippína, learning of this, became alarmed and made haste to forestall anything of the sort by poisoning Cláudius. But since, owing to the great quantity of wine he was forever drinking and his general habits of life, such as all emperors as a rule adopt for their protection, he could not easily be harmed, she sent for a famous dealer in poisons, a woman named Lucústa, who had recently been convicted on this very charge; and preparing with her aid a poison whose effect was sure, she put it in one of the vegetables called mushrooms. Then she herself ate of the others, but made her husband eat of the one which contained the poison; for it was the largest and finest of them. And so the victim of the plot was carried from the banquet apparently quite overcome by strong drink, a thing that had happened many times before; but during the night the poison took effect and he passed away, without having been able to say or hear a word. It was the thirteenth of October, and he had lived sixty-three years, two months, and thirteen days, having been emperor thirteen years, eight months and twenty days.

Cássius Dío, *Róman History*, 61.34 (translated by Earnest Carey)

Néro Murders His Mother, Agrippína

14.3 Néro accordingly avoided secret interviews with her, and when she withdrew to her gardens or to her estates at Túsculum and Ántium, he praised her for courting repose. At last, convinced that she would be too formidable, wherever she might dwell, he resolved to destroy her, merely deliberating whether it was to be accomplished by poison, or by the sword, or by any other violent means. Poison at first seemed best, but, were it to be administered at the imperial table, the result could not be referred to chance after the recent circumstances of the death of Británnicus. Again, to tamper with the servants of a woman who, from her familiarity with crime, was on her guard against treachery, appeared to be extremely difficult, and then, too, she had fortified her constitution by the use of antidotes. How again the dagger and its work were to be kept secret, no one could suggest, and it was feared too that whoever might be chosen to execute such a crime would spurn the order.

An ingenious suggestion was offered by Anicétus, a freedman, commander of the fleet at Misénum, who had been tutor to Néro in boyhood and had a hatred of Agrippína which she reciprocated. He explained that a vessel could be constructed, from which a part might by a contrivance be detached, when out at sea, so as to plunge her unawares into the water. "Nothing," he said, "allowed of accidents so much as the sea, and should she be overtaken by shipwreck, who would be so unfair as to impute to crime an offence committed by the winds and waves? The emperor would add the honor of a temple and of shrines to the deceased lady, with every other display of filial affection."

14.4 Néro liked the device, favored as it also was by the particular time, for he was celebrating Minérva's five days' festival at Báiæ. Thither he enticed his mother by repeated assurances that children ought to bear with the irritability of parents and to soothe their tempers, wishing thus to spread a rumor of reconciliation and to secure Agrippína's acceptance through the feminine credulity... As she approached, he went to the shore to meet her (she was coming from Ántium), welcomed her with outstretched hand and embrace, and conducted her to Báuli. This was the name of a country house, washed by a bay of the sea, between the promontory of Misénum and the lake of Báiæ.

Here was a vessel distinguished from others by its equipment, seemingly meant, among other things, to do honor to his mother; for she had been accustomed to sail in a tríreme, with a crew of marines. And now she was invited to a banquet, that night might serve to conceal the crime. It was well known that somebody had been found to betray it, that Agrippína had heard of the plot, and in doubt whether she was to believe it, was conveyed to Báiæ in her litter. There some soothing words allayed her fear; she was graciously received, and seated at table above the emperor. Néro prolonged the banquet with various conversation, passing from a youth's playful familiarity to an air of constraint, which seemed to indicate serious thought, and then, after protracted festivity, escorted her on her departure, clinging with kisses to her eyes and bosom, either to crown his hypocrisy or because the last sight of a mother on the eve of destruction caused a lingering even in that brutal heart.

14.5 A night of brilliant starlight with the calm of a tranquil sea was granted by heaven, seemingly, to convict the crime. The vessel had not gone far, Agrippína having with her two of her intimate attendants, one of whom, Creperéius Gállus, stood near the helm, while Acerrónia, reclining at Agrippína's feet as she reposed herself, spoke joyfully of her son's repentance and of the recovery of the mother's influence, when at a given signal the ceiling of the place, which was loaded with a quantity of lead, fell in, and Creperéius was crushed and instantly killed. Agrippína and Acerrónia were protected by the projecting sides of the couch, which happened to be too strong to yield under the weight. But this was not followed by the breaking up of the vessel; for all were bewildered, and those too, who were in the plot, were hindered by the unconscious majority. The crew then thought it best to throw the vessel on one side and so sink it, but they could not themselves promptly unite to face the emergency, and others, by counteracting the attempt, gave an opportunity of a gentler fall into the sea. Acerrónia, however, thoughtlessly exclaiming that she was Agrippína, and imploring help for the emperor's mother, was dispatched with poles and oars, and such naval implements as chance offered. Agrippína was silent and was thus the less recognized; still, she received a wound in her shoulder. She swam, then met with some small boats which conveyed her to the Lúcrine lake, and so entered her house.

14.6 There she reflected how for this very purpose she had been invited by a lying letter and treated with conspicuous honor, how also it was near the shore, not from being driven by winds or dashed on rocks, that the vessel had in its upper part collapsed, like a mechanism anything but nautical. She pondered too the death of Acerrónia; she looked at her own wound, and saw that her only safeguard against treachery was to ignore it. Then she sent her freedman Agerínus to tell her son how by heaven's favor and his good fortune she had escaped a terrible disaster; that she begged him, alarmed, as he might be, by his mother's peril, to put off the duty of a visit, as for the present she needed repose. Meanwhile, pretending that she felt secure, she applied remedies to her wound, and fomentations to her person. She then ordered search to be made for the will of Acerrónia, and her property to be sealed, in this alone throwing off disguise.

14.7 Néro, meantime, as he waited for tidings of the consummation of the deed, received information that she had escaped with the injury of a slight wound, after having so far encountered the peril that there could be no question as to its author. Then, paralyzed with terror and protesting that she would show herself the next moment eager for vengeance, either arming the slaves or stirring up the soldiery, or hastening to the Senate and the people, to charge him with the wreck, with her wound, and with the destruction of her friends, he asked what resource he had against all this, unless something could be at once devised by Búrrus and Séneca. He had instantly summoned both of them, and possibly they were already in the secret. There was a long silence on their part; they feared they might remonstrate in vain, or believed the crisis to be such that Néro must perish, unless Agrippína were at once crushed.

Thereupon Séneca was so far the more prompt as to glance back on Búrrus, as if to ask him whether the bloody deed must be required of the soldiers. Búrrus replied "that the prætorians were attached to the whole family of the Cæsars, and remembering Germánicus would not dare a savage deed on his offspring. It was for Anicétus to accomplish his promise." Anicétus, without a pause, claimed for himself the consummation of the crime. At those words, Néro declared that that day gave him empire, and that a freedman was the author of this mighty boon. "Go," he said, "with all speed and take with you the men readiest to execute your orders." He himself, when he had heard of the arrival of Agrippína's messenger, Agerínus, contrived a theatrical mode of accusation, and, while the man was repeating his message, threw down a sword at his feet, then ordered him to be put in irons, as a detected criminal, so that he might invent a story how his mother had plotted the emperor's destruction and in the shame of discovered guilt had by her own choice sought death.

14.8 Meantime, Agrippína's peril being universally known and taken to be an accidental occurrence, everybody, the moment he heard of it, hurried down to the beach. Some climbed projecting piers; some the nearest vessels; others, as far as their stature allowed, went into the sea; some, again, stood with outstretched arms, while the whole shore rung with wailings, with prayers and cries, as different questions were asked and uncertain answers given. A vast multitude streamed to the spot with torches, and as soon as all knew that she was safe, they at once prepared to wish her joy, till the sight of an armed and threatening force scared them away. Anicétus then surrounded the house with a guard, and having burst open the gates, dragged off the slaves who met him, till he came to the door of her chamber, where a few still stood, after the rest had fled in terror at the attack. A small lamp was in the room, and one slave-girl with Agrippína, who grew more and more anxious, as no messenger came from her son, not even Agerínus, while the appearance of the shore was changed, a solitude one moment, then sudden bustle and tokens of the worst catastrophe. As the girl rose to depart, she exclaimed, "Do you too forsake me?" and looking round saw Anicétus, who had with him the captain of the tríreme, Herculéius, and Obáritus, a centúrion of marines. "If," said she, "you have come to see me, take back word that I have recovered, but if you are here to do a crime, I believe nothing about my son; he has not ordered his mother's murder." The assassins closed in round her couch, and the captain of the tríreme first struck her head violently with a club. Then, as the centúrion bared his sword for the fatal deed, presenting her person, she exclaimed, "Smite my womb," and with many wounds she was slain.

14.9 So far our accounts agree. That Néro gazed on his mother after her death and praised her beauty, some have related, while others deny it. Her body was burnt that same night on a dining couch, with a mean funeral; nor, as long as Néro was in power, was the earth raised into a mound, or even decently closed. Subsequently, she received from the solicitude of her domestics, a humble sepulcher on the road to Misénum, near the country house of Cæsar the Dictator, which from a great height commands a view of the bay beneath. As soon as the funeral pile was lighted, one of her freedmen, surnamed Mnéster, ran himself through with a sword, either from love of his mistress or from the fear of destruction. Many years before Agrippína had anticipated this end for herself and had spurned the thought. For when she consulted the astrologers about Néro, they replied that he would be emperor and kill his mother. "Let him kill her," she said, "provided he is emperor."

14.10. But the emperor, when the crime was at last accomplished, realized its portentous guilt. The rest of the night, now silent and stupefied, now and still oftener starting up in terror, bereft of reason, he awaited the dawn as if it would bring with it his doom. He was first encouraged to hope by the flattery addressed to him, at the prompting of Búrrus, by the centúrions and tríbunes, who again and again pressed his hand and congratulated him on his having escaped an unforeseen danger and his mother's daring crime. Then his friends went to the temples, and, an example having once been set, the neighboring towns of testified their joy with sacrifices and deputations. He himself, with an opposite phase of hypocrisy, seemed sad, and almost angry at his own deliverance, and shed tears over his mother's death. But as the aspects of places change not, as do the looks of men, and as he had ever before his eyes the dreadful sight of that sea with its shores (some too believed that the notes of a funereal trumpet were heard from the surrounding heights, and wailings from the mother's grave), he retired to Neápolis and sent a letter to the Senate, the drift of which was that Agerínus, one of Agrippína's confidential freedmen, had been detected with the dagger of an assassin, and that in the consciousness of having planned the crime she had paid its penalty.

14.11 He even revived the charges of a period long past, how she had aimed at a share of empire, and at inducing the prætórian cohorts to swear obedience to a woman, to the disgrace of the Senate and people; how, when she was disappointed, in her fury with the soldiers, the Senate, and the populace, she opposed the usual donative and largess, and organized perilous prosecutions against distinguished citizens. What efforts had it cost him to hinder her from bursting into the Senate-house and giving answers to foreign nations! He glanced too with indirect censure at the days of Cláudius, and ascribed all the abominations of that reign to his mother, thus seeking to show that it was the State's good fortune which had destroyed her. For he actually told the story of the shipwreck; but who could be so stupid as to believe that it was accidental, or that a shipwrecked woman had sent one man with a weapon to break through an emperor's guards and fleets? So now it was not Néro, whose brutality was far beyond any remonstrance, but Séneca who was in ill repute, for having written a confession in such a style.

14.12 Still there was a marvelous rivalry among the nobles in decreeing thanksgivings at all the shrines, and the celebration with annual games of Minérva's festival, as the day on which the plot had been discovered; also, that a golden image of Minérva with a statue of the emperor by its side should be set up in the Senate-house, and that Agrippína's birthday should be classed among the inauspicious days. Thraséa Pǽtus, who had been used to pass over previous flatteries in silence or with brief assent, then walked out of the Senate, thereby imperiling himself, without communicating to the other senators any impulse towards freedom. There occurred too a thick succession of portents, which meant nothing. A woman gave birth to a snake, and another was killed by a thunderbolt in her husband's embrace. Then the sun was suddenly darkened and the fourteen districts of the city were struck by lightning. All this happened quite without any providential design; so much so, that for many subsequent years Néro prolonged his reign and his crimes. Still, to deepen the popular hatred towards his mother, and prove that since her removal, his clemency had increased, he restored to their ancestral homes two distinguished ladies, Júnia and Calpúrnia, with two ex-prǽtors, Valérius Cápito and Licínius Gábolus, whom Agrippína had formerly banished. He also allowed the ashes of Lóllia Paulína to be brought back and a tomb to be built over them. Itúrius and Calvísius, whom he had himself temporarily exiled, he now released from their penalty. Silána indeed had died a natural death at Taréntum, whither she had returned from her distant exile, when the power of Agrippína, to whose enmity she owed her fall, began to totter, or her wrath was at last appeased.

14.13 While Néro was lingering in the towns of Campánia, doubting how he should enter Rome, whether he would find the Senate submissive and the populace enthusiastic, all the vilest courtiers, and of these never had a court a more abundant crop, argued against his hesitation by assuring him that Agrippína's name was hated and that her death had heightened his popularity. "He might go without a fear," they said, "and experience in his person men's veneration for him." They insisted at the same time on preceding him. They found greater enthusiasm than they had promised, the tribes coming forth to meet him, the Senate in holiday attire, troops of their children and wives arranged according to sex and age, tiers of seats raised for the spectacle, where he was to pass, as a triumph is witnessed. Thus elated and exulting over his people's slavery, he proceeded to the Cápitol, performed the thanksgiving, and then plunged into all the excesses, which, though ill-restrained, some sort of respect for his mother had for a while delayed.

Tácitus, *Annals*, 14.3-14.13 (translated by Alfred John Church and William Jackson Brodribb)

Néro's Amusements

14.14 He had long had a fancy for driving a four-horse chariot, and a no less degrading taste for singing to the harp, in a theatrical fashion, when he was at dinner. This he would remind people was a royal custom, and had been the practice of ancient chiefs; it was celebrated too in the praises of poets and was meant to show honor to the gods. Songs indeed, he said, were sacred to Apóllo, and it was in the dress of a singer that that great and prophetic deity was seen in Róman temples as well as in Greek cities. He could no longer be restrained, when Séneca and Búrrus thought it best to concede one point that he might not persist in both. A space was enclosed in the Vátican valley where he might manage his horses, without the spectacle being public. Soon he actually invited all the people of Rome, who extolled him in their praises, like a mob which craves for amusements and rejoices when a prince draws them the same way.

However, the public exposure of his shame acted on him as an incentive instead of sickening him, as men expected. Imagining that he mitigated the scandal by disgracing many others, he brought on the stage descendants of noble families, who sold themselves because they were paupers. As they have ended their days, I think it due to their ancestors not to hand down their names. And indeed the infamy is his who gave them wealth to reward their degradation rather than to deter them from degrading themselves. He prevailed too on some well-known Róman knights, by immense presents, to offer their services in the amphitheater; only pay from one who is able to command, carries with it the force of compulsion.

14.15 Still, not yet wishing to disgrace himself on a public stage, he instituted some games under the title of "juvenile sports," for which people of every class gave in their names. Neither rank nor age nor previous high promotion hindered any one from practicing the art of a Greek or Látin actor and even stooping to gestures and songs unfit for a man. Noble ladies too actually played disgusting parts, and in the grove, with which Augústus had surrounded the lake for the naval fight, there were erected places for meeting and refreshment, and every incentive to excess was offered for sale. Money too was distributed, which the respectable had to spend under sheer compulsion and which the profligate gloried in squandering. Hence a rank growth of abominations and of all infamy. Never did a more filthy rabble add a worse licentiousness to our long corrupted morals.

Even, with virtuous training, purity is not easily upheld; far less amid rivalries in vice could modesty or propriety or any trace of good manners be preserved. Last of all, the emperor himself came on the stage, tuning his lute with elaborate care and trying his voice with his attendants. There were also present, to complete the show, a guard of soldiers with centúrions and tríbunes, and Búrrus, who grieved and yet applauded. Then it was that Róman knights were first enrolled under the title of Augustáni, men in their prime and remarkable for their strength, some, from a natural frivolity, others from the hope of promotion. Day and night they kept up a thunder of applause, and applied to the emperor's person and voice the epithets of deities. Thus they lived in fame and honor, as if on the strength of their merits.

14.16 Néro however, that he might not be known only for his accomplishments as an actor, also affected a taste for poetry, and drew round him persons who had some skill in such compositions, but not yet generally recognized. They used to sit with him, stringing together verses prepared at home, or extemporized on the spot, and fill up his own expressions, such as they were, just as he threw them off. This is plainly shown by the very character of the poems, which have no vigor or inspiration, or unity in their flow. He would also bestow some leisure after his banquets on the teachers of philosophy, for he enjoyed the wrangles of opposing dogmatists. And some there were who liked to exhibit their gloomy faces and looks, as one of the amusements of the court.

Tácitus, *Annals*, 14.14-14.16 (translated by Alfred John Church and William Jackson Brodribb)

Séneca Falls from Favor

14.51 But while the miseries of the State were daily growing worse, its supports were becoming weaker. Búrrus died, whether from illness or from poison was a question. It was supposed to be illness from the fact that from the gradual swelling of his throat inwardly and the closing up of the passage he ceased to breathe. Many positively asserted that by Néro's order his throat was smeared with some poisonous drug under the pretense of the application of a remedy, and that Búrrus, who saw through the crime, when the emperor paid him a visit, recoiled with horror from his gaze, and merely replied to his question, "I indeed am well." Rome felt for him a deep and lasting regret, because of the remembrance of his worth, because too of the merely passive virtue of one of his successors and the very flagrant iniquities of the other. For the emperor had appointed two men to the command of the prætorian cohorts, Fænius Rúfus, for a vulgar popularity, which he owed to his administration of the corn-supplies without profit to himself; and Sofónius Tigellínus, whose inveterate shamelessness and infamy were an attraction to him. As might have been expected from their known characters, Tigellínus had the greater influence with the prince, and was the associate of his most secret profligacy, while Rúfus enjoyed the favor of the people and of the soldiers, and this, he found, prejudiced him with Néro.

14.52 The death of Búrrus was a blow to Séneca's power, for virtue had not the same strength when one of its companions, so to say, was removed, and Néro too began to lean on worse advisers. They assailed Séneca with various charges, representing that he continued to increase a wealth which was already so vast as to be beyond the scale of a subject, and was drawing to himself the attachment of the citizens, while in the picturesqueness of his gardens and the magnificence of his country houses he almost surpassed the emperor. They further alleged against him that he claimed for himself alone the honors of eloquence, and composed poetry more assiduously, as soon as a passion for it had seized on Néro. "Openly inimical to the prince's amusements, he disparaged his ability in driving horses, and ridiculed his voice whenever he sang. When was there to be an end of nothing being publicly admired but what Séneca was thought to have originated? Surely Néro's boyhood was over, and he was all but in the prime of youthful manhood. He ought to shake off a tutor, furnished as he was with sufficiently noble instructors in his own ancestors."

14.53 Séneca, meanwhile, aware of these slanders, which were revealed to him by those who had some respect for merit, coupled with the fact that the emperor more and more shunned his intimacy, besought the opportunity of an interview. This was granted, and he spoke as follows: "It is fourteen years ago, Cæsar, that I was first associated with your prospects, and eight years since you have been emperor. In the interval, you have heaped on me such honors and riches that nothing is wanting to my happiness but a right use of it. I will refer to great examples taken not from my own but from your position. Your great-grandfather Augústus granted to Márcus Agríppa the calm repose of Mityléne, to Gáius Mæcénas what was nearly equivalent to a foreign retreat in the capital itself. One of these men shared his wars; the other struggled with many laborious duties at Rome; both received awards which were indeed splendid, but only proportioned to their great merits. For myself, what other recompense had I for your munificence, than a culture nursed, so to speak, in the shade of retirement, and to which a glory attaches itself, because I thus seem to have helped on the early training of your youth, an ample reward for the service. "You on the other hand have surrounded me with vast influence and boundless wealth, so that I often think within myself, Am I, who am but of an equestrian and provincial family, numbered among the chief men of Rome? Among nobles who can show a long succession of glories, has my new name become famous? Where is the mind once content with a humble lot? Is this the man who is building up his garden terraces, who paces grandly through these suburban parks, and revels in the affluence of such broad lands and such widely-spread investments? Only one apology occurs to me, that it would not have been right in me to have thwarted your bounty.

14.54 "And yet we have both filled up our respective measures, you in giving as much as a prince can bestow on a friend, and I in receiving as much as a friend can receive from a prince. All else only fosters envy, which, like all things human, sinks powerless beneath your greatness, though on me it weighs heavily. To me relief is a necessity. Just as I should implore support if exhausted by warfare or travel, so in this journey of life, old as I am and unequal even to the lightest cares, since I cannot any longer bear the burden of my wealth, I crave assistance. Order my property to be managed by your agents and to be included in your estate. Still I shall not sink myself into poverty, but having surrendered the splendors which dazzle me, I will henceforth again devote to my mind all the leisure and attention now reserved for my gardens and country houses. You have yet before you a vigorous prime, and that on which for so many years your eyes were fixed, supreme power. We, your older friends, can answer for our quiet behavior. It will likewise redound to your honor that you have raised to the highest places men who could also bear moderate fortune."

14.55 Néro's reply was substantially this: "My being able to meet your elaborate speech with an instant rejoinder is, I consider, primarily your gift, for you taught me how to express myself not only after reflection but at a moment's notice. My great-grandfather Augústus allowed Agríppa and Mæcénas to enjoy rest after their labors, but he did it at an age carrying with it an authority sufficient to justify any boon, of any sort, he might have bestowed. But neither of them did he strip of the rewards he had given. It was by war and its perils they had earned them; for in these the youth of Augústus was spent. And if I had passed my years in arms, your sword and right hand would not have failed me. But, as my actual condition required, you watched over my boyhood, then over my youth, with wisdom, counsel, and advice. And indeed your gifts to me will, as long as life holds out, be lasting possessions; those which you owe to me, your parks, investments, your country houses, are liable to accidents. Though they seem much, many far inferior to you in merit have obtained more. I am ashamed to quote the names of freedmen who parade a greater wealth. Hence I actually blush to think that, standing as you do first in my affections, you do not as yet surpass all in fortune.

14.56 "Yours too is a still vigorous manhood, quite equal to the labors of business and to the fruit of those labors; and, as for myself, I am but treading the threshold of empire. But perhaps you count yourself inferior to Vitéllius, thrice a cónsul, and me to Cláudius. Such wealth as long thrift has procured for Volúsius, my bounty, you think, cannot fully make up to you. Why not rather, if the frailty of my youth goes in any respect astray, call me back and guide yet more zealously with your help the manhood which you have instructed? It will not be your moderation, if you restore me your wealth, not your love of quiet, if you forsake your emperor, but my avarice, the fear of my cruelty, which will be in all men's mouths. Even if your self-control were praised to the utmost, still it would not be seemly in a wise man to get glory for himself in the very act of bringing disgrace on his friend." To these words the emperor added embraces and kisses; for he was formed by nature and trained by habit to veil his hatred under delusive flattery. Séneca thanked him, the usual end of an interview with a despot. But he entirely altered the practices of his former greatness; he kept the crowds of his visitors at a distance, avoided trains of followers, seldom appeared in Rome, as though weak health or philosophical studies detained him at home.

Tácitus, *Annals*, 14.51-14.56 (translated by Alfred John Church and William Jackson Brodribb)

The Great Fire of Rome

15.38 A disaster followed, whether accidental or treacherously contrived by the emperor, is uncertain, as authors have given both accounts, worse, however, and more dreadful than any which have ever happened to this city by the violence of fire. It had its beginning in that part of the círcus which adjoins the Pálatine and Cǽlian hills, where, amid the shops containing inflammable wares, the conflagration both broke out and instantly became so fierce and so rapid from the wind that it seized in its grasp the entire length of the círcus. For here there were no houses fenced in by solid masonry, or temples surrounded by walls, or any other obstacle to interpose delay. The blaze in its fury ran first through the level portions of the city, then rising to the hills, while it again devastated every place below them, it outstripped all preventive measures; so rapid was the mischief and so completely at its mercy the city, with those narrow winding passages and irregular streets, which characterized old Rome.

Added to this were the wailings of terror-stricken women, the feebleness of age, the helpless inexperience of childhood, the crowds who sought to save themselves or others, dragging out the infirm or waiting for them, and by their hurry in the one case, by their delay in the other, aggravating the confusion. Often, while they looked behind them, they were intercepted by flames on their side or in their face. Or if they reached a refuge close at hand, when this too was seized by the fire, they found that, even places, which they had imagined to be remote, were involved in the same calamity. At last, doubting what they should avoid or whither betake themselves, they crowded the streets or flung themselves down in the fields, while some who had lost their all, even their very daily bread, and others out of love for their kinsfolk, whom they had been unable to rescue, perished, though escape was open to them. And no one dared to stop the mischief, because of incessant menaces from a number of persons who forbade the extinguishing of the flames, because again others openly hurled brands, and kept shouting that there was one who gave them authority, either seeking to plunder more freely, or obeying orders.

15.39 Néro at this time was at Ántium, and did not return to Rome until the fire approached his house, which he had built to connect the palace with the gardens of Mæcénas. It could not, however, be stopped from devouring the palace, the house, and everything around it. However, to relieve the people, driven out homeless as they were, he threw open to them the Cámpus Mártius and the public buildings of Agríppa, and even his own gardens, and raised temporary structures to receive the destitute multitude. Supplies of food were brought up from Óstia and the neighboring towns, and the price of corn was reduced to three sésterces a peck. These acts, though popular, produced no effect, since a rumor had gone forth everywhere that, at the very time when the city was in flames, the emperor appeared on a private stage and sang of the destruction of Troy, comparing present misfortunes with the calamities of antiquity.

15.40 At last, after five days, an end was put to the conflagration at the foot of the Ésquiline hill, by the destruction of all buildings on a vast space, so that the violence of the fire was met by clear ground and an open sky. But before people had laid aside their fears, the flames returned, with no less fury this second time, and especially in the spacious districts of the city. Consequently, though there was less loss of life, the temples of the gods, and the porticoes which were devoted to enjoyment, fell in a yet more widespread ruin. And to this conflagration there attached the greater infamy because it broke out on the Æmílian property of Tigellínus, and it seemed that Néro was aiming at the glory of founding a new city and calling it by his name. Rome, indeed, is divided into fourteen districts, four of which remained uninjured, three were level to the ground, while in the other seven were left only a few shattered, half-burnt relics of houses.

15.41 It would not be easy to enter into a computation of the private mansions, the blocks of tenements, and of the temples, which were lost. Those with the oldest ceremonial, as that dedicated by Sérvius Túllius to Lúna, the great altar and shrine raised by the Arcádian Evánder to the visibly appearing Hércules, the temple of Júpiter the Stayer, which was vowed by Rómulus, Núma's royal palace, and the sanctuary of Vésta, with the tutelary deities of the Róman people, were burnt. So too were the riches acquired by our many victories, various beauties of Greek art, then again the ancient and genuine historical monuments of men of genius, and, notwithstanding the striking splendor of the restored city, old men will remember many things which could not be replaced. Some persons observed that the beginning of this conflagration was on the 19th of July, the day on which the Sénones captured and fired Rome. Others have pushed a curious inquiry so far as to reduce the interval between these two conflagrations into equal numbers of years, months, and days.

15.42 Néro meanwhile availed himself of his country's desolation, and erected a mansion in which the jewels and gold, long familiar objects, quite vulgarized by our extravagance, were not so marvelous as the fields and lakes, with woods on one side to resemble a wilderness, and, on the other, open spaces and extensive views. The directors and contrivers of the work were Sevérus and Céler, who had the genius and the audacity to attempt by art even what nature had refused, and to fool away an emperor's resources. They had actually undertaken to sink a navigable canal from the lake Avérnus to the mouths of the Tíber along a barren shore or through the face of hills, where one meets with no moisture which could supply water, except the Pómptine marshes. The rest of the country is broken rock and perfectly dry. Even if it could be cut through, the labor would be intolerable, and there would be no adequate result. Néro, however, with his love of the impossible, endeavored to dig through the nearest hills to Avérnus, and there still remain the traces of his disappointed hope.

15.43 Of Rome meanwhile, so much as was left unoccupied by his mansion, was not built up, as it had been after its burning by the Gauls, without any regularity or in any fashion, but with rows of streets according to measurement, with broad thoroughfares, with a restriction on the height of houses, with open spaces, and the further addition of colonnades, as a protection to the frontage of the blocks of tenements. These colonnades Néro promised to erect at his own expense, and to hand over the open spaces, when cleared of the debris, to the ground landlords. He also offered rewards proportioned to each person's position and property, and prescribed a period within which they were to obtain them on the completion of so many houses or blocks of building. He fixed on the marshes of Óstia for the reception of the rubbish, and arranged that the ships which had brought up corn by the Tíber, should sail down the river with cargoes of this rubbish. The buildings themselves, to a certain height, were to be solidly constructed, without wooden beams, of stone from Gábii or Álba, that material being impervious to fire. And to provide that the water which individual license had illegally appropriated, might flow in greater abundance in several places for the public use, officers were appointed, and everyone was to have in the open court the means of stopping a fire. Every building, too, was to be enclosed by its own proper wall, not by one common to others. These changes which were liked for their utility, also added beauty to the new city. Some, however, thought that its old arrangement had been more conducive to health, inasmuch as the narrow streets with the elevation of the roofs were not equally penetrated by the sun's heat, while now the open space, unsheltered by any shade, was scorched by a fiercer glow.

Tácitus, *Annals*, 15.38-15.43 (translated by Alfred John Church and William Jackson Brodribb)

Néro Blames the Great Fire on the Chrístians

15.44 Such indeed were the precautions of human wisdom. The next thing was to seek means of propitiating the gods, and recourse was had to the Síbylline books, by the direction of which prayers were offered to Vulcánus, Céres, and Prosérpina. Júno, too, was entreated by the matrons, first, in the Cápitol, then on the nearest part of the coast, whence water was procured to sprinkle the fane and image of the goddess. And there were sacred banquets and nightly vigils celebrated by married women. But all human efforts, all the lavish gifts of the emperor, and the propitiations of the gods, did not banish the sinister belief that the conflagratión was the result of an order.

Consequently, to get rid of the report, Néro fastened the guilt and inflicted the most exquisite tortures on a class hated for their abominations, called Chrístians by the populace. Chrístus, from whom the name had its origin, suffered the extreme penalty during the reign of Tibérius at the hands of one of our procurators, Póntius Pilátus, and a most mischievous superstition, thus checked for the moment, again broke out not only in Judǽa, the first source of the evil, but even in Rome, where all things hideous and shameful from every part of the world find their center and become popular. Accordingly, an arrest was first made of all who pleaded guilty; then, upon their information, an immense multitude was convicted, not so much of the crime of firing the city, as of hatred against mankind. Mockery of every sort was added to their deaths. Covered with the skins of beasts, they were torn by dogs and perished, or were nailed to crosses, or were doomed to the flames and burnt, to serve as a nightly illumination, when daylight had expired. Néro offered his gardens for the spectacle, and was exhibiting a show in the círcus, while he mingled with the people in the dress of a charioteer or stood aloft on a car. Hence, even for criminals who deserved extreme and exemplary punishment, there arose a feeling of compassion; for it was not, as it seemed, for the public good, but to glut one man's cruelty, that they were being destroyed.

15.45 Meanwhile Ítaly was thoroughly exhausted by contributions of money, the provinces were ruined, as also the allied nations and the free states, as they were called. Even the gods fell victims to the plunder; for the temples in Rome were despoiled and the gold carried off, which, for a triumph or a vow, the Róman people in every age had consecrated in their prosperity or their alarm. Throughout Ásia and Acháia not only votive gifts, but the images of deities were seized, Acrátus and Secúndus Carínas having been sent into those provinces. The first was a freedman ready for any wickedness; the latter, as far as speech went, was thoroughly trained in Greek learning, but he had not imbued his heart with sound principles. Séneca, it was said, to avert from himself the obloquy of sacrilege, begged for the seclusion of a remote rural retreat, and, when it was refused, feigning ill health, as though he had a nervous ailment, would not quit his chamber. According to some writers, poison was prepared for him at Néro's command by his own freedman, whose name was Cleónicus. This Séneca avoided through the freedman's disclosure, or his own apprehension, while he used to support life on the very simple diet of wild fruits, with water from a running stream when thirst prompted.

Tácitus, *Annals*, 15.44-15.45 (translated by Alfred John Church and William Jackson Brodribb)

The Death of Séneca

15.60 In quick succession Néro added the murder of Pláutius Lateránus, cónsul-elect, so promptly that he did not allow him to embrace his children or to have the brief choice of his own death. He was dragged off to a place set apart for the execution of slaves, and butchered by the hand of the tríbune Státius, maintaining a resolute silence, and not reproaching the tríbune with complicity in the plot. Then followed the destruction of Annǽus Séneca, a special joy to the emperor, not because he had convicted him of the conspiracy, but anxious to accomplish with the sword what poison had failed to do. It was, in fact, Natális alone who divulged Séneca's name, to this extent, that he had been sent to Séneca when ailing, to see him and remonstrate with him for excluding Píso from his presence, when it would have been better to have kept up their friendship by familiar intercourse; that Séneca's reply was that mutual conversations and frequent interviews were to the advantage of neither, but still that his own life depended on Píso's safety. Gávius Silvánus, tríbune of a prætórian cohort, was ordered to report this to Séneca and to ask him whether he acknowledged what Natális said and his own answer. Either by chance or purposely Séneca had returned on that day from Campánia, and had stopped at a country house four miles from Rome. Thither the tríbune came next evening, surrounded the house with troops of soldiers, and then made known the emperor's message to Séneca as he was at dinner with his wife, Pompéia Paulína, and two friends.

15.61 Séneca replied that Natális had been sent to him and had complained to him in Píso's name because of his refusal to see Píso, upon which he excused himself on the ground of failing health and the desire of rest. "He had no reason," he said, for "preferring the interest of any private citizen to his own safety, and he had no natural aptitude for flattery. No one knew this better than Néro, who had oftener experienced Séneca's free-spokenness than his servility." When the tríbune reported this answer in the presence of Poppæa and Tigellínus, the emperor's most confidential advisers in his moments of rage, he asked whether Séneca was meditating suicide. Upon this the tríbune asserted that he saw no signs of fear, and perceived no sadness in his words or in his looks. He was accordingly ordered to go back and to announce sentence of death. Fábius Rústicus tells us that he did not return the way he came, but went out of his course to Fænius, the commander of the guard, and having explained to him the emperor's orders, and asked whether he was to obey them, was by him admonished to carry them out, for a fatal spell of cowardice was on them all. For this very Silvánus was one of the conspirators, and he was now abetting the crimes which he had united with them to avenge. But he spared himself the anguish of a word or of a look, and merely sent in to Séneca one of his centúrions, who was to announce to him his last doom.

15.62 Séneca, quite unmoved, asked for tablets on which to inscribe his will, and, on the centúrion's refusal, turned to his friends, protesting that as he was forbidden to requite them, he bequeathed to them the only, but still the noblest possession yet remaining to him, the pattern of his life, which, if they remembered, they would win a name for moral worth and steadfast friendship. At the same time he called them back from their tears to manly resolution, now with friendly talk, and now with the sterner language of rebuke. "Where," he asked again and again, "are your maxims of philosophy, or the preparation of so many years' study against evils to come? Who knew not Néro's cruelty? After a mother's and a brother's murder, nothing remains but to add the destruction of a guardian and a tutor."

15.63 Having spoken these and like words, meant, so to say, for all, he embraced his wife; then softening awhile from the stern resolution of the hour, he begged and implored her to spare herself the burden of perpetual sorrow, and, in the contemplation of a life virtuously spent, to endure a husband's loss with honorable consolations. She declared, in answer, that she too had decided to die, and claimed for herself the blow of the executioner. There upon Séneca, not to thwart her noble ambition, from an affection too which would not leave behind him for insult one whom he dearly loved, replied: "I have shown you ways of smoothing life; you prefer the glory of dying. I will not grudge you such a noble example. Let the fortitude of so courageous an end be alike in both of us, but let there be more in your decease to win fame." Then by one and the same stroke they sundered with a dagger the arteries of their arms. Séneca, as his aged frame, attenuated by frugal diet, allowed the blood to escape but slowly, severed also the veins of his legs and knees. Worn out by cruel anguish, afraid too that his sufferings might break his wife's spirit, and that, as he looked on her tortures, he might himself sink into irresolution, he persuaded her to retire into another chamber. Even at the last moment his eloquence failed him not; he summoned his secretaries, and dictated much to them which, as it has been published for all readers in his own words, I forbear to paraphrase.

15.64 Néro meanwhile, having no personal hatred against Paulína and not wishing to heighten the odium of his cruelty, forbade her death. At the soldiers' prompting, her slaves and freedmen bound up her arms, and stanched the bleeding, whether with her knowledge is doubtful. For as the vulgar are ever ready to think the worst, there were persons who believed that, as long as she dreaded Néro's relentlessness, she sought the glory of sharing her husband's death, but that after a time, when a more soothing prospect presented itself, she yielded to the charms of life. To this she added a few subsequent years, with a most praiseworthy remembrance of her husband, and with a countenance and frame white to a degree of pallor which denoted a loss of much vital energy. Séneca meantime, as the tedious process of death still lingered on, begged Státius Annæus, whom he had long esteemed for his faithful friendship and medical skill, to produce a poison with which he had some time before provided himself, same drug which extinguished the life of those who were condemned by a public sentence of the people of Áthens. It was brought to him and he drank it in vain, chilled as he was throughout his limbs, and his frame closed against the efficacy of the poison. At last he entered a pool of heated water, from which he sprinkled the nearest of his slaves, adding the exclamation, "I offer this liquid as a libation to Júpiter the Deliverer." He was then carried into a bath, with the steam of which he was suffocated, and he was burnt without the usual funeral rites. So he had directed in a codicil of his will, when even in the height of his wealth and power he was thinking of his life's close.

Tácitus, *Annals*, 15.60-64 (translated by Alfred John Church and William Jackson Brodribb)

The Death of Petrónius

16.18 With regard to Gáius Petrónius, I ought to dwell a little on his antecedents. His days he passed in sleep, his nights in the business and pleasures of life. Indolence had raised him to fame, as energy raises others, and he was reckoned not a debauchee and spendthrift, like most of those who squander their substance, but a man of refined luxury. And indeed his talk and his doings, the freer they were and the more show of carelessness they exhibited, were the better liked, for their look of natural simplicity. Yet as proconsul of Bithýnia and soon afterwards as consul, he showed himself a man of vigor and equal to business. Then falling back into vice or affecting vice, he was chosen by Néro to be one of his few intimate associates, as a critic in matters of taste, while the emperor thought nothing charming or elegant in luxury unless Petrónius had expressed to him his approval of it. Hence jealousy on the part of Tigellínus, who looked on him as a rival and even his superior in the science of pleasure. And so he worked on the prince's cruelty, which dominated every other passion, charging Petrónius with having been the friend of Scævínus, bribing a slave to become informer, robbing him of the means of defense, and hurrying into prison the greater part of his domestics.

16.19 It happened at the time that the emperor was on his way Campánia and that Petrónius, after going as far as Cúmæ, was there detained. He bore no longer the suspense of fear or of hope. Yet he did not fling away life with precipitate haste, but having made an incision in his veins and then, according to his humor, bound them up, he again opened them, while he conversed with his friends, not in a serious strain or on topics that might win for him the glory of courage. And he listened to them as they repeated, not thoughts on the immortality of the soul or on the theories of philosophers, but light poetry and playful verses. To some of his slaves he gave liberal presents, a flogging to others. He dined, indulged himself in sleep, that death, though forced on him, might have a natural appearance. Even in his will he did not, as did many in their last moments, flatter Néro or Tigellínus or any other of the men in power. On the contrary, he described fully the prince's shameful excesses... Then he broke his signet-ring, that it might not be subsequently available for imperiling others.

Tácitus, *Annals*, 16.18-19 (translated by Alfred John Church and William Jackson Brodribb)

The Suicide of Néro

49 At last, while his companions one and all urged him to save himself as soon as possible from the indignities that threatened him, he bade them dig a grave in his presence, proportioned to the size of his own person, and at the same time bring water and wood for presently disposing of his body. As each of these things was done, he wept and said again and again: "What an artist the world is losing!"

While he hesitated, a letter was brought to Pháon by one of his couriers. Néro snatching it from his hand read that he had been pronounced a public enemy by the senate, and that they were seeking him to punish in the ancient fashion; and he asked what manner of punishment that was. When he learned that the criminal was stripped, fastened by the neck in a fork and then beaten to death with rods, in mortal terror he seized two daggers which he had brought with him, and then, after trying the point of each, put them up again, pleading that the fatal hour had not yet come. Now he would beg Spórus to begin to lament and wail, and now entreat someone to help him take his life by setting him the example; anon he reproached himself for his cowardice in such words as these: "To live is a scandal and a shame—this does not become Néro, does not become him—one should be resolute at such times—come, rouse thyself!" And now the horsemen were at hand who had orders to take him off alive. When he heard them, he quavered: "Hark, now strikes on my ear the trampling of swift-footed coursers!" and drove a dagger into his throat, aided by Epaphrodítus, his private secretary. He was all but dead when a centúrion rushed in, and as he placed a cloak to the wound, pretending that he had come to aid him, Néro merely gasped: "Too late!" and "This is fidelity!" With these words he was gone, with eyes so set and starting from their sockets that all who saw him shuddered with horror. First and beyond all else he had forced from his companions a promise to let no one have his head, but to contrive in some way that he be buried unmutilated. And this was granted by Icélus, Gálba's freedman, who had shortly before been released from the bondage to which he was consigned at the beginning of the revolt.

Suetónius, Lives of the Twelve Cæsars, Néro 49 (translated by J. C. Rolfe)

CHAPTER XXV

THE FLÁVIAN EMPERORS: VESPÁSIAN TO DOMÍTIAN

The Disputed Succession, I.—The Reign of Vespásian (A.D. 69-79), II.—The Reign of Títus (A.D. 79-81), III. Life and Manners of the Rómans, IV.—The Reign of Domítian (A.D. 81-96), V.

The Accession of Gálba

Iphícrates the Athénian used to say that it is best to have a mercenary soldier fond of money and of pleasures, for thus he will fight the more boldly, to procure the means to gratify his desires. But most have been of opinion, that the body of an army, as well as the natural one, when in its healthy condition, should make no efforts apart, but in compliance with its head. Wherefore they tell us that Æmílius Páullus, on taking command of the forces in Macedónia, and finding them talkative and impertinently busy, as though they were all commanders, issued out his orders that they should have only ready hands and keen swords, and leave the rest to him. And Pláto, who can discern no use of a good ruler or general, if his men are not on their part obedient and conformable (the virtue of obeying, as of ruling, being in his opinion one that does not exist without first a noble nature, and then a philosophic education, where the eager and active powers are allayed with the gentler and humaner sentiments), may claim in confirmation of his doctrines sundry mournful instances elsewhere, and, in particular, the events that followed among the Rómans upon the death of Néro, in which plain proofs were given that nothing is more terrible than a military force moving about in an empire upon uninstructed and unreasoning impulses. Demádes, after the death of Alexánder, compared the Macedónian army to the Cýclops after his eye was out, seeing their many disorderly and unsteady motions. But the calamities of the Róman government might be likened to the motions of the giants that assailed heaven, convulsed as it was, and distracted, and from every side recoiling, as it were, upon itself, not so much by the ambition of those who were proclaimed emperors, as by the covetousness and license of the soldiery, who drove commander after commander out, like nails one upon another.

For, as already related, Nymphídius Sabínus, captain of the guards, together with Tigellínus, after Néro's circumstances were now desperate, and it was perceived that he designed to fly into Égypt, persuaded the troops to declare Gálba emperor, as if Néro had been already gone, promising to all the court and prætórian soldiers, as they are called, seven thousand five hundred dráchmas apiece, and to those in service abroad twelve hundred and fifty dráchmas each; so vast a sum for a largess as it was impossible any one could raise, but he must be infinitely more exacting and oppressive than ever Néro was. This quickly brought Néro to his grave, and soon after Gálba too; they murdered the first in expectation of the promised gift, and not long after the other because they did not obtain it from him; and then, seeking about to find some one who would purchase at such a rate, they consumed themselves in a succession of treacheries and rebellions before they obtained their demands. But to give a particular relation of all that passed would require a history in full form; I have only to notice what is properly to my purpose, namely, what the Cǽsars did and suffered.

Sulpícius Gálba is owned by all to have been the richest private person that ever came to the imperial seat. And besides the additional honor of being of the family of the Sérvii, he valued himself more especially for his relationship to Cátulus, the most eminent citizen of his time both for virtue and renown, however he may have voluntarily yielded to others as regards power and authority. Gálba was also a kin to Lívia, the wife of Augústus, by whose interest he was preferred to the cónsulship by the emperor. It is said of him that he commanded the troops well in Gérmany, and, being made procónsul in Líbya, gained a reputation that few ever had. But his quiet manner of living and his sparingness in expenses and his disregard of appearance gave him, when he became emperor, an ill-name for meanness, being, in fact, his worn-out credit for regularity and moderation.

Plútarch, Life of Gálba (translated by John Dryden)

The Character of Vespásian

12 In other matters he was unassuming and lenient from the very beginning of his reign until its end, never trying to conceal his former lowly condition, but often even parading it. Indeed, when certain men tried to trace the origin of the Flávian family to the founders of Reate and a companion of Hércules whose tomb still stands on the Vía Salária, he laughed at them for their pains. So far was he from a desire for pomp and show, that on the day of his triumph, he did not hesitate to say: "It serves me right for being such a fool as to want a triumph in my old age, as if it were due to my ancestors or had ever been among my own ambitions." He did not even assume the tribunícian power at once nor the title of Father of his Country until late. As for the custom of searching those who came to pay their morning calls, he gave that up before the civil war was over.

13 He bore the frank language of his friends, the quips of pleaders, and the impudence of the philosophers with the greatest patience. Though Licínius Muciánus, a man of notorious unchastity, presumed upon his services to treat Vespásian with scant respect, he never had the heart to criticize him except privately... When Sálvius Liberális ventured to say while defending a rich client, "What is it to Cǽsar if Hippárchus had a hundred millions," he personally commended him. When the Cýnic Demétrius met him abroad after being condemned to banishment, and without deigning to rise in his presence or to salute him, even snarled out some insult, he merely called him "cur."

14 He was not inclined to remember or to avenge affronts or enmities, but made a brilliant match for the daughter of his enemy Vitéllius, and even provided her with a dowry and a house-keeping outfit. When he was in terror at being forbidden Néro's court, and asked what on earth he was to do or where he was to go, one of the ushers put him out and told him to "go to Morbóvia"; but when the man later begged for forgiveness, Vespásian confined his resentment to words, and those of about the same number and purport. Indeed, so far was he from being led by any suspicion or fear to cause anyone's death, that when his friends warned him that he must keep an eye on Méttius Pompusiánus, since it was commonly believed that he had an imperial horoscope, he even made him cónsul, guaranteeing that he would one day be mindful of the favor.

Suetónius, Lives of the Twelve Cǽsars, Vespásian 12-14 (translated by J. C. Rolfe)

Póntius Pílate and Jésus Christ

18.3.1 But now Pílate, the procurator of Judéa, removed the army from Cǽsaréa to Jerúsalem, to take their winter quarters there, in order to abolish the Jéwish laws. So he introduced Cǽsar's effigies, which were upon the ensigns, and brought them into the city; whereas our law forbids us the very making of images; on which account the former procurators were wont to make their entry into the city with such ensigns as had not those ornaments. Pílate was the first who brought those images to Jerúsalem, and set them up there; which was done without the knowledge of the people, because it was done in the night time; but as soon as they knew it, they came in multitudes to Cǽsaréa, and interceded with Pílate many days that he would remove the images; and when he would not grant their requests, because it would tend to the injury of Cǽsar, while yet they persevered in their request, on the sixth day he ordered his soldiers to have their weapons privately, while he came and sat upon his judgment-seat, which seat was so prepared in the open place of the city, that it concealed the army that lay ready to oppress them; and when the Jews petitioned him again, he gave a signal to the soldiers to encompass them routed, and threatened that their punishment should be no less than immediate death, unless they would leave off disturbing him,

145

and go their ways home. But they threw themselves upon the ground, and laid their necks bare, and said they would take their death very willingly, rather than the wisdom of their laws should be transgressed; upon which Pílate was deeply affected with their firm resolution to keep their laws inviolable, and presently commanded the images to be carried back from Jerúsalem to Cæsaréa.

18.3.2 But Pílate undertook to bring a current of water to Jerúsalem, and did it with the sacred money, and derived the origin of the stream from the distance of two hundred furlongs. However, the Jews were not pleased with what had been done about this water; and many ten thousands of the people got together, and made a clamor against him, and insisted that he should leave off that design. Some of them also used reproaches, and abused the man, as crowds of such people usually do. So he habited a great number of his soldiers in their habit, who carried daggers under their garments, and sent them to a place where they might surround them. So he bid the Jews himself go away; but they boldly casting reproaches upon him, he gave the soldiers that signal which had been beforehand agreed on; who laid upon them much greater blows than Pílate had commanded them, and equally punished those that were tumultuous, and those that were not; nor did they spare them in the least: and since the people were unarmed, and were caught by men prepared for what they were about, there were a great number of them slain by this means, and others of them ran away wounded. And thus an end was put to this sedition.

18.3.3 Now there was about this time Jésus, a wise man, if it be lawful to call him a man; for he was a doer of wonderful works, a teacher of such men as receive the truth with pleasure. He drew over to him both many of the Jews and many of the Géntiles. He was [the] Christ. And when Pílate, at the suggestion of the principal men amongst us, had condemned him to the cross, those that loved him at the first did not forsake him; for he appeared to them alive again the third day; as the divine prophets had foretold these and ten thousand other wonderful things concerning him. And the tribe of Chrístians, so named from him, are not extinct at this day.

Joséphus, *Antiquities of the Jews, 18.3.1-18.3.3 (translated by William Whiston)*

A Description of the Temple in Jerúsalem

5.5.1 Now this temple, as I have already said, was built upon a strong hill. At first the plain at the top was hardly sufficient for the holy house and the altar, for the ground about it was very uneven, and like a precipice; but when king Sólomon, who was the person that built the temple, had built a wall to it on its east side, there was then added one cloister founded on a bank cast up for it, and on the other parts the holy house stood naked. But in future ages the people added new banks, and the hill became a larger plain. They then broke down the wall on the north side, and took in as much as sufficed afterward for the compass of the entire temple. And when they had built walls on three sides of the temple round about, from the bottom of the hill, and had performed a work that was greater than could be hoped for, (in which work long ages were spent by them, as well as all their sacred treasures were exhausted, which were still replenished by those tributes which were sent to God from the whole habitable earth,) they then encompassed their upper courts with cloisters, as well as they [afterward] did the lowest [court of the] temple.

The lowest part of this was erected to the height of three hundred cubits, and in some places more; yet did not the entire depth of the foundations appear, for they brought earth, and filled up the valleys, as being desirous to make them on a level with the narrow streets of the city; wherein they made use of stones of forty cubits in magnitude; for the great plenty of money they then had, and the liberality of the people, made this attempt of theirs to succeed to an incredible degree; and what could not be so much as hoped for as ever to be accomplished, was, by perseverance and length of time, brought to perfection.

5.5.2 Now for the works that were above these foundations, these were not unworthy of such foundations; for all the cloisters were double, and the pillars to them belonging were twenty-five cubits in height, and supported the cloisters. These pillars were of one entire stone each of them, and that stone was white marble; and the roofs were adorned with cedar, curiously graven. The natural magnificence, and excellent polish, and the harmony of the joints in these cloisters, afforded a prospect that was very remarkable; nor was it on the outside adorned with any work of the painter or engraver. The cloisters [of the outmost court] were in breadth thirty cubits, while the entire compass of it was by measure six furlongs, including the tower of Antónia; those entire courts that were exposed to the air were laid with stones of all sorts. When you go through these [first] cloisters, unto the second [court of the] temple, there was a partition made of stone all round, whose height was three cubits: its construction was very elegant; upon it stood pillars, at equal distances from one another, declaring the law of purity, some in Greek, and some in Róman letters, that "no foreigner should go within that sanctuary" for that second [court of the] temple was called "the Sanctuary," and was ascended to by fourteen steps from the first court.

This court was four-square, and had a wall about it peculiar to itself; the height of its buildings, although it were on the outside forty cubits, was hidden by the steps, and on the inside that height was but twenty-five cubits; for it being built over against a higher part of the hill with steps, it was no further to be entirely discerned within, being covered by the hill itself. Beyond these thirteen steps there was the distance of ten cubits; this was all plain; whence there were other steps, each of five cubits a-piece, that led to the gates, which gates on the north and south sides were eight, on each of those sides four, and of necessity two on the east. For since there was a partition built for the women on that side, as the proper place wherein they were to worship, there was a necessity for a second gate for them: this gate was cut out of its wall, over against the first gate. There was also on the other sides one southern and one northern gate, through which was a passage into the court of the women; for as to the other gates, the women were not allowed to pass through them; nor when they went through their own gate could they go beyond their own wall. This place was allotted to the women of our own country, and of other countries, provided they were of the same nation, and that equally. The western part of this court had no gate at all, but the wall was built entire on that side. But then the cloisters which were betwixt the gates extended from the wall inward, before the chambers; for they were supported by very fine and large pillars. These cloisters were single, and, excepting their magnitude, were no way inferior to those of the lower court.

5.5.3 Now nine of these gates were on every side covered over with gold and silver, as were the jambs of their doors and their lintels; but there was one gate that was without the [inward court of the holy house, which was of Corínthian brass, and greatly excelled those that were only covered over with silver and gold. Each gate had two doors, whose height was severally thirty cubits, and their breadth fifteen. However, they had large spaces within of thirty cubits, and had on each side rooms, and those, both in breadth and in length, built like towers, and their height was above forty cubits. Two pillars did also support these rooms, and were in circumference twelve cubits. Now the magnitudes of the other gates were equal one to another; but that over the Corínthian gate, which opened on the east over against the gate of the holy house itself, was much larger; for its height was fifty cubits; and its doors were forty cubits; and it was adorned after a most costly manner, as having much richer and thicker plates of silver and gold upon them than the other. These nine gates had that silver and gold poured upon them by Alexánder, the father of Tibérius. Now there were fifteen steps, which led away from the wall of the court of the women to this greater gate; whereas those that led thither from the other gates were five steps shorter.

5.5.4 As to the holy house itself, which was placed in the midst [of the inmost court], that most sacred part of the temple, it was ascended to by twelve steps; and in front its height and its breadth were equal, and each a hundred cubits, though it was behind forty cubits narrower; for on its front it had what may be styled shoulders on each side, that passed twenty cubits further. Its first gate was seventy cubits high, and twenty-five cubits broad; but this gate had no doors; for it represented the universal visibility of heaven, and that it cannot be excluded from any place. Its front was covered with gold all over, and through it the first part of the house, that was more inward, did all of it appear; which, as it was very large, so did all the parts about the more inward gate appear to shine to those that saw them; but then, as the entire house was divided into two parts within, it was only the first part of it that was open to our view. Its height extended all along to ninety cubits in height, and its length was fifty cubits, and its breadth twenty.

But that gate which was at this end of the first part of the house was, as we have already observed, all over covered with gold, as was its whole wall about it; it had also golden vines above it, from which clusters of grapes hung as tall as a man's height. But then this house, as it was divided into two parts, the inner part was lower than the appearance of the outer, and had golden doors of fifty-five cubits altitude, and sixteen in breadth; but before these doors there was a veil of equal largeness with the doors. It was a Babylónian curtain, embroidered with blue, and fine linen, and scarlet, and purple, and of a contexture that was truly wonderful. Nor was this mixture of colors without its mystical interpretation, but was a kind of image of the universe; for by the scarlet there seemed to be enigmatically signified fire, by the fine flax the earth, by the blue the air, and by the purple the sea; two of them having their colors the foundation of this resemblance; but the fine flax and the purple have their own origin for that foundation, the earth producing the one, and the sea the other. This curtain had also embroidered upon it all that was mystical in the heavens, excepting that of the [twelve] signs, representing living creatures.

5.5.5 When any persons entered into the temple, its floor received them. This part of the temple therefore was in height sixty cubits, and its length the same; whereas its breadth was but twenty cubits: but still that sixty cubits in length was divided again, and the first part of it was cut off at forty cubits, and had in it three things that were very wonderful and famous among all mankind, the candlestick, the table [of show-bread], and the altar of incense. Now the seven lamps signified the seven planets; for so many there were springing out of the candlestick. Now the twelve loaves that were upon the table signified the circle of the zodiac and the year; but the altar of incense, by its thirteen kinds of sweet-smelling spices with which the sea replenished it, signified that God is the possessor of all things that are both in the uninhabitable and habitable parts of the earth, and that they are all to be dedicated to his use.

But the inmost part of the temple of all was of twenty cubits. This was also separated from the outer part by a veil. In this there was nothing at all. It was inaccessible and inviolable, and not to be seen by any; and was called the Holy of Holies. Now, about the sides of the lower part of the temple, there were little houses, with passages out of one into another; there were a great many of them, and they were of three stories high; there were also entrances on each side into them from the gate of the temple. But the superior part of the temple had no such little houses any further, because the temple was there narrower, and forty cubits higher, and of a smaller body than the lower parts of it. Thus we collect that the whole height, including the sixty cubits from the floor, amounted to a hundred cubits.

5.5.6 Now the outward face of the temple in its front wanted nothing that was likely to surprise either men's minds or their eyes; for it was covered all over with plates of gold of great weight, and, at the first rising of the sun, reflected back a very fiery splendor, and made those who forced themselves to look upon it to turn their eyes away, just as they would have done at the sun's own rays. But this temple appeared to strangers, when they were coming to it at a distance, like a mountain covered with snow; for as to those parts of it that were not gilt, they were exceeding white. On its top it had spikes with sharp points, to prevent any pollution of it by birds sitting upon it. Of its stones, some of them were forty-five cubits in length, five in height, and six in breadth.

Before this temple stood the altar, fifteen cubits high, and equal both in length and breadth; each of which dimensions was fifty cubits. The figure it was built in was a square, and it had corners like horns; and the passage up to it was by an insensible acclivity. It was formed without any iron tool, nor did any such iron tool so much as touch it at any time. There was also a wall of partition, about a cubit in height, made of fine stones, and so as to be grateful to the sight; this encompassed the holy house and the altar, and kept the people that were on the outside off from the priests. Moreover, those that had ... the leprosy were excluded out of the city entirely; women also, when their courses were upon them, were shut out of the temple; nor when they were free from that impurity, were they allowed to go beyond the limit before-mentioned; men also, that were not thoroughly pure, were prohibited to come into the inner [court of the] temple; nay, the priests themselves that were not pure were prohibited to come into it also.

5.5.7 Now all those of the stock of the priests that could not minister by reason of some defect in their bodies, came within the partition, together with those that had no such imperfection, and had their share with them by reason of their stock, but still made use of none except their own private garments; for nobody but he that officiated had on his sacred garments; but then those priests that were without any blemish upon them went up to the altar clothed in fine linen. They abstained chiefly from wine, out of this fear, lest otherwise they should transgress some rules of their ministration. The high priest did also go up with them; not always indeed, but on the seventh days and new moons, and if any festivals belonging to our nation, which we celebrate every year, happened. When he officiated, he had on a pair of breeches that reached beneath his privy parts to his thighs, and had on an inner garment of linen, together with a blue garment, round, without seam, with fringe work, and reaching to the feet. There were also golden bells that hung upon the fringes, and pomegranates intermixed among them. The bells signified thunder, and the pomegranates lightning. But that girdle that tied the garment to the breast was embroidered with five rows of various colors, of gold, and purple, and scarlet, as also of fine linen and blue, with which colors we told you before the veils of the temple were embroidered also.

The like embroidery was upon the ephod; but the quantity of gold therein was greater. Its figure was that of a stomacher for the breast. There were upon it two golden buttons like small shields, which buttoned the ephod to the garment; in these buttons were enclosed two very large and very excellent sardonyxes, having the names of the tribes of that nation engraved upon them: on the other part there hung twelve stones, three in a row one way, and four in the other; a sardius, a topaz, and an emerald; a carbuncle, a jasper, and a sapphire; an agate, an amethyst, and a ligure; an onyx, a beryl, and a chrysolite; upon every one of which was again engraved one of the aforementioned names of the tribes. A miter also of fine linen encompassed his head, which was tied by a blue ribbon, about which there was another golden crown, in which was engraved the sacred name [of God]: it consists of four vowels. However, the high priest did not wear these garments at other times, but a more plain habit; he only did it when he went into the most sacred part of the temple, which he did but once in a year, on that day when our custom is for all of us to keep a fast to God. And thus much concerning the city and the temple; but for the customs and laws hereto relating, we shall speak more accurately another time; for there remain a great many things thereto relating which have not been here touched upon.

5.5.8 Now as to the tower of Antónia, it was situated at the corner of two cloisters of the court of the temple; of that on the west, and that on the north; it was erected upon a rock of fifty cubits in height, and was on a great precipice; it was the work of king Hérod, wherein he demonstrated his natural magnanimity. In the first place, the rock itself was covered over with smooth pieces of stone, from its foundation, both for ornament, and that any one who would either try to get up or to go down it might not be able to hold his feet upon it. Next to this, and before you come to the edifice of the tower itself, there was a wall three cubits high; but within that wall all the space of the tower of Antónia itself was built upon, to the height of forty cubits. The inward parts had the largeness and form of a palace, it being parted into all kinds of rooms and other conveniences, such as courts, and places for bathing, and broad spaces for camps; insomuch that, by having all conveniences that cities wanted, it might seem to be composed of several cities, but by its magnificence it seemed a palace.

And as the entire structure resembled that of a tower, it contained also four other distinct towers at its four corners; whereof the others were but fifty cubits high; whereas that which lay upon the southeast corner was seventy cubits high, that from thence the whole temple might be viewed; but on the corner where it joined to the two cloisters of the temple, it had passages down to them both, through which the guard (for there always lay in this tower a Róman légion) went several ways among the cloisters, with their arms, on the Jéwish festivals, in order to watch the people, that they might not there attempt to make any innovations; for the temple was a fortress that guarded the city, as was the tower of Antónia a guard to the temple; and in that tower were the guards of those three. There was also a peculiar fortress belonging to the upper city, which was Hérod's palace; but for the hill Bézetha, it was divided from the tower Antónia, as we have already told you; and as that hill on which the tower of Antónia stood was the highest of these three, so did it adjoin to the new city, and was the only place that hindered the sight of the temple on the north. And this shall suffice at present to have spoken about the city and the walls about it, because I have proposed to myself to make a more accurate description of it elsewhere.

Joséphus, The Wars of the Jews, 5.5.1-5.5.8 (translated by William Whiston)

The Horrors of Famine During the Siege

5.6.1 As Joséphus was speaking thus with a loud voice, the seditious would neither yield to what he said, nor did they deem it safe for them to alter their conduct; but as for the people, they had a great inclination to desert to the Rómans; accordingly, some of them sold what they had, and even the most precious things that had been laid up as treasures by them, for every small matter, and swallowed down pieces of gold, that they might not be found out by the robbers... for Títus let a great number of them go away into the country, whither they pleased. And the main reasons why they were so ready to desert were these: That now they should be freed from those miseries which they had endured in that city, and yet should not be in slavery to the Rómans: however, John and Símon, with their factions, did more carefully watch these men's going out than they did the coming in of the Rómans; and if any one did but afford the least shadow of suspicion of such an intention, his throat was cut immediately.

5.6.2 But as for the richer sort, it proved all one to them whether they stayed in the city, or attempted to get out of it; for they were equally destroyed in both cases; for every such person was put to death under this pretense, that they were going to desert, but in reality that the robbers might get what they had. The madness of the seditious did also increase together with their famine, and both those miseries were every day inflamed more and more; for there was no corn which anywhere appeared publicly, but the robbers came running into, and searched men's private houses; and then, if they found any, they tormented them, because they had denied they had any; and if they found none, they tormented them worse, because they supposed they had more carefully concealed it. The indication they made use of whether they had any or not was taken from the bodies of these miserable wretches; which, if they were in good case, they supposed they were in no want at all of food; but if they were wasted away, they walked off without searching any further; nor did they think it proper to kill such as these, because they saw they would very soon die of themselves for want of food. Many there were indeed who sold what they had for one measure; it was of wheat, if they were of the richer sort; but of barley, if they were poorer. When these had so done, they shut themselves up in the inmost rooms of their houses, and ate the corn they had gotten; some did it without grinding it, by reason of the extremity of the want they were in, and others baked bread of it, according as necessity and fear dictated to them: a table was nowhere laid for a distinct meal, but they snatched the bread out of the fire, half-baked, and ate it very hastily.

5.6.3 It was now a miserable case, and a sight that would justly bring tears into our eyes, how men stood as to their food, while the more powerful had more than enough, and the weaker were lamenting [for want of it.] But the famine was too hard for all other passions, and it is destructive to nothing so much as to modesty; for what was otherwise worthy of reverence was in this case despised; insomuch that children pulled the very morsels that their fathers were eating out of their very mouths, and what was still more to be pitied, so did the mothers do as to their infants; and when those that were most dear were perishing under their hands, they were not ashamed to take from them the very last drops that might preserve their lives: and while they ate after this manner, yet were they not concealed in so doing; but the seditious everywhere came upon them immediately, and snatched away from them what they had gotten from others; for when they saw any house shut up, this was to them a signal that the people within had gotten some food; whereupon they broke open the doors, and ran in, and took pieces of what they were eating almost up out of their very throats, and this by force: the old men, who held their food fast, were beaten; and if the women hid what they had within their hands, their hair was torn for so doing; nor was there any commiseration shown either to the aged or to the infants, but they lifted up children from the ground as they hung upon the morsels they had gotten, and shook them down upon the floor.

But still they were more barbarously cruel to those that had prevented their coming in, and had actually swallowed down what they were going to seize upon, as if they had been unjustly defrauded of their right. They also invented terrible methods of torments to discover where any food was, and they were these to stop up the passages of the privy parts of the miserable wretches, and to drive sharp stakes up their fundaments; and a man was forced to bear what it is terrible even to hear, in order to make him confess that he had but one loaf of bread, or that he might discover a handful of barley-meal that was concealed; and this was done when these tormentors were not themselves hungry; for the thing had been less barbarous had necessity forced them to it; but this was done to keep their madness in exercise, and as making preparation of provisions for themselves for the following days. These men went also to meet those that had crept out of the city by night, as far as the Róman guards, to gather some plants and herbs that grew wild; and when those people thought they had got clear of the enemy, they snatched from them what they had brought with them, even while they had frequently entreated them, and that by calling upon the tremendous name of God, to give them back some part of what they had brought; though these would not give them the least crumb, and they were to be well contented that they were only spoiled, and not slain at the same time.

5.6.4 These were the afflictions which the lower sort of people suffered from these tyrants' guards; but for the men that were in dignity, and withal were rich, they were carried before the tyrants themselves; some of whom were falsely accused of laying treacherous plots, and so were destroyed; others of them were charged with designs of betraying the city to the Rómans; but the readiest way of all was this, to suborn somebody to affirm that they were resolved to desert to the enemy. And he who was utterly despoiled of what he had by Símon was sent back again to John, as of those who had been already plundered by John, Símon got what remained; insomuch that they drank the blood of the populace to one another, and divided the dead bodies of the poor creatures between them; so that although, on account of their ambition after dominion, they contended with each other, yet did they very well agree in their wicked practices; for he that did not communicate what he got by the miseries of others to the other tyrant seemed to be too little guilty, and in one respect only; and he that did not partake of what was so communicated to him grieved at this, as at the loss of what was a valuable thing, that he had no share in such barbarity.

5.6.5 It is therefore impossible to go distinctly over every instance of these men's iniquity. I shall therefore speak my mind here at once briefly: That neither did any other city ever suffer such miseries, nor did any age ever breed a generation more fruitful in wickedness than this was, from the beginning of the world. Finally, they brought the Hébrew nation into contempt, that they might themselves appear comparatively less impious with regard to strangers. They confessed what was true, that they were the slaves, the scum, and the spurious and abortive offspring of our nation, while they overthrew the city themselves, and forced the Rómans, whether they would or no, to gain a melancholy reputation, by acting gloriously against them, and did almost draw that fire upon the temple, which they seemed to think came too slowly; and indeed when they saw that temple burning from the upper city, they were neither troubled at it, nor did they shed any tears on that account, while yet these passions were discovered among the Rómans themselves; which circumstances we shall speak of hereafter in their proper place, when we come to treat of such matters.

Joséphus, *The Wars of the Jews*, 5.6.1-5.6.5 (translated by William Whiston)

The Torture of Those Caught by the Rómans

5.11.1 So now Títus's banks were advanced a great way, notwithstanding his soldiers had been very much distressed from the wall. He then sent a party of horsemen, and ordered they should lay ambushes for those that went out into the valleys to gather food. Some of these were indeed fighting men, who were not contented with what they got by rapine; but the greater part of them were poor people, who were deterred from deserting by the concern they were under for their own relations; for they could not hope to escape away, together with their wives and children, without the knowledge of the seditious; nor could they think of leaving these relations to be slain by the robbers on their account; nay, the severity of the famine made them bold in thus going out; so nothing remained but that, when they were concealed from the robbers, they should be taken by the enemy; and when they were going to be taken, they were forced to defend themselves for fear of being punished; as after they had fought, they thought it too late to make any supplications for mercy; so they were first whipped, and then tormented with all sorts of tortures, before they died, and were then crucified before the wall of the city.

This miserable procedure made Títus greatly to pity them, while they caught every day five hundred Jews; nay, some days they caught more: yet it did not appear to be safe for him to let those that were taken by force go their way, and to set a guard over so many he saw would be to make such as great deal them useless to him. The main reason why he did not forbid that cruelty was this, that he hoped the Jews might perhaps yield at that sight, out of fear lest they might themselves afterwards be liable to the same cruel treatment. So the soldiers, out of the wrath and hatred they bore the Jews, nailed those they caught, one after one way, and another after another, to the crosses, by way of jest, when their multitude was so great, that room was wanting for the crosses, and crosses wanting for the bodies.

5.11.2 But so far were the seditious from repenting at this sad sight, that, on the contrary, they made the rest of the multitude believe otherwise; for they brought the relations of those that had deserted upon the wall, with such of the populace as were very eager to go over upon the security offered them, and showed them what miseries those underwent who fled to the Rómans; and told them that those who were caught were supplicants to them, and not such as were taken prisoners. This sight kept many of those within the city who were so eager to desert, till the truth was known; yet did some of them run away immediately as unto certain punishment, esteeming death from their enemies to be a quiet departure, if compared with that by famine. So Títus commanded that the hands of many of those that were caught should be cut off, that they might not be thought deserters, and might be credited on account of the calamity they were under, and sent them in to John and Símon, with this exhortation, that they would now at length leave off, and not force him to destroy the city, whereby they would have those advantages of repentance, even in their utmost distress, that they would preserve their own lives, and so find a city of their own, and that temple which was their peculiar.

He then went round about the banks that were cast up, and hastened them, in order to show that his words should in no long time be followed by his deeds. In answer to which the seditious cast reproaches upon Cæsar himself, and upon his father also, and cried out, with a loud voice, that they contemned death, and did well in preferring it before slavery; that they would do all the mischief to the Rómans they could while they had breath in them; and that for their own city, since

152

they were, as he said, to be destroyed, they had no concern about it, and that the world itself was a better temple to God than this. That yet this temple would be preserved by him that inhabited therein, whom they still had for their assistant in this war, and did therefore laugh at all his threatenings, which would come to nothing, because the conclusion of the whole depended upon God only. These words were mixed with reproaches, and with them they made a mighty clamor.

Joséphus, The Wars of the Jews, 5.11.1-5.11.2 (translated by William Whiston)

Títus Pities the Besieged

5.12.3 So all hope of escaping was now cut off from the Jews, together with their liberty of going out of the city. Then did the famine widen its progress, and devoured the people by whole houses and families; the upper rooms were full of women and children that were dying by famine, and the lanes of the city were full of the dead bodies of the aged; the children also and the young men wandered about the market-places like shadows, all swelled with the famine, and fell down dead, wheresoever their misery seized them. As for burying them, those that were sick themselves were not able to do it; and those that were hearty and well were deterred from doing it by the great multitude of those dead bodies, and by the uncertainty there was how soon they should die themselves; for many died as they were burying others, and many went to their coffins before that fatal hour was come. Nor was there any lamentations made under these calamities, nor were heard any mournful complaints; but the famine confounded all natural passions; for those who were just going to die looked upon those that were gone to rest before them with dry eyes and open mouths.

A deep silence also, and a kind of deadly night, had seized upon the city; while yet the robbers were still more terrible than these miseries were themselves; for they brake open those houses which were no other than graves of dead bodies, and plundered them of what they had; and carrying off the coverings of their bodies, went out laughing, and tried the points of their swords in their dead bodies; and, in order to prove what metal they were made of they thrust some of those through that still lay alive upon the ground; but for those that entreated them to lend them their right hand and their sword to dispatch them, they were too proud to grant their requests, and left them to be consumed by the famine. Now every one of these died with their eyes fixed upon the temple, and left the seditious alive behind them. Now the seditious at first gave orders that the dead should be buried out of the public treasury, as not enduring the stench of their dead bodies. But afterwards, when they could not do that, they had them cast down from the walls into the valleys beneath.

5.12.4 However, when Títus, in going his rounds along those valleys, saw them full of dead bodies, and the thick putrefaction running about them, he gave a groan; and, spreading out his hands to heaven, called God to witness that this was not his doing; and such was the sad case of the city itself. But the Rómans were very joyful, since none of the seditious could now make sallies out of the city, because they were themselves disconsolate, and the famine already touched them also. These Rómans besides had great plenty of corn and other necessaries out of Sýria, and out of the neighboring provinces; many of whom would stand near to the wall of the city, and show the people what great quantities of provisions they had, and so make the enemy more sensible of their famine, by the great plenty, even to satiety, which they had themselves.

However, when the seditious still showed no inclinations of yielding, Títus, out of his commiseration of the people that remained, and out of his earnest desire of rescuing what was still left out of these miseries, began to raise his banks again, although materials for them were hard to be come at; for all the trees that were about the city had been already cut down for the making of the former banks. Yet did the soldiers bring with them other materials from the distance of ninety furlongs, and thereby raised banks in four parts, much greater than the former, though this was done only at the tower of Antónia. So Cǽsar went his rounds through the légions, and hastened on the works, and showed the robbers that they were now in his hands. But these men, and these only, were incapable of repenting of the wickednesses they had been guilty of; and separating their souls from their bodies, they used them both as if they belonged to other folks, and not to themselves. For no gentle affection could touch their souls, nor could any pain affect their bodies, since they could still tear the dead bodies of the people as dogs do, and fill the prisons with those that were sick.

Joséphus, The Wars of the Jews, 5.12.3-5.12.4 (translated by William Whiston)

Títus Offers to Spare the Temple

6.2.4 Now Títus was deeply affected with this state of things, and reproached John and his party, and said to them, "Have not you, vile wretches that you are, by our permission, put up this partition-wall before your sanctuary? Have not you been allowed to put up the pillars thereto belonging, at due distances, and on it to engrave in Greek, and in your own letters, this prohibition, that no foreigner should go beyond that wall. Have not we given you leave to kill such as go beyond it, though he were a Róman? And what do you do now, you pernicious villains? Why do you trample upon dead bodies in this temple? and why do you pollute this holy house with the blood of both foreigners and Jews themselves? I appeal to the gods of my own country, and to every god that ever had any regard to this place; (for I do not suppose it to be now regarded by any of them;) I also appeal to my own army, and to those Jews that are now with me, and even to yourselves, that I do not force you to defile this your sanctuary; and if you will but change the place whereon you will fight, no Róman shall either come near your sanctuary, or offer any affront to it; nay, I will endeavor to preserve you your holy house, whether you will or not."

Joséphus, The Wars of the Jews, 6.2.4 (translated by William Whiston)

The Temple of Jerúsalem is Razed

6.4.5. So Títus retired into the tower of Antónia, and resolved to storm the temple the next day, early in the morning, with his whole army, and to encamp round about the holy house. But as for that house, God had, for certain, long ago doomed it to the fire; and now that fatal day was come, according to the revolution of ages; it was the tenth day of the month Lous, [Ab,] upon which it was formerly burnt by the king of Bábylon; although these flames took their rise from the Jews themselves, and were occasioned by them; for upon Títus's retiring, the seditious lay still for a little while, and then attacked the Rómans again, when those that guarded the holy house fought with those that quenched the fire that was burning the inner [court of the] temple; but these Rómans put the Jews to flight, and proceeded as far as the holy house itself. At which time one of the soldiers, without staying for any orders, and without any concern or dread upon him at so great an undertaking, and being hurried on by a certain divine fury, snatched somewhat out of the materials that were on fire, and being lifted up by another soldier, he set fire to a golden window, through which there was a passage to the rooms that were round about the holy house, on the north side of it. As the flames went upward, the Jews made a great clamor, such as so mighty an affliction required, and ran together to prevent it; and now they spared not their lives any longer, nor suffered any thing to restrain their force, since that holy house was perishing, for whose sake it was that they kept such a guard about it.

6.4.6 And now a certain person came running to Títus, and told him of this fire, as he was resting himself in his tent after the last battle; whereupon he rose up in great haste, and, as he was, ran to the holy house, in order to have a stop put to the fire; after him followed all his commanders, and after them followed the several légions, in great astonishment; so there was a great clamor and tumult raised, as was natural upon the disorderly motion of so great an army. Then did Cæsar, both by calling to the soldiers that were fighting, with a loud voice, and by giving a signal to them with his right hand, order them to quench the fire. But they did not hear what he said, though he spoke so loud, having their ears already dimmed by a greater noise another way; nor did they attend to the signal he made with his hand neither, as still some of them were distracted with fighting, and others with passion.

But as for the légions that came running thither, neither any persuasions nor any threatenings could restrain their violence, but each one's own passion was his commander at this time; and as they were crowding into the temple together, many of them were trampled on by one another, while a great number fell among the ruins of the cloisters, which were still hot and smoking, and were destroyed in the same miserable way with those whom they had conquered; and when they were come near the holy house, they made as if they did not so much as hear Cæsar's orders to the contrary; but they encouraged those that were before them to set it on fire. As for the seditious, they were in too great distress already to afford their assistance [towards quenching the fire]; they were every where slain, and every where beaten; and as for a great part of the people, they were weak and without arms, and had their throats cut wherever they were caught. Now round about the altar lay dead bodies heaped one upon another, as at the steps going up to it ran a great quantity of their blood, whither also the dead bodies that were slain above [on the altar] fell down.

6.4.7 And now, since Cæsar was no way able to restrain the enthusiastic fury of the soldiers, and the fire proceeded on more and more, he went into the holy place of the temple, with his commanders, and saw it, with what was in it, which he found to be far superior to what the relations of foreigners contained, and not inferior to what we ourselves boasted of and believed about it. But as the flame had not as yet reached to its inward parts, but was still consuming the rooms that were about the holy house, and Títus supposing what the fact was, that the house itself might yet he saved, he came in haste and endeavored to persuade the soldiers to quench the fire, and gave order to Liberálius the centúrion, and one of those spearmen that were about him, to beat the soldiers that were refractory with their staves, and to restrain them; yet were their passions too hard for the regards they had for Cæsar, and the dread they had of him who forbade them, as was their hatred of the Jews, and a certain vehement inclination to fight them, too hard for them also. Moreover, the hope of plunder induced many to go on, as having this opinion, that all the places within were full of money, and as seeing that all round about it was made of gold. And besides, one of those that went into the place prevented Cæsar, when he ran so hastily out to restrain the soldiers, and threw the fire upon the hinges of the gate, in the dark; whereby the flame burst out from within the holy house itself immediately, when the commanders retired, and Cæsar with them, and when nobody any longer forbade those that were without to set fire to it. And thus was the holy house burnt down, without Cæsar's approbation.

6.4.8 Now although any one would justly lament the destruction of such a work as this was, since it was the most admirable of all the works that we have seen or heard of, both for its curious structure and its magnitude, and also for the vast wealth bestowed upon it, as well as for the glorious reputation it had for its holiness; yet might such a one comfort himself with this thought, that it was fate that decreed it so to be, which is inevitable, both as to living creatures, and as to works and places also. However, one cannot but wonder at the accuracy of this period thereto relating; for the same month and day were now observed, as I said before, wherein the holy house was burnt formerly by the Babylónians. Now the number of years that passed from its first foundation, which was laid by king Sólomon, till this its destruction, which happened in the second year of the reign of Vespásian, are collected to be one thousand one hundred and thirty, besides seven months and fifteen days; and from the second building of it, which was done by Hággai, in the second year of Cýrus the king, till its destruction under Vespásian, there were six hundred and thirty-nine years and forty-five days.

6.5.2 And now the Rómans, judging that it was in vain to spare what was round about the holy house, burnt all those places, as also the remains of the cloisters and the gates, two excepted; the one on the east side, and the other on the south; both which, however, they burnt afterward. They also burnt down the treasury chambers, in which was an immense quantity of money, and an immense number of garments, and other precious goods there reposited; and, to speak all in a few words, there it was that the entire riches of the Jews were heaped up together, while the rich people had there built themselves chambers [to contain such furniture]. The soldiers also came to the rest of the cloisters that were in the outer [court of the] temple, whither the women and children, and a great mixed multitude of the people, fled, in number about six thousand.

But before Cæsar had determined any thing about these people, or given the commanders any orders relating to them, the soldiers were in such a rage, that they set that cloister on fire; by which means it came to pass that some of these were destroyed by throwing themselves down headlong, and some were burnt in the cloisters themselves. Nor did any one of them escape with his life. A false prophet was the occasion of these people's destruction, who had made a public proclamation in the city that very day, that God commanded them to get upon the temple, and that there they should receive miraculous signs of their deliverance. Now there was then a great number of false prophets suborned by the tyrants to impose on the people, who denounced this to them, that they should wait for deliverance from God; and this was in order to keep them from deserting, and that they might be buoyed up above fear and care by such hopes. Now a man that is in adversity does easily comply with such promises; for when such a seducer makes him believe that he shall be delivered from those miseries which oppress him, then it is that the patient is full of hopes of such his deliverance.

Joséphus, *The Wars of the Jews*, 6.4.5-6.4.8, 6.5.2 (translated by William Whiston)

Jerúsalem is Taken

6.9.1 Now when Títus was come into this [upper] city, he admired not only some other places of strength in it, but particularly those strong towers which the tyrants in their mad conduct had relinquished; for when he saw their solid altitude, and the largeness of their several stones, and the exactness of their joints, as also how great was their breadth, and how extensive their length, he expressed himself after the manner following: "We have certainly had God for our assistant in this war, and it was no other than God who ejected the Jews out of these fortifications; for what could the hands of men or any machines do towards overthrowing these towers?" At which time he had many such discourses to his friends; he also let such go free as had been bound by the tyrants, and were left in the prisons. To conclude, when he entirely demolished the rest of the city, and overthrew its walls, he left these towers as a monument of his good fortune, which had proved his auxiliaries, and enabled him to take what could not otherwise have been taken by him.

6.9.2 And now, since his soldiers were already quite tired with killing men, and yet there appeared to be a vast multitude still remaining alive, Cæsar gave orders that they should kill none but those that were in arms, and opposed them, but should take the rest alive. But, together with those whom they had orders to slay, they slew the aged and the infirm; but for those that were in their flourishing age, and who might be useful to them, they drove them together into the temple, and shut them up within the walls of the court of the women; over which Cæsar set one of his freed-men, as also Frónto, one of his own friends; which last was to determine every one's fate, according to his merits. So this Frónto slew all those that had been seditious and robbers, who were impeached one by another; but of the young men he chose out the tallest and most beautiful, and reserved them for the triumph; and as for the rest of the multitude that were above seventeen years old, he put them into bonds, and sent them to the Egýptian mines. Títus also sent a great number into the provinces, as a present to them, that they might be destroyed upon their theatres, by the sword and by the wild beasts; but those that were under seventeen years of age were sold for slaves. Now during the days wherein Frónto was distinguishing these men, there perished, for want of food, eleven thousand; some of whom did not taste any food, through the hatred their guards bore to them; and others would not take in any when it was given them. The multitude also was so very great, that they were in want even of corn for their sustenance.

6.9.3 Now the number of those that were carried captive during this whole war was collected to be ninety-seven thousand; as was the number of those that perished during the whole siege eleven hundred thousand, the greater part of whom were indeed of the same nation [with the citizens of Jerúsalem], but not belonging to the city itself; for they were come up from all the country to the feast of unleavened bread, and were on a sudden shut up by an army, which, at the very first, occasioned so great a straightness among them, that there came a pestilential destruction upon them, and soon afterward such a famine, as destroyed them more suddenly. And that this city could contain so many people in it, is manifest by that number of them which was taken under Céstius, who being desirous of informing Néro of the power of the city, who otherwise was disposed to contemn that nation, entreated the high priests, if the thing were possible, to take the number of their whole multitude. So these high priests, upon the coming of that feast which is called the Passover, when they slay their sacrifices, from the ninth hour till the eleventh, but so that a company not less than ten belong to every sacrifice, (for it is not lawful for them to feast singly by themselves,) and many of us are twenty in a company, found the number of sacrifices was two hundred and fifty-six thousand five hundred; which, upon the allowance of no more than ten that feast together, amounts to two millions seven hundred thousand and two hundred persons that were pure and holy...

6.9.4 Now this vast multitude is indeed collected out of remote places, but the entire nation was now shut up by fate as in prison, and the Róman army encompassed the city when it was crowded with inhabitants. Accordingly, the multitude of those that therein perished exceeded all the destructions that either men or God ever brought upon the world; for, to speak only of what was publicly known, the Rómans slew some of them, some they carried captives, and others they made a search for under ground, and when they found where they were, they broke up the ground and slew all they met with. There were also found slain there above two thousand persons, partly by their own hands, and partly by one another, but chiefly destroyed by the famine; but then the ill savor of the dead bodies was most offensive to those that lighted upon them, insomuch that some were obliged to get away immediately, while others were so greedy of gain, that they would go in among the dead bodies that lay on heaps, and tread upon them; for a great deal of treasure was found in these caverns, and the hope of gain made every way of getting it to be esteemed lawful. Many also of those that had been put in prison by the tyrants were now brought out; for they did not leave off their barbarous cruelty at the very last: yet did God avenge himself upon them both, in a manner agreeable to justice. As for John, he wanted food, together with his brethren, in these caverns, and begged that the Rómans would now give him their right hand for his security, which he had often proudly rejected before; but for Símon, he struggled hard with the distress he was in, till he was forced to surrender himself, as we shall relate hereafter; so he was reserved for the triumph, and to be then slain; as was John condemned to perpetual imprisonment. And now the Rómans set fire to the extreme parts of the city, and burnt them down, and entirely demolished its walls.

6.10.1 And thus was Jerúsalem taken, in the second year of the reign of Vespásian, on the eighth day of the month Gorpéius [Elul]. It had been taken five times before, though this was the second time of its desolation; for Shíshak, the king of Égypt, and after him Antíochus, and after him Pómpey, and after them Sósius and Hérod, took the city, but still preserved it; but before all these, the king of Bábylon conquered it, and made it desolate, one thousand four hundred and sixty-eight years and six months after it was built. But he who first built it was a potent man among the Cánaanites, and is in our own tongue called [Melchísedek], the Righteous King, for such he really was; on which account he was [there] the first priest of God, and first built a temple [there], and called the city Jerúsalem, which was formerly called Sálem. However, David, the king of the Jews, ejected the Cánaanites, and settled his own people therein. It was demolished entirely by the Babylónians, four hundred and seventy-seven years and six months after him. And from king Dávid, who was the first of the Jews who reigned therein, to this destruction under Títus, were one thousand one hundred and seventy-nine years; but from its first building, till this last destruction, were two thousand one hundred and seventy-seven years; yet hath not its great antiquity, nor its vast riches, nor the diffusion of its nation over all the habitable earth, nor the greatness of the veneration paid to it on a religious account, been sufficient to preserve it from being destroyed. And thus ended the siege of Jerúsalem.

Joséphus, The Wars of the Jews, 6.9.1-6.9.4, 6.10.1 (translated by William Whiston)

The Destruction of Jerúsalem

7.1.1 Now as soon as the army had no more people to slay or to plunder, because there remained none to be the objects of their fury, (for they would not have spared any, had there remained any other work to be done,) Cǽsar gave orders that they should now demolish the entire city and temple, but should leave as many of the towers standing as were of the greatest eminency; that is, Phasǽlus, and Híppicus, and Mariámne; and so much of the wall as enclosed the city on the west side. This wall was spared, in order to afford a camp for such as were to lie in garrison, as were the towers also spared, in order to demonstrate to posterity what kind of city it was, and how well fortified, which the Róman valor had subdued; but for all the rest of the wall, it was so thoroughly laid even with the ground by those that dug it up to the foundation, that there was left nothing to make those that came thither believe it had ever been inhabited. This was the end which Jerúsalem came to by the madness of those that were for innovations; a city otherwise of great magnificence, and of mighty fame among all mankind.

Joséphus, The Wars of the Jews, 7.1.1 (translated by William Whiston)

Vespásian and Títus Celebrate a Triumph

7.5.4 Now all the soldiery marched out beforehand by companies, and in their several ranks, under their several commanders, in the night time, and were about the gates, not of the upper palaces, but those near the temple of Isis; for there it was that the emperors had rested the foregoing night. And as soon as ever it was day, Vespásian and Títus came out crowned with laurel, and clothed in those ancient purple habits which were proper to their family, and then went as far as Octávian's Walks; for there it was that the senate, and the principal rulers, and those that had been recorded as of the equestrian order, waited for them. Now a tribunal had been erected before the cloisters, and ivory chairs had been set upon it, when they came and sat down upon them. Whereupon the soldiery made an acclamation of joy to them immediately, and all gave them attestations of their valor; while they were themselves without their arms, and only in their silken garments, and crowned with laurel: then Vespásian accepted of these shouts of theirs; but while they were still disposed to go on in such acclamations, he gave them a signal of silence. And when every body entirely held their peace, he stood up, and covering the greatest part of his head with his cloak, he put up the accustomed solemn prayers; the like prayers did Títus put up also; after which prayers Vespásian made a short speech to all the people, and then sent away the soldiers to a dinner prepared for them by the emperors. Then did he retire to that gate which was called the Gate of the Pomp, because pompous shows do always go through that gate; there it was that they tasted some food, and when they had put on their triumphal garments, and had offered sacrifices to the gods that were placed at the gate, they sent the triumph forward, and marched through the theatres, that they might be the more easily seen by the multitudes.

7.5.5 Now it is impossible to describe the multitude of the shows as they deserve, and the magnificence of them all; such indeed as a man could not easily think of as performed, either by the labor of workmen, or the variety of riches, or the rarities of nature; for almost all such curiosities as the most happy men ever get by piece-meal were here one heaped on another, and those both admirable and costly in their nature; and all brought together on that day demonstrated the vastness of the dominions of the Rómans; for there was here to be seen a mighty quantity of silver, and gold, and ivory, contrived into all sorts of things, and did not appear as carried along in pompous show only, but, as a man may say, running along like a river. Some parts were composed of the rarest purple hangings, and so carried along; and others accurately represented to the life what was embroidered by the arts of the Babylónians.

There were also precious stones that were transparent, some set in crowns of gold, and some in other ouches, as the workmen pleased; and of these such a vast number were brought, that we could not but thence learn how vainly we imagined any of them to be rarities. The images of the gods were also carried, being as well wonderful for their largeness, as made very artificially, and with great skill of the workmen; nor were any of these images of any other than very costly materials; and many species of animals were brought, every one in their own natural ornaments. The men also who brought every one of these shows were great multitudes, and adorned with purple garments, all over interwoven with gold; those that were chosen for carrying these pompous shows having also about them such magnificent ornaments as were both extraordinary and surprising. Besides these, one might see that even the great number of the captives was not unadorned, while the variety that was in their garments, and their fine texture, concealed from the sight the deformity of their bodies.

But what afforded the greatest surprise of all was the structure of the pageants that were borne along; for indeed he that met them could not but be afraid that the bearers would not be able firmly enough to support them, such was their magnitude; for many of them were so made, that they were on three or even four stories, one above another. The magnificence also of their structure afforded one both pleasure and surprise; for upon many of them were laid carpets of gold. There was also wrought gold and ivory fastened about them all; and many resemblances of the war, and those in several ways, and variety of contrivances, affording a most lively portraiture of itself. For there was to be seen a happy country laid waste, and entire squadrons of enemies slain; while some of them ran away, and some were carried into captivity; with walls of great altitude and magnitude overthrown and ruined by machines; with the strongest fortifications taken, and the walls of most populous cities upon the tops of hills seized on, and an army pouring itself within the walls; as also every place full of slaughter, and supplications of the enemies, when they were no longer able to lift up their hands in way of opposition.

Fire also sent upon temples was here represented, and houses overthrown, and falling upon their owners: rivers also, after they came out of a large and melancholy desert, ran down, not into a land cultivated, nor as drink for men, or for cattle, but through a land still on fire upon every side; for the Jews related that such a thing they had undergone during this war. Now the workmanship of these representations was so magnificent and lively in the construction of the things, that it exhibited what had been done to such as did not see it, as if they had been there really present. On the top of every one of these pageants was placed the commander of the city that was taken, and the manner wherein he was taken. Moreover, there followed those pageants a great number of ships; and for the other spoils, they were carried in great plenty. But for those that were taken in the temple of Jerúsalem, they made the greatest figure of them all; that is, the golden table, of the weight of many talents; the candlestick also, that was made of gold, though its construction were now changed from that which we made use of; for its middle shaft was fixed upon a basis, and the small branches were produced out of it to a great length, having the likeness of a trident in their position, and had every one a socket made of brass for a lamp at the tops of them. These lamps were in number seven, and represented the dignity of the number seven among the Jews; and the last of all the spoils, was carried the Law of the Jews. After these spoils passed by a great many men, carrying the images of Victory, whose structure was entirely either of ivory or of gold. After which Vespásian marched in the first place, and Títus followed him; Domítian also rode along with them, and made a glorious appearance, and rode on a horse that was worthy of admiration.

7.5.6 Now the last part of this pompous show was at the temple of Júpiter Capitolínus, whither when they were come, they stood still; for it was the Rómans' ancient custom to stay till somebody brought the news that the general of the enemy was slain. This general was Símon, the son of Gióras, who had then been led in this triumph among the captives; a rope had also been put upon his head, and he had been drawn into a proper place in the fórum, and had withal been tormented by those that drew him along; and the law of the Rómans required that malefactors condemned to die should be slain there. Accordingly, when it was related that there was an end of him, and all the people had set up a shout for joy, they then began to offer those sacrifices which they had consecrated, in the prayers used in such solemnities; which when they had finished, they went away to the palace. And as for some of the spectators, the emperors entertained them at their own feast; and for all the rest there were noble preparations made for feasting at home; for this was a festival day to the city of Rome, as celebrated for the victory obtained by their army over their enemies, for the end that was now put to their civil miseries, and for the commencement of their hopes of future prosperity and happiness.

7.5.7 After these triumphs were over, and after the affairs of the Rómans were settled on the surest foundations, Vespásian resolved to build a temple to Peace, which was finished in so short a time, and in so glorious a manner, as was beyond all human expectation and opinion: for he having now by Providence a vast quantity of wealth, besides what he had formerly gained in his other exploits, he had this temple adorned with pictures and statues; for in this temple were collected and deposited all such rarities as men aforetime used to wander all over the habitable world to see, when they had a desire to see one of them after another; he also laid up therein those golden vessels and instruments that were taken out of the Jéwish temple, as ensigns of his glory. But still he gave order that they should lay up their Law, and the purple veils of the holy place, in the royal palace itself, and keep them there.

Joséphus, The Wars of the Jews, 7.5.4-7.5.7 (translated by William Whiston)

The Siege of Masáda

7.8.2 For now it was that the Róman general came, and led his army against Eleázar and those Sicárii who held the fortress Masáda together with him; and for the whole country adjoining, he presently gained it, and put garrisons into the most proper places of it; he also built a wall quite round the entire fortress, that none of the besieged might easily escape; he also set his men to guard the several parts of it; he also pitched his camp in such an agreeable place as he had chosen for the siege, and at which place the rock belonging to the fortress did make the nearest approach to the neighboring mountain, which yet was a place of difficulty for getting plenty of provisions; for it was not only food that was to be brought from a great distance [to the army], and this with a great deal of pain to those Jews who were appointed for that purpose, but water was also to be brought to the camp, because the place afforded no fountain that was near it. When therefore Sílva had ordered these affairs beforehand, he fell to besieging the place; which siege was likely to stand in need of a great deal of skill and pains, by reason of the strength of the fortress, the nature of which I will now describe.

7.8.3 There was a rock, not small in circumference, and very high. It was encompassed with valleys of such vast depth downward, that the eye could not reach their bottoms; they were abrupt, and such as no animal could walk upon, excepting at two places of the rock, where it subsides, in order to afford a passage for ascent, though not without difficulty. Now, of the ways that lead to it, one is that from the lake Aspháltiris, towards the sun-rising, and another on the west, where the ascent is easier: the one of these ways is called the *Serpent*, as resembling that animal in its narrowness and its perpetual windings; for it is broken off at the prominent precipices of the rock, and returns frequently into itself, and lengthening again by little and little, hath much ado to proceed forward; and he that would walk along it must first go on one leg, and then on the other;

there is also nothing but destruction, in case your feet slip; for on each side there is a vastly deep chasm and precipice, sufficient to quell the courage of every body by the terror it infuses into the mind. When, therefore, a man hath gone along this way for thirty furlongs, the rest is the top of the hill—not ending at a small point, but is no other than a plain upon the highest part of the mountain.

Upon this top of the hill, Jónathan the high priest first of all built a fortress, and called it Masáda: after which the rebuilding of this place employed the care of king Hérod to a great degree; he also built a wall round about the entire top of the hill, seven furlongs long; it was composed of white stone; its height was twelve, and its breadth eight cubits; there were also erected upon that wall thirty-eight towers, each of them fifty cubits high; out of which you might pass into lesser edifices, which were built on the inside, round the entire wall; for the king reserved the top of the hill, which was of a fat soil, and better mold than any valley for agriculture, that such as committed themselves to this fortress for their preservation might not even there be quite destitute of food, in case they should ever be in want of it from abroad. Moreover, he built a palace therein at the western ascent; it was within and beneath the walls of the citadel, but inclined to its north side.

Now the wall of this palace was very high and strong, and had at its four corners towers sixty cubits high. The furniture also of the edifices, and of the cloisters, and of the baths, was of great variety, and very costly; and these buildings were supported by pillars of single stones on every side; the walls and also the floors of the edifices were paved with stones of several colors. He also had cut many and great pits, as reservoirs for water, out of the rocks, at every one of the places that were inhabited, both above and round about the palace, and before the wall; and by this contrivance he endeavored to have water for several uses, as if there had been fountains there. Here was also a road dug from the palace, and leading to the very top of the mountain, which yet could not be seen by such as were without [the walls]; nor indeed could enemies easily make use of the plain roads; for the road on the east side, as we have already taken notice, could not be walked upon, by reason of its nature; and for the western road, he built a large tower at its narrowest place, at no less a distance from the top of the hill than a thousand cubits; which tower could not possibly be passed by, nor could it be easily taken; nor indeed could those that walked along it without any fear (such was its contrivance) easily get to the end of it; and after such a manner was this citadel fortified, both by nature and by the hands of men, in order to frustrate the attacks of enemies.

7.8.4 As for the furniture that was within this fortress, it was still more wonderful on account of its splendor and long continuance; for here was laid up corn in large quantities, and such as would subsist men for a long time; here was also wine and oil in abundance, with all kinds of pulse and dates heaped up together; all which Eleázar found there, when he and his Sicárii got possession of the fortress by treachery. These fruits were also fresh and full ripe, and no way inferior to such fruits newly laid in, although they were little short of a hundred years from the laying in these provisions [by Hérod], till the place was taken by the Rómans; nay, indeed, when the Rómans got possession of those fruits that were left, they found them not corrupted all that while; nor should we be mistaken, if we supposed that the air was here the cause of their enduring so long; this fortress being so high, and so free from the mixture of all terrain and muddy particles of matter.

There was also found here a large quantity of all sorts of weapons of war, which had been treasured up by that king, and were sufficient for ten thousand men; there was east iron, and brass, and tin, which show that he had taken much pains to have all things here ready for the greatest occasions; for the report goes how Hérod thus prepared this fortress on his own account, as a refuge against two kinds of danger; the one for fear of the multitude of the Jews, lest they should depose him, and restore their former kings to the government; the other danger was greater and more terrible, which arose from Cleopátra queen of Égypt, who did not conceal her intentions, but spoke often to Ántony, and desired him to cut off Hérod, and entreated him to bestow the kingdom of Judéa upon her. And certainly it is a great wonder that Ántony did never comply with her commands in this point, as he was so miserably enslaved to his passion for her; nor should any one have been surprised if she had been gratified in such her request. So the fear of these dangers made Hérod rebuild Masáda, and thereby leave it for the finishing stroke of the Rómans in this Jéwish war.

7.8.5 Since therefore the Róman commander Sílva had now built a wall on the outside, round about this whole place, as we have said already, and had thereby made a most accurate provision to prevent any one of the besieged running away, he undertook the siege itself, though he found but one single place that would admit of the banks he was to raise; for behind that tower which secured the road that led to the palace, and to the top of the hill from the west; there was a certain eminency of the rock, very broad and very prominent, but three hundred cubits beneath the highest part of Masáda; it was called the White Promontory. Accordingly, he got upon that part of the rock, and ordered the army to bring earth; and when they fell to that work with alacrity, and abundance of them together, the bank was raised, and became solid for two hundred cubits in height. Yet was not this bank thought sufficiently high for the use of the engines that were to be set upon it; but still another elevated work of great stones compacted together was raised upon that bank; this was fifty cubits, both in breadth and height. The other machines that were now got ready were like to those that had been first devised by Vespásian, and afterwards by Títus, for sieges. There was also a tower made of the height of sixty cubits, and all over plated with iron, out of which the Rómans threw darts and stones from the engines, and soon made those that fought from the walls of the place to retire, and would not let them lift up their heads above the works. At the same time Sílva ordered that great battering ram which he had made to be brought thither, and to be set against the wall, and to make frequent batteries against it, which with some difficulty broke down a part of the wall, and quite overthrew it.

However, the Sicárii made haste, and presently built another wall within that, which should not be liable to the same misfortune from the machines with the other; it was made soft and yielding, and so was capable of avoiding the terrible blows that affected the other. It was framed after the following manner: They laid together great beams of wood lengthways, one close to the end of another, and the same way in which they were cut: there were two of these rows parallel to one another, and laid at such a distance from each other as the breadth of the wall required, and earth was put into the space between those rows. Now, that the earth might not fall away upon the elevation of this bank to a greater height, they further laid other beams over cross them, and thereby bound those beams together that lay lengthways. This work of theirs was like a real edifice; and when the machines were applied, the blows were weakened by its yielding; and as the materials by such concussion were shaken closer together, the pile by that means became firmer than before.

When Sílva saw this, he thought it best to endeavor the taking of this wall by setting fire to it; so he gave order that the soldiers should throw a great number of burning torches upon it: accordingly, as it was chiefly made of wood, it soon took fire; and when it was once set on fire, its hollowness made that fire spread to a mighty flame. Now, at the very beginning of this fire, a north wind that then blew proved terrible to the Rómans; for by bringing the flame downward, it drove it upon them, and they were almost in despair of success, as fearing their machines would be burnt: but after this, on a sudden the wind changed into the south, as if it were done by Divine Providence, and blew strongly the contrary way, and carried the flame, and drove it against the wall, which was now on fire through its entire thickness. So the Rómans, having now assistance from God, returned to their camp with joy, and resolved to attack their enemies the very next day; on which occasion they set their watch more carefully that night, lest any of the Jews should run away from them without being discovered.

7.8.6 However, neither did Eleázar once think of flying away, nor would he permit any one else to do so; but when he saw their wall burned down by the fire, and could devise no other way of escaping, or room for their further courage, and setting before their eyes what the Rómans would do to them, their children, and their wives, if they got them into their power, he consulted about having them all slain. Now as he judged this to be the best thing they could do in their present circumstances, he gathered the most courageous of his companions together, and encouraged them to take that course by a speech which he made to them in the manner following: "Since we, long ago, my generous friends, resolved never to be servants to the Rómans, nor to any other than to God himself, who alone is the true and just Lord of mankind, the time is now come that obliges us to make that resolution true in practice. And let us not at this time bring a reproach upon ourselves for self-contradiction, while we formerly would not undergo slavery, though it were then without danger, but must now, together with slavery, choose such punishments also as are intolerable; I mean this, upon the supposition that the Rómans once reduce us under their power while we are alive. We were the very first that revolted from them, and we are the last that fight against them; and I cannot but esteem it as a favor that God hath granted us, that it is still in our power to die bravely, and in a state of freedom, which hath not been the case of others, who were conquered unexpectedly. It is very plain that we shall be taken within a day's time; but it is still an eligible thing to die after a glorious manner, together with our dearest friends. This is what our enemies themselves cannot by any means hinder, although they be very desirous to take us alive. Nor can we propose to ourselves any more to fight them, and beat them.

"It had been proper indeed for us to have conjectured at the purpose of God much sooner, and at the very first, when we were so desirous of defending our liberty, and when we received such sore treatment from one another, and worse treatment from our enemies, and to have been sensible that the same God, who had of old taken the Jéwish nation into his favor, had now condemned them to destruction; for had he either continued favorable, or been but in a lesser degree displeased with us, he had not overlooked the destruction of so many men, or delivered his most holy city to be burnt and demolished by our enemies. To be sure we weakly hoped to have preserved ourselves, and ourselves alone, still in a state of freedom, as if we had been guilty of no sins ourselves against God, nor been partners with those of others; we also taught other men to preserve their liberty.

"Wherefore, consider how God hath convinced us that our hopes were in vain, by bringing such distress upon us in the desperate state we are now in, and which is beyond all our expectations; for the nature of this fortress which was in itself unconquerable, hath not proved a means of our deliverance; and even while we have still great abundance of food, and a great quantity of arms, and other necessaries more than we want, we are openly deprived by God himself of all hope of deliverance; for that fire which was driven upon our enemies did not of its own accord turn back upon the wall which we had built; this was the effect of God's anger against us for our manifold sins, which we have been guilty of in a most insolent and extravagant manner with regard to our own countrymen; the punishments of which let us not receive from the Rómans, but from God himself, as executed by our own hands; for these will be more moderate than the other. Let our wives die before they are abused, and our children before they have tasted of slavery; and after we have slain them, let us bestow that glorious benefit upon one another mutually, and preserve ourselves in freedom, as an excellent funeral monument for us. But first let us destroy our money and the fortress by fire; for I am well assured that this will be a great grief to the Rómans, that they shall not be able to seize upon our bodies, and shall fall of our wealth also; and let us spare nothing but our provisions; for they will be a testimonial when we are dead that we were not subdued for want of necessaries, but that, according to our original resolution, we have preferred death before slavery."

7.8.7 This was Eleázar's speech to them. Yet did not the opinions of all the auditors acquiesce therein; but although some of them were very zealous to put his advice in practice, and were in a manner filled with pleasure at it, and thought death to be a good thing, yet had those that were most effeminate a commiseration for their wives and families; and when these men were especially moved by the prospect of their own certain death, they looked wistfully at one another, and by the tears that were in their eyes declared their dissent from his opinion. When Eleázar saw these people in such fear, and that their souls were dejected at so prodigious a proposal, he was afraid lest perhaps these effeminate persons should, by their lamentations and tears, enfeeble those that heard what he had said courageously; so he did not leave off exhorting them, but stirred up himself, and recollecting proper arguments for raising their courage, he undertook to speak more briskly and fully to them, and that concerning the immortality of the soul...

Joséphus, *The Wars of the Jews*, 7.8.2-7.8.7 (translated by William Whiston)

Masáda is Taken

7.9.1 Now as Eleázar was proceeding on in this exhortation, they all cut him off short, and made haste to do the work, as full of an unconquerable ardor of mind, and moved with a demoniacal fury. So they went their ways, as one still endeavoring to be before another, and as thinking that this eagerness would be a demonstration of their courage and good conduct, if they could avoid appearing in the last class; so great was the zeal they were in to slay their wives and children, and themselves also! Nor indeed, when they came to the work itself, did their courage fail them, as one might imagine it would have done, but they then held fast the same resolution, without wavering, which they had upon the hearing of Eleázar's speech, while yet every one of them still retained the natural passion of love to themselves and their families, because the reasoning they went upon appeared to them to be very just, even with regard to those that were dearest to them; for the husbands tenderly embraced their wives, and took their children into their arms, and gave the longest parting kisses to them, with tears in their eyes.

Yet at the same time did they complete what they had resolved on, as if they had been executed by the hands of strangers; and they had nothing else for their comfort but the necessity they were in of doing this execution, to avoid that prospect they had of the miseries they were to suffer from their enemies. Nor was there at length any one of these men found that scrupled to act their part in this terrible execution, but every one of them dispatched his dearest relations. Miserable men indeed were they! whose distress forced them to slay their own wives and children with their own hands, as the lightest of those evils that were before them. So they being not able to bear the grief they were under for what they had done any longer, and esteeming it an injury to those they had slain, to live even the shortest space of time after them, they presently laid all they had upon a heap, and set fire to it. They then chose ten men by lot out of them to slay all the rest; every one of whom laid himself down by his wife and children on the ground, and threw his arms about them, and they offered their necks to the stroke of those who by lot executed that melancholy office; and when these ten had, without fear, slain them all, they made the same rule for casting lots for themselves, that he whose lot it was should first kill the other nine, and after all should kill himself.

Accordingly, all these had courage sufficient to be no way behind one another in doing or suffering; so, for a conclusion, the nine offered their necks to the executioner, and he who was the last of all took a view of all the other bodies, lest perchance some or other among so many that were slain should want his assistance to be quite dispatched, and when he perceived that they were all slain, he set fire to the palace, and with the great force of his hand ran his sword entirely through himself, and fell down dead near to his own relations. So these people died with this intention, that they would not leave so much as one soul among them all alive to be subject to the Rómans. Yet was there an ancient woman, and another who was of kin to Eleázar, and superior to most women in prudence and learning, with five children, who had concealed themselves in caverns under ground, and had carried water thither for their drink, and were hidden there when the rest were intent upon the slaughter of one another. Those others were nine hundred and sixty in number, the women and children being withal included in that computation. This calamitous slaughter was made on the fifteenth day of the month Xánthicus.

7.9.2 Now for the Rómans, they expected that they should be fought in the morning, when, accordingly, they put on their armor, and laid bridges of planks upon their ladders from their banks, to make an assault upon the fortress, which they did; but saw nobody as an enemy, but a terrible solitude on every side, with a fire within the place, as well as a perfect silence. So they were at a loss to guess at what had happened. At length they made a shout, as if it had been at a blow given by the battering ram, to try whether they could bring any one out that was within; the women heard this noise, and came out of their under-ground cavern, and informed the Rómans what had been done, as it was done; and the second of them clearly described all both what was said and what was done, and this manner of it; yet did they not easily give their attention to such a desperate undertaking, and did not believe it could be as they said; they also attempted to put the fire out, and quickly cutting themselves a way through it, they came within the palace, and so met with the multitude of the slain, but could take no pleasure in the fact, though it were done to their enemies. Nor could they do other than wonder at the courage of their resolution, and the immovable contempt of death which so great a number of them had shown, when they went through with such an action as that was.

Joséphus, The Wars of the Jews, 7.9.1-7.9.2 (translated by William Whiston)

An Account of the Eruption of Vesúvius

Your request that I would send you an account of my uncle's death, in order to transmit a more exact relation of it to posterity, deserves my acknowledgments; for, if this accident shall be celebrated by your pen, the glory of it, I am well assured, will be rendered for ever illustrious. And notwithstanding he perished by a misfortune, which, as it involved at the same time a most beautiful country in ruins, and destroyed so many populous cities, seems to promise him an everlasting remembrance; notwithstanding he has himself composed many and lasting works; yet I am persuaded, the mentioning of him in your immortal writings, will greatly contribute to render his name immortal. Happy I esteem those to be to whom by provision of the gods has been granted the ability either to do such actions as are worthy of being related or to relate them in a manner worthy of being read; but peculiarly happy are they who are blessed with both these uncommon talents: in the number of which my uncle, as his own writings and your history will evidently prove, may justly be ranked. It is with extreme willingness, therefore, that I execute your commands; and should indeed have claimed the task if you had not enjoined it. He was at that time with the fleet under his command at Misénum.

On the 24th of August, about one in the afternoon, my mother desired him to observe a cloud which appeared of a very unusual size and shape. He had just taken a turn in the sun, and, after bathing himself in cold water, and making a light luncheon, gone back to his books: he immediately arose and went out upon a rising ground from whence he might get a better sight of this very uncommon appearance. A cloud, from which mountain was uncertain, at this distance (but it was found afterwards to come from Mount Vesúvius), was ascending, the appearance of which I cannot give you a more exact description of than by likening it to that of a pine-tree, for it shot up to a great height in the form of a very tall trunk, which spread itself out at the top into a sort of branches; occasioned, I imagine, either by a sudden gust of air that impelled it, the force of which decreased as it advanced upwards, or the cloud itself, being pressed back again by its own weight, expanded in the manner I have mentioned; it appeared sometimes bright and sometimes dark and spotted, according as it was either more or less impregnated with earth and cinders. This phenomenon seemed to a man of such learning and research as my uncle extraordinary and worth further looking into. He ordered a light vessel to be got ready, and gave me leave, if I liked, to accompany him. I said I had rather go on with my work; and it so happened, he had himself given me something to write out.

As he was coming out of the house, he received a note from Rectína, the wife of Bássus, who was in the utmost alarm at the imminent danger which threatened her; for her villa lying at the foot of Mount Vesúvius, there was no way of escape but by sea; she earnestly entreated him therefore to come to her assistance. He accordingly changed his first intention, and what he had begun from a philosophical, he now carries out in a noble and generous spirit. He ordered the galleys to be put to sea, and went himself on board with an intention of assisting not only Rectína, but the several other towns which lay thickly strewn along that beautiful coast.

Hastening then to the place from whence others fled with the utmost terror, he steered his course direct to the point of danger, and with so much calmness and presence of mind as to be able to make and dictate his observations upon the motion and all the phenomena of that dreadful scene. He was now so close to the mountain that the cinders, which grew thicker and hotter the nearer he approached, fell into the ships, together with pumice-stones, and black pieces of burning rock: they were in danger too not only of being aground by the sudden retreat of the sea, but also from the vast fragments which rolled down from the mountain, and obstructed all the shore. Here he stopped to consider whether he should turn back again; to which the pilot advising him, "Fortune," said he, "favors the brave; steer to where Pomponiánus is." Pomponiánus was then at Stábiæ, separated by a bay, which the sea, after several insensible windings, forms with the shore.

He had already sent his baggage on board; for though he was not at that time in actual danger, yet being within sight of it, and indeed extremely near, if it should in the least increase, he was determined to put to sea as soon as the wind, which was blowing dead inshore, should go down. It was favorable, however, for carrying my uncle to Pomponiánus, whom he found in the greatest consternation: he embraced him tenderly, encouraging and urging him to keep up his spirits, and, the more effectually to soothe his fears by seeming unconcerned himself, ordered a bath to be got ready, and then, after having bathed, sat down to supper with great cheerfulness, or at least (what is just as heroic) with every appearance of it. Meanwhile broad flames shone out in several places from Mount Vesúvius, which the darkness of the night contributed to render still brighter and clearer. But my uncle, in order to soothe the apprehensions of his friend, assured him it was only the burning of the villages, which the country people had abandoned to the flames: after this he retired to rest, and it is most certain he was so little disquieted as to fall into a sound sleep: for his breathing, which, on account of his corpulence, was rather heavy and sonorous, was heard by the attendants outside. The court which led to his apartment being now almost filled with stones and ashes, if he had continued there any time longer, it would have been impossible for him to have made his way out. So he was awoke and got up, and went to Pomponiánus and the rest of his company, who were feeling too anxious to think of going to bed.

They consulted together whether it would be most prudent to trust to the houses, which now rocked from side to side with frequent and violent concussions as though shaken from their very foundations; or fly to the open fields, where the calcined stones and cinders, though light indeed, yet fell in large showers, and threatened destruction. In this choice of dangers they resolved for the fields: as resolution which, while the rest of the company were hurried into by their fears, my uncle embraced upon cool and deliberate consideration. They went out then, having pillows tied upon their heads with napkins; and this was their whole defense against the storm of stones that fell round them. It was now day everywhere else, but *there* a deeper darkness prevailed than in the thickest night; which, however, was in some degree alleviated by torches and other lights of various kinds. They thought proper to go farther down upon the shore to see if they might safely put out to sea, but found the waves still running extremely high, and boisterous.

There my uncle, laying himself down upon a sail-cloth, which was spread for him, called twice for some cold water, which he drank, when immediately the flames, preceded by a strong whiff of sulphur, dispersed the rest of the party, and obliged him to rise. He raised himself up with the assistance of two of his servants, and instantly fell down dead; suffocated, as I conjecture, by some gross and noxious vapor, having always had a weak throat, which was often inflamed. As soon as it was light again, which was not till the third day after this melancholy accident, his body was found entire, and without any marks of violence upon it, in the dress in which he fell, and looking more like a man asleep than dead. During all this time my mother and I, who were at Misénum— but this has no connection with your history, and you did not desire any particulars besides those of my uncle's death; so I will end here, only adding that I have faithfully related to you what I was either an eye-witness of myself or received immediately after the accident happened, and before there was time to vary the truth. You will pick out of this narrative whatever is most important: for a letter is one thing, a history another; it is one thing writing to a friend, another thing writing to the public. Farewell.

Plíny the Younger, *Letter 65, To Tácitus* (translated by William Melmoth)

The Difficulties of the Historian in a Corrupt Age

1 To bequeath to posterity a record of the deeds and characters of distinguished men is an ancient practice which even the present age, careless as it is of its own sons, has not abandoned whenever some great and conspicuous excellence has conquered and risen superior to that failing, common to petty and to great states, blindness and hostility to goodness. But in days gone by, as there was a greater inclination and a more open path to the achievement of memorable actions, so the man of highest genius was led by the simple reward of a good conscience to hand on without partiality or self-seeking the remembrance of greatness. Many too thought that to write their own lives showed the confidence of integrity rather than presumption. Of Rutílius and Scáurus no one doubted the honesty or questioned the motives. So true is it that merit is best appreciated by the age in which it thrives most easily. But in these days, I, who have to record the life of one who has passed away, must crave an indulgence, which I should not have had to ask had I only to inveigh against an age so cruel, so hostile to all virtue.

2 We have only to read that the panegyrics pronounced by Arulénus Rústicus on Pǽtus Thraséa, and by Herénnius Senécio on Príscus Helvídius, were made capital crimes, that not only their persons but their very books were objects of rage, and that the triúmvirs were commissioned to burn in the fórum those works of splendid genius. They fancied, forsooth, that in that fire the voice of the Róman people, the freedom of the Senate, and the conscience of the human race were perishing, while at the same time they banished the teachers of philosophy, and exiled every noble pursuit, that nothing good might anywhere confront them. Certainly we showed a magnificent example of patience; as a former age had witnessed the extreme of liberty, so we witnessed the extreme of servitude, when the informer robbed us of the interchanges of speech, and hearing. We should have lost memory as well as voice, had it been as easy to forget as to keep silence.

3 Now at last our spirit is returning. And yet, though at the dawn of a most happy age Nérva Cǽsar blended things once irreconcilable, sovereignty and freedom; though Nérva Trájan is now daily augmenting the prosperity of the time, and though the public safety has not only our hopes and good wishes, but has also the certain pledge of their fulfillment: still, from the necessary condition of human frailty, the remedy works less quickly than the disease. As our bodies grow but slowly, perish in a moment, so it is easier to crush than to revive genius and its pursuits. Besides, the charm of indolence steals over us, and the idleness which at first we loathed we afterwards love. What if during those fifteen years, a large portion of human life, many were cut off by ordinary casualties, and the ablest fell victim to the Emperor's rage, if a few of us survive, though there have been taken from the midst of life those many years which brought the young in dumb silence to old age, and the old almost to the very verge and end of existence! Yet we shall not regret that we have told, though in language unskillful and unadorned, the story of past servitude, and borne our testimony to present happiness. Meanwhile this book, intended to do honor to Agrícola, my father-in-law, will, as an expression of filial regard, be commended, or at least excused.

Públius Cornélius Tácitus, *Agrícola*, 1-3
(translated by Alfred John Church and William Jackson Brodribb)

The Virtues of Agrícola

9 As he was returning from the command of the légion, Vespásian admitted him into the patrícian order, and then gave him the province of Aquitánia, a preeminently splendid appointment both from the importance of its duties and the prospect of the cónsulate to which the Emperor destined him. Many think the genius of the soldier wants subtlety, because military law, which is summary and blunt, and apt to appeal to the sword, finds no exercise for the refinements of the fórum. Yet Agrícola, from his natural good sense, though called to act among civilians, did his work with ease and correctness. And, besides, the times of business and relaxation were kept distinct. When his public and judicial duties required it, he was dignified, thoughtful, austere, and yet often merciful; when business was done with, he wore no longer the official character. He was altogether without harshness, pride, or the greed of gain. With a most rare felicity, his good nature did not weaken his authority, nor his strictness the attachment of his friends. To speak of uprightness and purity in such a man would be an insult to his virtues.

Fame itself, of which even good men are often weakly fond, he did not seek by an ostentation of virtue or by artifice. He avoided rivalry with his colleagues, contention with his procurator, thinking such victories no honor and defeat disgrace. For somewhat less than three years he was kept in his governorship, and was then recalled with an immediate prospect of the cónsulate. A general belief went with him that the province of Brítain was to be his, not because he had himself hinted it, but because he seemed worthy of it. Public opinion is not always mistaken; sometimes even it chooses the right man. He was cónsul, and I but a youth, when he betrothed to me his daughter, a maiden even then of noble promise. After his cónsulate he gave her to me in marriage, and was then at once appointed to the government of Brítain, with the addition of the sacred office of the pontificate.

Públius Cornélius Tácitus, *Agrícola*, 9
(translated by Alfred John Church and William Jackson Brodribb)

Agrícola's Pacification of Brítain

17 When however Vespásian had restored to unity Brítain as well as the rest of the world, in the presence of the great generals and renowned armies the enemy's hopes were crushed. They were at once panic-stricken by the attack of Petílius Ceriális on the state of the Brigántes, said to be the most prosperous in the entire province. There were many battles, some by no means bloodless, and his conquests, or at least his wars, embraced a large part of the territory of the Brigántes. Indeed he would have altogether thrown into the shade the activity and renown of any other successor; but Július Fróntus was equal to the burden, a great man as far as greatness was then possible, who subdued by his arms the powerful and warlike tribe of the Sílures, surmounting the difficulties of the country as well as the valor of the enemy.

18 Such was the state of Brítain, and such were the vicissitudes of the war, which Agrícola found on his crossing over about midsummer. Our soldiers made it a pretext for carelessness, as if all fighting was over, and the enemy were biding their time. The Ordóvices, shortly before Agrícola's arrival, had destroyed nearly the whole of a squadron of allied cavalry quartered in their territory. Such a beginning raised the hopes of the country, and all who wished for war approved the precedent, and anxiously watched the temper of the new governor. Meanwhile Agrícola, though summer was past and the detachments were scattered throughout the province, though the soldiers' confident anticipation of inaction for that year would be a source of delay and difficulty in beginning a campaign, and most advisers thought it best simply to watch all weak points, resolved to face the peril. He collected a force of veterans and a small body of auxiliaries; then as the Ordóvices would not venture to descend into the plain, he put himself in front of the ranks to inspire all with the same courage against a common danger, and led his troops up a hill. The tribe was all but exterminated.

Well aware that he must follow up the prestige of his arms, and that in proportion to his first success would be the terror of the other tribes, he formed the design of subjugating the island of Móna, from the occupation of which Paulínus had been recalled, as I have already related, by the rebellion of the entire province. But, as his plans were not matured, he had no fleet. The skill and resolution of the general accomplished the passage. With some picked men of the auxiliaries, disencumbered of all baggage, who knew the shallows and had that national experience in swimming which enables the Brítons to take care not only of themselves but of their arms and horses, he delivered so unexpected an attack that the astonished enemy who were looking for a fleet, a naval armament, and an assault by sea, thought that to such assailants nothing could be formidable or invincible. And so, peace having been sued for and the island given up, Agrícola became great and famous as one who, when entering on his province, a time which others spend in vain display and a round of ceremonies, chose rather toil and danger. Nor did he use his success for self-glorification, or apply the name of campaigns and victories to the repression of a conquered people. He did not even describe his achievements in a laurelled letter. Yet by thus disguising his renown he really increased it, for men inferred the grandeur of his aspirations from his silence about services so great.

19 Next, with thorough insight into the feelings of his province, and taught also, by the experience of others, that little is gained by conquest if followed by oppression, he determined to root out the causes of war. Beginning first with himself and his dependents, he kept his household under restraint, a thing as hard to many as ruling a province. He transacted no public business through freedmen or slaves; no private leanings, no recommendations or entreaties of friends, moved him in the selection of centúrions and soldiers, but it was ever the best man whom he thought most trustworthy. He knew everything, but did not always act on his knowledge. Trifling errors he treated with leniency, serious offences with severity. Nor was it always punishment, but far oftener penitence, which satisfied him. He preferred to give office and power to men who would not transgress, rather than have to condemn a transgressor. He lightened the exaction of corn and tribute by an equal distribution of the burden, while he got rid of those contrivances for gain which were more intolerable than the tribute itself. Hitherto the people had been compelled to endure the farce of waiting by the closed granary and of purchasing corn unnecessarily and raising it to a fictitious price. Difficult byroads and distant places were fixed for them, so that states with a winter-camp close to them had to carry corn to remote and inaccessible parts of the country, until what was within the reach of all became a source of profit to the few.

20 Agrícola, by the repression of these abuses in his very first year in office, restored to peace its good name, when, from either the indifference or the harshness of his predecessors, it had come to be as much dreaded as war. When, however, summer came, assembling his forces, he continually showed himself in the ranks, praised good discipline, and kept the stragglers in order. He would himself choose the position of the camp, himself explore the estuaries and forests. Meanwhile he would allow the enemy no rest, laying waste his territory with sudden incursions, and, having sufficiently alarmed him, would then by forbearance display the allurements of peace. In consequence, many states, which up to that time had been independent, gave hostages, and laid aside their animosities; garrisons and forts were established among them with a skill and diligence with which no newly-acquired part of Brítain had before been treated.

21 The following winter passed without disturbance, and was employed in salutary measures. For, to accustom to rest and repose through the charms of luxury a population scattered and barbarous and therefore inclined to war, Agrícola gave private encouragement and public aid to the building of temples, courts of justice and dwelling-houses, praising the energetic, and reproving the indolent. Thus an honorable rivalry took the place of compulsion. He likewise provided a liberal education for the sons of the chiefs, and showed such a preference for the natural powers of the Brítons over the industry of the Gauls that they who lately disdained the tongue of Rome now coveted its eloquence. Hence, too, a liking sprang up for our style of dress, and the "tóga" became fashionable. Step by step they were led to things which dispose to vice, the lounge, the bath, the elegant banquet. All this in their ignorance they called civilization, when it was but a part of their servitude.

Públius Cornélius Tácitus, *Agrícola*, 17-21
(translated by Alfred John Church and William Jackson Brodribb)

Domítian's Envy of Agrícola

39 Of this series of events, though not exaggerated in the dispatches of Agrícola by any boastfulness of language, Domítian heard, as was his wont, with joy in his face but anxiety in his heart. He felt conscious that all men laughed at his late mock triumph over Gérmany, for which there had been purchased from traders people whose dress and hair might be made to resemble those of captives, whereas now a real and splendid victory, with the destruction of thousands of the enemy, was being celebrated with just applause. It was, he thought, a very alarming thing for him that the name of a subject should be raised above that of the Emperor; it was to no purpose that he had driven into obscurity the pursuit of forensic eloquence and the graceful accomplishments of civic life, if another were to forestall the distinctions of war. To other glories he could more easily shut his eyes, but the greatness of a good general was a truly imperial quality. Harassed by these anxieties, and absorbed in an incommunicable trouble, a sure prognostic of some cruel purpose, he decided that it was best for the present to suspend his hatred until the freshness of Agrícola's renown and his popularity with the army should begin to pass away.

40 For Agrícola was still the governor of Brítain. Accordingly the Emperor ordered that the usual triumphal decorations, the honor of a laurelled statue, and all that is commonly given in place of the triumphal procession, with the addition of many laudatory expressions, should be decreed in the senate, together with a hint to the effect that Agrícola was to have the province of Sýria, then vacant by the death of Atílius Rúfus, a man of cónsular rank, and generally reserved for men of distinction. It was believed by many persons that one of the freedmen employed on confidential services was sent to Agrícola, bearing a dispatch in which Sýria was offered him, and with instructions to deliver it should he be in Brítain; that this freedman in crossing the straights met Agrícola, and without even saluting him made his way back to Domítian; though I cannot say whether the story is true, or is only a fiction invented to suit the Emperor's character.

Meanwhile Agrícola had handed over his province in peace and safety to his successor. And not to make his entrance into Rome conspicuous by the concourse of welcoming throngs, he avoided the attentions of his friends by entering the city at night, and at night too, according to orders, proceeded to the palace, where, having been received with a hurried embrace and without a word being spoken, he mingled in the crowd of courtiers. Anxious henceforth to temper the military renown, which annoys men of peace, with other merits, he studiously cultivated retirement and leisure, simple in dress, courteous in conversation, and never accompanied but by one or two friends, so that the many who commonly judge of great men by their external grandeur, after having seen and attentively surveyed him, asked the secret of a greatness which but few could explain.

41 During this time he was frequently accused before Domítian in his absence, and in his absence acquitted. The cause of his danger lay not in any crime, nor in any complaint of injury, but in a ruler who was the foe of virtue, in his own renown, and in that worst class of enemies— the men who praise. And then followed such days for the commonwealth as would not suffer Agrícola to be forgotten; days when so many of our armies were lost in Mœsia, Dácia, Gérmany, and Pannónia, through the rashness or cowardice of our generals, when so many of our officers were besieged and captured with so many of our auxiliaries, when it was no longer the boundaries of empire and the banks of rivers which were imperiled, but the winter-quarters of our légions and the possession of our territories. And so when disaster followed upon disaster, and the entire year was marked by destruction and slaughter, the voice of the people called Agrícola to the command; for they all contrasted his vigor, firmness, and experience in war, with the inertness and timidity of other generals. This talk, it is quite certain, assailed the ears of the Emperor himself, while affection and loyalty in the best of his freedmen, malice and envy in the worst, kindled the anger of a prince ever inclined to evil. And so at once, by his own excellences and by the faults of others, Agrícola was hurried headlong to a perilous elevation.

42 The year had now arrived in which the pro-cónsulate of Ásia or África was to fall to him by lot, and, as Cívica had been lately murdered, Agrícola did not want a warning, or Domítian a precedent. Persons well acquainted with the Emperor's feelings came to ask Agrícola, as if on their own account, whether he would go. First they hinted their purpose by praises of tranquility and leisure; then offered their services in procuring acceptance for his excuses; and at last, throwing off all disguise, brought him by entreaties and threats to Domítian. The Emperor, armed beforehand with hypocrisy, and assuming a haughty demeanor, listened to his prayer that he might be excused, and having granted his request allowed himself to be formally thanked, nor blushed to grant so sinister a favor. But the salary usually granted to a pro-cónsul, and which he had himself given to some governors, he did not bestow on Agrícola, either because he was offended at its not having been asked, or was warned by his conscience that he might be thought to have purchased the refusal which he had commanded.

It is, indeed, human nature to hate the man whom you have injured; yet the Emperor, notwithstanding his irascible temper and an implacability proportioned to his reserve, was softened by the moderation and prudence of Agrícola, who neither by a perverse obstinacy nor an idle parade of freedom challenged fame or provoked his fate. Let it be known to those whose habit it is to admire the disregard of authority, that there may be great men even under bad emperors, and that obedience and submission, when joined to activity and vigor, may attain a glory which most men reach only by a perilous career, utterly useless to the state, and closed by an ostentatious death.

43 The end of his life, a deplorable calamity to us and a grief to his friends, was regarded with concern even by strangers and those who knew him not. The common people and this busy population continually inquired at his house, and talked of him in public places and in private gatherings. No man when he heard of Agrícola's death could either be glad or at once forget it. Men's sympathy was increased by a prevalent rumor that he was destroyed by poison. For myself, I have nothing which I should venture to state for fact. Certainly during the whole of his illness the Emperor's chief freedmen and confidential physicians came more frequently than is usual with a court which pays its visits by means of messengers. This was, perhaps, solicitude, perhaps espionage. Certain it is, that on the last day the very agonies of his dying moments were reported by a succession of couriers, and no one believed that there would be such haste about tidings which would be heard with regret. Yet in his manner and countenance the Emperor displayed some signs of sorrow, for he could now forget his enmity, and it was easier to conceal his joy than his fear. It was well known that on reading the will, in which he was named co-heir with Agrícola's excellent wife and most dutiful daughter, he expressed delight, as if it had been a complimentary choice. So blinded and perverted was his mind by incessant flattery, that he did not know that it was only a bad Emperor whom a good father would make his heir.

44 Agrícola was born on the 13th of June, in the third cónsulate of Gáius Cæsar; he died on the 23rd of August, during the cónsulate of Colléga and Príscus, being in the fifty-sixth year of his age. Should posterity wish to know something of his appearance, it was graceful rather than commanding. There was nothing formidable in his appearance; a gracious look predominated. One would easily believe him a good man, and willingly believe him to be great. As for himself, though taken from us in the prime of a vigorous manhood, yet, as far as glory is concerned, his life was of the longest. Those true blessings, indeed, which consist in virtue, he had fully attained; and on one who had reached the honors of a cónsulate and a triumph, what more had fortune to bestow? Immense wealth had no attractions for him, and wealth he had, even to splendor. As his daughter and his wife survived him, it may be thought that he was even fortunate—fortunate, in that while his honors had suffered no eclipse, while his fame was at its height, while his kindred and his friends still prospered, he escaped from the evil to come. For, though to survive until the dawn of this most happy age and to see a Trájan on the throne was what he would speculate upon in previsions and wishes confided to my ears, yet he had this mighty compensation for his premature death, that he was spared those later years during which Domítian, leaving now no interval or breathing space of time, but, as it were, with one continuous blow, drained the life-blood of the Commonwealth.

45 Agrícola did not see the senate-house besieged, or the senate hemmed in by armed men, or so many of Rome's noblest ladies exiles and fugitives. Cárus Métius had as yet the distinction of but one victory, and the noisy counsels of Messalínus were not heard beyond the walls of Álba, and Mássa Bæbius was then answering for his life. It was not long before our hands dragged Helvídius to prison, before we gazed on the dying looks of Mánricus and Rústicus, before we were steeped in Senécio's innocent blood. Even Néro turned his eyes away, and did not gaze upon the atrocities which he ordered; with Domítian it was the chief part of our miseries to see and to be seen, to know that our sighs were being recorded, to have, ever ready to note the pallid looks of so many faces, that savage countenance reddened with the hue with which he defied shame. Thou wast indeed fortunate, Agrícola, not only in the splendor of thy life, but in the opportune moment of thy death. Thou submittedst to thy fate, so they tell us who were present to hear thy last words, with courage and cheerfulness, seeming to be doing all thou couldst to give thine Emperor full acquittal. As for me and thy daughter, besides all the bitterness of a father's loss, it increases our sorrow that it was not permitted us to watch over thy failing health, to comfort thy weakness, to satisfy ourselves with those looks, those embraces. Assuredly we should have received some precepts, some utterances to fix in our inmost hearts. This is the bitterness of our sorrow, this the smart of our wound, that from the circumstance of so long an absence thou wast lost to us four years before. Doubtless, best of fathers, with that most loving wife at thy side, all the dues of affection were abundantly paid thee, yet with too few tears thou wast laid to thy rest, and in the light of thy last day there was something for which thine eyes longed in vain.

46 If there is any dwelling-place for the spirits of the just; if, as the wise believe, noble souls do not perish with the body, rest thou in peace; and call us, thy family, from weak regrets and womanish laments to the contemplation of thy virtues, for which we must not weep nor beat the breast. Let us honor thee not so much with transitory praises as with our reverence, and, if our powers permit us, with our emulation. That will be true respect, that the true affection of thy nearest kin. This, too, is what I would enjoin on daughter and wife, to honor the memory of that father, that husband, by pondering in their hearts all his words and acts, by cherishing the features and lineaments of his character rather than those of his person. It is not that I would forbid the likenesses which are wrought in marble or in bronze; but as the faces of men, so all similitudes of the face are weak and perishable things, while the fashion of the soul is everlasting, such as may be expressed not in some foreign substance, or by the help of art, but in our own lives. Whatever we loved, whatever we admired in Agrícola, survives, and will survive in the hearts of men, in the succession of the ages, in the fame that waits on noble deeds. Over many indeed, of those who have gone before, as over the inglorious and ignoble, the waves of oblivion will roll; Agrícola, made known to posterity by history and tradition, will live for ever.

Públius Cornélius Tácitus, *Agrícola*, 39-46
(translated by Alfred John Church and William Jackson Brodribb)

CHAPTER XXVI

THE FIVE GOOD EMPERORS: NÉRVA TO MÁRCUS AURÉLIUS

The Reign of Nérva (A.D. 96-98), I.—The Reign of Trájan (A.D. 98-117), II.
The Reign of Hádrian (A.D. 117-138), III.—The Reign of Antonínus Píus (A.D. 138-161), IV.
The Reign of Márcus Aurélius (A.D. 161-180), V.

The Accession of Trájan

68.5 When he became emperor, he sent a letter to the senate, written with his own hand, in which he declared, among other things, that he would not slay nor disfranchise any good man; and he confirmed this by oaths not only at the time but also later. He sent for Æliánus and the Prætórians who had mutinied against Nérva, pretending that he was going to employ them for some purpose, and then put them out of the way. When he came to Rome, he did much to reform the administration of affairs and much to please the better element; to the public business he gave unusual attention, making many grants, for example, to the cities in Ítaly for the support of their children, and upon the good citizens he conferred many favors. When Plotína, his wife, first entered the palace, she turned around so as to face the stairway and the populace and said: "I enter here such a woman as I would fain be when I depart." And she conducted herself during the entire reign in such a manner as to incur no censure.

Cássius Dío, Róman History, 68.5 (translated by Earnest Carey)

Trájan and Súra

68.15 When Licínius Súra died, Trájan bestowed upon him a public funeral and a statue. This man had attained to such a degree of wealth and pride that he had built a gymnasium for the Rómans; yet so great was the friendship and confidence which he showed toward Trájan and Trájan toward him, that, although he was often slandered—as naturally happens in the case of all those who possess any influence with the emperors—Trájan never felt any suspicion or hatred toward him. On the contrary, when those who envied Súra became very insistent, the emperor went uninvited to his house to dinner, and having dismissed his whole body-guard, he first called Súra's physician and caused him to anoint his eyes, and then his barber, whom he caused to shave his chin (for the emperors themselves as well as all the rest used to follow this ancient practice; it was Hádrian who first set the fashion of wearing a beard); and after doing all this, he next took a bath and had dinner. Then on the following day he said to his friends who were constantly in the habit of making disparaging remarks about Súra: "If Súra had desired to kill me, he would have killed me yesterday."

Cássius Dío, Róman History, 68.15 (translated by Earnest Carey)

A Letter of Plíny to Trájan Concerning the Christians

It is my invariable rule, Sir, to refer to you in all matters where I feel doubtful; for who is more capable of removing my scruples, or informing my ignorance? Having never been present at any trials concerning those who profess Christiánity, I am unacquainted not only with the nature of their crimes, or the measure of their punishment, but how far it is proper to enter into an examination concerning them. Whether, therefore, any difference is usually made with respect to ages, or no distinction is to be observed between the young and the adult; whether repentance entitles them to a pardon, or, if a man has been once a Chrístian, it avails nothing to desist from his error; whether the very profession of Christianity, unattended with any criminal act, or only the crimes themselves inherent in the profession are punishable; on all these points I am in great doubt.

In the meanwhile, the method I have observed towards those who have been brought before me as Christians is this: I asked them whether they were Christians; if they admitted it, I repeated the question twice, and threatened them with punishment; if they persisted, I ordered them to be at once punished: for I was persuaded, whatever the nature of their opinions might be, a contumacious and inflexible obstinacy certainly deserved correction. There were others also brought before me possessed with the same infatuation, but being Roman citizens, I directed them to be sent to Rome.

But this crime spreading (as is usually the case) while it was actually under prosecution, several instances of the same nature occurred. An anonymous information was laid before me containing a charge against several persons, who upon examination denied they were Christians, or had ever been so. They repeated after me an invocation to the gods, and offered religious rites with wine and incense before your statue (which for that purpose I had ordered to be brought, together with those of the gods), and even reviled the name of Christ: whereas there is no forcing, it is said, those who are really Christians into any of these compliances: I thought it proper, therefore, to discharge them. Some among those who were accused by a witness in person at first confessed themselves Christians, but immediately after denied it; the rest owned indeed that they had been of that number formerly, but had now (some above three, others more, and a few above twenty years ago) renounced that error.

They all worshipped your statue and the images of the gods, uttering imprecations at the same time against the name of Christ. They affirmed the whole of their guilt, or their error, was, that they met on a stated day before it was light, and addressed a form of prayer to Christ, as to a divinity, binding themselves by a solemn oath, not for the purposes of any wicked design, but never to commit any fraud, theft, or adultery, never to falsify their word, nor deny a trust when they should be called upon to deliver it up; after which it was their custom to separate, and then reassemble, to eat in common a harmless meal. From this custom, however, they desisted after the publication of my edict, by which, according to your commands, I forbade the meeting of any assemblies. After receiving this account, I judged it so much the more necessary to endeavor to extort the real truth, by putting two female slaves to the torture, who were said to officiate in their religious rites: but all I could discover was evidence of an absurd and extravagant superstition.

I deemed it expedient, therefore, to adjourn all further proceedings, in order to consult you. For it appears to be a matter highly deserving your consideration, more especially as great numbers must be involved in the danger of these prosecutions, which have already extended, and are still likely to extend, to persons of all ranks and ages, and even of both sexes. In fact, this contagious superstition is not confined to the cities only, but has spread its infection among the neighboring villages and country. Nevertheless, it still seems possible to restrain its progress. The temples, at least, which were once almost deserted, begin now to be frequented; and the sacred rites, after a long intermission, are again revived; while there is a general demand for the victims, which till lately found very few purchasers. From all this it is easy to conjecture what numbers might be reclaimed if a general pardon were granted to those who shall repent of their error.

The Reply of Trájan to Plíny Concerning the Christians

You have adopted the right course, my dearest Secúndus, in investigating the charges against the Christians who were brought before you. It is not possible to lay down any general rule for all such cases. Do not go out of your way to look for them. If indeed they should be brought before you, and the crime is proved, they must be punished; with the restriction, however, that where the party denies he is a Christian, and shall make it evident that he is not, by invoking our gods, let him (notwithstanding any former suspicion) be pardoned upon his repentance. Anonymous information ought not to be received in any sort of prosecution. It is introducing a very dangerous precedent, and is quite foreign to the spirit of our age.

Plíny the Younger, Letters, Correspondence with Trájan, 97, 98
(translated by William Melmoth, revised by F. C. T. Bosanquet)

The Character of Márcus Aurélius

72.35 His education was of great assistance to him, for he had been trained both in rhetoric and in philosophical disputation. In the former he had Cornélius Frónto and Cláudius Heródes for teachers, and, in the latter, Június Rústicus and Apóllonius of Nicomédia, both of whom professed Zéno's doctrines. As a result, great numbers pretended to pursue philosophy, hoping that they might be enriched by the emperor. Most of all, however, he owed his advancement to his own natural gifts; for even before he associated with those teachers he had a strong impulse towards virtue. Indeed, while still a boy he so pleased all his relatives, who were numerous, influential and wealthy, that he was loved by them all; and when Hádrian, chiefly for this reason, had adopted him, he did not become haughty, but, though young and a Cæsar, served Antonínus most loyally throughout all the latter's reign and without giving offence showed honor to the others who were foremost in the State. He used always to salute the most worthy men in the House of Tibérius, where he lived, before visiting his father, not only without putting on the attire befitting his rank, but actually dressed as a private citizen, and receiving them in the very apartment where he slept. He used to visit many who were sick, and never missed going to his teachers. He would wear a dark cloak whenever he went out unaccompanied by his father, and he never employed a torch-bearer for himself alone. Upon being appointed leader of the knights he entered the Fórum with the rest, although he was a Cæsar. This shows how excellent was his natural disposition, though it was greatly aided by his education. He was always steeping himself in Greek and Látin rhetorical and philosophical learning, even after he had reached man's estate and had hopes of becoming emperor.

72.36 Even before he was appointed Cæsar he had a dream in which he seemed to have shoulders and arms of ivory, and to use them in all respect like his other members. As a result of his close application and study he was extremely frail in body, though in the beginning he had been so vigorous that he used to fight in armor, and on the chase would strike down wild boars while on horseback; and not only in his early youth but even later he wrote most of his letters to his intimate friends with his own hand. However, he did not meet with the good fortune that he deserved, for he was not strong in body and was involved in a multitude of troubles throughout practically his entire reign. But for my part, I admire him all the more for this very reason, that amid unusual and extraordinary difficulties he both survived himself and preserved the empire. Just one thing prevented him from being completely happy, namely, that after rearing and educating his son in the best possible way he was vastly disappointed in him. This matter must be our next topic; for our history now descends from a kingdom of gold to one of iron and rust, as affairs did for the Rómans of that day.

Cássius Dío, Róman History, 72.35-72.36 (translated by Earnest Carey)

Márcus Aurélius Credits His Teachers

From my grandfather Vérus I learned good morals and the government of my temper.

From the reputation and remembrance of my father, modesty and a manly character.

From my mother, piety and beneficence, and abstinence, not only from evil deeds, but even from evil thoughts; and further, simplicity in my way of living, far removed from the habits of the rich.

From my great-grandfather, not to have frequented public schools, and to have had good teachers at home, and to know that on such things a man should spend liberally.

From my governor, to be neither of the green nor of the blue party at the games in the Círcus, nor a partisan either of the Parmulárius or the Scutárius at the gladiators' fights; from him too I learned endurance of labor, and to want little, and to work with my own hands, and not to meddle with other people's affairs, and not to be ready to listen to slander.

From Diognétus, not to busy myself about trifling things, and not to give credit to what was said by miracle-workers and jugglers about incantations and the driving away of dæmons and such things; and not to breed quails for fighting, nor to give myself up passionately to such things; and to endure freedom of speech; and to have become intimate with philosophy; and to have been a hearer, first of Bácchius, then of Tandásis and Marciánus; and to have written dialogues in my youth; and to desired a plank bed and skin, and whatever else of the kind belongs to the Grécian discipline.

From Rústicus I received the impression that my character required improvement and discipline; and from him I learned not to be led astray to sophistic emulation, nor to writing on speculative matters, nor to delivering little hortatory orations, nor to showing myself off as a man who practices much discipline, or does benevolent acts in order to make a display; and to abstain from rhetoric, and poetry, and fine writing; and not to walk about in the house in my outdoor dress, nor to do other things of the kind; and to write my letters with simplicity, like the letter which Rústicus wrote from Sinuéssa to my mother; and with respect to those who have offended me by words, or done me wrong, to be easily disposed to be pacified and reconciled, as soon as they have shown a readiness to be reconciled; and to read carefully, and not to be satisfied with a superficial understanding of a book; nor hastily to give my assent to those who talk overmuch; and I am indebted to him for being acquainted with the discourses of Epictétus, which he communicated to me out of his own collection.

From Apollónius I learned freedom of will and undeviating steadiness of purpose; and to look to nothing else, not even for a moment, except to reason; and to be always the same, in sharp pains, on the occasion of the loss of a child, and in long illness; and to see clearly in a living example that the same man can be both most resolute and yielding, and not peevish in giving his instruction; and to have had before my eyes a man who clearly considered his experience and his skill in expounding philosophical principles as the smallest of his merits; and from him I learned how to receive from friends what are esteemed favors, without being either humbled by them or letting them pass unnoticed.

From Séxtus, a benevolent disposition, and the example of a family governed in a fatherly manner, and the idea of living conformably to nature; and gravity without affectation, and to look carefully after the interests of friends, and to tolerate ignorant persons, and those who form opinions without consideration: he had the power of readily accommodating himself to all, so that intercourse with him was more agreeable than any flattery; and at the same time he was most highly venerated by those who associated with him: and he had the faculty both of discovering and ordering, in an intelligent and methodical way, the principles necessary for life; and he never showed anger or any other passion, but was entirely free from passion, and also most affectionate; and he could express approbation without noisy display, and he possessed much knowledge without ostentation.

From Alexánder the grammarian, to refrain from fault-finding, and not in a reproachful way to chide those who uttered any barbarous or solecistic or strange-sounding expression; but dexterously to introduce the very expression which ought to have been used, and in the way of answer or giving confirmation, or joining in an inquiry about the thing itself, not about the word, or by some other fit suggestion.

From Frónto I learned to observe what envy, and duplicity, and hypocrisy are in a tyrant, and that generally those among us who are called Patrícians are rather deficient in paternal affection.

From Alexánder the Platónist, not frequently nor without necessity to say to any one, or to write in a letter, that I have no leisure; nor continually to excuse the neglect of duties required by our relation to those with whom we live, by alleging urgent occupations.

From Cátulus, not to be indifferent when a friend finds fault, even if he should find fault without reason, but to try to restore him to his usual disposition; and to be ready to speak well of teachers, as it is reported of Domítius and Athenódotus; and to love my children truly.

From my brother Sevérus, to love my kin, and to love truth, and to love justice; and through him I learned to know Thraséa, Helvídius, Cáto, Díon, Brútus; and from him I received the idea of a polity in which there is the same law for all, a polity administered with regard to equal rights and equal freedom of speech, and the idea of a kingly government which respects most of all the freedom of the governed; I learned from him also consistency and undeviating steadiness in my regard for philosophy; and a disposition to do good, and to give to others readily, and to cherish good hopes, and to believe that I am loved by my friends; and in him I observed no concealment of his opinions with respect to those whom he condemned, and that his friends had no need to conjecture what he wished or did not wish, but it was quite plain.

From Máximus I learned self-government, and not to be led aside by anything; and cheerfulness in all circumstances, as well as in illness; and a just admixture in the moral character of sweetness and dignity, and to do what was set before me without complaining. I observed that everybody believed that he thought as he spoke, and that in all that he did he never had any bad intention; and he never showed amazement and surprise, and was never in a hurry, and never put off doing a thing, nor was perplexed nor dejected, nor did he ever laugh to disguise his vexation, nor, on the other hand, was he ever passionate or suspicious. He was accustomed to do acts of beneficence, and was ready to forgive, and was free from all falsehood; and he presented the appearance of a man who could not be diverted from right rather than of a man who had been improved. I observed, too, that no man could ever think that he was despised by Máximus, or ever venture to think himself a better man. He had also the art of being humorous in an agreeable way.

In my father I observed mildness of temper, and unchangeable resolution in the things which he had determined after due deliberation; and no vainglory in those things which men call honors; and a love of labor and perseverance; and a readiness to listen to those who had anything to propose for the common weal; and undeviating firmness in giving to every man according to his deserts; and a knowledge derived from experience of the occasions for vigorous action and for remission. And I observed that ... he considered himself no more than any other citizen...

I observed too his habit of careful inquiry in all matters of deliberation, and his persistency, and that he never stopped his investigation through being satisfied with appearances which first present themselves; and that his disposition was to keep his friends, and not to be soon tired of them, nor yet to be extravagant in his affection; and to be satisfied on all occasions, and cheerful; and to foresee things a long way off, and to provide for the smallest without display; and to check immediately popular applause and all flattery; and to be ever watchful over the things which were necessary for the administration of the empire, and to be a good manager of the expenditure, and patiently to endure the blame which he got for such conduct; and he was neither superstitious with respect to the gods, nor did he court men by gifts or by trying to please them, or by flattering the populace; but he showed sobriety in all things and firmness, and never any mean thoughts or action, nor love of novelty. And the things which conduce in any way to the commodity of life, and of which fortune gives an abundant supply, he used without arrogance and without excusing himself; so that when he had them, he enjoyed them without affectation, and when he had them not, he did not want them.

No one could ever say of him that he was either a sophist or a home-bred flippant slave or a pedant; but every one acknowledged him to be a man ripe, perfect, above flattery, able to manage his own and other men's affairs. Besides this, he honored those who were true philosophers, and he did not reproach those who pretended to be philosophers, nor yet was he easily led by them. He was also easy in conversation, and he made himself agreeable without any offensive affectation. He took a reasonable care of his body's health, not as one who was greatly attached to life, nor out of regard to personal appearance, nor yet in a careless way, but so that, through his own attention, he very seldom stood in need of the physician's art or of medicine or external applications. He was most ready to give way without envy to those who possessed any particular faculty, such as that of eloquence or knowledge of the law or of morals, or of anything else; and he gave them his help, that each might enjoy reputation according to his deserts; and he always acted conformably to the institutions of his country, without showing any affectation of doing so.

Further, he was not fond of change nor unsteady, but he loved to stay in the same places, and to employ himself about the same things; and after his paroxysms of headache he came immediately fresh and vigorous to his usual occupations. His secrets were not but very few and very rare, and these only about public matters; and he showed prudence and economy in the exhibition of the public spectacles and the construction of public buildings, his donations to the people, and in such things, for he was a man who looked to what ought to be done, not to the reputation which is got by a man's acts... There was in him nothing harsh, nor implacable, nor violent, nor, as one may say, anything carried to the sweating point; but he examined all things severally, as if he had abundance of time, and without confusion, in an orderly way, vigorously and consistently. And that might be applied to him which is recorded of Sócrates, that he was able both to abstain from, and to enjoy, those things which many are too weak to abstain from, and cannot enjoy without excess. But to be strong enough both to bear the one and to be sober in the other is the mark of a man who has a perfect and invincible soul, such as he showed in the illness of Máximus...

Márcus Aurélius, *Meditations*, Book 1 (translated by George Long)

CHAPTER XXVII

THE DECLINE OF THE EMPIRE

The Times of the Sevéri, I.—The Disintegration of the Empire, II.—The Illýrian Emperors, III.

Caracálla's Murder of Géta

77.2 Antonínus [Caracálla] wished to murder his brother at the Saturnália, but was unable to do so; for his evil purpose had already become too manifest to remain concealed, and so there now ensued many sharp encounters between the two, each of whom felt that the other was plotting against him, and many defensive measures were taken on both sides. Since many soldiers and athletes, therefore, were guarding Géta, both abroad and at home, day and night alike, Antonínus induced his mother to summon them both, unattended, to her apartment, with a view to reconciling them.

Thus Géta was persuaded, and went in with him; but when they were inside, some centúrions, previously instructed by Antonínus, rushed in a body and struck down Géta, who at sight of them had run to his mother, hung about her neck and clung to her bosom and breasts, lamenting and crying: "Mother that didst bear me, mother that didst bear me, help! I am being murdered." And so she, tricked in this way, saw her son perishing in the most impious fashion in her arms, and received him at his death into the very womb, as it were, whence he had been born; for she was all covered with his blood, so that she took no note of the wound she had received on her hand. But she was not permitted to mourn or weep for her son, though he had met so miserable an end before his time (he was only twenty-two years and nine months old), but, on the contrary, she was compelled to rejoice and laugh as though at some great good fortune; so closely were all her words, gestures, and changes of color observed. Thus she alone, the Augústa, wife of the emperor and mother of the emperors, was not permitted to shed tears even in private over so great a sorrow.

Cássius Dío, *Róman History*, 77.2 (translated by Earnest Carey)

Aurélian and Zenóbia

26. After this he directed his march toward Palmýra, in order that, by storming it, he might put an end to his labors. But frequently on the march his army met with a hostile reception from the brigands of Sýria, and after suffering many mishaps he incurred great danger during the siege, being even wounded by an arrow.

A letter of his is still in existence ... in which, without the wonted reserve of an emperor he confesses the difficulty of this war:

> The Rómans are saying that I am merely waging a war with a woman, just as if Zenóbia alone and with her own forces only were fighting against me, and yet, as a matter of fact, there is as great a force of the enemy as if I had to make war against a man, while she, because of her fear and her sense of guilt, is a much baser foe. It cannot be told what a store of arrows is here, what great preparations for war, what a store of spears and of stones; there is no section of the wall that is not held by two or three engines of war, and their machines can even hurl fire. Why say more? She fears like a woman, and fights as one who fears punishment. I believe, however, that the gods will truly bring aid to the Róman commonwealth, for they have never failed our endeavors.

Finally, exhausted and worn out by reason of ill-success, he dispatched a letter to Zenóbia asking her to surrender and promising to spare her life; of this letter I have inserted a copy:

> From Aurélian, Emperor of the Róman world and recoverer of the East, to Zenóbia and all others who are bound to her by alliance in war. You should have done of your own free will what I now command in my letter. For I bid you surrender, promising that your lives shall be spared, and with the condition that you, Zenóbia, together with your children shall dwell wherever I, acting in accordance with the wish of the most noble senate, shall appoint a place. Your jewels, your gold, your silver, your silks, your horses, your camels, you shall all hand over to the Róman treasury. As for the people of Palmýra, their rights shall be preserved.

27. On receiving this letter Zenóbia responded with more pride and insolence than befitted her fortunes, I suppose with a view to inspiring fear; for a copy of her letter, too, I have inserted:

> From Zenóbia, Queen of the East, to Aurélian Augústus. None save yourself has ever demanded by letter what you now demand. Whatever must be accomplished in matters of war must be done by valor alone. You demand my surrender as though you were not aware that Cleopátra preferred to die a Queen rather than remain alive, however high her rank. We shall not lack reinforcements from Pérsia, which we are even now expecting. On our side are the Sáracens, on our side, too, the Arménians. The brigands of Sýria have defeated your army, Aurélian. What more need be said? If those forces, then, which we are expecting from every side, shall arrive, you will, of a surety, lay aside that arrogance with which you now command my surrender, as though victorious on every side.

This letter, Nicómachus says, was dictated by Zenóbia herself and translated by him into Greek from the Sýrian tongue. For that earlier letter of Aurélian's was written in Greek.

28. On receiving this letter Aurélian felt no shame, but rather was angered, and at once he gathered together from every side his soldiers and leaders and laid siege to Palmýra; and that brave man gave his attention to everything that seemed incomplete or neglected. For he cut off the reinforcements which the Pérsians had sent, and he tampered with the squadrons of Sáracens and Arménians, bringing them over to his own side, some by forcible means and some by cunning. Finally, by a mighty effort he conquered that most powerful woman. Zenóbia, then, conquered, fled away on camels (which they call dromedaries), but while seeking to reach the Pérsians she was captured by the horseman sent after her, and thus she was brought into the power of Aurélian.

And so Aurélian, victorious and in possession of the entire East, more proud and insolent now that he held Zenóbia in chains, dealt with the Pérsians, Arménians, and Sáracens as the needs of the occasion demanded. Then were brought in those garments, encrusted with jewels, which we now see in the Temple of the Sun, then, too, the Pérsian dragon-flags and head-dresses, and a purple such as no nation ever afterward offered or the Róman world beheld.

30. But to return to my undertaking: despite all this, there arose a terrible uproar among all the soldiers, who demanded Zenóbia for punishment. Aurélian, however, deeming it improper that a woman should be put to death, killed many who had advised her to begin and prepare and wage the war, but the woman he saved for his triumph, wishing to show her to the eyes of the Róman people. It was regarded as a cruel thing that Longínus the philosopher should have been among those who were killed. He, it is said, was employed by Zenóbia as her teacher in Greek letters, and Aurélian is said to have slain him because he was told that that over-proud letter of hers had been dictated in accord with his counsel, although, in fact, it was composed in the Sýrian tongue...

32. At length, now more secure, he returned again to Éurope, and there, with his well-known valor, he crushed all the enemies who were roving about. Meanwhile, when Aurélian was performing great deeds in the provinces of Thrace as well as in all Éurope, there rose up a certain Fírmus, who laid claim to Égypt, but without the imperial insignia and as though he purposed to make it into a free state. Without delay Aurélian turned back against him, and there also his wonted good-fortune did not abandon him. For he recovered Égypt at once and took vengeance on the enterprise, violent in temper, as he always was; and then, being greatly angered that Tétricus still held the provinces of Gaul, he departed to the West and there took over the légions which were surrendered to him, for Tétricus betrayed his own troops since he could not endure their evil deeds. And so Aurélian, now ruler over the entire world, having subdued both the East and the Gauls, and victor in all lands, turned his march toward Rome, that he might present to the gaze of the Rómans a triumph over both Zenóbia and Tétricus, that is, over both East and West.

33. It is not without advantage to know what manner of triumph Aurélian had, for it was a most brilliant spectacle. There were three royal chariots, of which the first, carefully wrought and adorned with silver and gold and jewels, had belonged to Odænáthus, the second, also wrought with similar care, had been given to Aurélian by the king of the Pérsians, and the third Zenóbia had made for herself, hoping in it to visit the city of Rome. And this hope was not unfulfilled; for she did, indeed, enter the city in it, but vanquished and led in triumph.

There was also another chariot, drawn by four stags and said to have once belonged to the king of the Goths. In this, so many have handed down to memory, Aurélian rode up to the Cápitol, purposing there to slay the stags, which he had captured along with this chariot and then vowed, it was said, to Júpiter Óptimus Máximus. There advanced, moreover, twenty elephants, and two hundred tamed beasts of divers kinds from Líbya and Pálestine, which Aurélian at once presented to private citizens, that the privy-purse might not be burdened with the cost of their food; furthermore, there were led along in order four tigers and also giraffes and elks and other such animals, also eight hundred pairs of gladiators besides the captives from the barbarian tribes... There also advanced among them certain men of Palmýra, who had survived its fall, the foremost of the State, and Egýptians, too, because of their rebellion.

34. There were led along also ten women, who, fighting in male attire, had been captured among the Goths after many others had fallen; these a placard declared to be of the race of the Ámazons, for placards were borne before all, displaying the names of their nations. In the procession was Tétricus also, arrayed in scarlet cloak, a yellow tunic, and Gállic trousers, and with him his son, whom he had proclaimed in Gaul as emperor. And there came Zenóbia, too, decked with jewels and in golden chains, the weight of which was borne by others. There were carried aloft golden crowns presented by all the cities, made known by placards carried aloft. Then came the Róman people itself, the flags of the guilds and the camps, the mailed cuirassiers, the wealth of the kings, the entire army, and, lastly, the senate (albeit somewhat sadly, since they saw senators, too, being led in triumph), all adding much to the splendor of the procession. Scarce did they reach the Cápitol by the ninth hour of the day, and when they arrived at the Palace it was late indeed. On the following days amusements were given to the populace, plays in the theatres, races in the Círcus, wild-beast hunts, gladiatorial fights and also a naval battle.

Históría Augústa, *The Deified Aurélian*, 26-34 (translated by translated by David Magie)

Tertúllian on the Spread of Christiánity

37. ...We are but of yesterday, and we have filled every place among you—cities, islands, fortresses, towns, market-places, the very camp, tribes, companies, palace, senate, fórum—we have left nothing to you but the temples of your gods. For what wars should we not be fit, not eager, even with unequal forces, we who so willingly yield ourselves to the sword, if in our religion it were not counted better to be slain than to slay? Without arms even, and raising no insurrectionary banner, but simply in enmity to you, we could carry on the contest with you by an ill-willed severance alone. For if such multitudes of men were to break away from you, and betake themselves to some remote corner of the world, why, the very loss of so many citizens, whatever sort they were, would cover the empire with shame; nay, in the very forsaking, vengeance would be inflicted. Why, you would be horror-struck at the solitude in which you would find yourselves, at such an all-prevailing silence, and that stupor as of a dead world. You would have to seek subjects to govern. You would have more enemies than citizens remaining. For now it is the immense number of Chrístians which makes your enemies so few—almost all the inhabitants of your various cities being followers of Christ. Yet you choose to call us enemies of the human race, rather than of human error...

Tertúllian, *Apology*, 37 (translated by Sydney Thelwall)

Tertúllian on the Persecution of Chrístians

50. ... Nor does your cruelty, however exquisite, avail you; it is rather a temptation to us. The oftener we are mown down by you, the more in number we grow; the blood of Chrístians is seed. Many of your writers exhort to the courageous bearing of pain and death, as Cícero in the *Túsculans*, as Séneca in his *Chances*, as Diógenes, Pýrrhus, Callínicus; and yet their words do not find so many disciples as Chrístians do, teachers not by words, but by their deeds. That very obstinacy you rail against is the preceptress. For who that contemplates it, is not excited to inquire what is at the bottom of it? who, after inquiry, does not embrace our doctrines? and when he has embraced them, desires not to suffer that he may become partaker of the fulness of God's grace, that he may obtain from God complete forgiveness, by giving in exchange his blood? For that secures the remission of all offences. On this account it is that we return thanks on the very spot for your sentences. As the divine and human are ever opposed to each other, when we are condemned by you, we are acquitted by the Highest.

Tertúllian, *Apology*, 50 (translated by Sydney Thelwall)

Tertúllian on Pagan Learning

For philosophy it is which is the material of the world's wisdom, the rash interpreter of the nature and the dispensation of God. Indeed heresies are themselves instigated by philosophy. From this source came the Æons, and I known not what infinite forms, and the Trinity of Man in the system of Valentínus, who was of Pláto's school. From the same source came Márcion's better god, with all his tranquility; he came of the Stóics. Then, again, the opinion that the soul dies is held by the Epicuréans; while the denial of the restoration of the body is taken from the aggregate school of all the philosophers; also, when matter is made equal to God, then you have the teaching of Zéno; and when any doctrine is alleged touching a god of fire, then Heraclítus comes in. The same matter is discussed over and over again by the heretics and the philosophers; the same arguments are involved. Whence comes evil? Why is it permitted? What is the origin of Man? And in what way does he come? Besides the question which Valentínus has very lately proposed— Whence comes God? Which he settles with the answer: From *enthymésis* and *éctroma*.

Unhappy Áristotle! who invented for these men dialectics, the art of building up and pulling down; an art so evasive in its propositions, so far-fetched in its conjectures, so harsh, in its arguments, so productive of contentions, embarrassing even to itself, retracting everything, and really treating of nothing! Whence spring those "fables and endless genealogies," and "unprofitable questions," and "words which spread like a cancer?" From all these, when the Apostle would restrain us, he expressly names philosophy as that which he would have us be on our guard against. Writing to the *Colóssians*, he says, "See that no one beguile you through philosophy and vain deceit, after the tradition of men, and contrary to the wisdom of the Holy Ghost." He had been at Áthens, and had in his interviews (with its philosophers) become acquainted with that human wisdom which pretends to know the truth, while it only corrupts it, and is itself divided into its own manifold heresies, by the variety of its mutually repugnant sects.

What indeed has Áthens to do with Jerúsalem? What concord is there between the Acádemy and the Church? What between heretics and Chrístians? Our instruction comes from "the porch of Sólomon," who had himself taught that "the Lord should be sought in simplicity of heart." Away with all attempts to produce a mottled Christiánity of Stóic, Platónic, and dialectic composition! We want no curious disputation after possessing Christ Jésus, no inquisition after enjoying the gospel! With our faith, we desire no further belief. For this is our primary faith, that there is nothing which we ought to believe besides!

Tertúllian, On the Proscription of Heretics (translated by T. Herbert Bindley)

The Martyrdom of Saints Perpétua and Felícity

3. When, she said, we were still under legal surveillance and my father was liked to vex me with his words and continually strove to hurt my faith because of his love: Father, said I, Do you see (for examples) this vessel lying, a pitcher or whatsoever it may be? And he said, I see it. And I said to him, Can it be called by any other name than that which it is? And he answered, No. So can I call myself naught other than that which I am, a Christian. Then my father angry with this word came upon me to tear out my eyes; but he only vexed me, and he departed vanquished, he and the arguments of the devil. Then because I was without my father for a few days I gave thanks unto the Lord; and I was comforted because of his absence. In this same space of a few days we were baptized, and the Spirit declared to me, I must pray for nothing else after that water save only endurance of the flesh.

After a few days we were taken into prison, and I was much afraid because I had never known such darkness. O bitter day! There was a great heat because of the press, there was cruel handling of the soldiers. Lastly I was tormented there by care for the child. Then Tértius and Pompónius, the blessed deacons who ministered to us, obtained with money that for a few hours we should be taken forth to a better part of the prison and be refreshed. Then all of them going out from the dungeon took their pleasure; I suckled my child that was now faint with hunger. And being careful for him, I spoke to my mother and strengthened my brother and commended my son unto them. I pined because I saw they pined for my sake. Such cares I suffered for many days; and I obtained that the child should abide with me in prison; and straightway I became well and was lightened of my labor and care for the child; and suddenly the prison was made a palace for me, so that I would sooner be there than anywhere else...

5. A few days after, the report went abroad that we were to be tried. Also my father returned from the city spent with weariness; and he came up to me to cast down my faith saying: Have pity, daughter, on my grey hairs; have pity on your father, if I am worthy to be, called father by you; if with these hands I have brought you unto this flower of youth and I have preferred you before all your brothers; give me not over to the reproach of men. Look upon your brothers; look upon your mother and mother's sister; look upon your son, who will not endure to live after you. Give up your resolution; do not destroy us all together; for none of us will speak openly against men again if you suffer aught. This he said fatherly in his love, kissing my hands and groveling at my feet; and with tears he named me, not daughter, but lady. And I was grieved for my father's case because he would not rejoice at my passion out of all my kin; and I comforted him, saying: That shall be done at this tribunal, whatsoever God shall please; for know that we are not established in our own power, but in God's. And he went from me very sorrowful.

6. Another day as we were at meal we were suddenly snatched away to be tried; and we came to the fórum. Therewith a report spread abroad through the parts near to the fórum, and a very great multitude gathered together. We went up to the tribunal. The others being asked, confessed. So they came to me. And my father appeared there also, with my son, and would draw me from the step, saying: Perform the Sacrifice; have mercy on the child. And Hilárian the procurator—he that after the death of Minúcius Timínian the procónsul had received in his room the right and power of the sword—said: Spare your father's grey hairs; spare the infancy of the boy. Make sacrifice for the Emperors' prosperity. And I answered: I am a Christian. And when my father stood by me yet to cast down my faith, he was bidden by Hilárian to be cast down and was smitten with a rod. And I sorrowed for my father's harm as though I had been smitten myself; so sorrowed I for his unhappy old age. Then Hilárian passed sentence upon us all and condemned us to the beasts; and cheerfully we went down to the dungeon. Then because my child had been used to being breastfed and to staying with me in the prison, straightway I sent Pompónius the deacon to my father, asking for the child. But my father would not give him. And as God willed, no longer did he need to be suckled, nor did I take fever; that I might not be tormented by care for the child and by the pain of my breasts...

18. Now dawned the day of their victory, and they went forth from the prison into the amphitheater as it were into heaven, cheerful and bright of countenance; if they trembled at all, it was for joy, not for fear. Perpétua followed behind, glorious of presence, as a true spouse of Christ and darling of God; at whose piercing look all cast down their eyes. Felícity likewise, rejoicing that she had borne a child in safety, that she might fight with the beasts, came now from blood to blood, from the midwife to the gladiator, to wash after her travail in a second baptism. And when they had been brought to the gate and were being compelled to put on, the men the dress of the priests of Sáturn, the women the dress of the priestesses of Céres, the noble Perpétua remained of like firmness to the end, and would not. For she said: For this cause came we willingly unto this, that our liberty might not be obscured. For this cause have we devoted our lives, that we might do no such thing as this; this we agreed with you. Injustice acknowledged justice; the tríbune suffered that they should be brought forth as they were, without more ado. Perpétua began to sing, as already treading on the Egýptian's head. Revocátus and Saturnínus and Sáturus threatened the people as they gazed. Then when they came into Hilárian's sight, they began to say to Hilárian, stretching forth their hands and nodding their heads: You judge us, they said, and God you. At this the people being enraged besought that they should be vexed with scourges before the line of gladiators (those namely who fought with beasts). Then truly they gave thanks because they had received somewhat of the sufferings of the Lord.

19. But He who had said *Ask and you shall receive* [John 16:24] gave to them asking that end which each had desired. For whenever they spoke together of their desire in their martyrdom, Saturnínus for his part would declare that he wished to be thrown to every kind of beast, that so indeed he might wear the more glorious crown. At the beginning of the spectacle therefore himself with Revocátus first had ado with a leopard and was afterwards torn by a bear on a raised bridge. Now Sáturus detested nothing more than a bear, but was confident already he should die by one bite of a leopard. Therefore when he was being given to a boar, the gladiator instead who had bound him to the boar was torn asunder by the same beast and died after the days of the games; nor was Sáturus more than dragged. Moreover when he had been tied on the bridge to be assaulted by a bear, the bear would not come forth from his den. So Sáturus was called back unharmed a second time.

20. But for the women the devil had made ready a most savage bull, prepared for this purpose against all custom; so they were called back and clothed in loose robes. Perpétua was first thrown, and fell upon her loins. And when she had sat upright, her robe being rent at the side, she drew it over to cover her thigh, mindful rather of modesty than of pain. Next, looking for a pin, she likewise pinned up her disheveled hair; for it was not meet that a martyr should suffer with hair disheveled, lest she should seem to grieve in her glory. So she stood up; and when she saw Felícity smitten down, she went up and gave her hand and raised her up.. And both of them stood up together and the (hardness of the people being now subdued) were called back to the Gate of Life. There Perpétua being received by one named Rústicus, then a catechúmen, who stood close at her side, and as now awakening from sleep (so much was she in the Spirit and in ecstasy) began first to look about her; and then (which amazed all there), When, forsooth, she asked, are we to be thrown to the bull? And when she heard that this had been done already, she would not believe till she perceived some marks of mauling on her body and on her dress. Thereupon she called her brother to her, and that catechúmen, and spoke to them, saying: Stand fast in the faith, and love you all one another; and be not offended because of our passion.

21. Sáturus also at another gate exhorted Púdens the soldier, saying: So then indeed, as I trusted and foretold, I have felt no assault of beasts until now. And now believe with all your heart. Behold, I go out thither and shall perish by one bite of the leopard. And immediately at the end of the spectacle, the leopard being released, with one bite of his he was covered with so much blood that the people (in witness to his second baptism) cried out to him returning: Well washed, well washed. Truly it was well with him who had washed in this wise. Then said he to Púdens the soldier: Farewell; remember the faith and me; and let not these things trouble you, but strengthen you.

And therewith he took from Púdens' finger a little ring, and dipping it in his wound gave it back again for an heirloom, leaving him a pledge and memorial of his blood. Then as the breath left him he was cast down with the rest in the accustomed place for his throat to be cut. And when the people besought that they should be brought forward, that when the sword pierced through their bodies their eyes might be joined thereto as witnesses to the slaughter, they rose of themselves and moved, whither the people willed them, first kissing one another, that they might accomplish their martyrdom with the rites of peace. The rest not moving and in silence received the sword; Sáturus much earlier gave up the ghost; for he had gone up earlier also, and now he waited for Perpétua likewise.

But Perpétua, that she might have some taste of pain, was pierced between the bones and shrieked out; and when the swordsman's hand wandered still (for he was a novice), herself set it upon her own neck. Perchance so great a woman could not else have been slain (being feared of the unclean spirit) had she not herself so willed it. O most valiant and blessed martyrs! O truly called and elected unto the glory of Our Lord Jésus Christ! Which glory he that magnifies, honors and adores, ought to read these witnesses likewise, as being no less than the old, unto the Church's edification; that these new wonders also may testify that one and the same Holy Spirit works ever until now, and with Him God the Father Almighty, and His Son Jésus Christ Our Lord, to Whom is glory and power unending for ever and ever. Amen.

Perpétua et. al., *The Passion of Perpétua and Felícity* (translated by W.H. Shewring)

CHAPTER XXVIII

THE REORGANIZATION OF THE EMPIRE

The Reign of Dioclétian (A.D. 284-305), I.—The Reign of Cónstantine (A.D. 313-337), II.
The Successors of Cónstantine (337-395), III.

Cónstantine Receives a Sign

1.25 As soon then as he was established on the throne, he began to care for the interests of his paternal inheritance, and visited with much considerate kindness all those provinces which had previously been under his father's government. Some tribes of the barbarians who dwelt on the banks of the Rhine, and the shores of the Western ocean, having ventured to revolt, he reduced them all to obedience, and brought them from their savage state to one of gentleness. He contented himself with checking the inroads of others, and drove from his dominions, like untamed and savage beasts, those whom he perceived to be altogether incapable of the settled order of civilized life. Having disposed of these affairs to his satisfaction, he directed his attention to other quarters of the world, and first passed over to the Brítish nations, which lie in the very bosom of the ocean. These he reduced to submission, and then proceeded to consider the state of the remaining portions of the empire, that he might be ready to tender his aid wherever circumstances might require it.

1.26 While, therefore, he regarded the entire world as one immense body, and perceived that the head of it all, the royal city of the Róman empire, was bowed down by the weight of a tyrannous oppression; at first he had left the task of liberation to those who governed the other divisions of the empire, as being his superiors in point of age. But when none of these proved able to afford relief, and those who had attempted it had experienced a disastrous termination of their enterprise, he said that life was without enjoyment to him as long as he saw the imperial city thus afflicted, and prepared himself for the overthrowal of the tyranny.

1.27 Being convinced, however, that he needed some more powerful aid than his military forces could afford him, on account of the wicked and magical enchantments which were so diligently practiced by the tyrant, he sought Divine assistance, deeming the possession of arms and a numerous soldiery of secondary importance, but believing the co-operating power of Deity invincible and not to be shaken. He considered, therefore, on what God he might rely for protection and assistance. While engaged in this enquiry, the thought occurred to him, that, of the many emperors who had preceded him, those who had rested their hopes in a multitude of gods, and served them with sacrifices and offerings, had in the first place been deceived by flattering predictions, and oracles which promised them all prosperity, and at last had met with an unhappy end, while not one of their gods had stood by to warn them of the impending wrath of heaven; while one alone who had pursued an entirely opposite course, who had condemned their error, and honored the one Supreme God during his whole life, had found I him to be the Savior and Protector of his empire, and the Giver of every good thing. Reflecting on this, and well weighing the fact that they who had trusted in many gods had also fallen by manifold forms of death, without leaving behind them either family or offspring, stock, name, or memorial among men: while the God of his father had given to him, on the other hand, manifestations of his power and very many tokens: and considering farther that those who had already taken arms against the tyrant, and had marched to the battle-field under the protection of a multitude of gods, had met with a dishonorable end (for one of them had shamefully retreated from the contest without a blow, and the other, being slain in the midst of his own troops, became, as it were, the mere sport of death); reviewing, I say, all these considerations, he judged it to be folly indeed to join in the idle worship of those who were no gods, and, after such convincing evidence, to err from the truth; and therefore felt it incumbent on him to honor his father's God alone.

1.28 Accordingly he called on him with earnest prayer and supplications that he would reveal to him who he was, and stretch forth his right hand to help him in his present difficulties. And while he was thus praying with fervent entreaty, a most marvelous sign appeared to him from heaven, the account of which it might have been hard to believe had it been related by any other person. But since the victorious emperor himself long afterwards declared it to the writer of this history, when he was honored with his acquaintance and society, and confirmed his statement by an oath, who could hesitate to accredit the relation, especially since the testimony of after-time has established its truth? He said that about noon, when the day was already beginning to decline, he saw with his own eyes the trophy of a cross of light in the heavens, above the sun, and bearing the inscription, "Conquer by this." At this sight he himself was struck with amazement, and his whole army also, which followed him on this expedition, and witnessed the miracle.

1.29 He said, moreover, that he doubted within himself what the import of this apparition could be. And while he continued to ponder and reason on its meaning, night suddenly came on; then in his sleep the Christ of God appeared to him with the same sign which he had seen in the heavens, and commanded him to make a likeness of that sign which he had seen in the heavens, and to use it as a safeguard in all engagements with his enemies.

1.30 At dawn of day he arose, and communicated the marvel to his friends: and then, calling together the workers in gold and precious stones, he sat in the midst of them, and described to them the figure of the sign he had seen, bidding them represent it in gold and precious stones. And this representation I myself have had an opportunity of seeing.

1.31 Now it was made in the following manner. A long spear, overlaid with gold, formed the figure of the cross by means of a transverse bar laid over it. On the top of the whole was fixed a wreath of gold and precious stones; and within this, the symbol of the Savior's name, two letters indicating the name of Christ by means of its initial characters, the letter P being intersected by X in its center: and these letters the emperor was in the habit of wearing on his helmet at a later period. From the cross-bar of the spear was suspended a cloth, a royal piece, covered with a profuse embroidery of most brilliant precious stones; and which, being also richly interlaced with gold, presented an indescribable degree of beauty to the beholder. This banner was of a square form, and the upright staff, whose lower section was of great length, bore a golden half-length portrait of the pious emperor and his children on its upper part, beneath the trophy of the cross, and immediately above the embroidered banner.

The emperor constantly made use of this sign of salvation as a safeguard against every adverse and hostile power, and commanded that others similar to it should be carried at the head of all his armies.

Eusébius, *The Life of the Blessed Emperor Cónstantine*, 1.25-1.31
(translated by Ernest Cushing Richardson)

Cónstantine's Conversion and the Defeat of Maxéntius

1.32 These things were done shortly afterwards. But at the time above specified, being struck with amazement at the extraordinary vision, and resolving to worship no other God save Him who had appeared to him, he sent for those who were acquainted with the mysteries of His doctrines, and enquired who that God was, and what was intended by the sign of the vision he had seen. They affirmed that He was God, the only begotten Son of the one and only God: that the sign which had appeared was the symbol of immortality, and the trophy of that victory over death which He had gained in time past when sojourning on earth. They taught him also the causes of His advent, and explained to him the true account of His incarnation. Thus he was instructed in these matters, and was impressed with wonder at the divine manifestation which had been presented to his sight. Comparing, therefore, the heavenly vision with the interpretation given, he found his judgment confirmed; and, in the persuasion that the knowledge of these things had been imparted to him by Divine teaching, he determined thenceforth to devote himself to the reading of the Inspired writings.

Moreover, he made the priests of God his counselors, and deemed it incumbent on him to honor the God who had appeared to him with all devotion. And after this, being fortified by well-grounded hopes in Him, he hastened to quench the threatening fire of tyranny.

1.33 For [Maxéntius] who had tyrannically possessed himself of the imperial city, had proceeded to great lengths in impiety and wickedness, so as to venture without hesitation on every vile and impure action...

1.35 All men, therefore, both people and magistrates, whether of high or low degree, trembled through fear of him whose daring wickedness was such as I have described, and were oppressed by his grievous tyranny. Nay, though they submitted quietly, and endured this bitter servitude, still there was no escape from the tyrant's sanguinary cruelty. For at one time, on some trifling pretense, he exposed the populace to be slaughtered by his own body-guard; and countless multitudes of the Róman people were slain in the very midst of the city by the lances and weapons, not of Scýthians or barbarians, but of their own fellow-citizens. And besides this, it is impossible to calculate the number of senators whose blood was shed with a view to the seizure of their respective estates, for at different times and on various fictitious charges, multitudes of them suffered death.

1.36 But the crowning point of the tyrant's wickedness was his having recourse to sorcery: sometimes for magic purposes ripping up women with child, at other times searching into the bowels of new-born infants. He slew lions also, and practiced certain horrid arts for evoking demons, and averting the approaching war, hoping by these means to get the victory. In short, it is impossible to describe the manifold acts of oppression by which this tyrant of Rome enslaved his subjects: so that by this time they were reduced to the most extreme penury and want of necessary food, a scarcity such as our contemporaries do not remember ever before to have existed at Rome.

1.37 Cónstantine, however, filled with compassion on account of all these miseries, began to arm himself with all warlike preparation against the tyranny. Assuming therefore the Supreme God as his patron, and invoking His Christ to be his preserver and aid, and setting the victorious trophy, the salutary symbol, in front of his soldiers and body-guard, he marched with his whole forces, trying to obtain again for the Rómans the freedom they had inherited from their ancestors.

And whereas, Maxéntius, trusting more in his magic arts than in the affection of his subjects, dared not even advance outside the city gates, but had guarded every place and district and city subject to his tyranny, with large bodies of soldiers, the emperor, confiding in the help of God, advanced against the first and second and third divisions of the tyrant's forces, defeated them all with ease at the first assault, and made his way into the very interior of Ítaly.

1.38 And already he was approaching very near Rome itself, when, to save him from the necessity of fighting with all the Rómans for the tyrant's sake, God himself drew the tyrant, as it were by secret cords, a long way outside the gates. And now those miracles recorded in Holy Writ, which God of old wrought against the ungodly (discredited by most as fables, yet believed by the faithful), did he in every deed confirm to all alike, believers and unbelievers, who were eye-witnesses of the wonders. For as once in the days of Móses and the Hébrew nation, who were worshipers of God, "Pháraoh's chariots and his host hath he cast into the sea and his chosen chariot-captains are drowned in the Red Sea," so at this time Maxéntius, and the soldiers and guards with him, "went down into the depths like stone," when, in his flight before the divinely-aided forces of Cónstantine, he essayed to cross the river which lay in his way, over which, making a strong bridge of boats, he had framed an engine of destruction, really against himself, but in the hope of ensnaring thereby him who was beloved by God. For his God stood by the one to protect him, while the other, godless, proved to be the miserable contriver of these secret devices to his own ruin. So that one might well say, "He hath made a pit, and dug it, and is fallen into the ditch which he made. His mischief shall return upon his own head, and his violence shall come down upon his own pate." Thus, in the present instance, under divine direction, the machine erected on the bridge, with the ambuscade concealed therein, giving way unexpectedly before the appointed time, the bridge began to sink, and the boats with the men in them went bodily to the bottom. And first the wretch himself, then his armed attendants and guards, even as the sacred oracles had before described, "sank as lead in the mighty waters." So that they who thus obtained victory from God might well, if not in the same words, yet in fact in the same spirit as the people of his great servant Móses, sing and speak as they did concerning the impious tyrant of old: "Let us sing unto the Lord, for he hath been glorified exceedingly: the horse and his rider hath he thrown into the sea. He is become my helper and my shield unto salvation." And again, "Who is like unto thee, O Lord, among the gods? who is like thee, glorious in holiness, marvelous in praises, doing wonders?"

Eusébius, *The Life of the Blessed Emperor Cónstantine*, 1.32-1.38
(translated by Ernest Cushing Richardson)

The Deeds of Cónstantine

1.39 Having then at this time sung these and suchlike praises to God, the Ruler of all and the Author of victory, after the example of his great servant Móses, Cónstantine entered the imperial city in triumph. And here the whole body of the senate, and others of rank and distinction in the city, freed as it were from the restraint of a prison, along with the whole Róman populace, their countenances expressive of the gladness of their hearts, received him with acclamations and abounding joy; men, women, and children, with countless multitudes of servants, greeting him as deliverer, preserver, and benefactor, with incessant shouts. But he, being possessed of inward piety toward God, was neither rendered arrogant by these plaudits, nor uplifted by the praises he heard: but, being sensible that he had received help from God, he immediately rendered a thanksgiving to him as the Author of his victory.

1.40 Moreover, by loud proclamation and monumental inscriptions he made known to all men the salutary symbol, setting up this great trophy of victory over his enemies in the midst of the imperial city, and expressly causing it to be engraved in indelible characters, that the salutary symbol was the safeguard of the Róman government and of the entire empire. Accordingly, he immediately ordered a lofty spear in the figure of a cross to be placed beneath the hand of a statue representing himself, in the most frequented part of Rome, and the following inscription to be engraved on it in the Látin language: by virtue of this salutary sign, which is the true test of valor, I have preserved and liberated your city from the yoke of tyranny. I have also set at liberty the Róman senate and people, and restored them to their ancient distinction and splendor.

1.41 Thus the pious emperor, glorying in the confession of the victorious cross, proclaimed the Son of God to the Rómans with great boldness of testimony. And the inhabitants of the city, one and all, senate and people, reviving, as it were, from the pressure of a bitter and tyrannical domination, seemed to enjoy purer rays of light, and to be born again into a fresh and new life. All the nations, too, as far as the limit of the western ocean, being set free from the calamities which had heretofore beset them, and gladdened by joyous festivals, ceased not to praise him as the victorious, the pious, the common benefactor: all, indeed, with one voice and one mouth, declared that Cónstantine had appeared by the grace of God as a general blessing to mankind. The imperial edict also was everywhere published, whereby those who had been wrongfully deprived of their estates were permitted again to enjoy their own, while those who had unjustly suffered exile were recalled to their homes. Moreover, he freed from imprisonment, and from every kind of danger and fear, those who, by reason of the tyrant's cruelty, had been subject to these sufferings.

1.42 The emperor also personally inviting the society of God's ministers, distinguished them with the highest possible respect and honor, showing them favor in deed and word as persons consecrated to the service of his God. Accordingly, they were admitted to his table, though mean in their attire and outward appearance; yet not so in his estimation, since he thought he saw not the man as seen by the vulgar eye, but the God in him. He made them also his companions in travel, believing that He whose servants they were would thus help him. Besides this, he gave from his own private resources costly benefactions to the churches of God, both enlarging and heightening the sacred edifices, and embellishing the august sanctuaries of the church with abundant offerings.

1.43 He likewise distributed money largely to those who were in need, and besides these showing himself philanthropist and benefactor even to the heathen, who had no claim on him; and even for the beggars in the fórum, miserable and shiftless, he provided, not with money only, or necessary food, but also decent clothing. But in the case of those who had once been prosperous, and had experienced a reverse of circumstances, his aid was still more lavishly bestowed. On such persons, in a truly royal spirit, he conferred magnificent benefactions; giving grants of land to some, and honoring others with various dignities.

Orphans of the unfortunate he cared for as a father, while he relieved the destitution of widows, and cared for them with special solicitude. Nay, he even gave virgins, left unprotected by their parents' death, in marriage to wealthy men with whom he was personally acquainted. But this he did after first bestowing on the brides such portions as it was fitting they should bring to the communion of marriage. In short, as the sun, when he rises upon the earth, liberally imparts his rays of light to all, so did Cónstantine, proceeding at early dawn from the imperial palace, and rising as it were with the heavenly luminary, impart the rays of his own beneficence to all who came into his presence. It was scarcely possible to be near him without receiving some benefit, nor did it ever happen that any who had expected to obtain his assistance were disappointed in their hope.

Eusébius, *The Life of the Blessed Emperor Cónstantine*, 1.39-1.43

(translated by Ernest Cushing Richardson)

The Edict of Toleration of Galérius (A.D. 311)

34 Among other arrangements which we are always accustomed to make for the prosperity and welfare of the republic, we had desired formerly to bring all things into harmony with the ancient laws and public order of the Rómans, and to provide that even the Chrístians who had left the religion of their fathers should come back to reason; since, indeed, the Chrístians themselves, for some reason, had followed such a caprice and had fallen into such a folly that they would not obey the institutes of antiquity, which perchance their own ancestors had first established; but at their own will and pleasure, they would thus make laws unto themselves which they should observe and would collect various peoples in diverse places in congregations. Finally when our law had been promulgated to the effect that they should conform to the institutes of antiquity, many were subdued by the fear of danger, many even suffered death. And yet since most of them persevered in their determination, and we saw that they neither paid the reverence and awe due to the gods nor worshipped the God of the Chrístians, in view of our most mild clemency and the constant habit by which we are accustomed to grant indulgence to all, we thought that we ought to grant our most prompt indulgence also to these, so that they may again be Chrístians and may hold their conventicles, provided they do nothing contrary to good order. But we shall tell the magistrates in another letter what they ought to do.

Wherefore, for this our indulgence, they ought to pray to their God for our safety, for that of the republic, and for their own, that the republic may continue uninjured on every side, and that they may be able to live securely in their homes.

35 This edict is published at Nicomédia on the day before the Kálends of May, in our eighth cónsulship and the second of Maxímínus.

Lactántius, *On the Deaths of the Persecutors*, 34-35
(translated by University of Pennsylvania Department of History)

Cónstantine's Edict of Milán (A.D. 313)

48 When I, Cónstantine Augústus, as well as I, Licínius Augústus, had fortunately met near Mediolánum (Milán), and were considering everything that pertained to the public welfare and security, we thought, among other things which we saw would be for the good of many, those regulations pertaining to the reverence of the Divinity ought certainly to be made first, so that we might grant to the Chrístians and others full authority to observe that religion which each preferred; whence any Divinity whatsoever in the seat of the heavens may be propitious and kindly disposed to us and all who are placed under our rule And thus by this wholesome counsel and most upright provision we thought to arrange that no one whatsoever should be denied the opportunity to give his heart to the observance of the Chrístian religion, of that religion which he should think best for himself, so that the Supreme Deity, to whose worship we freely yield our hearts) may show in all things His usual favor and benevolence.

Therefore, your Worship should know that it has pleased us to remove all conditions whatsoever, which were in the rescripts formerly given to you officially, concerning the Chrístians and now any one of these who wishes to observe Chrístian religion may do so freely and openly, without molestation. We thought it fit to commend these things most fully to your care that you may know that we have given to those Chrístians free and unrestricted opportunity of religious worship. When you see that this has been granted to them by us, your Worship will know that we have also conceded to other religions the right of open and free observance of their worship for the sake of the peace of our times, that each one may have the free opportunity to worship as he pleases; this regulation is made we that we may not seem to detract from any dignity or any religion.

Moreover, in the case of the Chrístians especially we esteemed it best to order that if it happens anyone heretofore has bought from our treasury from anyone whatsoever, those places where they were previously accustomed to assemble, concerning which a certain decree had been made and a letter sent to you officially, the same shall be restored to the Chrístians without payment or any claim of recompense and without any kind of fraud or deception, Those, moreover, who have obtained the same by gift, are likewise to return them at once to the Chrístians. Besides, both those who have purchased and those who have secured them by gift, are to appeal to the vicar if they seek any recompense from our bounty, that they may be cared for through our clemency. All this property ought to be delivered at once to the community of the Chrístians through your intercession, and without delay. And since these Chrístians are known to have possessed not only those places in which they were accustomed to assemble, but also other property, namely the churches, belonging to them as a corporation and not as individuals, all these things which we have included under the above law, you will order to be restored, without any hesitation or controversy at all, to these Chrístians, that is to say to the corporations and their conventicles: providing, of course, that the above arrangements be followed so that those who return the same without payment, as we have said, may hope for an indemnity from our bounty.

In all these circumstances you ought to tender your most efficacious intervention to the community of the Chrístians, that our command may be carried into effect as quickly as possible, whereby, moreover, through our clemency, public order may be secured. Let this be done so that, as we have said above, Divine favor towards us, which, under the most important circumstances we have already experienced, may, for all time, preserve and prosper our successes together with the good of the state. Moreover, in order that the statement of this decree of our good will may come to the notice of all, this rescript, published by your decree, shall be announced everywhere and brought to the knowledge of all, so that the decree of this, our benevolence, cannot be concealed.

Lactántius, *On the Deaths of the Persecutors*, 48
(translated by University of Pennsylvania Department of History)

The Site of Byzántium (Constantinóple)

4.38 The site of Byzántium is as regards the sea more favorable security and prosperity than that of any other city in the world known to us, but as regards the land it is most disadvantageous in both respects. For, as concerning the sea, it completely blocks the mouth of the Póntus in such a manner that no one can sail in or out without the consent of the Býzantines. So that they have complete control over the supply of all those many products furnished by the Póntus which men in general require in their daily life. For as regards necessities it is an undisputed fact that most plentiful supplies and best qualities of cattle and slaves reach us from the countries lying round the Póntus, while among luxuries the same countries furnish us with abundance of honey, wax, and preserved fish, while of the superfluous produce of our countries they take olive-oil and every kind of wine. As for corn there is a give-and-take, they sometimes supplying us when we require it and sometimes importing it from us. The Greeks, then, would entirely lose all this commerce or it would be quite unprofitable to them, if the Býzantines were disposed to be deliberately unfriendly to them, and had made common cause formerly with the Gauls and more especially at present with the Thrácians, or if they had abandoned the place altogether. For, owing to the narrowness of the strait and the numbers of the barbarians on its banks, it would evidently be impossible for our ships to sail into the Póntus. Though perhaps the Býzantines themselves are the people who derive most financial benefit from the situation of their town, since they can readily export all their superfluous produce and import whatever they require on advantageous terms and without any danger or hardship, yet, as I said, they are of great service to other peoples. Therefore, as being the common benefactors of all, they naturally not only should meet with gratitude from the Greeks, but with general support when they are exposed to peril from the barbarians.

Polýbius, *Histories*, 4.38 (translated by W. R. Paton)

The Corruption of Róman Morals

14.6.2 And since I think it likely that foreigners who may read this account (if, indeed, any such should meet with it) are likely to wonder how it is that, when my history has reached the point of narrating what was done at Rome, nothing is spoken of but seditions, and shops, and cheapness, and other similarly inconsiderable matters, I will briefly touch upon the causes of this, never intentionally departing from the strict truth.

14.6.3 At the time when Rome first rose into mundane brilliancy—that Rome which was fated to last as long as mankind shall endure, and to be increased with a sublime progress and growth—virtue and fortune, though commonly at variance, agreed upon a treaty of eternal peace, as far as she was concerned. For if either of them had been wanting to her, she would never have reached her perfect and complete supremacy.

14.6.4 Her people, from its very earliest infancy to the latest moment of its youth, a period which extends over about three hundred years, carried on a variety of wars with the natives around its walls. Then, when it arrived at its full-grown manhood, after many and various labors in war, it crossed the Alps and the sea, till, as youth and man, it had carried the triumphs of victory into every country in the world.

14.6.5 And now that it is declining into old age, and often owes its victories to its mere name, it has come to a more tranquil time of life. Therefore the venerable city, after having bowed down

193

the haughty necks of fierce nations, and given laws to the world, to be the foundations and eternal anchors of liberty, like a thrifty parent, prudent and rich, entrusted to the Cæsars, as to its own children, the right of governing their ancestral inheritance.

14.6.6 And although the tribes are indolent, and the countries peaceful, and although there are no contests for votes, but the tranquility of the age of Núma has returned, nevertheless, in every quarter of the world Rome is still looked up to as the mistress and the queen of the earth, and the name of the Róman people is respected and venerated.

14.6.7 But this magnificent splendor of the assemblies and councils of the Róman people is defaced by the inconsiderate levity of a few, who never recollect where they have been born, but who fall away into error and licentiousness, as if a perfect impunity were granted to vice. For as the lyric poet Simónides teaches us, the man who would live happily in accordance with perfect reason, ought above all things to have a glorious country.

14.6.8 Of these men, some thinking that they can be handed down to immortality by means of statues, are eagerly desirous of them, as if they would obtain a higher reward from brazen figures unendowed with sense than from a consciousness of upright and honorable actions; and they even are anxious to have them plated over with gold, a thing which is reported to have been first done in the instance of Acílius Glábrio, who by his wisdom and valor had subdued King Antíochus. But how really noble a thing it is to despise all these inconsiderable and trifling things, and to bend one's attention to the long and toilsome steps of true glory, as the poet of Áscra has sung, and Cáto the Cénsor has shown by his example. For when he was asked how it was that while many other nobles had statues he had none, replied: "I had rather that good men should marvel how it was that I did not earn one, than (what would be a much heavier misfortune) inquire how it was that I had obtained one."

14.6.9 Others place the height of glory in having a coach higher than usual, or splendid apparel; and so toil and sweat under a vast burden of cloaks, which are fastened to their necks by many clasps, and blow about from the excessive fineness of the material; showing a desire, by the continual wriggling of their bodies, and especially by the waving of the left hand, to make their long fringes and tunics, embroidered in multiform figures of animals with threads of various colors, more conspicuous.

14.6.10 Others, with not any one asking them, put on a feigned severity of countenance, and extol their patrimonial estates in a boundless degree, exaggerating the yearly produce of their fruitful fields, which they boast of possessing in numbers from east to west, being forsooth ignorant that their ancestors, by whom the greatness of Rome was so widely extended, were not eminent for riches; but through a course of dreadful wars overpowered by their valor all who were opposed to them, though differing but little from the common soldiers either in riches, or in their mode of life, or in the costliness of their garments.

14.6.11 This is how it happened that Valérius Publícola was buried by the contributions of his friends, and that the destitute wife of Régulus was, with her children, supported by the aid of the friends of her husband, and that the daughter of Scípio had a dowry provided for her out of the public treasury, the other nobles being ashamed to see the beauty of this full-grown maiden, while her moneyless father was so long absent on the service of his country.

14.6.12 But now if you, as an honorable stranger, should enter the house of any one well off, and on that account full of pride, for the purpose of saluting him, at first, indeed, you will be hospitably received, as though your presence had been desired; and after having had many questions put to you, and having been forced to tell a number of lies, you will wonder, since the man had never seen you before, that one of high rank should pay such attention to you who are but an unimportant individual; so that by reason of this as a principal source of happiness, you begin to repent of not having come to Rome ten years ago.

14.6.13 And when relying on this affability you do the same thing the next day, you will stand waiting as one utterly unknown and unexpected, while he who yesterday encouraged you to repeat your visit, counts upon his fingers who you can be, marveling, for a long time, whence you come, and what you want. But when at length you are recognized and admitted to his acquaintance, if you should devote yourself to the attention of saluting him for three years consecutively, and after this intermit your visits for an equal length of time, then if you return to repeat a similar course, you will never be questioned about your absence any more than if you had been dead, and you will waste your whole life in submitting to court the humors of this blockhead.

14.6.14 But when those long and unwholesome banquets, which are indulged in at certain intervals, begin to be prepared, or the distribution of the usual dole-baskets takes place, then it is discussed with anxious deliberation whether when those to whom a return is due are to be entertained, it is proper to invite also a stranger; and if, after the matter has been thoroughly sifted, it is determined that it may be done, that person is preferred who waits all night before the houses of charioteers, or who professes a skill in dice, or pretends to be acquainted with some peculiar secrets.

14.6.15 For such entertainers avoid all learned and sober men as unprofitable and useless; with this addition, that the nomenclators also, who are accustomed to make a market of these invitations and of similar favors, selling them for bribes, do for gain thrust in mean and obscure men at these dinners.

14.6.16 The whirlpools of banquets, and the various allurements of luxury, I omit, that I may not be too prolix, and with the object of passing on to this fact, that some people, hastening on without fear of danger, drive their horses, as if they were post-horses, with a regular license, as the saying is, through the wide streets of the city, over the roads paved with flint, dragging behind them large bodies of slaves like bands of robbers...

14.6.17 And many matrons, imitating these men, gallop over every quarter of the city with their heads covered, and in close carriages. And as skillful conductors of battles place in the van their densest and strongest battalions, then their light-armed troops, behind them the darters, and in the extreme rear troops of reserve, ready to join in the attack if necessity should arise; so, according to the careful arrangements of the stewards of those city households, who are conspicuous by wands fastened to their right hands, as if a regular watchword had been issued from the camp, first of all, near the front of the carriage march all the slaves concerned in spinning and working; next to them come the blackened crew employed in the kitchen; then the whole body of slaves promiscuously mixed up with a gang of idle plebéians from the neighborhood...

14.6.18 And as this is the case, those few houses which were formerly celebrated for the serious cultivation of becoming studies, are now filled with the ridiculous amusements of torpid indolence, re-echoing with the sound of vocal music and the tinkle of flutes and lyres. Lastly, instead of a philosopher, you find a singer; instead of an orator, some teacher of ridiculous arts is summoned; and the libraries closed for ever, like so many graves; organs to be played by water-power are made; and lyres of so vast a size, that they look like wagons; and flutes, and ponderous machines suited for the exhibitions of actors.

14.6.19 Last of all, they have arrived at such a depth of unworthiness, that when, no very long time ago, on account of an apprehended scarcity of food, the foreigners were driven in haste from the city; those who practiced liberal accomplishments, the number of whom was exceedingly small, were expelled without a moment's breathing-time; yet the followers of actresses, and all who at that time pretended to be of such a class, were allowed to remain; and three thousand dancing-girls had not even a question put to them, but stayed unmolested with the members of their choruses, and a corresponding number of dancing masters.

14.6.20 And wherever you turn your eyes, you may see a multitude of women with their hair curled, who, as far as their age goes, might, if they had married, been by this time the mothers of three children, sweeping the pavements with their feet till they are weary, whirling round in rapid gyrations, while representing innumerable groups and figures which the theatrical plays contain.

14.6.21 It is a truth beyond all question, that, when at one time Rome was the abode of all the virtues, many of the nobles, like the Lotóphagi, celebrated in Hómer, who detained men by the deliciousness of their fruit, allured foreigners of free birth by manifold attentions of courtesy and kindness.

14.6.22 But now, in their empty arrogance, some persons look upon everything as worthless which is born outside of the walls of the city, except only the childless and the unmarried. Nor can it be conceived with what a variety of obsequious observance men without children are courted at Rome.

14.6.23 And since among them, as is natural in a city so great as to be the metropolis of the world, diseases attain to such an insurmountable degree of violence, that all the skill of the physician is ineffectual even to mitigate them; a certain assistance and means of safety has been devised, in the rule that no one should go to see a friend in such a condition, and to a few precautionary measures a further remedy of sufficient potency has been added, that men should not readmit into their houses servants who have been sent to inquire how a man's friends who may have been seized with an illness of this kind are, until they have cleansed and purified their persons in the bath. So that a taint is feared, even when it has only been seen with the eyes of another.

14.6.24 But nevertheless, when these rules are observed thus stringently, some persons, if they be invited to a wedding, though the vigor of their limbs be much diminished, yet, when gold is offered in the hollow palm of the right hand, will go actively as far as Spolétum. These are the customs of the nobles.

14.6.25 But of the lower and most indigent class of the populace some spend the whole night in the wine shops. Some lie concealed in the shady arcades of the theatres; which Cátulus was in his ædileship the first person to raise, in imitation of the lascivious manners of Campánia, or else they play at dice so eagerly as to quarrel over them; snuffing up their nostrils and making unseemly noises by drawing back their breath, into their noses; or (and this is their favorite pursuit of all others) from sunrise to evening they stay gaping through sunshine or rain, examining in the most careful manner the most sterling good or bad qualities of the charioteers and horses.

14.6.26 And it is very wonderful to see an innumerable multitude of people with great eagerness of mind intent upon the event of the contests in the chariot race. These pursuits, and others of like character, prevent anything worth mentioning or important from being done at Rome. Therefore we must return to our original subject.

Ammiánus Marcellínus, *Róman History*, 14.6.1-14.6.26 (translated by Charles Duke Yonge)

Further Vices of the People of Rome

28.4.6 And in the first place we will speak of the faults of the nobles, as we have already repeatedly done as far as our space permitted; and then we will proceed to the faults of the common people, touching, however, only briefly and rapidly on either.

28.4.7 Some men, conspicuous for the illustriousness of their ancestry as they think, gave themselves immoderate airs, and call themselves Rebúrri, and Fabúnii, and Pagónii, and Geriónes, Dálii, Tarrácii, or Perrásii, and other finely-sounding appellations, indicating the antiquity of their family.

28.4.10 Some of these, when any one meets and begins to salute them, toss their heads like bulls preparing to butt, offering their flatterers their knees or hands to kiss, thinking that quite enough for their perfect happiness; while they deem it sufficient attention and civility to a stranger who may happen to have laid them under some obligation to ask him what warm or cold bath he frequents, or what house he lives in.

28.4.11 And while they are so solemn, looking upon themselves as especial cultivators of virtue, if they learn that any one has brought intelligence that any fine horses or skillful coachmen are coming from any place, they rush with as much haste to see them, examine them, and put questions concerning them, as their ancestors showed on beholding the twin-brothers Tyndáridæ, when they filled the whole city with joy by the announcement of that ancient victory.

28.4.12 A number of idle chatterers frequent their houses, and, with various pretended modes of adulation, applaud every word uttered by men of such high fortune; resembling the parasites in a comedy, for as they puff up bragging soldiers, attributing to them, as rivals of the heroes of old, sieges of cities, and battles, and the death of thousands of enemies, so these men admire the construction of the lofty pillars, and the walls inlaid with stones of carefully chosen colors, and extol these grandees with superhuman praises.

28.4.13 Sometimes scales are sent for at their entertainments to weigh the fish, or the birds, or the dormice which are set on the table; and then the size of them is dwelt on over and over again, to the great weariness of those present, as something never seen before; especially when near thirty secretaries stand by, with tablets and memorandum books, to record all these circumstances; so that nothing seems to be wanting but a schoolmaster.

28.4.14 Some of them, hating learning as they hate poison, read Júvenal and Márius Máximus with tolerably careful study; though, in their profound laziness, they never touch any other volumes; why, it does not belong to my poor judgment to decide.

28.4.15 For, in consideration of their great glories and long pedigrees, they ought to read a great variety of books; in which, for instance, they might learn that Sócrates, when condemned to death and thrown into prison, asked some one who was playing a song of the Greek poet Stesíchorus with great skill, to teach him also to do that, while it was still in his power; and when the musician asked him of what use this skill could be to him, as he was to die the next day, he answered, "that I may know something more before I die."

28.4.10. And there are among them some who are such severe judges of offences, that if a slave is too long in bringing them hot water, they will order him to be scourged with three hundred stripes; but should he intentionally have killed a man, while numbers insist that he ought to be unhesitatingly condemned as guilty, his master will exclaim, "What can the poor wretch do? what can one expect from a good-for-nothing fellow like that?" But should any one else venture to do anything of the kind, he would be corrected.

28.4.17 Their ideas of civility are such that a stranger had better kill a man's brother than send an excuse to them if he be asked to dinner; for a senator fancies that he has suffered a terrible grievance, equal to the loss of his entire patrimony, if any guest be absent, whom, after repeated deliberations, he has once invited.

28.4.18 Some of them, if they have gone any distance to see their estates in the country, or to hunt at a meeting collected for their amusement by others, think they have equaled the marches of Alexánder the Great, or of Cæsar; or if they have gone in some painted boats from Lake Avérnus to Putéoli or Caiéta, especially if they have ventured on such an exploit in warm weather. Where if, amid their golden fans, a fly should perch on the silken fringes, or if a slender ray of the sun should have pierced through a hole in their awning, they complain that they were not born among the Cimmérians.

28.4.19 Then, when they come from the bath of Silvárius, or the waters of Mamǽa, which are so good for the health, after they come out of the water, and have wiped themselves with cloths of the finest linen, they open the presses, and take out of them robes so delicate as to be transparent, selecting them with care, till they have got enough to clothe eleven persons; and at length, after they have picked out all they choose, they wrap themselves up in them, and take the rings which they had given to their attendants to hold, that they might not be injured by the damp; and then they depart when their fingers are properly cooled.

28.4.21 Some of them, though not many, wish to avoid the name of gamblers, and prefer to be called dice-players; the difference being much the same as that between a thief and a robber. But this must be confessed that, while all friendships at Rome are rather cool, those alone which are engendered by dice are sociable and intimate, as if they had been formed amid glorious exertions, and were firmly cemented by exceeding affection; to which it is owing that some of this class of gamblers live in such harmony that you might think them the brothers Quintílii. And so you may sometimes see a man of base extraction, who knows all the secrets of the dice, as grave as Pórcius Cáto when he met with a repulse which he had never expected nor dreamt of, when a candidate for the prætorship, with affected solemnity and a serious face, because at some grand entertainment or assembly some man of procónsular rank has been preferred to himself.

28.4.22 Some lay siege to wealthy men, whether old or young, childless or unmarried, or even with wives and children (for with such an object no distinction is ever regarded by them), seeking by most marvelous tricks to allure them to make their wills; and then if, after observing all the forms of law, they bequeath to these persons what they have to leave, being won over by them to this compliance, they speedily die.

28.4.23 Another person, perhaps only in some subordinate office, struts along with his head up, looking with so slight and passing a glance upon those with whom he was previously acquainted, that you might fancy it must be Márcus Marcéllus just returned from the capture of Sýracuse.

28.4.24. Many among them deny the existence of a superior Power in heaven, and yet neither appear in public, nor dine, nor think that they can bathe with any prudence, before they have carefully cónsulted an almanac, and learnt where (for example) the planet Mércury is, or in what portion of Cáncer the moon is as she passes through the heavens.

28.4.25 Another man, if he perceives his creditor to be importunate in demanding a debt, flies to a charioteer who is bold enough to venture on any audacious enterprise, and takes care that he shall be harassed with dread of persecution as a poisoner; from which he cannot be released without giving bail and incurring a very heavy expense. One may add to this, that he includes under this head a debtor who is only so through the engagements into which he has entered to avoid a prosecution, as if he were a real debtor, and that he never lets him go till he has obtained the discharge of the debt.

28.4.26 On the other side, a wife, who, as the old proverb has it, hammers on the same anvil day and night, to compel her husband to make his will, and then the husband is equally urgent that his wife shall do the same. And men learned in the law are procured on each side, the one in the bedchamber, and his opponent in the dining-room, to draw up counter-documents. And under their employ are placed ambiguous interpreters of the contracts of their victims, who, on the one side, promise with great liberality high offices, and the funerals of wealthy matrons; and from these they proceed to the obsequies of the husbands, giving hints that everything necessary ought to be prepared; and .... as Cícero says, "Nor in the affairs of men do they understand anything good, except what is profitable; and they love those friends most (as they would prefer sheep) from whom they expect to derive the greatest advantage."

28.4.27 And when they borrow anything, they are so humble and cringing, you would think you were at a comedy, and seeing Mícon or Láches; when they are constrained to repay what they have borrowed, they become so turgid and bombastic that you would take them for those descendants of Hércules, Cresphóntes and Teménus. This is enough to say of the senatorial older.

28.4.28 And let us come to the idle and lazy common people, among whom some, who have not even got shoes, boast of high-sounding names ... These men spend their whole lives in drinking, and gambling, and brothels, and pleasures, and public spectacles; and to them the Círcus Maximus is their temple, their home, their public assembly; in fact, their whole hope and desire.

28.4.29 And you may see in the fórum, and roads, and streets, and places of meeting, knots of people collected, quarrelling violently with one another, and objecting to one another, and splitting themselves into violent parties.

28.4.30 Among whom those who have lived long, having influence by reason of their age, their gray hairs and wrinkles, are continually crying out that the republic cannot stand, if in the contest which is about to take place, the skillful charioteer, whom some individual backs, is not foremost in the race, and does not dexterously shave the turning-post with the trace-horses.

28.4.31 And when there is so much ruinous carelessness, when the wished-for day of the equestrian games dawns, before the sun has visibly risen, they all rush out with headlong haste, as if with their speed they would outstrip the very chariots which are going to race; while as to the event of the contest they are all torn asunder by opposite wishes, and the greater part of them, through their anxiety, pass sleepless nights.

28.4.32 From hence, if you go to some cheap theatre the actors on the stage are driven off by hisses, if they have not taken the precaution to conciliate the lowest of the people by gifts of money. And if there should be no noise, then, in imitation of the people in the Táuric Chérsonese, they raise an outcry that the strangers ought to be expelled (on whose assistance they have always relied for their principal support), using foul and ridiculous expressions; such as are greatly at variance with the pursuits and inclinations of that populace of old, whose many facetious and elegant expressions are recorded by tradition and by history.

28.4.34 Among these men are many chiefly addicted to fattening themselves up by gluttony, who, following the scent of any delicate food, and the shrill voices of the women who, from cockcrow, cry out with a shrill scream, like so many peacocks, and gliding over the ground on tiptoe, get an entrance into the halls, biting their nails while the dishes are getting cool. Others fix their eyes intently on the tainted meat which is being cooked, that you might fancy Demócritus, with a number of anatomists, was gazing into the entrails of sacrificed victims, in order to teach posterity how best to relieve internal pains.

Ammiánus Marcellínus, *Róman History*, 28.4.1-28.4.35 (translated by Charles Duke Yonge)

The Battle of Adrianóple

31.13.1 And while arms and missiles of all kinds were meeting in fierce conflict, and Bellóna, blowing her mournful trumpet, was raging more fiercely than usual, to inflict disaster on the Rómans, our men began to retreat; but presently, roused by the reproaches of their officers, they made a fresh stand, and the battle increased like a conflagration, terrifying our soldiers, numbers of whom were pierced by strokes from the javelins hurled at them, and from arrows.

31.13.2 Then the two lines of battle dashed against each other, like the beaks (or rams) of ships, and thrusting with all their might, were tossed to and fro, like the waves of the sea. Our left wing had advanced actually up to the wagons, with the intent to push on still further if they were properly supported; but they were deserted by the rest of the cavalry, and so pressed upon by the superior numbers of the enemy, that they were overwhelmed and beaten down, like the ruin of a vast rampart. Presently our infantry also was left unsupported, while the different companies became so huddled together that a soldier could hardly draw his sword, or withdraw his hand after he had once stretched it out. And by this time such clouds of dust arose that it was scarcely possible to see the sky, which resounded with horrible cries; and in consequence, the darts, which were bearing death on every side, reached their mark, and fell with deadly effect, because no one could see them beforehand so as to guard against them.

31.13.3 But when the barbarians, rushing on with their enormous host, beat down our horses and men, and left no spot to which our ranks could fall back to deploy, while they were so closely packed that it was impossible to escape by forcing a way through them, our men at last began to despise death, and again took to their swords and slew all they encountered, while with mutual blows of battle-axes, helmets and breastplates were dashed in pieces.

31.13.4 Then, you might see the barbarian towering in his fierceness, hissing or shouting, fall with his legs pierced through, or his right hand cut off, sword and all, or his side transfixed, and still, in the last gasp of life, casting round him defiant glances. The plain was covered with carcasses, strewing the mutual ruin of the combatants; while the groans of the dying, or of men fearfully wounded, were intense, and caused great dismay all around.

31.13.5 Amidst all this great tumult and confusion our infantry were exhausted by toil and danger, till at last they had neither strength left to fight, nor spirits to plan anything; their spears were broken by the frequent collisions, so that they were forced to content themselves with their drawn swords, which they thrust into the dense battalions of the enemy, disregarding their own safety, and seeing that every possibility of escape was cut off from them.

31.13.6 The ground, covered with streams of blood, made their feet slip, so that all that they endeavored to do was to sell their lives as dearly as possible; and with such vehemence did they resist their enemies who pressed on them, that some were even killed by their own weapons. At last one black pool of blood disfigured everything, and wherever the eye turned, it could see nothing but piled-up heaps of dead, and lifeless corpses trampled on without mercy.

31.13.7 The sun being now high in the heavens, having traversed the sign of Léo, and reached the abode of the heavenly Vírgo, scorched the Rómans, who were emaciated by hunger, worn out with toil, and scarcely able to support even the weight of their armor. At last our columns were entirely beaten back by the overpowering weight of the barbarians, and so they took to disorderly flight, which is the only resource in extremity, each man trying to save himself as well as he could.

31.13.8 While they were all flying and scattering themselves over roads with which they were unacquainted, the emperor, bewildered with terrible fear, made his way over heaps of dead, and fled to the battalions of the Lanceárii and the Mattiárii, who, till the superior numbers of the enemy became wholly irresistible, stood firm and immovable. As soon as he saw him, Trájan exclaimed that all hope was lost, unless the emperor, thus deserted by his guards, could be protected by the aid of his foreign allies.

31.13.9 When this exclamation was heard, a count named Víctor hastened to bring up with all speed the Batávians, who were placed in the reserve, and who ought to have been near at hand, to the emperor's assistance; but as none of them could be found, he too retreated, and in a similar manner Richómeres and Saturnínus saved themselves from danger.

31.13.10 So now, with rage flashing in their eyes, the barbarians pursued our men, who were in a state of torpor, the warmth of their veins having deserted them. Many were slain without knowing who smote them; some were overwhelmed by the mere weight of the crowd which pressed upon them; and some were slain by wounds inflicted by their own comrades. The barbarians spared neither those who yielded nor those who resisted.

31.13.11 Besides these, many half slain lay blocking up the roads, unable to endure the torture of their wounds; and heaps of dead horses were piled up and filled the plain with their carcasses. At last a dark moonless night put an end to the irremediable disaster which cost the Róman state so dear.

31.13.12 Just when it first became dark, the emperor being among a crowd of common soldiers, as it was believed— for no one said either that he had seen him, or been near him—was mortally wounded with an arrow, and, very shortly after, died, though his body was never found. For as some of the enemy loitered for a long time about the field in order to plunder the dead, none of the defeated army or of the inhabitants ventured to go to them.

31.13.13 A similar fate befell the Cæsar Décius, when fighting vigorously against the barbarians; for he was thrown by his horse falling, which he had been unable to hold, and was plunged into a swamp, out of which he could never emerge, nor could his body be found.

31.13.14 Others report that Válens did not die immediately, but that he was borne by a small body of picked soldiers and eunuchs to a cabin in the neighborhood, which was strongly built, with two stories; and that while these unskillful hands were tending his wounds, the cottage was surrounded by the enemy, though they did not know who was in it; still, however, he was saved from the disgrace of being made a prisoner.

31.13.15 For when his pursuers, while vainly attempting to force the barred doors, were assailed with arrows from the roof, they, not to lose by so inconvenient a delay the opportunity of collecting plunder, gathered some bundles and stubble, and setting fire to them, burnt down the building, with those who were in it.

31.13.16 But one of the soldiers dropped from the windows, and, being taken prisoner by the barbarians, revealed to them what had taken place, which caused them great concern, because they looked upon themselves as defrauded of great glory in not having taken the ruler of the Róman state alive. This same young man afterwards secretly returned to our people, and gave this account of the affair.

31.13.17 When Spain had been recovered after a similar disaster, we are told that one of the Scípios was lost in a fire, the tower in which he had taken refuge having been burnt. At all events it is certain that neither Scípio nor Válens enjoyed that last honor of the dead—a regular funeral.

31.13.18 Many illustrious men fell in this disastrous defeat, and among them one of the most remarkable was Trájan, and another was Sebástian; there perished also thirty-five tríbunes who had no particular command, many captains of battalions, and Valeriánus and Equítius, one of whom was master of the horse and the other high steward. Poténtius, too, tríbune of the promoted officers, fell in the flower of his age, a man respected by all persons of virtue, and recommended by the merits of his father, Ursicínus, who had formerly been commander of the forces, as well as by his own. Scarcely one-third of the whole army escaped.

31.13.19 Nor, except the battle of Cánnæ, is so destructive a slaughter recorded in our annals; though, even in the times of their prosperity, the Rómans have more than once had to deplore the uncertainty of war, and have for a time succumbed to evil Fortune; while the well-known dirges of the Greeks have bewailed many disastrous battles.

Ammiánus Marcellínus, *Róman History*, 31.13.1-31.13.19 (translated by Charles Duke Yonge)

CHAPTER XXIX

THE EXTINCTION OF THE WESTERN EMPIRE

The Great Invasions, I.—The Fall of the Western Empire, II.

The Meeting of Áttila and Pope Léo the Great

Áttila, the leader of the Huns, who was called the scourge of God, came into Ítaly, inflamed with fury, after he had laid waste with most savage frenzy Thrace and Illýricum, Macedónia and Mœsia, Acháia and Greece, Pannónia and Gérmany. He was utterly cruel in inflicting torture, greedy in plundering, insolent in abuse... He destroyed Aquiléia from the foundations and razed to the ground those regal cities, Pávia and Milán; he laid waste many other towns, and was rushing down upon Rome.

Then Léo had compassion on the calamity of Ítaly and Rome, and with one of the cónsuls and a large part of the Róman senate he went to meet Áttila. The old man of harmless simplicity, venerable in his gray hair and his majestic garb, ready of his own will to give himself entirely for the defense of his flock, went forth to meet the tyrant who was destroying all things. He met Áttila, it is said, in the neighborhood of the river Míncio, and he spoke to the grim monarch, saying "The senate and the people of Rome, once conquerors of the world, now indeed vanquished, come before thee as suppliants. We pray for mercy and deliverance. O Áttila, thou king of kings, thou couldst have no greater glory than to see suppliant at thy feet this people before whom once all peoples and kings lay suppliant. Thou hast subdued, O Áttila, the whole circle of the lands which it was granted to the Rómans, victors over all peoples, to conquer. Now we pray that thou, who hast conquered others, shouldst conquer thyself The people have felt thy scourge; now as suppliants they would feel thy mercy."

As Léo said these things Áttila stood looking upon his venerable garb and aspect, silent, as if thinking deeply. And lo, suddenly there were seen the apostles Peter and Paul, clad like bishops, standing by Léo, the one on the right hand, the other on the left. They held swords stretched out over his head, and threatened Áttila with death if he did not obey the pope's command. Wherefore Áttila was appeased, he who had raged as one mad. He, by Léo's intercession, straightway promised a lasting peace and withdrew beyond the Dánube.

Anonymous Account (translated by J. H. Robinson)

PUBLIC DOMAIN TRANSLATION CREDITS

Agrícola, Públius Cornélius Tácitus, translated by Alfred John Church and William Jackson Brodribb (London, New York: Macmillan, 1877)

Annals, Públius Cornélius Tácitus, translated by Alfred John Church and William Jackson Brodribb (London, New York: Macmillan, 1888)

Apology, Tertúllian, translated by Sydney Thelwell, Ante-Nicene Fathers, Volume III (Grand Rapids, Michigan: Eerdmans Publishing Company, 1993)

The City of God, St. Áugustine, translated by Rev. Marcus Dods, Ante-Nicene Fathers, Volume II (Grand Rapids, Michigan: Eerdmans Publishing Company, 1993)

Civil Wars, Áppian, translated by Horace White, *Loeb Classical Library*, Cambridge (MA: Harvard University Press, 1912-1913)

Commentaries on the Gállic War, Gáius Július Cæsar, translated by W.A. McDevitte and W.S. Bohn (New York: Harper & Brothers, 1869)

Conspiracy of Cátiline, Gáius Sallústius Críspus, translated by Rev. John Selby Watson (New York: Harper & Brothers, 1867)

On the Deaths of the Persecutors, Lactántius, translated in University of Pennsylvania. Dept. of History: *Translations and Reprints from the Original Sources of Európéan History* (Philadelphia: University of Pennsylvania Press, 1897-1907, Vol. 4:, 1, pp. 28-30)

Foreign Wars, Áppian, translated by Horace White, *Loeb Classical Library*, Cambridge (MA: Harvard University Press, 1912-1913)

História Augústa, translated by David Magie, *Loeb Classical Library* (Cambridge, MA: Harvard University Press, 1921, 1924, 1932)

Histories, Polýbius, translated by W. R. Paton, *Loeb Classical Library* (Cambridge, MA: Harvard University Press, 1922 through 1927)

History of Rome, Lívy, translated by Rev. Canon Roberts, *Everyman's Library* (London: J.M. Dent and Sons, 1912)

Letters, Plíny the Younger, translated by William Melmoth, revised by F. C. T. Bosanquet, *The Harvard Classics* (New York: P.F. Collier & Son, 1909–14)

The Life of the Blessed Emperor Cónstantine, Eusébius, translated by Ernest Cushing Richardson, Ph.D., *A Select Library of Nícene and Post-Nícene Fathers of the Christian Church*, 2nd series, vol. 1, 1890

Lives, Plútarch, translated by John Dryden, edited by A.H. Clough (Boston: Little Brown and Co., 1906)

Lives of the Twelve Cæsars, Gáius Suetónius Tranquíllus, translated by J. C. Rolfe, *Loeb Classical Library* (Cambridge, MA: Harvard University Press, 1913)

Meditations, Márcus Aurélius, translated by George Long, *Harvard Classics* (Cambridge, MA: Harvard University Press, 1862)

The Natural History, Plíny the Elder, translated by John Bostock and H. T. Riley (London: Taylor and Francis, Red Lion Court, Fleet Street, 1855)

The Orations of Márcus Túllius Cícero, translated by C. D. Yonge, Vol. 2. (London: G. Bell and Sons, 1913-21)

The Passion of Perpétua and Felícity, Perpétua *et al.*, translated by W.H. Shewring (London: 1931)

On the Proscription of Heretics, Tertúllian, translated by T. Herbert Bindley, (London: SPCK, 1914)

Readings in European History, translated by J. H. Robinson (Boston: Ginn, 1905)

Res Géstæ Dívi Augústi, Augústus Cæsar, translated by Frederick W. Shipley, *Loeb Classical Library* (Cambridge, MA: Harvard University Press, 1924)

Róman Antiquities, Dionýsius of Halicarnássus, translated by Earnest Carey, *Loeb Classical Library* (Cambridge, MA: Harvard University Press, 1940)

Róman History, Ammiánus Marcellínus, translated by Charles Duke Yonge, (London: 1862)

Róman History, Cássius Dío, translated by Earnest Carey, *Loeb Classical Library* (Cambridge, MA: Harvard University Press, 1914)

The Róman History, Gáius Velléius Patérculus, translated by Frederick W. Shipley (Cambridge, MA: Harvard University Press, 1924)

The War with Jugúrtha, Gáius Sallústius Críspus, translated by John C. Rolfe, *Loeb Classical Library* (Cambridge, MA: Harvard University Press, 1921, revised 1931)

The Works of Flávius Joséphus, Flávius Joséphus, translated by William Whiston, A.M. (Auburn and Buffalo: John E. Beardsley, 1895)

Made in the USA
Columbia, SC
29 September 2019